The Happiness
Advantage

The Seven Principles that Fuel Success
and Performance at Work

Shawn Achor

First published in the United States in 2010 by Crown Business, an imprint of the Crown
Publishing Group, a division of Random House, Inc., New York

First published in the UK in 2010 by Virgin Books, an imprint of Ebury Publishing
A Random House Group Company

This edition published in 2011 by Virgin Books

www.randomhouse.co.uk

Addresses for companies within The Random House Group Limited can be found at
www.randomhouse.co.uk/offices.htm

The Random House Group Limited Reg. No. 954009

A CIP catalogue record for this book is
available from the British Library

ISBN 9780753539477

Penguin Random House is committed to a sustainable future for
our business, our readers and our planet. This book is made from
Forest Stewardship Council® certified paper.

Printed and bound in Great Britain by Clays Ltd, St Ives plc

To my parents, both teachers,

who have dedicated their lives to the belief that we can all

shine brighter

ACKNOWLEDGMENTS

■ ■ ■

This section has been the most fun part of writing this book. I am humbled and excited knowing that every word in this book has been shaped by the people in my life. I hope I have written in such a way that you can still hear their voices.

Thank you to my mentor, Dr. Tal Ben-Shahar. I remember meeting him at a café in Harvard Square to discuss a new class on happiness. I found him to be a kind, mild, and unimposing man. Little did I know this humble stranger would soon transform Harvard, and my life in the process. It took him only one tall coffee to reorient my entire world, helping me see how my study of religious ethics at the divinity school paralleled the questions asked in the science of positive psychology. He encouraged my growth and forgave my failings. Knowing him is one of my daily gratitudes; for without him, I would not be in this field nor be writing this book today.

Thank you to Elizabeth Peterson, one of my former students from the Positive Psychology class at Harvard, who later came to join my company. She, like Tal, is a loyal guardian of positive psychology, believing that it must not only remain a science, but must also be lived. Liz has painstakingly edited every word of this book for a year, and has in the midst of this challenge remained a true friend.

Thank you to my mother, a high school English teacher and now college freshmen advisor at Baylor University, and to my father, a professor of psychology also at Baylor, who gave me the twin gift of a love for learning and a love for teaching. I am grateful to my sister, Amy, and brother, Bobo, who have kept the fires burning bright enough to remind me that I still had a home as I traveled nonstop for two years through forty countries.

Thank you to Mr. Hollis, who offered his genius as a public high school teacher; he made me fall in love with academia. Thank you to Brian Little, who was the best professor I had at Harvard and who I studied fervently as his Teaching Fellow, trying to learn the art of lecturing from a master. Thank you to Professor Phil Stone for inspiring Tal and me. Thank you to Professor Ellen Langer for letting me join her lab and to learn how to think outside of the norms of what academia expects. Thank you to my literary agent, Rafe Sagalyn, for making this book possible; Tal said he was the best and he was right. Thank you to Roger Scholl at Broadway Books, who believed in this book, and to Talia Krohn at Broadway, who edited this book assiduously and with great insight.

Thank you to the Young Presidents Organization for helping me meet so many new friends all over the world from Asia to South America. Thank you to Salim Dewji for arranging my speaking tour through Africa, a lifelong dream. Thank you to Michelle Blieberg at UBS and Lisanne Biolos at KPMG for their friendship and for inviting me into their companies to test our theories. Thank you to John Galvin and Steven Schragis, who started my speaking career, propelling me out of the classroom and into the public with talks at One Day University. Thank you to Michelle Lemmons, Greg Kaiser, and Greg Ray from International Speakers Bureau for partnering with me and for caring so much for building up their speakers. Thank you to my friends at the Washington Speakers Bureau and to C. J. Lonoff at Speaking Matters for helping bring this message worldwide. Thank you to Carrie Callahan for her help with PR for me. And thank you to Dini Coffin and Stewart Clifford from Enterprise Media for bringing this science to video.

I have been blessed with a network of friends too large to name here, but a special thank you to the following people whose friendship and encouragement have be integral to my happiness and success over the past year: Angie Koban, Alia Crum, Laura Babbitt and Mike Lampert, Jessica Glazer, Max Weisbuch and Amanda Youmans, Judy and Russ Miller and Caroline Sami, Caleb Merkl, Olivia Shabb, and Brent Furl.

If you have never written an acknowledgement page, try taking an afternoon to do it. I have just found that you cannot help but be happy and humbled being reminded that we are loved and that we do nothing alone.

I look forward to the new friendships and community this book creates.

CONTENTS

. . .

PART ONE: POSITIVE PSYCHOLOGY AT WORK

PART TWO: SEVEN PRINCIPLES

PART THREE: THE RIPPLE EFFECT

The Happiness
Advantage

PART 1

POSITIVE
PSYCHOLOGY
AT WORK

■ ■ ■

INTRODUCTION

· · ·

I f you observe the people around you, you'll find most individuals follow a formula that has been subtly or not so subtly taught
to them by their schools, their company, their parents, or society. That is: If you work hard, you will become successful, and once
you become successful, *then* you'll be happy. This pattern of belief
explains what most often motivates us in life. We think: If I just get
that raise, or hit that next sales target, I'll be happy. If I can just get
that next good grade, I'll be happy. If I lose that five pounds, I'll be
happy. And so on. Success first, happiness second.

The only problem is that this formula is broken.

If success causes happiness, then every employee who gets a
promotion, every student who receives an acceptance letter, everyone who has ever accomplished a goal of any kind should be happy.
But with each victory, our goalposts of success keep getting pushed
further and further out, so that happiness gets pushed over the
horizon.

Even more important, the formula is broken because it is backward. More than a decade of groundbreaking research in the fields
of positive psychology and neuroscience has proven in no uncertain
terms that the relationship between success and happiness works
the other way around. Thanks to this cutting-edge science, we now
know that happiness is the precursor to success, not merely the result. And that happiness and optimism actually *fuel* performance

and achievement—giving us the competitive edge that I call the Happiness Advantage.

Waiting to be happy limits our brain's potential for success, whereas cultivating positive brains makes us more motivated, efficient, resilient, creative, and productive, which drives performance upward. This discovery has been confirmed by thousands of scientific studies and in my own work and research on 1,600 Harvard students and dozens of Fortune 500 companies worldwide. In this book, you will learn not only why the Happiness Advantage is so powerful, but how you can use it on a daily basis to increase your success at work. But I'm getting excited and jumping ahead of myself. I begin this book where I began my research, at Harvard, where the Happiness Advantage was born.

DISCOVERING THE HAPPINESS ADVANTAGE

. . .

applied to Harvard on a dare.

I was raised in Waco, Texas, and never really expected to leave. Even as I was applying to Harvard, I was setting down roots and training to be a local volunteer firefighter. For me, Harvard was a place from the movies, the place mothers joke about their kids going to when they grow up. The chances of actually getting in were infinitesimally small. I told myself I'd be happy just to tell my kids someday, offhandedly at dinner, that I had even *applied* to Harvard. (I imagined my imaginary children being quite impressed.)

When I unexpectedly got accepted, I felt thrilled and humbled by the privilege. I wanted to do the opportunity justice. So I went to Harvard, and I stayed . . . for the next twelve years.

When I left Waco, I had been out of Texas four times and never out of the country (though Texans consider anything out of Texas foreign travel). But as soon as I stepped out of the T in Cambridge and into Harvard Yard, I fell in love. So after getting my BA, I found a way to stay. I went to grad school, taught sections in sixteen different courses, and then began delivering lectures. As I pursued my graduate studies, I also became a Proctor, an officer of Harvard hired to live in residence with undergraduates to help them navigate the difficult path to both academic success and happiness within the Ivory Tower. This effectively meant that I lived in a college dorm for a total of 12 years of my life (not a fact I brought up on first dates).

I tell you this for two reasons. First, because I saw Harvard as such a privilege, it fundamentally changed the way my brain processed my experience. I felt grateful for every moment, even in the midst of stress, exams, and blizzards (something else I had only seen in the movies). Second, my 12 years teaching in the classrooms and living in the dorms afforded me a comprehensive view of how thousands of other Harvard students advanced through the stresses and challenges of their college years. That's when I began noticing the patterns.

PARADISE LOST AND FOUND

Around the time that Harvard was founded, John Milton wrote in *Paradise Lost*, "The Mind is its own place, and in itself can make a heaven of hell, a hell of heaven."

Three hundred years later, I observed this principle come to life. Many of my students saw Harvard as a privilege, but others quickly lost sight of that reality and focused only on the workload, the competition, the stress. They fretted incessantly about their future, despite the fact that they were earning a degree that would open so many doors. They felt overwhelmed by every small setback instead of energized by the possibilities in front of them. And after watching enough of those students struggle to make their way through, something dawned on me. Not only were these students the ones who seemed most susceptible to stress and depression, they were the ones whose grades and academic performance were suffering the most.

Years later, in the fall of 2009, I was invited to go on a month-long speaking tour throughout Africa. During the trip, a CEO from South Africa named Salim took me to Soweto, a township just outside of Johannesburg that many inspiring people, including Nelson Mandela and Archbishop Desmond Tutu, have called their home.

We visited a school next to a shantytown where there was no electricity and scarce running water. Only when I was in front of the children did it dawn on me that none of the stories I normally use in my talks would work. Sharing the research and experiences of privileged American college students and wealthy, powerful business leaders seemed inappropriate. So I tried to open a dialogue. Struggling for points of common experience, I asked in a very clearly tongue-in-cheek tone, "Who here likes to do schoolwork?" I thought the seemingly universal distaste for schoolwork would bond us together. But to my shock, 95 percent of the children raised their hands and started smiling genuinely and enthusiastically.

Afterward, I jokingly asked Salim why the children of Soweto were so weird. "They see schoolwork as a privilege," he replied, "one that many of their parents did not have." When I returned to Harvard two weeks later, I saw students complaining about the very thing the Soweto students saw as a privilege. I started to realize just how much our interpretation of reality changes our experience of that reality. The students who were so focused on the stress and the pressure—the ones who saw learning as a chore—were missing out on all the opportunities right in front of them. But those who saw attending Harvard as a privilege seemed to shine even brighter. Almost unconsciously at first, and then with ever-increasing interest, I became fascinated with what caused those high potential individuals to develop a positive mindset to excel, especially in such a competitive environment. And likewise, what caused those who succumbed to the pressure to fail—or stay stuck in a negative or neutral position.

RESEARCHING HAPPINESS AT HOGWARTS

For me, Harvard remains a magical place, even after twelve years. When I invite friends from Texas to visit, they claim that eating in the freshman dining hall is like being at Hogwarts, Harry Potter's fantastical school of magic. Add in the other beautiful buildings, the university's abundant resources, and the seemingly endless opportunities it offers, and my friends often end up asking, "Shawn, why would you waste your time studying happiness at Harvard? Seriously, what does a Harvard student possibly have to be *un*happy about?"

In Milton's time, Harvard had a motto that reflected the school's religious roots: *Veritas, Christo et Ecclesiae* (Truth, for Christ and the Church). For many years now, that motto has been truncated to a single word: *Veritas,* or just truth. There are now many truths at Harvard, and one of them is that despite all its magnificent facilities, a wonderful faculty, and a student body made up of some of America's (and the world's) best and brightest, it is home to many chronically unhappy young men and women. In 2004, for instance, a *Harvard Crimson* poll found that as many as 4 in 5 Harvard students suffer from depression at least once during the school year, and nearly half of all students suffer from depression so debilitating they can't function.[1]

This unhappiness epidemic is not unique to Harvard. A Conference Board survey released in January of 2010 found that only 45 percent of workers surveyed were happy at their jobs, the lowest in 22 years of polling.[2] Depression rates today are ten times higher than they were in 1960.[3] Every year the age threshold of unhappiness sinks lower, not just at universities but across the nation. Fifty years ago, the mean onset age of depression was 29.5 years old. Today, it is almost exactly half that: 14.5 years old. My friends wanted to know, Why study happiness at Harvard? The question I asked in response was: Why *not* start there?

So I set out to find the students, those 1 in 5 who were truly flourishing—the individuals who were above the curve in terms of their happiness, performance, achievement, productivity, humor, energy, or resilience—to see what exactly was giving them such an advantage over their peers. What was it that allowed these people to escape the gravitational pull of the norm? Could patterns be teased out of their lives and experience to help others in all walks of life to be more successful in an increasingly stressful and negative world? As it turns out, they could.

Scientific discovery is a lot about timing and luck. I serendipitously found three mentors—Harvard professors Phil Stone, Ellen Langer, and Tal Ben-Shahar—who happened to be at the vanguard of a brand new field called positive psychology. Breaking with traditional psychology's focus on what makes people *un*happy and how they can return to "normal," these three were applying the same scientific rigor to what makes people thrive and excel—the very same questions I wanted to answer.

ESCAPING THE CULT OF THE AVERAGE

The graph below may seem boring, but it is the very reason I wake up excited every morning. (Clearly, I live a very exciting life.) It is also the basis of the research underlying this book.

This is a scatter-plot diagram. Each dot represents an individual, and each axis represents some variable. This particular diagram could be plotting anything: weight in relation to height, sleep in relation to energy, happiness in relation to success, and so on. If we got this data back as researchers, we would be thrilled because

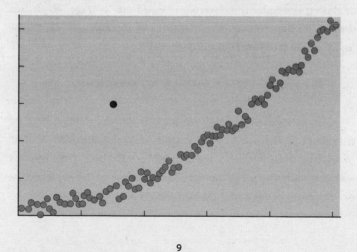

very clearly there is a trend going on here, and that means that we can get published, which in the academic world is all that really matters. The fact that there is one weird red dot—what we call an outlier—up above the curve is no problem. It's no problem because we can just delete it. We can delete it because it's clearly a measurement error—and we know that it's an error because it's screwing up our data.

One of the very first things students in intro psychology, statistics, or economics courses learn is how to "clean up the data." If you are interested in observing the general trend of what you are researching, then outliers mess up your findings. That's why there exist countless formulas and statistics packages to help enterprising researchers eliminate these "problems." And to be clear, this is not cheating; these are statistically valid procedures—if, that is, one is interested only in the general trend. I am not.

The typical approach to understanding human behavior has always been to look for the average behavior or outcome. But in my view this misguided approach has created what I call the "cult of the average" in the behavioral sciences. If someone asks a question such as "How fast can a child learn how to read in a classroom?" science changes that question to "How fast does the *average* child learn to read in the classroom?" We then ignore the children who read faster or slower, and tailor the classroom toward the "average" child. This is what Tal Ben-Shahar calls "the error of the average." That's the first mistake traditional psychology makes.

If we study merely what is average, we will remain merely average.

Conventional psychology consciously ignores outliers because they don't fit the pattern. I've sought to do the opposite: Instead of deleting these outliers, I want to learn from them. (This concept was originally described by Abraham Maslow as he explains the need to study the growing tip of the curve.)

TOO FOCUSED ON THE NEGATIVE

True, there are psychology researchers out there who don't just study what is average. They tend to focus on those who fall only on one side of average—below it. According to Ben-Shahar in *Happier*, this is the second mistake traditional psychology makes. Of course, the people who fall below normal are the ones who tend to need the most help—to be relieved of depression or alcohol abuse or chronic stress. As a result, psychologists understandably have spent considerable effort studying how they can help these people recover and get back to normal. Valuable as such work is, it still only yields half the picture.

You can eliminate depression without making someone happy. You can cure anxiety without teaching someone optimism. You can return someone to work without improving their job performance. If all you strive for is diminishing the bad, you'll only attain the average and you'll miss out entirely on the opportunity to exceed the average.

You can study gravity forever without learning how to fly.

Extraordinarily, as late as 1998, there was a 17-to-1 negative-to-positive ratio of research in the field of psychology. In other words, for every one study about happiness and thriving there were 17 studies on depression and disorder. This is very telling. As a society, we know very well how to be unwell and miserable and so little about how to thrive.

A few years back, one event in particular really drove this home for me. I had been asked to speak at the "Wellness Week" at one of the most elite New England boarding schools. The topics to be discussed: Monday, eating disorders; Tuesday, depression; Wednesday, drugs and violence; Thursday, risky sex; and Friday, who knew? That's not a wellness week; that's a sickness week.

This pattern of focusing on the negative pervades not only our research and schools but our society. Turn on the news, and the majority of airtime is spent on accidents, corruption, murders, abuse. This focus on the negative tricks our brains into believing that this sorry ratio is reality, that most of life is negative. Ever heard of Medical School Syndrome? In the first year of medical school, as students listen to all the diseases and symptoms that can befall a person, many aspiring doctors become suddenly convinced that they have come down with ALL of them. A few years ago, my brother-in-law called me from Yale Medical School and told me that he had "leprosy" (which even at Yale is extremely rare). But I had no idea how to console him because he had just gotten over a week of menopause and was very sensitive. The point is, as we will see throughout this book, what we spend our time and mental energy focusing on can indeed become our reality.

It is not healthy nor scientifically responsible only to study the negative half of human experience. In 1998, Martin Seligman, then president of the American Psychological Association, announced that it was finally time to shift the traditional approach to psychology and start to focus more on the positive side of the curve. That we needed to study what works, not just what is broken. Thus, "positive psychology" was born.

GOING HUNGRY AT HARVARD

In 2006, Dr. Tal Ben-Shahar asked if I would serve as his head teaching fellow to help design and teach a course called Positive Psychology. Tal was not yet internationally well-known; his best-selling book *Happier* wouldn't be published until the following spring. Under the circumstances, we thought we'd be lucky to lure in a hundred undergraduates brave enough to risk a hit on their transcripts by foregoing a credit in, say, advanced economic theory for one in happiness.

Over the next two semesters, nearly 1,200 Harvard students

enrolled in the class—that's one in every six students at one of the most hard-driving universities in the world. We quickly began to realize that these students were there because they were hungry. They were starving to be happier, not sometime in the future, but in the present. And they were there because despite all the advantages they enjoyed, they still felt unfulfilled.

Take a moment to imagine one of these students: By age one, many were lying in their cribs wearing a onesie saying "Bound for Harvard" or maybe a cute little Yale hat (in case something terrible happened). Since they were in pre-pre-kindergarten—which in some cases they were enrolled in even before being conceived—they were in the top 1 percent of their class, and then the top 1 percent of those who took standardized testing along the way. They won awards, they broke records. This kind of high achievement was not just encouraged, it was expected. I know one Harvard student whose mother would keep every handwriting exercise and restaurant placemat drawing he ever did, because "this is going to be in a museum someday." (That was a lot of pressure on me, Mom.)

And then they get into Harvard, walk confidently into that Hogwarts-like freshman dining hall on the first day of college, and have a terrible realization: *50 percent of them are suddenly below average.*

I like to tell my advisees: If my calculations are correct, 99 percent of Harvard students do not graduate in the top 1 percent. They don't find that joke very funny.

With so much pressure to be great, it is no surprise to find that when these kids fall, they fall hard. To make matters worse, this pressure—and the depression that follows—pulls people inward, away from their friends, families, and social supports, at a time when they need the support most. They skip meals, shut themselves in their rooms or the library, emerging only for the occasional kegger (and then in an attempt to blow off steam they get too drunk to even enjoy themselves—or at least remember enjoying themselves). They even seem too busy, too preoccupied, and too stressed to reach out for love. Based on my study of Harvard undergraduates, the average number of romantic relationships over four years is less than one. The average number of sexual partners, if you're curious, is 0.5 per student. (I have no idea what 0.5 sexual partners means, but it sounds like the scientific equivalent of second base.) In my survey, I found that among these brilliant Harvard students, 24 percent are *unaware* if they are currently involved in any romantic relationship.

What was going on here was that like so many people in contemporary society, along the way to gaining their superb educations, and their shiny opportunities, they had absorbed the wrong lessons. They had mastered formulas in calculus and chemistry. They had read great books and learned world history and become fluent in foreign languages. But they had never formally been taught how to maximize their brains' potential or how to find meaning and happiness. Armed with iPhones and personal digital assistants, they had multitasked their way through a storm of résumé-building experiences, often at the expense of actual ones. In their pursuit of high achievement, they had isolated themselves from their peers and loved ones and thus compromised the very support systems they so ardently needed. Repeatedly, I noticed these patterns in my own students, who often broke down under the tyranny of expectations we place on ourselves and those around us.

Brilliant people sometimes do the most unintelligent thing possible. In the midst of stress, rather than investing, these individuals *divested* from the greatest predictor of success and happiness: their social support network. Countless studies have found that social relationships are the best guarantee of heightened well-being and lowered stress, both an antidote for depression and a prescription for high performance. But instead, these students had somehow learned that when the going gets tough, the tough get going—to an isolated cubicle in the library basement.

These best and brightest willingly sacrificed happiness for success because, like so many of us, they had been taught that if you work hard you will be successful—and only then, once you are successful, will you be happy. They had been taught that happiness is the reward you get only when you become partner of an investment firm, win the Nobel Prize, or get elected to Congress.

But in fact, as you will learn throughout this book, new research in psychology and neuroscience shows that it works the other way around: We become more successful *when* we are happier and more positive. For example, doctors put in a positive mood before making a diagnosis show almost three times more intelligence and creativity than doctors in a neutral state, and they make accurate diagnoses 19 percent faster. Optimistic salespeople outsell their pessimistic counterparts by 56 percent. Students primed to feel happy before taking math achievement tests far outperform their neutral peers. *It turns out that our brains are literally hardwired to perform at their best not when they are negative or even neutral, but when they are positive.*

Yet in today's world, we ironically sacrifice happiness for success only to lower our brains' success rates. Our hard-driving lives leave us feeling stressed, and we feel swamped by the mounting pressure to succeed at any cost.

LISTENING TO POSITIVE OUTLIERS

The more I studied the research emerging from the field of positive psychology, the more I learned how wrongheaded we are (not just the Harvard students, but all of us) in our beliefs about personal and professional fulfillment. Studies conclusively showed that the quickest way to high achievement is *not* a single-minded concentration on work, and that the best way to motivate employees is *not* to bark orders and foster a stressed and fearful workforce. Instead, radical new research on happiness and optimism were turning both the academic and corporate worlds upside down. I immediately saw an opportunity—I could test these ideas out on my students. I could design a study to see if these new ideas indeed explained why some students were thriving while others succumbed to stress and depression. By studying the patterns and habits of people above the curve, I could glean information about not just how to move us up to average, but how to move the entire average up.

Luckily, I was in a unique position to conduct this research. As a freshman proctor, I'd been blessed for a dozen years with an incredible close-up view of these students—what their habits are, what makes them tick, and what we can learn from their experiences to apply to our own lives. I'd been able to read all the admissions files, see the admissions committee's comments, watch the students progress intellectually and socially, and see what jobs they received after college. I also ended up grading a large percentage of them in the classroom as a teaching fellow for sixteen different courses. To get to know the students beyond just their exams and transcripts, I began meeting with students at my "coffice" in Starbucks to hear their stories. By my calculation, I have sat for more than a half hour individually with over 1,100 Harvard students—enough caffeine to get an entire Olympic team disqualified for decades.

I then took these observations and used them to design and conduct my own empirical survey of 1,600 high achieving undergraduates—one of the largest studies on happiness ever performed on students at Harvard. At the same time, I continued to steep myself in the positive psychology research that was suddenly exploding out of my own institution and out of university laboratories all around the world. The result? Surprising and exciting conclusions about what causes some to rise to the top and thrive in challenging environments while others sink down and never become what they have in them to be. What I found, and what you're about to read, was revealing, not just for Harvard, but for all of us in the working world.

THE SEVEN PRINCIPLES

Once I'd finished gathering and analyzing this massive amount of research, I was able to isolate seven specific, actionable, and proven patterns that predict success and achievement.

The Happiness Advantage—Because positive brains have a biological advantage over brains that are neutral or negative, this principle teaches us how to retrain our brains to capitalize on positivity and improve our productivity and performance.

The Fulcrum and the Lever—How we experience the world, and our ability to succeed within it, constantly changes based on our mindset. This principle teaches us how we can adjust our mindset (our fulcrum) in a way that gives us the power (the lever) to be more fulfilled and successful.

The Tetris Effect—When our brains get stuck in a pattern that focuses on stress, negativity, and failure, we set ourselves up to fail. This principle teaches us how to retrain our brains to spot patterns of possibility, so we can see—and seize—opportunity wherever we look.

Falling Up—In the midst of defeat, stress, and crisis, our brains map different paths to help us cope. This principle is about finding the mental path that not only leads us up out of failure or suffering, but teaches us to be happier and more successful because of it.

The Zorro Circle—When challenges loom and we get overwhelmed, our rational brains can get hijacked by emotions. This principle teaches us how to regain control by focusing first on small, manageable goals, and then gradually expanding our circle to achieve bigger and bigger ones.

The 20-Second Rule—Sustaining lasting change often feels impossible because our willpower is limited. And when willpower fails, we fall back on our old habits and succumb to the path of least resistance. This principle shows how, by making small energy adjustments, we can reroute the path of least resistance and replace bad habits with good ones.

Social Investment—In the midst of challenges and stress, some people choose to hunker down and retreat within themselves. But the most successful people invest in their friends, peers, and family members to propel themselves forward. This principle teaches us how to invest more in one of the greatest predictors of success and excellence—our social support network.

Together, these Seven Principles helped Harvard students (and later, tens of thousands of people in the "real world") overcome obstacles, reverse bad habits, become more efficient and productive, make the most of opportunities, conquer their most ambitious goals, and reach their fullest potential.

OUT OF THE IVORY TOWER

While I loved working with students, what I really wanted was to see if these same principles could also drive happiness and success in the real world. To bridge the gap between academia and business, I formed a small consulting firm, called Aspirant, to deliver and test this research at companies and nonprofit organizations.

A month later, the global economy began to collapse.

THE HAPPINESS ADVANTAGE AT WORK

. . .

Flying over the savannahs of Zimbabwe in the fall of 2008, I suddenly began to feel nervous. How could I lecture to people on happiness research in a country that had just been devastated by the complete implosion of their financial system, not to mention one ruled by a dictator, Robert Mugabe? When I landed in the city of Harare, I was taken to dinner by some local business leaders. In the dim candlelight, one of them asked me, "Shawn, how many trillionaires do you know?" I said jokingly, very few. He then said, "Raise your hand if you were a trillionaire." Everyone sitting on the floor at the dinner table raised their hands. Seeing my shocked response, another person explained, "Don't be impressed. The very last time I used a Zim dollar, I spent a trillion to buy a chocolate bar."

Zimbabwe had just been devastated by the complete collapse of its currency. All the financial institutions were struggling to survive; the country had even moved to a barter system for a while. In the midst of this, I worried that my research would fall on ears deafened by the concussions of repeated crisis. But to my surprise, I found people more eager than ever to hear about the research behind the principles. They wanted to bounce back from this challenge stronger than before, and they knew they needed a whole new set of tools to do so.

THE REAL WORLD

While I've since found that my seven principles of positive psychology have extraordinary applications in the workplace in both good
times and bad, the economic collapse very quickly crystallized the
need, not just to help businesses and professionals preserve their
well-being, but to help them maximize their energy, productivity,
and performance when they needed it the most. They recognized it,
too, for I suddenly found many once invincible businesses reaching
out their hands for help.

Within one year, I had spoken to businesses in forty countries
across five continents and found that the same principles that predicted success at Harvard worked everywhere I went. For a boy
from Waco who hadn't traveled much, it was a humbling experience
to meet so many people across the world, each with a different story
of happiness, hardship, and resilience. It was also a time of great
learning. I learned more about happiness during my travels to Africa and the Middle East in the midst of a crisis than in twelve years
of sheltered study. The fruit of that labor and research is this book.
From Wall Street traders to Tanzanian schoolteachers to salespeople in Rome—they all could use the now crisis-tempered principles
to propel themselves forward.

In October 2008, I was brought in to American Express to speak
to a group of vice presidents. AIG had just become a ward of the
Federal Reserve. Lehman Brothers had gone under. The Dow was at
a record low. So when I walked into the room at AmEx, the mood
was grim. Tired-looking executives looked at me ashen-faced, and
their Blackberries, usually chirping incessantly at the start of these
events, had fallen silent. Massive layoffs, leadership reorganization,
and a decision to restructure into a bank had been announced 30
minutes before my 90-minute talk on happiness. This was *not* going
to be a receptive audience. Or so I thought.

I assumed, just as I had in Zimbabwe, that the last thing a
group of people so distraught and unnerved would be interested in

hearing about was positive psychology. Yet again, it turned out to be one of the most engaged and receptive groups I have ever encountered. The 90 minutes turned into nearly three hours as executives canceled appointments and postponed meetings. Like the nearly thousand students who showed up for that first Harvard class on the subject, these highly sophisticated financiers were hungry to understand the new science of happiness and how it could bring them success in their jobs and careers.

The earliest adopters of the Happiness Advantage were the world's largest banks, as they were the first to get hit. I began researching and teaching the principles in this book to thousands of senior leaders, managing directors, and CEOs at some of the world's biggest (and most battered) financial institutions. Then I began to branch out to people and companies in all other sectors who had been hit hard by the meltdown. These were not happy times nor happy audiences. But regardless of their industry, company, or rank in the organization, rather than resistance, I found people almost universally open to learning how to use positive psychology to rethink the way they did their work.

INOCULATING AGAINST STRESS

Meanwhile, positive psychology researchers had finished a "meta-analysis," a study of nearly every scientific happiness study available—over 200 studies on 275,000 people worldwide.[1] Their findings exactly matched the principles I was teaching—that happiness leads to success in nearly every domain, including work, health, friendship, sociability, creativity, and energy. This encouraged me to apply the principles to other populations.

Tax auditors, for instance, are not known for happiness. But if we are going to test the effectiveness of the Happiness Advantage in the working world, I wanted to see if teaching the seven principles could raise the happiness, well-being, and resilience of an accounting firm right before they went into the most stressful tax season in decades. So in December of 2008, I gave three hours of positive psychology training to 250 managers at KPMG. Then I returned to see if the training had helped inoculate these individuals against the negative effects of stress. Testing showed that the principles did just that, and in very short order; the group of auditors who had gone through the training reported significantly higher life satisfaction scores, and lower stress scores, than a control group who had not received the training.

So it went at UBS, Credit Suisse, Morgan Stanley, and countless other beleaguered giants. In the midst of the largest downturn in modern memory, companies were instituting no-fly restrictions for their employees—similar to wartime, when you think about it—tightening their belts, trying to survive. Yet they found room in their budgets for my trainings on this research. The leaders of these companies recognized that more than just technical skills would be required to help their company rise above challenging circumstances.

Soon law schools and law firms also began knocking at the door. Understandably so; researchers have discovered that lawyers have more than three times the depression rate of the average occupational group and that law students suffer from dangerously elevated levels of mental distress.[2] Several Harvard Law School students told me that they often studied at the smaller Education School library because just being in the same room with other law students, even if no one said a word, spread negative stress like secondhand smoke.

To attack this thorny reality, I taught the seven principles to focus groups of lawyers and law students across the country. We talked about how using a positive mindset could gain them a competitive edge, how building up their social-support systems could eradicate anxiety, and how they could buffer themselves against the negativity that spread rapidly from one library cubicle to another. Again, the results were immediate and impressive. Even in the midst of their heavy workloads and tyranny of impossible expectations, these hard-driving individuals were able to use the Happiness Advantage to reduce stress and achieve more in their academic and professional lives.

SPREADING THE WORD

Despite the academic explosion of positive psychology, its ground-breaking findings are still mostly a secret. When I started in graduate school, Tal told me the head of his Ph.D. program estimated the average academic journal article is read by only seven people. This is an extraordinarily depressing statistic, because I know that number has to include the researcher's mom. That means we're down to about six people who read these studies. This is a travesty because scientists are making discoveries daily that reveal how the human brain works best and how we can best relate to one another—and yet only six people and one proud mom are privy to this information.

The more I traveled, the more I found that the groundbreaking findings of positive psychology are still mostly unknown in the business and professional fields. Lawyers who suffer from unbearable stress are unaware that specific techniques have already been developed to buffer them against this occupational hazard. Teachers in inner-city schools don't know about the study that isolated the top two patterns of successful teaching. Fortune 500 companies are still using incentive programs that were proven ineffective almost a generation ago.

As a result, they miss an incredible opportunity to get ahead. If a study has proven how CEOs can become 15 percent more productive, or how managers can improve customer satisfaction by 42 percent, then I think the people in the trenches should know about it, not just a handful of academics. The point of this book is to arm you with that research, so that you *will* know exactly how you can use the principles of positive psychology to gain a competitive edge in your career and in the workplace.

RAISING PERFORMANCE, NOT DELUSION

Grounded in two decades of research that has revolutionized the field of psychology, and further shaped by my own study of the science of happiness and success, the principles that form the core of this book have also been field-tested and refined through my work with everyone from global financiers to grade-schoolers, surgeons to attorneys, accountants to UN ambassadors. In essence, they are a set of tools that anyone, no matter their profession or calling, can use to achieve more every day. The best part about them is that they don't only work in a business setting. They can help you overcome obstacles, reverse bad habits, become more efficient and productive, make the most of opportunities, and help you to conquer your most ambitious goals—in life *and* in work. In essence, they are a set of seven tools you can use to achieve more every day.

Here is what they will *not* do. They will not tell you to paint on a happy face, use "positive thinking" to wish away your problems, or worse, to pretend your problems don't exist. I'm not here to tell you that everything always comes up roses. If there's anything the past few years have taught me, it's that this view is deluded. As I once heard a managing director at a large financial institution complain: "It's one P.M., and six times today I have heard that 'the company has turned the corner.' If we've turned the corner six times, I don't know where we are."

The Happiness Advantage starts at a different place. It asks us to be realistic about the present while maximizing our potential for the future. It is about learning how to cultivate the mindset and behaviors that have been empirically proven to fuel greater success and fulfillment. It is a work ethic.

Happiness is not the belief that we don't need to change;
it is the realization that we can.

CHANGE IS POSSIBLE

. . .

A behavioral riddle:

You are in a cage, behind bars. The bars are made of titanium, and your cage is empty. To survive you must consume 240 tiny pellets of food every hour. The pellets are provided to you but unfortunately are located in very small holes outside of your cage, so the process of reaching through the bars and actually grabbing a pellet initially takes you 30 seconds per pellet. If you can't learn to complete the task faster, you will only consume half the amount of nutrition you need, and will eventually starve. What do you do?

The answer: Expand the part of your brain in charge of this task so you can become faster at retrieving pellets.

Impossible, right? Well, not so fast. This riddle is, in fact, based upon a famous study from the field of neuroscience, only the subjects in the experiment were not humans but squirrel monkeys.[1] After 500 tries, the monkeys had become very adept at retrieving the pellets, even as the size of the hole continually decreased. So even though the task became harder, through practice they began to master it, like a young piano student who learns to master a scale. Intuitively, this makes sense. We've all heard the saying "practice makes perfect." But where it gets really interesting is when researchers looked at what was happening in the monkeys' brains as they got faster and faster at retrieving the pellets.

Using strategically placed electrodes, researchers were able to

25

establish the areas of the brain that showed activity when a monkey was first faced with this conundrum. Then they tracked their brain function as the monkeys reached for pellets over and over. When the researchers looked at the brain scans at the end of the experiment, they found that the amount of cortical area being activated by the task had increased several times over. In other words, through mere practice, each monkey had literally expanded the section of its brain necessary for accomplishing this task. And not over countless generations through the process of evolution, but over the course of one experiment conducted over just a few months.

Great, you might say, for squirrel monkeys—but for the most part, we don't hire monkeys in our organizations (at least not on purpose). But recent advances in neuroscience have proven that this process works identically in humans.

A SHORT COURSE IN NEUROPLASTICITY

"I'm wired to be unhappy." "You can't teach an old dog new tricks." "Some people are just born cynical and will never change." "Women are not good at math." "I'm just not a funny person." "She's a born athlete." Or so goes the established train of thought in our culture. Our potential is biologically fixed. Once a brain reaches maturity, it's pointless to try to change it.

Without the ability to make lasting positive change, a book like *The Happiness Advantage* would be a cruel joke—a nice pat on the back for the already happy and successful among us, but useless for the rest. What good is the discovery that happiness fuels success if we can't actually become happier?

The belief that we are just our genes is one of the most pernicious myths in modern culture—the insidious notion that people come into the world with a fixed set of abilities and that they, and their brains, cannot change. The scientific community is partly to blame for this because for decades scientists refused to see what potential for change was staring them right in the face.

To explain, let me take you back to Africa.

THE AFRICAN UNICORN

In ancient Egypt, carvings and writings spoke of a mythical creature, half-zebra, half-giraffe. When nineteenth century British traders found these carvings, they described this beast as "the African Unicorn," a fantasy creature and biological impossibility. However, natives of the Congo Basin insisted that they had sighted exactly such an animal deep within the forest. Even without the aid of modern genetics, the British explorers knew that was ridiculous. Giraffes simply did not mate with zebras, and certainly did not produce offspring. (Zebras might think giraffes have great personalities, but they just don't find them attractive.) For years, Western biologists scoffed at the ignorance and superstition of the natives for thinking that such a mythical beast was possible.

In 1901, the intrepid Sir Harry Johnston came upon some pygmy natives who had been kidnapped by a German explorer. Appalled by this atrocity, Johnston intervened, offering to pay handsomely for the pygmies' freedom. In gratitude, the freed natives gave him pelts and skulls they claimed were from the African Unicorn. Unsurprisingly, when he brought them back to Europe, he was ridiculed. There was no way these were the furs of an African Unicorn, people scoffed, because the African Unicorn didn't exist. When Johnston protested that although he never saw the creature, the pygmies had shown him its tracks, the scientific community dismissed his claims and debated for years about his sanity.

Then, in 1918, a live okapi—indeed a cross between the giraffe and the zebra—was captured in the wild and showcased in Europe. A decade later, the first okapi was successfully mated in Antwerp.

Today, the "mythical" okapis, which apparently weren't so mythical after all, are now quite common in zoos across the world.

In the 1970s, the Dalai Lama claimed that mere thought could change our brain structure. Even without the aid of modern brain scans and fMRIs, Western scientists knew this was ridiculous. While it might be comforting to believe our brains can change, they said, it was only a myth. And certainly, if the brain *could* change, it couldn't do so through mere thought or force of will alone. For most of the twentieth century, it was a commonly held notion in the most esteemed research circles that after adolescence our brains were fixed and unyielding. Neuroplasticity, the idea that the brain is malleable and can therefore change throughout our lives, was essentially the "Western Unicorn."

A few years later, some researchers began discovering tracks of what they claimed was this mythical chimera. This time scientists found clues not in the skull of an okapi, but inside the skull of a cabbie. Researchers were studying the brains of taxi cab drivers who lived in London.[2] (Small wonder scientists get mocked at dinner parties for their overly specific research subjects.) They found something previously unimaginable: The cab drivers' brains had significantly larger hippocampi, the brain structure devoted to spatial memory, than the average person's.

Why would this happen? To learn the answer, I went to the source—a living London cabbie. He explained to me that streets in London are not based on a grid system like much of Manhattan or Washington, D.C. As a result, navigating London is like navigating a Byzantine maze and requires that the driver have a vast internal spatial map. (It's so difficult, drivers are forced to take a navigational test called The Knowledge before being licensed to drive one of the city's famous black cabs.)

Who cares? While a bigger hippocampus may not seem exciting to you, it forced scientists to confront the "myth" of neuroplasticity, that brain change is possible depending on how you live your life. Faced with this data, a scientist who held rigid to a fixed-state brain model, which said that your brain does not change after adolescence, would be left with an awkward choice.

Either he would have to argue that (a) from birth, some people's genes develop a larger hippocampus because they know that they will one day grow up to become taxi cab drivers in London, or concede that (b) the hippocampus can increase in size *as a result of* many hours of practice driving a taxi cab in maze-like surroundings.

As brain scans became more sophisticated and accurate, more tracks of the mythical "Western Unicorn" kept appearing. Imagine someone we'll call Roger, who could see normally growing up but then suddenly lost his vision after toxic chemicals were splashed in his eyes during a high-school chemistry experiment.[3] After the accident, Roger was forced to learn how to read braille, which required him to use his primary index finger to feel every word he read. When neuroscientists put someone like Roger in an fMRI machine to scan his brain, they made some startling discoveries. When they poked at the index finger of Roger's *non*-reading hand, nothing out of the ordinary happened: A small part of his brain would simply light up, just like it would if someone tapped on any of our fingers. But then came the extraordinary part: When researchers tapped on Roger's braille-reading finger, a relatively enormous area of cortical mass would light up, like a halogen lamp clicking on in his brain.

To explain this, scientists again were left with two options. Either (a) from birth, our genes are smart enough to anticipate a freak chemistry lab experiment and thus arrange for a well-hardwired index finger on just one hand, or (b) our brains change in response to our actions and circumstances.

The answer in both cases above is obvious and inescapable. Brain change, once thought impossible, is now a well-known fact, one that is supported by some of the most rigorous and cutting-edge research in neuroscience.[4] And the implications are far-reaching. Once our brains were discovered to have such built-in plasticity, our potential for intellectual and personal growth suddenly became equally malleable. As you're about to read over the next seven sections, studies have found numerous ways we can rewire our brains to be more positive, creative, resilient, and productive—to see more possibility wherever we look. Indeed, if our thoughts, daily activities, and behaviors can change our brain, the great question becomes not *if,* but *how much* change is possible?

FROM POSSIBLE TO PROBABLE

What is the longest sequence of numbers a person can remember? How tall can a human being grow? How much money can one make? How long can a person live? The *Guinness Book of World Records* lists many of the greatest records set—the greatest potentials ever achieved. But, the *Guinness Book of World Records* is a fossil record. It speaks only to what *has* been done, not how much *can* be done. That is why it has to be constantly updated—records are forever being broken, so it is forever out of date.

Take the fascinating case of the British middle distance runner Roger Bannister. In the 1950s, after rigorous testing and mathematical computations of the physics of our anatomy, experts concluded that the human body could not run a mile in under four minutes. A physical impossibility, the scientists said. Then along came Roger Bannister, who in 1954 seemed to have no qualms proving that it could in fact be run in 3:59.4. And once Bannister broke the imaginary barrier, suddenly the floodgates opened; scores of runners started besting the four-minute mark every year, each one faster than the next. How fast does a human have the potential to run the mile—or swim the 100-meter, or complete the marathon—today? We honestly don't know. That is why we hold our breath during every Olympic competition, to see if a new world record has been established.

The point is, we do not know the limits of human potential. Just as we can't know the limit for how fast a human can run or predict which student will grow up to win a Nobel Prize, we still don't know the limits of our brain's enormous potential to grow and adapt to changing circumstances. All we know is that this kind of change *is* possible. The rest of this book is about how we can capitalize on our brain's capacity to change so that we can reap the benefits of the Happiness Advantage.

LASTING POSITIVE CHANGE

If change is possible, the natural question is, how long does it last? Can utilizing these principles make a real, lasting difference in our lives? In a word, yes. As you will read over the next seven chapters, studies have confirmed numerous ways we can permanently raise our happiness baseline and adopt a more positive mindset. Since this book is about the Happiness Advantage, it's more than a little comforting to know that people *can* become happier, that pessimists *can* become optimists, and that stressed and negative brains *can* be trained to see more possibility. The competitive edge is available to all who put in the effort.

I have also performed my own testing on the lasting effectiveness of positive psychology training. As previously mentioned, tests one week after the trainings at KPMG confirmed that employees were significantly less stressed, happier, and more optimistic as they began to implement the seven principles. But once the "honeymoon effect" dissipated, did it make any real difference in their lives? Or did they just go back to their old habits once the workload rose? To answer this question, I revisited KPMG four months later. Extraordinarily, the positive effects of the study held. The control group's spirits inevitably rose somewhat as the economy crawled back from its bleak December 2008 low. However, the managers who had had the training reported a significantly higher satisfaction with life, greater feelings of effectiveness, and less stress. The life satisfaction score, which is one of the most crucial predictors of productivity and performance in the workplace, had improved considerably for those who had the training; and, more important, statistical analysis revealed that the training was responsible for the positive effects. Again we saw that small positive interventions could create sustainable, long-term change at work.

FROM INFORMATION TO TRANSFORMATION

I once spoke with a sleep researcher who had data to show that the more you sleep, the more gracefully you age. "You must sleep 23 hours a day," I joked, as if he had never heard that one before. His faced turned serious. "Shawn, I'm a sleep researcher. I stay up all night watching people sleep. I never sleep." He revealed his age and it was true—he did look about ten years older than he really was. Far too often, just having the knowledge is not enough to change our behavior and create real, lasting change.

In the summer of 2009, I found myself suffering from this common pitfall myself. I was pushing so hard to bring this research to as many people as I could that I was crossing the Atlantic multiple times a month, cut off from my friends and family, and feeling overwhelmed. In short, the opposite of this book's prescription for success. It was a ten-hour plane ride from Zurich to Boston that finally broke this camel's back. Not just proverbially, but literally. Suddenly, a pain in my back and legs became so unbearable that I had to lie down in the back of the plane with help from the flight attendants. A hasty trip to the emergency room revealed that I had ruptured a disc in my back—so badly, in fact, that I spent the next month in a bed or lying on the floor. I had to get a massive cortisone epidural just so I could finally start walking again. Unable to travel or continue my research, I was forced to slow down, to finally spend some time putting these principles into practice in my own life. And I finally saw what I had been missing. These principles worked just as well for creating change for me in a personal crisis as they did for creating change for employees in the economic crisis. I will remain eternally grateful for that month, because it gave me time to practice what I had been preaching—to make those same changes in my own mindset and behavior that I had urged of so many others.

The point is that just reading this book is not enough. It takes actual focus and effort to put these principles into practice, and only then will the returns start pouring in. The good news is that the returns are indeed enormous. The fact that each principle is based on years of hard science means that these ideas have been tested, retested, and proven effective. Books about how to get ahead in the workplace can be inspirational but are often full of unproven strategies. On the other hand, science can be fascinating but is often impossible to understand, much less translate into action. My goal in writing this book has been to bridge that gap.

PART 2

THE SEVEN
PRINCIPLES

...

THE HAPPINESS ADVANTAGE

How Happiness Gives Your Brain—
and Your Organization—the Competitive Edge

In 1543, Nicolas Copernicus published *De Revolutionibus Orbium Coelestium* (On the Revolution of Celestial Spheres). Until then, most of the world had believed that the Earth was the center of the universe and that the sun revolved around the planet. But Copernicus famously argued that precisely the opposite was true—Earth revolved around the sun—a revelation that eventually changed the way humans saw the entire universe.

Today, a similar fundamental shift in the field of psychology is underway. For untold generations, we have been led to believe that happiness orbited around success. That if we work hard enough, we will be successful, and only if we are successful will we become happy. Success was thought to be the fixed point of the work universe, with happiness revolving around it. Now, thanks to breakthroughs in the burgeoning field of positive psychology, we are learning that the opposite is true. When we are happy—when our mindset and mood are positive—we are smarter, more motivated, and thus more successful. Happiness is the center, and success revolves around it.

Unfortunately, despite the decades of research that tell us otherwise, many businesses and their leaders still cling stubbornly to their belief in this flawed order. The ruling powers continue to tell us that if we just put our nose to the grindstone and work hard now, we will be successful, and therefore happier, in some distant future. As we work toward our goals, happiness is either irrelevant or an easily dispensable luxury or a reward only to be won after a lifetime of toil. Some even treat it as a weakness, a sign that we're not working hard enough. Every time we fall for this misguided creed, we undercut not only our mental and emotional well-being, but also our chances at success and achievement.

The most successful people, the ones with the competitive edge, don't look to happiness as some distant reward for their achievements, nor grind through their days on neutral or negative; they are the ones who capitalize on the positive and reap the rewards at every turn. This chapter will show you how they do it, why it works, and how you, too, can profit. In its own way, the Happiness Advantage, too, is a Copernican revolution—it shows us that success orbits around happiness, not the other way around.[1]

DEFINING HAPPINESS

No one would talk to me. I was minutes away from speaking about the connection between happiness and performance at work to a group of executives from the Korean company Samsung, just waiting for the HR manager to introduce me to the room. I usually enjoy getting to know people during this brief interlude before a talk, but on this day all the managers were staring ahead blankly, ignoring my repeated attempts at conversation. So I dejectedly pretended to fix my PowerPoint presentation (a surefire tactic for avoiding social awkwardness in these situations, though it works less well at cocktail parties). Finally, someone entered the room and introduced himself as Brian, the leader of the group. That's when I learned that the planners of the event had forgotten to mention one small detail: No one spoke any English.

As it turns out, the translator Samsung usually hired for these occasions was out sick, so Brian offered to translate for me. As we began, he leaned over and confided, "I'm not great with languages."

For the next three hours, I spoke in one-minute bursts, turning after each one to my "translator," who would proceed to either look very confused, or animatedly start speaking to the group, usually for about three minutes longer than I had. I have no idea how accurately he was translating, but I do know he got all the credit for my jokes. Given how bumpy this process was, I decided to stop talking and instead encourage the executives to talk to one another. "To study how happiness affects performance," I said, "we need a definition. So that's the question I pose to you: What is happiness?" Pleased with my little last-minute exercise, I waited for Brian to translate what I had just said. Instead, he looked confused and leaned toward me. "You don't know what happiness means?" he asked nervously.

My face froze. "No, I'm saying I'd like the *group* to come up with a definition of happiness."

He covered his microphone and leaned in again, clearly trying not to embarrass me. "I can Google it for you."

THE SCIENCE OF HAPPINESS

While I was appreciative of the offer, not even the all-knowing Google has a definitive answer to this question. That's because there *is* no single meaning; happiness is relative to the person experiencing it. This is why scientists often refer to it as "*subjective well-being*"—because it's based on how we each feel about our own lives.[2] In essence, the best judge of how happy you are is you. To empirically study happiness, then, scientists must rely on individual self-reports. Thankfully, after years of testing and honing survey questions on millions of people around the world, researchers have developed self-report metrics that accurately and reliably measure individual happiness.

So how do the scientists define happiness? Essentially, as the experience of positive emotions—pleasure combined with deeper feelings of meaning and purpose. Happiness implies a positive mood in the present and a positive outlook for the future. Martin

Seligman, the pioneer in positive psychology, has broken it down into three, measurable components: pleasure, engagement, and meaning.[3] His studies have confirmed (though most of us know this intuitively) that people who pursue only pleasure experience only part of the benefits happiness can bring, while those who pursue all three routes lead the fullest lives.[4] Perhaps the most accurate term for happiness, then, is the one Aristotle used: *eudaimonia,* which translates not directly to "happiness" but to "human flourishing." This definition really resonates with me because it acknowledges that happiness is not all about yellow smiley faces and rainbows. *For me, happiness is the joy we feel striving after our potential.*

The chief engine of happiness is positive emotions, since happiness is, above all else, a feeling. In fact, some researchers prefer the term "positive emotions" or "positivity" to "happiness" because, while they are essentially synonymous, happiness is a far more vague and unwieldy term. Barbara Fredrickson, a researcher at the University of North Carolina and perhaps the world's leading expert on the subject, describes the ten most common positive emotions: "joy, gratitude, serenity, interest, hope, pride, amusement, inspiration, awe, and love."[5] This paints a far richer picture of happiness than that ubiquitous yellow smiley face, which doesn't leave much room for nuance. Still, for ease of discussion, you will find that throughout this book the terms positive emotions, positivity, and happiness are all used interchangeably. Whatever you call it, our tireless pursuit of this feeling is part of our unique humanity, a fact that has been chronicled by writers and philosophers far more eloquent than I (including Thomas Jefferson in the United States' founding document). But as we are about to see, happiness is even more than a good feeling—it is also an indispensable ingredient of our success.

THE HAPPINESS ADVANTAGE AT WORK

In the Introduction, I mentioned the impressive meta-analysis of happiness research that brought together the results of over 200 scientific studies on nearly 275,000 people—and found that happiness leads to success in nearly every domain of our lives, including marriage, health, friendship, community involvement, creativity, and, in particular, our jobs, careers, and businesses.[6] Data abounds showing that happy workers have higher levels of productivity, produce higher sales, perform better in leadership positions, and receive higher performance ratings and higher pay. They also enjoy more job security and are less likely to take sick days, to quit, or to become burned out. Happy CEOs are more likely to lead teams of employees who are both happy and healthy, and who find their work climate conducive to high performance. The list of the benefits of happiness in the workplace goes on and on.

THE CHICKEN OR THE EGG

At this point you might be thinking: Maybe people are happy *because* they are more productive and earn higher pay. As psychology graduate students are taught to repeat ad nauseam: "Correlation is not causation." In other words, studies often only tell us that two things are related; to find out which causes which, we need to look at it more closely and find out which came first. So which comes first, the chicken or the egg? Does happiness come before success or success before happiness?

If happiness were just the end result of being successful, the prevailing creed at companies and schools would be correct: Focus on productivity and performance, even to the detriment of our emotional and physical well-being, and we will eventually become more successful, and therefore happier. But thanks to strides in positive psychology, this myth has been debunked. As the authors of the survey were able to say conclusively, "study after study shows that happiness *precedes* important outcomes and indicators of thriving."[7] In short, based on the wealth of data they compiled, they found that happiness *causes* success and achievement, not the opposite. Let's look more closely at how.

One way psychologists attempt to answer the chicken or the egg question is to follow people over long periods. One study, for example, measured the initial level of positive emotions in 272 employees, then followed their job performance over the next eighteen months.[8] And they found that even after controlling for other factors, those who were happier at the beginning ended up receiving better evaluations and higher pay later on. Another study found that how happy individuals were as college freshmen predicted how high their income was nineteen years later, regardless of their initial level of wealth.[9]

One of the most famous longitudinal studies on happiness comes from an unlikely place: the old diaries of Catholic nuns.[10] These 180 nuns from the School Sisters of Notre Dame, all born before 1917, were asked to write down their thoughts in autobiographical journal entries. More than five decades later, a clever group of researchers decided to code the entries for positive emotional content. Could their level of positivity as 20-year-olds predict how the rest of their lives turned out? In fact, yes. The nuns whose journal entries had more overtly joyful content lived nearly ten years longer than the nuns whose entries were more negative or neutral. By age 85, 90 percent of the happiest quartile of nuns were still alive, compared to only 34 percent of the least happy quartile.[11] Clearly, the nuns who were happy at 20 didn't feel that way because they knew they would go on to live longer; their superior health and longer life spans could only be the result of their happiness, not the cause.

This study highlights another clue to answering the chicken or the egg question: Happiness can improve our physical health, which in turn keeps us working faster and longer and therefore makes us more likely to succeed. This revelation provides companies an additional incentive to care about employee happiness, since healthy employees will be more productive on the job. Research shows that unhappy employees take more sick days, staying home an average of 1.25 more days per month, or 15 extra sick days a year.[12] And again, studies have determined that happiness functions as the cause, not just the result, of good health. In one study I'm glad I never volunteered to take part in, researchers gave subjects a survey designed to measure levels of happiness—then injected them with a strain of the cold virus.[13] A week later, the individuals who were happier before the start of the study had fought off the virus much better than the less happy individuals. They didn't just feel better, either; they actually had fewer objective symptoms of illness as measured by doctors—less sneezing, coughing, inflammation, and congestion. What this means is that companies and leaders who take measures to cultivate a happy workplace will not only have more productive and efficient workers—they'll have less absenteeism and lower healthcare expenditures.

YOUR BRAIN ON HAPPINESS

In addition to these longitudinal studies, scientists discovered more proof that happiness causes success when they started examining how positive emotions affect our brain function and change our behavior. Psychologists have long known that negative emotions narrow our thoughts and range of actions, which has served an important evolutionary purpose. In prehistoric times, if a saber-toothed tiger was running at you, fear and stress helped release chemicals that either prepared you to fight the tiger (which admittedly might not go very well) or flee from him (a contest you again might lose). Still, these were both better options than doing nothing and simply waiting to be attacked. So what evolutionary purpose would positive emotions have? Until recently, scientists were content to say that happiness merely makes us feel good, and end the inquiry there.

Thankfully, the last 20 years have changed all that. Extensive research has found that happiness actually has a very important evolutionary purpose, something Barbara Fredrickson has termed the "Broaden and Build Theory."[14] Instead of narrowing our actions down to fight or flight as negative emotions do, positive ones broaden the amount of possibilities we process, making us more thoughtful, creative, and open to new ideas. For instance, individuals who are "primed"—meaning scientists help evoke a certain mindset or emotion before doing an experiment—to feel either amusement or contentment can think of a larger and wider array of thoughts and ideas than individuals who have been primed to feel either anxiety or anger.[15] And when positive emotions broaden our scope of cognition and behavior in this way, they not only make us more creative, they help us build more intellectual, social, and physical resources we can rely upon in the future.

Recent research shows that this "broadening effect" is actually biological; that happiness gives us a real chemical edge on the competition. How? Positive emotions flood our brains with dopamine and serotonin, chemicals that not only make us feel good, but dial up the learning centers of our brains to higher levels. They help us organize new information, keep that information in the brain longer, and retrieve it faster later on. And they enable us to make and sustain more neural connections, which allows us to think more quickly and creatively, become more skilled at complex analysis and problem solving, and see and invent new ways of doing things.

We even quite literally see more of what's around us when we're feeling happy. A recent University of Toronto study found that our mood can actually change how our visual cortex—the part of the brain responsible for sight—processes information.[16] In this experiment, people were primed for either positivity or negativity, then asked to look at a series of pictures. Those who were put in a negative mood didn't process all the images in the pictures—missing substantial parts of the background—while those in a good mood saw everything. Eye-tracking experiments have shown the same thing: Positive emotions actually expand our peripheral line of vision.[17]

Think of the edge all this gives us in the workplace. After all, who wouldn't want to see out-of-the-box solutions, spot opportunities, and better see how to build upon the ideas of others? In today's innovation-driven knowledge economy, business success in practically every job or profession hinges on being able to find creative and novel solutions to problems. For example, when researchers at Merck first began studying the effects of a drug called Finasteride, they were intent on finding a cure for benign prostatic hyperplasia, otherwise known as an enlarged prostate. During checkups with the research subjects, though, they learned that many of the participants were experiencing a weird side effect: They were regrowing hair. Fortunately, the Merck researchers could see the billion-dollar product hiding in the unexpected side effect, and Propecia was born.

The Happiness Advantage is why cutting-edge software companies have foosball tables in the employee lounge, why Yahoo! has an in-house massage parlor, and why Google engineers are encouraged to bring their dogs to work. These aren't just PR gimmicks. Smart companies cultivate these kinds of working environments because every time employees experience a small burst of happiness, they get primed for creativity and innovation. They see solutions they might otherwise have missed. Famed CEO Richard Branson has said that, "more than any other element, fun is the secret of Virgin's success." This isn't just because fun is, well, fun. It's because fun also leads to bottom-line results.

JELL-O AT LUNCH

Positive emotions can begin to open our eyes and minds to new solutions and ideas even at a very young age. In one interesting study, researchers asked four-year-old children to complete a series of learning tasks, such as putting together blocks of different shapes.[18] The first group was given neutral instructions: Please put these blocks together as quickly as you can. The researchers gave the second group the same set of instructions, then asked them first to briefly think about something that makes them happy. Now, at only four years of age, these kids obviously don't have a wealth of happy experiences to choose from; they can't look back on career accomplishments or wedding days or first kisses (we hope). So most likely they thought about something along the lines of the Jell-O they had at lunch. Still, it was enough to make a difference. The children who were primed to be happy significantly outperformed the others, completing the task both more quickly and with fewer errors.

The benefits of priming the brain with positive thoughts don't end at childhood either. To the contrary, studies have found that across the board, in both academic and business settings, these same benefits persist throughout our adult lives. For instance, students who were told to think about the happiest day of their lives right before taking a standardized math test outperformed their peers.[19] And people who expressed more positive emotions while negotiating business deals did so more efficiently and successfully than those who were more neutral or negative.[20] The implications of these studies are undeniable: People who put their heads down and wait for work to bring eventual happiness put themselves at a huge disadvantage, while those who capitalize on positivity every chance they get come out ahead.

GIVE THE DOC A LOLLIPOP

In medical school, one way aspiring doctors are trained to make diagnoses is through a version of role-playing. They are asked to diagnose hypothetical patients, usually by reading a list of the patient's current symptoms and medical history. This is a skill that requires a good deal of creativity, because diagnostic errors often result from an inflexibility in thinking, or a phenomenon called "anchoring." Anchoring occurs when a doctor has trouble letting go of an initial diagnosis (the anchor point), even in the face of new information that contradicts the initial theory. If you've ever seen the television show *House M.D.*, you'll recognize how important creativity is in the field of medicine. The show's twists and turns demand that Dr. House switch from one diagnosis to another at warp speeds. (The show is exaggerated, of course, but in reality such changes are at many times necessary.) So to find out if positive emotions could possibly affect how well doctors make their diagnoses, a trio of researchers decided to send a group of experienced doctors back to school by giving them a series of these sets of symptoms to analyze.[21] The doctors were split into three groups: one primed to feel happy, one given neutral but medicine-related statements to read before the exercise, and one, the control group, given nothing.

The goal of the study was not only to see how fast they performed the correct diagnosis, but also how well they avoided anchoring. As it turned out, the happy doctors made the right diagnosis much faster and exhibited much more creativity. On average, they came to a correct diagnosis only 20 percent of the way through the manuscript—nearly twice as fast as the control group—and showed about two and half times less anchoring.

My favorite part of the study, though, is *how* the doctors were primed to be happy—with candy! It didn't take a cash reward or the promise of a promotion or an extra week of vacation to boost their moods enough to make them twice as effective and more than twice as creative; all it took was a small gift of candy right before they started the task. (And they didn't even get to eat the candy, to ensure that heightened blood sugar levels didn't affect the results.) This reveals something important about the Happiness Advantage in action: Even the smallest shots of positivity can give someone a serious competitive edge.

Two implications of these results immediately come to mind. First, perhaps patients should start offering their doctors lollipops, instead of the other way around. Second, and more important, perhaps hospitals should make a more concerted effort to improve the overall working conditions for doctors, by improving benefits, adding perks, or just allowing them shorter or more flexible shifts. If just a bit of candy makes our doctors more effective, imagine how much sharper, more efficient, and more creative a medical system we could have if hospital policies focused more on employee satisfaction (not just of doctors but also of nurses, med students, and technicians). It's not hard to see that this study, and all the others like it, have invaluable lessons to impart not just about how we should run our hospitals, but our businesses and schools as well.

THE UNDOING EFFECT

Bryan, a salesman in Des Moines, was already feeling nervous about his upcoming presentation when he heard a knock on his office door. "Big meeting at four," his boss reminded him. "You ready? This is huge—we need this account. Don't mess it up, buddy." As his boss proceeded down the hall, Bryan felt stress coursing through his body. Even though he already had the presentation down pat, he was now so nervous that he spent the next few hours going over it again and again, trying to anticipate where he might make mistakes, and reminding himself how terrible it would be for his company to lose this account.

Little did Bryan know that the more he focused his mind on the potentially disastrous effects of a bad presentation, the more he doomed himself to failure. While it may seem counterintuitive for many hardened businessmen, we now know that the best thing Bryan could have done in that situation is find a quick jolt of happiness.

Why does this work? Because in addition to broadening our intellectual and creative capacities, positive emotions also provide a swift antidote to physical stress and anxiety, what psychologists call "the undoing effect."[22] In one experiment, subjects were asked to make a difficult, time-pressured speech that they were told would be videotaped and evaluated by their peers.[23] As you might imagine, this induced considerable anxiety and measurable increases in heart rate and blood pressure—just how Bryan felt right before his presentation. The researchers then randomly assigned the participants to view one of four different videos: Two induced feelings of joy and contentment, one was neutral, and the fourth was sad. Indeed, the people primed with positive feelings experienced a faster recovery from the stress and its physical effects. Not only had the happy films made them feel better, but they had undone the physiological effects of stress. In other words, a quick burst of positive emotions doesn't just broaden our cognitive capacity; it also provides a quick and powerful antidote to stress and anxiety, which in turn improves our focus and our ability to function at our best level.

So instead of adding to Bryan's stress by reminding him of the high stakes of the presentation, his boss would have been better served by stressing the positives, with some encouraging words, or a reminder of the chief strengths Bryan brings to the table. Or Bryan himself could have employed any number of techniques to boost positivity and build confidence: visualizing himself giving a clear and cogent presentation, recalling a past instance when he made a successful business pitch, or taking a moment to do something entirely unrelated to his work that makes him happy—maybe making a quick call to a friend, reading a funny article online, watching a two-minute clip of *The Daily Show,* or taking a brisk walk around the block. Some of these suggestions may seem overly simple, or even ridiculous in a serious work setting, but given that their worth has proven scientifically unassailable, we'd be ridiculous not to use them. Everyone has one or two quick activities they know will make them smile, and however trivial they may feel, their benefits are worth it.

CAPITALIZING ON THE HAPPINESS ADVANTAGE

Obviously, there are people for whom this positivity comes more naturally. Once, after I had detailed the full extent of the Happiness Advantage at a corporate training, an exasperated executive stood up to say, "Well, that's great for happy people, Shawn, but what about the rest of us? We want that edge up too." His point is a good one, and he's right that if our level of happiness were set in stone, all this information would prove rather depressing news for the less positively inclined among us. Thankfully that's not the case. We can *all* reap the full benefits of the Happiness Advantage if we work hard enough at it. Remember, happiness is not just a mood—it's a work ethic.

Scientists once thought happiness was almost completely hereditary (dictated by a genetically determined "set point"). But thankfully, they have since discovered that in fact we have far more control over our own emotional well-being than previously believed.[24] While we each have a happiness baseline that we fluctuate around on a daily basis, with concerted effort, we can raise that baseline permanently so that even when we are going up and down, we are doing so at a higher level.

Each principle in this book contributes to at least one, if not many, of the things scientists have found to be most crucial to human happiness, like pursuing meaningful life goals, scanning the world for opportunities, cultivating an optimistic and grateful mindset, and holding on to rich social relationships.

As important as these larger shifts in thinking and behavior are, it's equally important to realize that the Happiness Advantage also lies in the small, momentary blips of positivity that pepper our lives each and every day. As we have seen, just a short humorous video clip, a quick conversation with a friend, or even a small gift of candy can produce significant and immediate boosts in cognitive power and job performance. As Barbara Fredrickson points out, while making big changes and pursuing lasting happiness is certainly a worthy goal, when we "look under the hood at the dynamics of the process" we've found that "we should be focusing on how we feel from day to day."[25]

With this in mind, here are a number of proven ways we can improve our moods and raise our levels of happiness throughout the day. Each activity listed below not only gives us a quick boost of positive emotions, improving our performance and focus in the moment; but if performed habitually over time, each has been shown to help permanently raise our happiness baseline. Of course, since happiness is subjective and not the same for everyone, we all have our own favorite happiness booster. Maybe yours is listening to a particular song, talking to a friend, playing basketball, petting a dog, or even cleaning your kitchen. My friend Abby gains an embarrassing amount of satisfaction from mopping the floor. Researchers have found that "person-activity fit" is often just as important as the activity itself, so if one of the tips below doesn't resonate with you, don't force it.[26] Find a personally tailored substitute instead. The goal is simply to lift your spirits and put you in a more positive mindset, so you can reap all the benefits of the Happiness Advantage.

Meditate. Neuroscientists have found that monks who spend years meditating actually grow their left prefrontal cortex, the part of the brain most responsible for feeling happy. But don't worry, you don't have to spend years in sequestered, celibate silence to experience a boost. Take just five minutes each day to watch your breath go in and out. While you do so, try to remain patient. If you find your mind drifting, just slowly bring it back to focus. Meditation takes practice, but it's one of the most powerful happiness interventions. Studies show that in the minutes right after meditating, we experience feelings of calm and contentment, as well as heightened awareness and empathy. And, research even shows that regular meditation can permanently rewire the brain to raise levels of happiness, lower stress, even improve immune function.[27]

Find Something to Look Forward To. One study found that people who just *thought about* watching their favorite movie actually raised their endorphin levels by 27 percent.[28] Often, the most enjoyable part of an activity is the anticipation. If you can't take the time for a vacation right now, or even a night out with friends, put something on the calendar—even if it's a month or a year down the road. Then whenever you need a boost of happiness, remind yourself about it. Anticipating future rewards can actually light up the pleasure centers in your brain much as the actual reward will.

Commit **Conscious** *Acts of Kindness*. A long line of empirical research, including one study of over 2,000 people, has shown that acts of altruism—giving to friends and strangers alike—decrease stress and strongly contribute to enhanced mental health.[29] Sonja Lyubomirsky, a leading researcher and author of *The How of Happiness*, has found that individuals told to complete five acts of kindness over the course of a day report feeling much happier than control groups and that the feeling lasts for many subsequent days, far after the exercise is over.[30] To try this yourself, pick one day a week and make a point of committing five acts of kindness. But if you want to reap the psychological benefit, make sure you do these things deliberately and consciously—you can't just look back over the last 24 hours and declare your acts post hoc. ("Oh yeah, I held the door for that guy coming out of the bank. That was nice.") And they need not be grand gestures, either. One of my favorite acts is paying the toll of someone behind me on the Mass Pike. Being able to counter the negative effects of traffic-induced stress is $2 well spent in my book.

Infuse Positivity Into Your Surroundings. As we'll read more about in the next chapter, our physical environment can have an enormous impact on our mindset and sense of well-being. While we may not always have complete control over our surroundings, we can make specific efforts to infuse them with positivity. Think about your office: What feelings does it inspire? People who flank their computers with pictures of loved ones aren't just decorating—they're ensuring a hit of positive emotion each time they glance in that direction. Making time to go outside on a nice day also delivers a huge advantage; one study found that spending 20 minutes outside in good weather not only boosted positive mood, but broadened thinking and improved working memory.[31] The smartest bosses encourage employees to get a breath of fresh air at least once a day, and they reap the benefits in heightened team performance.

We can also change our surroundings to keep negative emotions at bay. If stock tickers send your mood into a tailspin every time you glance their way, turn off CNBC. For that matter, you might also try watching less TV in general; studies have shown that the less negative TV we watch, specifically violent media, the happier we are. This doesn't mean shutting ourselves off from the real world or ignoring problems. Psychologists have found that people who watch less TV are actually *more* accurate judges of life's risks and rewards than those who subject themselves to the tales of crime, tragedy, and death that appear night after night on the ten o'clock news.[32] That's because these people are less likely to see sensationalized or one-sided sources of information, and thus see reality more clearly.

Exercise. You have probably heard that exercise releases pleasure-inducing chemicals called endorphins, but that's not its only benefit. Physical activity can boost mood and enhance our work performance in a number of other ways as well, by improving motivation and feelings of mastery, reducing stress and anxiety, and helping us get into flow—that "locked in" feeling of total engagement that we usually get when we're at our most productive. One study proved just how powerful exercise can be: Three groups of depressed patients were assigned to different coping strategies—one group took antidepressant medication, one group exercised for 45 minutes three times a week, and one group did a combination of both.[33] After four months, all three groups experienced similar improvements in happiness. The very fact that exercise proved just as helpful as anti-depressants is remarkable, but the story doesn't end here.

The groups were then tested six months later to assess their relapse rate. Of those who had taken the medication alone, 38 percent had slipped back into depression. Those in the combination group were doing only slightly better, with a 31 percent relapse rate. The biggest shock, though, came from the exercise group: Their relapse rate was only 9 percent! In short, physical activity is not just an incredibly powerful mood lifter, but a long-lasting one. Walk, bike, run, play, stretch, jump rope, pogo stick—it doesn't matter as long as you get moving.

Spend Money (but Not on Stuff). Contrary to the popular saying, money *can* buy happiness, but only if used to *do* things as opposed to simply *have* things. In his book *Luxury Fever*, Robert Frank explains that while the positive feelings we get from material objects are frustratingly fleeting, spending money on experiences, especially ones with other people, produces positive emotions that are both more meaningful and more lasting.[34] For instance, when researchers interviewed more than 150 people about their recent purchases, they found that money spent on activities—such as concerts and group dinners out—brought far more pleasure than material purchases like shoes, televisions, or expensive watches.[35]

Spending money on other people, called "prosocial spending," also boosts happiness. In one experiment, 46 students were given $20 to spend.[36] The ones who were told to spend the money on others (for instance, by treating a friend to lunch, buying a toy for a younger sister, or donating to charity) were happier at the end of the day than the ones who had been instructed to spend the money on themselves.

What are your own spending habits? Draw two columns on a piece of paper (or take ten minutes at work to create a nifty spreadsheet) and track your purchases over the next month. Are you spending more on things or on experiences? At the end of the month, look back over each column and think about the pleasure each purchase brought you, and for how long. You may quickly find yourself wanting to reapportion money from your "having" column to your "doing" column.

Exercise a Signature Strength. Everyone is good at something— perhaps you give excellent advice, or you're great with little kids, or you whip up a mean batch of blueberry pancakes. Each time we use a skill, whatever it is, we experience a burst of positivity. If you find yourself in need of a happiness booster, revisit a talent you haven't used in a while.

Even more fulfilling than using a skill, though, is exercising a strength of character, a trait that is deeply embedded in who we are. A team of psychologists recently catalogued the 24 cross-cultural character strengths that most contribute to human flourishing. They then developed a comprehensive survey that identifies an individual's top five, or "signature," strengths.[37] (To learn what's in your own top five, go to www.viasurvey.org and take the survey for free.) When 577 volunteers were encouraged to pick one of their signature strengths and use it in a new way each day for a week, they became significantly happier and less depressed than control groups.[38] And these benefits lasted: Even after the experiment was over, their levels of happiness remained heightened a full six months later. Studies have shown that the more you use your signature strengths in daily life, the happier you become.

One of mine is the "love of learning," and I feel noticeably depleted on the days I don't find an opportunity to use this strength. So, I find ways to incorporate learning into some of my boring daily tasks. For instance, I have to travel nearly 300 days a year for my work, and the continuous stream of airports and hotels can weigh on my mental health. I'd love to visit a museum in each new city, but unfortunately I often can't spare the time. So I decided that for each new place I visit, I would learn one historical fact. Even this small cognitive exercise makes an enormous difference in my mindset as I wing my way across the continents. So take the survey to find out your own signature strengths, then try to incorporate at least one of them into your life each day.

As you intergrate these happiness exercises into your daily life, you'll not only start to *feel* better, but you'll also start to notice how your enhanced positivity makes you more efficient, motivated, and productive, and opens up opportunities for greater achievement. But the Happiness Advantage doesn't end there. By changing the way you work, and the way you lead the people around you, you can enhance the success of your team and your whole organization.

PUTTING THE HORSE BEFORE THE CART: LEADING WITH THE HAPPINESS ADVANTAGE

Anyone can send ripples of positivity throughout their workplace. But one thing I've found in my work with managers and companies is that this is even more true for leaders or people in a position of authority—mainly because (a) they determine company policies and shape the workplace culture; (b) they are often expected to set an example for their employees; and (c) they tend to interact with the most people over the course of the day. Sadly, in the modern workplace, leaders often scoff at the idea that focusing on happiness can have real bottom-line results. Bosses and managers have a tendency to honor the employees who can go the longest without breaks or vacation and those who don't "waste" their time socializing. Few executives encourage their employees to take time out from their work days for exercise or meditation, or allow them to leave 30 minutes early one night a week to do some local volunteering—even though, as the research proves, the return on investment for each of these activities is huge.

Even more misguided, though, are the managers who discourage even the activities that involve relatively little time investment. Most of the people I work with admit that they would be embarrassed or ashamed if the boss walked by as they were laughing at a YouTube video, or talking to their five-year-old son on the phone, or telling a joke to colleagues in the hallway. And yet as we've seen, all these practices provide exactly the kinds of quick bursts of positive emotions that can improve our performance on the job. And the bosses who discourage positivity in their employees are at a double disadvantage, because these tend to be people who are most negative themselves. In short, sacrificing positivity in the name of time management and efficiency actually slows us down.

The best leaders use the Happiness Advantage as a tool to motivate their teams and maximize employee potential. We all know how this can be done on an organizational level. Google is famous for keeping scooters in the hallway, video games in the break room, and gourmet chefs in the cafeteria. The founder of Patagonia instituted a "Let My People Go Surfing" policy. (Should the mood strike you, he told employees, grab a surfboard from the office closet and hit the waves.) The data couldn't be clearer that these policies—as well as more conventional happiness boosters like gym memberships, health benefits, and on-site day care—consistently deliver big dividends. Coors Brewing Company, for example, reported a $6.15 return in profitability for every $1 spent on its corporate fitness program.[39] Toyota saw an instant jump in productivity at its North American Parts Center when it instituted a strength-based training for employees.[40] But it's true too that you don't have to make sweeping policy changes like these to capitalize on the Happiness Advantage. As we have seen, even the smallest moments of positivity in the workplace can enhance efficiency, motivation, creativity, and productivity.

One way to do this is simply to provide frequent recognition and encouragement. As studies have shown, managers who do so see a substantial increase in their employees' productivity. And not just by some small amount; one study found that project teams with encouraging managers performed 31 percent better than teams whose managers were less positive and less open with praise.[41] In fact, when recognition is specific and deliberately delivered, it is even more motivating than money.[42]

Recognition can be given in traditional ways—a complimentary e-mail, or a pat on the back for a job well done. But you can also get creative with it. One of my favorite examples is the one business consultant Alexander Kjerulf cites about a Danish car company that instituted "The Order of the Elephant."[43] The elephant is a two-foot-tall stuffed animal that any employee can give to another as a reward for doing something exemplary. The benefits come not just in the delivery and reception of well-earned praise, but afterward as well. As Kjerulf explains, "other employees stopping by immediately notice the elephant and go, 'Hey, you got the elephant. What'd you do?', which of course means that the good stories and best practices get told and re-told many times."

Chip Conley, CEO of a wildly successful chain of boutique hotels, makes time at the end of his executive meetings to allow one person to talk for one minute about someone in the company who deserves recognition.[44] It could be a peer or someone many ranks down, a manager or a maid. After the executive has spoken for one minute about why this employee deserves recognition, a different executive at the meeting volunteers to call, e-mail, or visit that employee to tell him or her what a great job that employee is doing. This isn't just a nicety; the benefits here are far-reaching. The recognized employee obviously feels great, as do both the executive who made the recommendation and the executive who gets to deliver the praise. Everyone else gets a mood boost as well—they get to hear about the good work being done at their company, and then they spend the next few days thinking about the good work of other employees they'd like to recommend during the next meeting.

Just as important as *what* you say to employees is *how* you say it—the best leaders know that delivering instructions in an angry, negative tone handicaps their employees before the task is even underway. One study done at the Yale School of Management paints this picture perfectly.[45] Student volunteers were put in teams to do business tasks together, with the goal of earning money for an imaginary company. Then in came the "manager" who was actually an actor instructed to speak in one of four ways: with "cheerful enthusiasm," "serene warmth," "depressed sluggishness," or "hostile irritability." Of these four groups, which two do you think not only became more positive themselves, but proved far more effective than the other groups, winning their companies more profit in the end?

Now think about which of these four tones you use most often. It might surprise you; we're often entirely unaware of the messages we're sending. I remember once, during a talk, one woman in the audience sat scowling at me the entire time. But then afterward, she was one of the people who waited in line to tell me personally how much she loved the presentation. I was shocked. Then I thought about how much negativity she was probably spreading to her employees on a daily basis, without even knowing it. So the next time you interact with a colleague or direct report, make an effort to adopt a more positive tone and facial expression. This does not mean you should be inauthentic, smother your true feelings, or paint an awkward smile on your face. But the more you make a genuine effort to avoid slipping into an apathetic or irritable tone, the more your team's performance will benefit.

This isn't only true in corporate settings. In environments thought to be even more stoic than corporate America—like the military—leaders who openly express their positivity get the most out of their teams. In the U.S. Navy, researchers found, annual prizes for efficiency and preparedness are far more frequently awarded to squadrons whose commanding officers are openly encouraging.[46] On the other hand, the squadrons receiving the lowest marks in performance are generally led by commanders with a negative, controlling, and aloof demeanor. Even in an environment where one would think the harsh "military taskmaster" style of leadership would be most effective, positivity wins out.

THE LOSADA LINE

Sure, there will always be naysayers and skeptics who admit that happiness may make work more enjoyable but resist the notion that it can give us a real, measurable competitive advantage. This is too bad. Maybe they think focusing on happiness in a serious business setting is unnatural, or a waste of time and effort, or maybe they believe that encouragement and recognition should be used as rewards for high performance, not as tools for driving it. And for some leaders, positivity simply comes less naturally than it does for others. As one London bank executive responded after I shared an idea for how he could infuse some positivity into his workplace, "That's a great idea. I'll never do it." To help these people capitalize on the Happiness Advantage, I often recommend that they keep one thing in mind: the number 2.9013. This may seem random, but a decade of research on high and low performance teams by psychologist and business consultant Marcial Losada shows just how important it is.[47] Based on Losada's extensive mathematical modeling, 2.9013 is the ratio of positive to negative interactions necessary to make a corporate team successful. This means that it takes about three positive comments, experiences, or expressions to fend off the languishing effects of one negative. Dip below this tipping point, now known as the Losada Line, and workplace performance quickly suffers. Rise above it—ideally, the research shows, to a ratio of 6 to 1—and teams produce their very best work.

This is not just some arcane mathematical formula, either. Losada himself observed countless examples of it in action. For instance, he once worked with a global mining company suffering from process losses greater than 10 percent; unsurprisingly, he found that their positivity ratio was only 1.15.[48] But after team leaders were instructed to give more positive feedback and encourage more positive interactions, their teams' average ratio increased to 3.56. And in turn, they made giant strides in production, improving their performance by over 40 percent.

Though originally skeptical, the company's CEO couldn't help but exult in the "notable transformation." He confided to Losada: "You untied knots that imprisoned us: Today we look at each other differently, we trust each other more, we learned to disagree without being disagreeable. We care not only about our personal success, but also about the success of others. Most important, we obtain tangible results."

Losada's mathematical ratio joins the increasingly long line of evidence in support of the Happiness Advantage—just one more way that groundbreaking science has triggered a Copernican revolution in the workplace. Once we accept this new order in the working universe—that happiness is the center around which success orbits—we can change the way we work, interact with colleagues, and lead our teams, to give our own careers, and our whole organizations, the competitive edge.

THE FULCRUM AND THE LEVER

Changing Your Performance by Changing Your Mindset

I fell for psychology the day my sister fell off the bed.

Once when I was seven years old, my sister Amy and I were playing on the top of our bunk beds. At the time, Amy was two years younger (incidentally, she still is), and at that time that meant she had to do whatever I wanted to do. I wanted to play war (I'm from Texas), so I lined up all my G.I. Joes and soldiers on my side of the top bunk against all her My Little Ponies and unicorns on the other side. I felt confident about the outcome; you don't have to know a lot about military history to know that very rarely have unicorns ever defeated soldiers on a battlefield.

However, there are differing accounts of what happened at the climax of the battle. I'm the one telling this story, so I will tell the true version. My sister got a little too excited and, without any help from me, fell off of the top bunk. I heard a crash on the floor and I nervously peered over the side of the bed to see what had befallen my fallen sibling.

Amy had landed on the floor on her hands and knees, on all fours. Now, I was nervous. First, because my sister was and is my best friend. More important, though, I had been charged by my parents with ensuring that my sister and I play as quietly and safely as possible, as they were settling down for a long winter's nap. I looked at my sister's face and noticed that a wail of pain and suffering was about to erupt from her mouth, threatening to wake my parents from their rest. Crisis is the mother of all invention, so I did the only thing my frantic little seven-year-old brain could think to do. I said, "Amy, wait! Wait. Did you see how you landed? No human lands on all fours like that. You . . . you're a unicorn!"

Now this was absolutely cheating, for I knew that there was nothing in the world my sister wanted more than for the world to realize that she was not Amy the five-year-old, but Amy the special unicorn. The wail froze in my sister's throat, as confusion took over her face. You could see the conflict in her eyes as her brain tried to decide whether to focus on the physical pain she was feeling or her excitement about her newfound identity as a unicorn. The latter won out. Instead of crying, waking my parents, and all the negative consequences that would have ensued, a smile spread across her face, and she proudly bound back up to the top of the bed with all the grace of a baby unicorn.

My sister and I had no idea that what we stumbled across at the tender age of five and seven would be at the vanguard of a scientific revolution occurring two decades later. No, we did not learn that you can lie to someone and manipulate them into being happy in the face of pain and suffering. What we learned was much more powerful: a scientific truth about the human brain.

Although we would never have used these words, my sister and I began to realize that our brains are like single processors capable of devoting only a finite amount of resources to experiencing the world. Because our brain's resources are limited, we are left with a choice: to use those finite resources to see only pain, negativity, stress, and uncertainty, or to use those resources to look at things through a lens of gratitude, hope, resilience, optimism, and meaning. In other words, while we of course can't change reality through sheer force of will alone, we can use our brain to change how we *process* the world, and that in turn changes how we react to it. Happiness is not about lying to ourselves, or turning a blind eye to the negative, but about adjusting our brain so that we see the ways to rise above our circumstances.

THE ARCHIMEDEAN FORMULA

Archimedes, the greatest scientist and mathematician of ancient Greece, famously posited, "Give me a lever long enough and a fulcrum on which to place it, and I shall move the world."

Twenty-two hundred years later, as I sat in a freshman dormitory watching students prepare for an exam, I had my own Eureka moment: Our brains, too, operate according to the Archimedean formula.

Take, for example, a seesaw. On a seesaw, the fulcrum is set at the exact center between the two seats. If two boys, each weighing 100 pounds, sit the same distance from the fulcrum on opposing seesaw seats, they will balance each other (until they start wiggling). Now, imagine two boys, one weighing 100 pounds and the other 150 pounds, in the same situation. The smaller boy is going to hang in the air until the larger one either pushes off with his feet from the ground or (as boys sometimes do) jumps off and lets his smaller companion crash earthward.

But what if we move the fulcrum? The closer we move the center point, the fulcrum, toward the heavier boy, the easier he is to lift. If we keep moving the fulcrum in that direction, eventually the lighter boy will effectively weigh more than his big-boned buddy. Move the fulcrum close enough to the heavier boy, and the lighter boy can climb off his seat and, with a single finger, use the seesaw lever to move his heavier friend up. In other words, by shifting this point around which energy is applied, we can effectively turn the seesaw from a balancing scale into a powerful lever.

That was exactly Archimedes' point. If we have a long enough lever and a good place to stand—a fulcrum point—we can move the entire world.

What I realized is that our brains work in precisely the same way. Our power to maximize our potential is based on two important things: (1) the length of our lever—how much potential power and possibility we believe we have, and (2) the position of our fulcrum—the mindset with which we generate the power to change.

What this means in practical terms is that whether you are a student striving for better grades, a junior executive striving for better pay, or a teacher hoping to better inspire students, you don't need to try so hard to generate power and produce results. Our potential, as we saw in Part 1, is not fixed. The more we move our fulcrum (or mindset), the more our lever lengthens and so the more power we generate. Move the fulcrum so that all the advantage goes to a negative mindset, and we never rise off the ground. Move the fulcrum to a positive mindset, and the lever's power is magnified—ready to move everything up.

Simply put, by changing the fulcrum of our mindset and lengthening our lever of possibility, we change what is possible. It's not the weight of the world that determines what we can accomplish. It is our fulcrum and lever.

MOVE THE FULCRUM, CHANGE REALITY

As a college senior, I took a class called "The Einsteinian Revolution," taught by one of the most passionate professors I've ever known, Peter Galison. On the first day of the course, every humanities major in the class trembled in anticipation of the difficult workload. I remember whispering to one of my friends during the introduction to the first lecture, "If this took Einstein 20 years, how are we supposed to get it before the midterm?" But somehow, Galison took one of the most complicated subjects in physics and made it come to life.

According to Einstein's Special Theory of Relativity, many of the seemingly inviolable laws of the universe become altered based on the observer. As a result, some amazing impossibilities in a seemingly "objective and fixed" world suddenly became possible. For example, take two people, one standing still and the other traveling close to the speed of light. Common sense might tell you that both will age at the same rate, but in fact, the person remaining still ages faster because time dilates with motion, relative from the stationary observer. In other words, time, once thought to be fixed and immutable, is actually relative to motion. According to Einstein, everything from length to distance to time is relative. If this sounds incredible, think about the impression it made on the nicely ordered world of classical physics.

Relativity doesn't end with mere physics. Every second of our own experience has to be measured through a relative and subjective brain. In other words, "reality" is merely our brain's relative understanding of the world based on where and how we are observing it. Most important, we can change this perspective at any moment, and by doing so change our experience of the world around us. This is what I mean by moving our fulcrum. Essentially, our mindset, and in turn our experience of the world, is never set in stone, but constantly in flux. If this is a startling realization for you, think of how shocking it was for a group of 75-year-old men who suddenly found themselves traveling back in time.

TURNING BACK THE CLOCK

If there is anything we thought we could be sure of, it's that time moves in only one direction. That was the prevailing view anyway, right up until my mentor Ellen Langer proved it wrong with one brilliant stroke.

In 1979, Langer designed a week-long experiment on a group of 75-year-old men.[1] The men knew little about the nature of the experiment except that they would be gone for a week at a retreat center, and they could bring along no pictures, newspapers, magazines, or books dated later than 1959.

When they arrived, the men were gathered into a room and

told that for the next week they were to pretend as though it was the year 1959—a time when these 75-year-old men were merely 55 years young. To reinforce the scenario, they were supposed to dress and act like they did at the time, and they were given ID badges with pictures of themselves in their mid-50s. Over the course of the week, they were instructed to talk about President Eisenhower and other events in their lives that had happened at that time. Some took to referring to their old jobs in the present tense, as if they had never retired. *Life* and *Saturday Evening Post* issues from 1959 were displayed on the coffee tables. In short, everything was designed to make them see the world through the lens of being 55.

Langer is a rogue psychologist. For nearly forty years, she has challenged the expectations of the scientific community in ways no one saw coming. True to form, in this case she had a truly radical hypothesis. She wanted to prove that our "mental construction"—the way we conceive of ourselves—has a direct influence upon the physical aging process. Langer had other words for it, but essentially she was arguing that by moving the fulcrum and lever of these 75-year-old men, she could change the "objective" reality of their age.

And that is exactly what happened. Before the retreat, the men were tested on every aspect we assume deteriorates with age: physical strength, posture, perception, cognition, and short-term memory. After the retreat, most of the men had improved in every category; they were significantly more flexible, had better posture, and even much-improved hand strength. Their average eyesight even improved by almost 10 percent, as did their performance on tests of memory. In over half the men, intelligence, long thought to be fixed from adolescence, moved up as well. Even their physical appearance changed; random people who didn't know anything about the experiment were shown pictures of the men both before and after the experiment, and asked to guess their age. Based on these objective ratings, the men looked, on average, three years younger than when they arrived. This flew in the face of everything we thought we understood about physiology and aging, and revealed radical new implications about the power of mindset to shape reality.

As we'll discover in this chapter, our external "reality" is far more malleable than many of us think, and far more dependent on the eyes through which we view it. With the right mindset, our power to dictate this reality—and in turn the results of our actions—increases exponentially.

SINGING EXECUTIVES, PLACEBOS, AND HOTEL MAIDS

As I looked out at the 70 managing and executive directors who had assembled for my talk at UBS in Stamford, Connecticut, I found many of them staring back at me skeptically. Their company was suffering massive restructuring and layoffs, legal battles, and a share price 80 percent off its high. And there I stood, asking this room full of battle-weary bankers to sing "Row, Row, Row Your Boat," over and over again. (At least this time I remembered to specify that they sing it in their own heads, not out loud—a detail I once forgot on Wall Street, where I quickly learned the true definition of "tone deaf.")

My instructions were simple: "Close your eyes and start singing the song in your head. When you get to the end, start again. Keep going until I say 'Stop.'" They did as they were told, though occasionally, the more cynical executives would peek to make sure I wasn't fooling with them or clandestinely wiring up electric shocks. In fact, I was fastidiously watching the clock. Finally, I told everyone to stop, open their eyes, and write down how long they thought the experiment had lasted, in minutes and seconds. One man guessed it had been two minutes, while another was sure it had been four. A woman in the back of the room guessed 45 seconds. There were 70 people in the room, and I heard 70 different answers, ranging from 30 seconds to 5 minutes. All of the executives were convinced that their estimate was right, but of course, there can only be one correct answer, which in this case was exactly 70 seconds.

I have done this experiment in nearly 40 countries, and every time I conduct it, I hear a tremendous range in answers. (Shanghai wins for the largest split: from 20 seconds to 7 minutes!) The point, of course, is that what feels like the blink of an eye to some can feel like an eternity to others. Depending on their mindset, each person experiences the objective reality of time differently. Perhaps those who think the song (or the exercise, or both) is stupid and boring, and are impatient to get back to work, tend to make longer guesses, while those who are interested and engaged in the talk or simply enjoy the brief period of relaxation tend to guess the time as being shorter. And as we all know, time flies when you're having fun.

The reason I enjoy this exercise is because psychology has shown that mindset doesn't just change how we feel about an experience—it actually changes the objective *results* of that experience. Anyone who has heard about the Placebo Effect already knows how powerfully this works. Countless studies show that when patients are given a sugar pill and told that it will help alleviate some symptom, it often does so—sometimes as effectively as the actual drug. In a *New York Times* article entitled "Placebos Prove So Powerful Even Experts are Surprised," doctors describe studies where fake hair product grew hair on balding heads and "sham surgery" diminished swelling in hurt knees.[2] Indeed, an empirical review of placebo studies found that "Placebos are about 55 percent to 60 percent as effective as most active medications like aspirin and codeine for controlling pain." The simple change in mindset—i.e., a belief that they are taking an actual drug—is powerful enough to make the objective symptom actually disappear.

Then there's what might be thought of as the reverse placebo effect, which is in many ways even more fascinating. In one of my favorite all-time experiments, Japanese researchers blindfolded a group of students and told them their right arms were being rubbed with a poison ivy plant.[3] Afterward, all 13 of the students' arms reacted with the classic symptoms of poison ivy: itching, boils, and redness. Not surprising . . . until you find out that the plant used for the study wasn't poison ivy at all, just a harmless shrub. The students' beliefs were actually strong enough to create the biological effects of poison ivy, even though no such plant had touched them.

Then, on the students' other arm, the researchers rubbed actual poison ivy, but told them it was a harmless plant. Even though all 13 students were highly allergic, only 2 of them broke out into the poison ivy rash! (I love this experiment, but the most staggering part is the fact that researchers somehow got permission to spread poison ivy on people who are highly allergic. I had to wait months for departmental permission to ask Harvard students to play charades.)

So how exactly is it that our relative perception of what is happening, or what we think will happen, can actually affect what does happen? One answer is that the brain is organized to act on what we predict will happen next, something psychologists call "Expectancy Theory." Dr. Marcel Kinsbourne, a neuroscientist at the New School for Social Research in New York, explains that our expectations create brain patterns that can be just as real as those created by events in the real world.[4] In other words, the expectation of an event causes the same complex set of neurons to fire as though the event were actually taking place, triggering a cascade of events in the nervous system that leads to a whole host of real physical consequences.

What this means in the workplace is that beliefs can actually change the concrete results of our efforts and our work. This isn't just a theory; it's been proven by a number of serious scientific studies. In one conducted a few years ago, Ali Crum, one of my former students and now research colleague from Yale University, teamed up with Ellen Langer to perform an experiment on the cleaning staff of seven different hotels.[5] They told half of the employees how much exercise they were getting every day through their work, how many calories their daily activities burned, how similar vacuuming is to a cardio workout, and so on. The other half of the cleaning staff, as the control group, was given no such good news.

At the end of the experiment, several weeks later, Crum and Langer found that those who had been primed to think of their work as exercise had actually lost weight; not only that, but their cholesterol had also dropped. These individuals had not done any more work, nor had they exercised any more than the control group. The only difference was in how their brains conceived of the work they were doing. That point is so important, it bears repeating: *The mental construction of our daily activities, more than the activity itself, defines our reality.*

MORE THAN 24 HOURS IN A DAY?

Given what we now know about the relative nature of time, ask yourself this: How much more efficient and productive (not to mention happy) could you be if you changed the way you view the hours in your workday? In a scenario where reality can be experienced any number of ways depending on where you put your fulcrum, the question becomes not "why are there only 24 hours in a day?" but "how can I use my *relative* experience of the workday to my best advantage?"

The most successful people adopt a mindset that not only makes their workdays more bearable, but also helps them work longer, harder, and faster than their negative mindset peers. In essence, these people use their positive mindsets to gain control (relatively speaking) of time itself. For them, 24/7 is only an objective clock-calendar measurement: They take the same units of time given to everyone and use their mindset to become more efficient and productive.

Think of the last interminable meeting you were forced to sit through (you probably won't have to think back very far). You may have decided in the first three minutes that the stated objective of the meeting was not going to be met, or that you didn't care about the objective to begin with. Those two hours that followed suddenly became a tremendous waste of time, a drain on your energy and productivity and probably also your motivation. But what if, instead, you chose to see the meeting as an opportunity, and created your own objective? What if you forced yourself to learn three new things before the meeting ended? If you can't learn them from the actual content of the meeting (and let's be honest, many meetings offer quite a low ratio of useful content to minutes spent sitting), be more creative: What can you learn from the speaker about how to (or not to) give a good presentation? How would you present this idea differently? What's the best way to handle difficult questions from colleagues? What's the best background color for PowerPoint slides?

Now think about other daily tasks you find just as tedious as meetings. I think you'll find that the more you think of them as drudgery, the more they become just that. I watched my own brain nearly succumb to this trap when I was researching this chapter. I generally love reading psychology books at coffee shops and then talking about their ideas with my colleagues and students. My brain considers that "fun" and "playtime." But because I had a deadline for finishing this book and I needed to read those studies for research, suddenly my mindset changed. Reading psychology books was now "work," and my brain attempted to avoid what I normally love. Tasks I once completed quickly and joyfully now made me feel as though I were wading through mental molasses.

I realized it was time to move the fulcrum. I thought about how I was defining the task mentally (menial labor) and consciously changed it (to reading for enrichment). I also changed the language I used to describe the activity to other people. After telling a few friends I was at Starbucks reading for pleasure, I started to realize that in fact I was. Altering my conception of the time constraints also proved helpful. Tal Ben-Shahar has pointed out that the term "deadline" is about as negative as you can get. How true! He likes to use the term "lifeline" instead. For me, the renewed enthusiasm for my work came when I ignored the constraint entirely and thought only of the intrinsic value I derived from the activity itself, instead of simply when it was "due." It also helped to stop focusing on how I would "use" the material I was reading later on. When we reconnect ourselves with the pleasure of the "means," as opposed to only focusing on the "ends," we adopt a mindset more conducive not only to enjoyment, but to better results. (I'm pleased to report that I did in fact turn my manuscript in on time, in case you're wondering.)

Just as our view of work affects our real experience of it, so too does our view of leisure. If our mindset conceives of free time, hobby time, or family time as non-productive, then we will, in fact, make it a waste of time. For example, many of the business leaders and Harvard students I work with exhibit the telltale symptoms of the "workaholic's curse." They conceive of all the time spent away from actual work to be a hindrance to their productivity, so they squander it. As one CEO of a telecommunications company in Malaysia told me: "I wanted to be productive because that's what makes me happy, so I tried to maximize the time I spent working. But, as I later realized, I had too narrowly defined what 'being productive' was. I started to feel guilty when I did anything that wasn't work. Nothing else, not exercise or time with my wife or relaxation, was productive. So I never had time to recharge my batteries, which meant that, ironically, the more I worked, the more my productivity plummeted."

As we learned in the last chapter, allowing ourselves to engage in activities we enjoy can actually greatly enhance our performance at work. But simply doing them is not enough to get results, just like it was not enough for the hotel maids who only went through the motions and didn't think about all the exercise they were getting. When your brain conceives of family dinner or Sudoku or fantasy football or a phone call with a friend as a "waste of time," it won't be able to reap its inherent benefits. But if you change the fulcrum so that you conceive of such free time as a chance to learn and practice new things, to recharge your batteries and connect with others, you'll be able to leverage the power of that rest time and return stronger than before.

THE LEVER OF POSSIBILITY

Just as your mindset about work affects your performance, so too does your mindset about your own ability. What I mean is that the more you believe in your own ability to succeed, the more likely it is that you will. This may seem like overly inspirational hokum to some (and in truth, the idea has been peddled by some less than reputable sources over the years). But the last few decades have seen an explosion of serious science in support of it.

Studies show that simply believing we can bring about positive change in our lives increases motivation and job performance; that success, in essence, becomes a self-fulfilling prophesy. One study of 112 entry-level accountants found that those who believed they could accomplish what they set out to do were the ones who ten months later scored the best job performance ratings from their supervisors.[6] Amazingly, their belief in their own ability was an even stronger predictor of job performance than the actual level of skill or training they had.

More important, our beliefs about our abilities are not necessarily innate, but can change, as our mindset is almost always in flux. In a study performed by Margaret Shih and her colleagues at Harvard, a group of Asian women were given similar math tests on two separate occasions.[7] The first time around, they were primed to think about the fact that they were women, stereotypically worse at math than men. The second time around, they were told to focus on their identity as Asians, generally thought to be math whizzes compared to other ethnic groups. The result: The women performed far better in the second situation than they did in the first. Their math

IQs hadn't changed and neither had the difficulty of the questions. But in the second instance they believed more in their ability, and this was enough to make a substantive difference in performance.

A fascinating real-life example of this emerged shortly after the 2008 presidential election. Decades of research have shown that internalizing racial stereotypes contributes to the achievement gap between black and white students. (For instance, African American students perform worse than whites on standardized tests when they are asked to fill out a form beforehand disclosing their race.) A team of researchers wondered if the ascendance of an African American to the country's highest office could lessen this phenomenon, so they administered a 20-question standardized test to more than 400 Americans, before the election and again right afterward.[8] On the first test, blacks did indeed score worse than whites overall, but on the second their scores improved so dramatically that the performance gap was erased entirely. As the *New York Times* reported, "the inspiring role model that Mr. Obama projected" erased the self-doubt that had hindered black performance. While this was only one study and its effects were probably temporary, it illustrates how strongly our beliefs can affect our abilities.

At the leadership training firm IDology, the trainers often ask their clients one question: "What identity are you wearing today?" If you're sporting self-doubt, you've undercut your performance before you even begin. So when faced with a difficult task or challenge, give yourself an immediate competitive advantage by focusing on all the reasons you will succeed, rather than fail. Remind yourself of the relevant skills you have, rather than those you lack. Think of a time you have been in a similar circumstance in the past and performed well. Years of research have shown that a specific and concerted focus on your strengths during a difficult task produces the best results.

You can use this technique in any situation. In charge of making Thanksgiving dinner but worry the food might not turn out as well as you'd like? Focus on the fact that you're good at time management and at following directions. Have to give a big presentation but believe you're a weak public speaker? Focus on how prepared you are, and how much research you've done on the material. This doesn't mean you should ignore your weaknesses or chant empty affirmations to yourself or take on tasks you can't handle, it just means to focus on what you are actually good at as you walk down the hallway. Remember your signature strengths from the last chapter? Pick one that applies to the challenge at hand. When I have to give a lecture on new material and I'm unsure how it will be received, I try to focus on the fact that I'm pretty good at reading people and how that helps me connect to an audience. There's a palpable difference in the quality of my talks when I remember to take this approach, as opposed to when I fall into the trap of lamenting my poor memorization skills or propensity to pace incessantly.

LEVERAGING INTELLIGENCE

More important still than believing in your own abilities is believing that you can *improve* these abilities. Few people have proven this theory more convincingly than Stanford psychologist Carol Dweck, whose studies show that whether or not someone believes their intelligence is changeable directly affects their achievement. Dweck found that people can be split into two categories: Those with a "fixed mindset" believe that their capabilities are already set, while those with a "growth mindset" believe that they can enhance their basic qualities through effort. A growth mindset is not dismissive of innate ability; it merely recognizes, as Dweck explains, that "although people may differ in every which way—in their initial talents and aptitudes, interests, or temperaments—everyone can change and grow through application and experience."[9] Her research has shown that people with fixed mindsets miss choice opportunities for improvement and consistently underperform, while those with a "growth mindset" watch their abilities move ever upward.

In one study, Dweck and her colleagues tested 373 students at the start of seventh grade to find out whether they had a fixed or a growth mindset.[10] The researchers then tracked their academic achievement over the next two years. They found that a student's mindset began to have an increasingly large effect on the math achievement scores as he or she progressed through seventh and eighth grade. The grade point average of students with a fixed theory of intelligence remained flat, while students with a growth mindset experienced an upward trajectory in their GPA—simply, those who believed they could improve, did. The researchers suggest a number of reasons a growth mindset propels students to further success, but it basically comes down to motivation. When we believe there will be a positive payoff for our effort, we work harder instead of succumbing to helplessness.

Beliefs are so powerful because they dictate our efforts and actions. In another of her studies—this one in Hong Kong—Dweck showed how growth mindsets lead people to maximize their potential, while fixed mindsets hold us back. At the University of Hong Kong, classes, textbooks, and exams are all in English, so you have to speak the language well to be successful. But many students are not fluent in English when they start classes, so as Dweck says, "it would make sense for them to do something about it in a hurry."[11] To these students, her team of researchers posed the question: "If the faculty offered a course for students who need to improve their English skills, would you take it?"

Then they also assessed each student's mindset: Did they think their intelligence was fixed and couldn't be changed? Or did they think they could improve their intelligence? It turns out that the students with a growth mindset were the ones who gave "an emphatic yes" to the opportunity to take the English course, while those with a fixed mindset chose on the whole to skip it. Those who simply believed in their own power to change followed a course of action that maximized their college performance. The others, given the same opportunity, squandered it.

Once we realize how much our reality depends on how we view it, it comes as less of a surprise that our external circumstances predict only about 10 percent of our total happiness.[12] This is why Sonja Lyubomirsky, a leader in the scientific study of well-being, has written that she prefers the phrase "creation or construction of happiness" to the more popular "pursuit," since "research shows that it's in our power to fashion it for ourselves."[13] As all these mindset studies have shown, this is true for positive outcomes and success in any other domain. By changing the way we perceive ourselves and our work, we can dramatically improve our results.

USING THE FULCRUM AND LEVER
TO FIND YOUR CALLING

Yale psychologist Amy Wrzesniewski has made a living out of studying how the mental conceptions we have of our jobs affect performance. After many years and hundreds of interviews with workers in every conceivable profession, she has found that employees have one of three "work orientations," or mindsets about our work. We view our work as a Job, a Career, or a Calling.[14] People with a "job" see work as a chore and their paycheck as the reward. They work because they have to and constantly look forward to the time they can spend away from their job. By contrast, people who view their work as a career work not only out of necessity, but also to advance and succeed. They are invested in their work and want to do well. Finally, people with a calling view work as an end in itself; their work is fulfilling not because of external rewards but because they feel it contributes to the greater good, draws on their personal strengths, and gives them meaning and purpose. Unsurprisingly, people with a calling orientation not only find their work more rewarding, but work harder and longer because of it. And as a result, these are the people who are generally more likely to get ahead.

For those who already see their work as a calling, this is great news. Those who don't, though, needn't despair. Wrzesniewski's most interesting finding is not just that people see their work in one of these three ways, but that it fundamentally doesn't matter what type of job one has. She found that there are doctors who see their work only as a job, and janitors who see their work as a calling. In fact, in one study of 24 administrative assistants, each orientation was represented in nearly equal thirds, even though their objective situations (job descriptions, salary, and level of education) were nearly identical.

What this means is that a calling orientation can have just as much to do with mindset as it does with the actual work being done. In other words, unhappy employees can find ways to improve their work life that don't involve quitting, changing jobs or careers, or going off to find themselves. Organizational psychologists call this "job crafting," but in essence, it involves simply adjusting one's mindset.[15] As Wrzesniewski says, "new possibilities open for the meaning of work" simply by the way "it is constructed by the individual."[16]

How does this work? Well, if you can't make actual changes to your daily work, ask yourself what potential meaning and pleasure already exist in what you do. Imagine two janitors at the local elementary school. One focuses only on the mess he must clean up each night, while the other believes that he is contributing to a cleaner and healthier environment for the students. They both undertake the same tasks every day, but their different mindsets dictate their work satisfaction, their sense of fulfillment, and ultimately how well they do their job.

In my consulting work with companies, I encourage employees to rewrite their "job description" into what Tal Ben-Shahar calls a "calling description." I have them think about how the same tasks might be written in a way that would entice others to apply for the job. The goal is not to misrepresent the work they do, but to highlight the meaning that can be derived from it. Then I ask them to think of their own personal goals in life. How can their current job tasks be connected to this larger purpose? Researchers have found that even the smallest tasks can be imbued with greater meaning when they are connected to personal goals and values. The more we can align our daily tasks with our personal vision, the more likely we are to see work as a calling.

Try this exercise: Turn a piece of paper horizontally, and on the left hand side write down a task you're forced to perform at work that feels devoid of meaning. Then ask yourself: What is the purpose of this task? What will it accomplish? Draw an arrow to the right and write this answer down. If what you wrote still seems unimportant, ask yourself again: What does this result lead to? Draw another arrow and write this down. Keep going until you get to a result that is meaningful to you. In this way, you can connect every small thing you do to the larger picture, to a goal that keeps you motivated and energized. If you're a law professor and you hate administrative work, draw your arrow until you can connect it to something you do care about, like providing a new generation of young lawyers with the resources they need to succeed.

Chip Conley, the innovative hotelier I mentioned in the last chapter, uses a similar strategy to engage his employees. He likes to tell each one: "Forget about your current job title. What would our customers call your job title if they described it by the impact you have on their lives?"[17] When you make these larger connections, your mundane tasks not only become more palatable, but you perform them with far greater dedication, and see greater returns in performance as a result.

WE AREN'T SAVING DOLPHINS

Before speaking at one Fortune 500 company in New York this past summer, I was introduced by a senior level executive who explained to the audience of 80 salespeople why I was invited. Having not heard my talk yet, he riffed on the importance of the training:

"Look, I understand that you are all here at work to make money, and you are frustrated that pay has been lowered over the past two quarters. So don't think about this as a session about happiness; think about how these strategies will help you make more money. To be honest, it has to be about money: We're not saving the dolphins here."

A few people laughed wryly, but I wasn't one of them. This executive had unwittingly primed his employees for failure. Here's what he had effectively said: "Saving the dolphins is meaningful and has a positive effect on the world, while the job you're in provides no meaning and worth beyond making you a lot of money." He had reminded everyone that they had jobs, not callings.

Sure enough, his dolphin quip had an immediate impact on the room. It was a poignant and humbling moment to see the group's mood deflate. Many of the employees who had moments ago seemed excited about discussing happiness at work suddenly gave off subtle but palpable signs of disappointment, chagrin, frustration, embarrassment, or disinterest. The fastest way to disengage an employee is to tell him his work is meaningful only because of the paycheck.

This is not to say that all jobs have equal meaning, but that even a rote or routine task can be meaningful if you find a good reason to be invested. You feel productive at the end of the day. You showed people you were smart or efficient. You made life easier for a client or customer. You improved your skill set. You learned from a mistake. I have met high school students bagging groceries at H-E-B near my house in Waco who sacked as if it was a calling. Of course, they didn't want to do that job their entire lives, but while they were doing their work, they were making the most of it. And I have worked with entrepreneurs who have built $100 million companies who view their job as soul-draining. You can have the best job in the world, but if you can't find the meaning in it, you won't enjoy it, whether you are a movie maker or an NFL playmaker.

CHANGING THE FULCRUM AND LEVER
OF THOSE AROUND YOU

As we have seen, a few choice words can alter a person's mindset, which in turn can alter their accomplishments. All it took for the hotel maids to lose weight was a short talk about how physically active they were. All it took for the Asian women to excel on a math test was a researcher reminding them of their innate intelligence. These studies show how mindset can affect performance, but also how we can affect the mindset of others. Sometimes a few key words here and there can make all the difference.

Imagine, then, the power we all have to influence the performance of those around us, positively or negatively. For instance, when researchers remind elderly people that cognition typically declines with age, they perform worse on memory tests than those who had no such reminder.[18] How many well-meaning managers shoot themselves in the foot when they similarly remind those under them at work of their weaknesses? Conversely, as we've seen, when a manager openly expresses his faith in an employee's skill, he doesn't just improve mood and motivation; he actually improves their likelihood of succeeding.

Even the way we describe seemingly straightforward tasks can make a difference in how people perform. In one experiment, subjects were asked to play either the "Wall Street Game" or the "Community Game," a task designed to measure people's willingness to cooperate under different conditions.[19] In reality, they were the exact same game. But those who had been primed to think of community were more likely to be cooperative than those thinking of Wall Street. What we expect from people (and from ourselves) manifests itself in the words we use, and those words can have a powerful effect on end results. This means, as you will continue to see in the coming chapters, that the best managers and leaders view each interaction as an opportunity to prime their employees for excellence.

THE PYGMALION EFFECT

According to the Roman poet Ovid, the sculptor Pygmalion could look at a piece of marble and see the sculpture trapped inside of it. In particular, Pygmalion had a vision of his ideal, the zenith of all of his hopes and desires—a woman he named Galatea. One day, he began to chisel the marble, crafting it to his vision. When he was finished, he stepped back and looked at his work. It was beautiful. Galatea was more than just a woman: The statue represented every hope, every dream, every possibility, every meaning—beauty itself. Inevitably, Pygmalion fell in love.

Now, Pygmalion was no fool. He was not in love with a stone woman; he was in love with the possibility of his ideal coming to life. So he asked the goddess of love, Venus, if she would grant him one wish and make his ideal a reality. And so she did, at least according to the myth.

Now fast-forward to the twentieth century, to one of the most well-known psychology experiments ever performed. A team of researchers led by Robert Rosenthal went into an elementary school and administered intelligence tests to the students.[20] The researchers then told the teachers in each of the classrooms which students—say, Sam, Sally, and Sarah—the data had identified as academic superstars, the ones with the greatest potential for growth. They asked the teachers not to mention the results of the study to the students, and not to spend any more or less time with them. (And, in fact, the teachers were warned they would be observed to make sure they did not.) At the end of the year, the students were tested again, and indeed, Sam, Sally, and Sarah posted off-the-chart intellectual ability.

This would be a predictable story, except for an O. Henry-type twist at the end. When Sam, Sally, and Sarah had been tested at the beginning of the experiment, they were found to be absolutely, wonderfully *ordinary*. The researchers had randomly picked their names and then lied to the teachers about their ability. But after the experiment, they had in fact turned into academic superstars. So what caused these ordinary students to become extraordinary? Although the teachers had said nothing directly to these children and had spent equal amounts of time with everyone, two crucial things had happened. The belief the teachers had in the students' potential had been unwittingly and nonverbally communicated. More important, these nonverbal messages were then digested by the students and transformed into reality.

This phenomenon is called the Pygmalion Effect: when our belief in another person's potential brings that potential to life. Whether we are trying to uncover the talent in a class of second graders or in the workers sitting around at the morning meeting, the Pygmalion Effect can happen anywhere. The expectations we have about our children, co-workers, and spouses—whether or not they are ever voiced—can make that expectation a reality.

MOTIVATING A TEAM WITH THE PYGMALION EFFECT

In the 1960s, MIT business professor Douglas McGregor famously posited that managers subscribe to one of two theories of human motivation. Theory X holds that people work because you pay them, and that if you don't watch them they will stop working. Theory Y holds the opposite: that people work for intrinsic motives, that they work harder and better when not being ordered around, and that they do it for the satisfaction they receive from good work.

When researchers try to study what happens when X (or Y) workers are exposed to leaders with the opposing view, they run into a very telling snag. Very few managers have employees with opposing theories. Managers who believe Theory X turn out to have workers who need constant supervision, while managers who hold to Theory Y have employees who work for the love of the job. Turns out that no matter what their motivations might have been before working for these managers, employees typically become the kind of worker their manager expects them to be. Here is the Pygmalion Effect in action.

This is a shining example of a self-fulfilling prophecy: People act as we expect them to act, which means that a leader's expectations about what he thinks will motivate his employees often end up coming true. The more that Fortune 500 executive assumed his employees worked for their paychecks and not to "save dolphins," the more their motivation shifted toward Theory X, further and further away from meaningful work. In fact, rarely have I seen an optimistic and motivated worker under the supervision of a pessimistic, apathetic manager. As the leaders go, so go their employees.

Naturally, the Pygmalion Effect can be a very powerful tool in business. So if you are a leader, whether of 3 people or 300, remember that the power to affect results rests not just in who's on your team, but how you leverage your team. Every Monday, ask yourself these three questions: (1) Do I believe that the intelligence and skills of my employees are not fixed, but can be improved with effort?; (2) Do I believe that my employees want to make that effort, just as they want to find meaning and fulfillment in their jobs?; and (3) How am I conveying these beliefs in my daily words and actions?

SUPERMAN'S CAPE

In some states, the Superman capes you can buy for Halloween are required to carry a warning that the capes won't actually help you fly. Sounds hilarious, but it's a useful reminder of the one caveat to the fulcrum and lever principle. While it's important to shift our fulcrum to a more positive mindset, we don't want to shift it too far—in other words, we have to be careful not to have unrealistic expectations about our potential. While so much of our experience is relative and dependent on mindset, there are of course still concrete restraints (like gravity, for one). But it returns us to the question I posed in the chapter "Change Is Possible": How do we know what our potential is, and what kind of limits should we put on it? Imagine, for example, running shoes that say: "Do not attempt to run a sub-four-minute mile—injuries could result."

Such warnings might sometimes be necessary, of course. It's when they cause us to artificially shorten our horizons that they cause a problem. My field of study attempts to push back at these illusory boundaries by looking at positive outliers who have already gone beyond them. We want to push the limits of possibility as far as they *can* go, not limit them in the way too many discouraging bosses, parents, teachers, or media stories tell us they *should* be limited. Sure, simply believing we can fly won't set us aloft. Yet if we don't believe, we have no chance of ever making it off the ground. And, as science has shown, when we believe we can do more and achieve more (or when others believe it for us), that is often the precise reason we *do* achieve more.

The heart of the challenge is to stop thinking of the world as fixed when reality is, in truth, relative. We have seen how 75-year-old men turned back their biological clocks, how a few choice words and beliefs can improve test scores, and how some employees find callings where others see only jobs. Yet this is still a relatively small glimpse into all the ways our mindset can shape the objective world around us. The next few chapters will show us precisely how we can cultivate a positive mindset—and capitalize on this positivity to move ever upward in our jobs, our careers, and our organizations.

THE TETRIS EFFECT

Training Your Brain to Capitalize on Possibility

One chilly Massachusetts morning, back in September of 2005, I walked out of Wigglesworth residence hall (yes, that's the real name) and almost attempted to steal a police car. Admittedly, this had all the earmarks of a bad career move, especially since part of my job description was to be a positive role model and help teach impressionable young undergraduates a sense of responsibility. So what could possibly have driven me to do such a thing? Unbelievably, it was a video game called Grand Theft Auto, which I had stayed up until 4.00 A.M. playing the night before.

For five straight hours, my brain had grown accustomed to the following pattern: find a car to steal, engage in a high-speed chase, reap the reward (in this case, fake money). Of course, this was just a stupid video game, and should have had absolutely no bearing on my behavior in the real world. But after so many hours of repeated play, when I woke up the next morning, my brain was still stuck in this way of thinking. Which is why I walked out onto Massachusetts Avenue and scanned my environment for a vulnerable car. To my brain's momentary delight, the best car to steal—a police car—was serendipitously parked not five feet from me. Yes! Before the rational part of my brain had time to get a word in edgewise, I found myself acting on the pattern I had been practicing the evening before.

Adrenaline shot through my body as I reached for the shiny handle of the Cambridge Police cruiser. The fact that there was a police officer sitting in the front seat . . . well, that was no problem.

I would just have to press X on the controller and it would automatically pull the officer out of the car. It took seeing my reflection in the window to finally jolt me out of Grand Theft Auto world and back into my senses.

True story. Blessedly, I did not go through with the crime. (Can you imagine the trial? "Harvard Adviser Tells Court: 'Brain Stuck in *Vice City*, Couldn't Help It.'") Yet while obviously I had no real desire to commit grand larceny that morning, for that one moment, I could only follow the pattern I had been practicing to see. And as I soon learned, this is not entirely uncommon; it has to do with the way our brains are programmed to work in the real world.

GETTING IN SHAPES

In September 2002, a British 23-year-old named Faiz Chopdat was jailed for four months after refusing to turn off his cell phone on a flight from Egypt to England. The crew had repeatedly requested that he switch off the phone so it wouldn't interfere with the plane's communications system, and he'd openly ignored them. The reason: He was playing Tetris.

Tetris, as you probably know, is a deceptively simple game in which four kinds of shapes fall from the top of the screen, and the player can rotate or move them until they hit the bottom. When these blocks create an unbroken horizontal line across the entire screen, that line disappears. The sole point of the game is to arrange the falling shapes in a way that will create as many unbroken lines as possible. Sounds boring, but as Chopdat learned the hard way, it can be surprisingly addictive.

In a study at Harvard Medical School's Department of Psychiatry, researchers paid 27 people to play Tetris for multiple hours a day, three days in a row.[1] Whenever I mention this to students, they can't believe they missed an opportunity to play video games for pay. But wait until you hear about the side effects, I tell them.

For days after the study, some participants literally couldn't stop dreaming about shapes falling from the sky. Others couldn't stop seeing these shapes everywhere, even in their waking hours. Quite simply, they couldn't stop seeing their world as being made up of sequences of Tetris blocks.

One Tetris addict wrote about his own experience in the *Philadelphia City Paper:* "Walking through the aisles at the local Acme, trying to decide between Honey Nut or the new Frosted Cheerios, I notice how perfectly one set of cereal boxes would fit in with the gap on the row below it. Running doggedly around the track at the Y, bored out of my mind, I find myself focusing on the brick wall and calculating which direction I'd have to rotate those slightly darker bricks to make them fit in with the uneven row of dark bricks a few feet lower down the wall. Going out to get some fresh air after hours of work, I rub my watery, stinging eyes, look up at the Philadelphia skyline, and wonder, 'If I flip the Victory Building on its side, would it fit into the gap between Liberties One and Two?'"² Gamers soon took to calling this bizarre condition the Tetris Effect.

What was going on here? Are Tetris addicts temporarily insane? Not at all. The Tetris Effect stems from a very normal physical process that repeated playing triggers in their brains. They become stuck in something called a "cognitive afterimage." You know those blue or green dots that cloud your vision for a few seconds after someone takes a flash photograph of you? This happens because the flash has momentarily burned an image onto your visual field so that as you look around at the world, you see that same light pattern—that afterimage—everywhere. When these kids played Tetris for an extended period, they similarly became stuck with something clouding their vision—in this case, a cognitive pattern that caused them to involuntarily see Tetris shapes wherever they looked (just as Grand Theft Auto had made me involuntarily see cars to lift). This isn't just a vision problem—playing hour after hour of Tetris actually changes the wiring of the brain. Specifically, as subsequent studies found, the consistent play was creating new neural pathways, new connections that warped the way they viewed real-life situations.

To be sure, this would be great news if these students were training for a Tetris tournament. But it proved extremely maladaptive when they were doing non-Tetris activities; and let's face it, very few jobs reward obsessive Tetris-playing. That's the way it is with our brains: They very easily get stuck in patterns of viewing the world, some more beneficial than others. But of course, the Tetris Effect isn't just about video games; as we're about to explain in more detail, it is a metaphor for the way our brains dictate the way we see the world around us.

THE TETRIS EFFECT AT WORK

Everyone knows someone stuck in some version of the Tetris Effect—someone who is unable to break a pattern of thinking or behaving. Often, this pattern can be negative. The friend who walks into any room and immediately finds the one thing to complain about. The boss who focuses on what an employee continues to do wrong, instead of how he's improving. The colleague who predicts doom before every meeting, no matter the circumstances. You know the type. Maybe you're even one of them.

In my work with Fortune 500 companies, I've learned something very valuable: These people usually aren't *trying* to be difficult or grumpy. Their brains are just really outstanding at scanning their environment for negatives—at immediately spotting the annoyances and stresses and hassles. And no small wonder, given that, like the Tetris players, their brains have been honed and trained to do so through years of practice. Unfortunately, our society only encourages this kind of training. Think about it: In the work world, as in our personal lives, we are often rewarded for noticing the problems that need solving, the stresses that need managing, and the injustices that need righting. Sometimes this can be very useful. The problem is that if we get stuck in only that pattern, always looking for and picking up on the negative, even a paradise can become a hell. And worse, the better we get at scanning for the negative, the more we miss out on the positive—those things in life that bring us greater happiness, and in turn fuel our success. The good news is that we can also train our brains to scan for the positive—for the possibilities dormant in every situation—and become experts at capitalizing on the Happiness Advantage.

During a break from one of my talks in Australia, I walked outside to get some fresh air and stumbled upon two employees, also on break. One glanced up at the sky and said, "It's nice that it's sunny today." The other one said, "I wish it wasn't so hot today." Both statements were based on reality. It *was* sunny and it *was* hot. But the second person was giving into a habit that would prove debilitating to his productivity and performance the second he walked back into his office. He literally couldn't see the positives in his life and in his work—the opportunities, the possibilities, the chances for growth—and as a result, he didn't have even a fighting chance of capitalizing on them. This is no small thing. Constantly scanning the world for the negative comes with a great cost. It undercuts our creativity, raises our stress levels, and lowers our motivation and ability to accomplish goals.

BRINGING THE TETRIS EFFECT HOME

Over the past year, as I have been working with the global tax-accounting firm KPMG to help their tax auditors and managers become happier, I began to realize that many of the employees were suffering from an unfortunate problem. Many of them had to spend 8 to 14 hours a day scanning tax forms for errors, and as they did, their brains were becoming wired to look for mistakes. This made them very good at their jobs, but they were getting so expert at seeing errors and potential pitfalls that this habit started to spill over into other areas of their lives.

Like the Tetris players who suddenly saw those blocks everywhere, these accountants experienced each day as a tax audit, always scanning the world for the worst. As you can imagine, this was no picnic, and what's more, it was undermining their relationships at work and at home. In performance reviews, they noticed only the faults of their team members, never the strengths. When they went home to their families, they noticed only the C's on their kids' report cards, never the A's. When they ate at restaurants, they could only notice that the potatoes were underdone—never that the steak was cooked perfectly. One tax auditor confided that he had been very depressed over the past quarter. As we discussed why, he mentioned in passing that one day during a break at work he had made an Excel spreadsheet listing all the mistakes his wife had made over the past six weeks. Imagine the reaction of his wife (or soon to be ex wife) when he brought that list of faults home in an attempt to make things better.

Tax auditors are far from the only ones who get stuck in this kind of pattern. Lawyers are just as susceptible, if not more so—which is one reason studies have found that they are 3.6 times more likely to suffer from major depressive disorder than the rest of the employed population.[3] (When I mentioned that statistic at a hospital in California, the doctors, not big fans of malpractice suits, burst into applause.) This might seem a relatively surprising finding given that lawyers have high levels of education, pay, and status, but in fact, given what they are required to do all day long, it's not that surprising at all.

The problem starts in law school, where levels of distress spike as soon as students settle into their classes and start learning the techniques of critical analysis.[4] Why? Because, as one study from *The Yale Journal of Health Policy, Law, and Ethics* explains: "Law schools teach students to look for flaws in arguments, and they train them to be critical rather than accepting."[5] And while this of course is "a crucial skill for lawyers in practice," when it starts to leak beyond the courtroom into their personal lives it can have "significant negative consequences." Trained to be on the lookout for the flaws in every argument, the holes in every case, they start "to overestimate the significance and permanence of the problems they encounter," the fastest route to depression and anxiety—which in turn interferes with their ability to do their job.

Over the years, I've talked with many lawyers who sheepishly admitted that they had a habit of "deposing" their children when they got home from work *("But if you were, as your alibi suggests, at the movies until 10:30, please explain to the court how you came to be 15 minutes late for curfew?").* Others have said they find themselves involuntarily thinking about quality time with their spouses in terms of quantified, billable hours. Even during their moments of leisure, the lawyers could tell you exactly how much money they had just wasted discussing the color of the new wallpaper. Like the fault-finding accountants, their brains get stuck in a pattern. And so it goes, in any profession or line of work. No one is immune. Athletes can't stop competing with their friends or families. Social workers who deal with domestic abuse can't stop distrusting men. Financial traders can't stop assessing the risk inherent in everything they do. Managers can't stop micromanaging their children's lives.

Admittedly, being stuck in these patterns might well make someone very successful in a particular aspect of his or her work. Tax auditors *should* look for errors. Athletes *should* be competitive. Traders *should* apply rigorous risk analysis. The problem comes when individuals cannot "compartmentalize" their abilities. And when that happens, not only do they miss out on the Happiness Advantage, but their pessimistic, fault-finding mindset makes them far more susceptible to depression, stress, poor physical health, and even substance abuse.

This is the essence of a Negative Tetris Effect: a cognitive pattern that *decreases* our overall success rates. But the Tetris Effect need not be maladaptive. Just as our brains can be wired in ways that hold us back, we can retrain them to scan for the good things in life—to help us see more possibility, to feel more energy, and to succeed at higher levels. The first step is understanding just how much of what we see is solely a matter of focus. As William James once said, "My experience is what I agree to attend to."

YOUR BRAIN AS SPAM FILTER

On a daily basis, we're bombarded with competing demands on our attention. Think about all the things our brains have to attend to even when we're engaged in a relatively passive activity, like sitting at Starbucks. We cannot possibly listen to the music, enjoy the taste of the coffee, eavesdrop on the conversation at the next table, and note the outfits of the people milling about, all while thinking about what we have to do at work later that day, what we're going to cook for dinner, and how we're going to pay for that big renovation we're doing on the house. To deal with this overload, our brains have a filter that only lets the most pertinent information through to our consciousness.

This filter is much like the spam blocker on your e-mail. Your spam blocker follows certain rules that tell it to delete noxious and unimportant e-mails without your even having to see or process them. The same thing goes on in our brains. Scientists estimate that we remember only one of every 100 pieces of information we receive; the rest effectively gets filtered out, dumped into the brain's spam file.[6] Now, all of this might work fine, if only we could trust our neural spam filter to know exactly what is best for us. Unfortunately, we can't. Spam filters, whether in our heads or our e-mail, scan only for what they are programmed to find. If we have programmed our brain's filter to delete the positive, that data will cease to exist for us as surely as the chain letters and advertisements cease to exist in our inbox. As you are about to learn, we see what we look for, and we miss the rest.

GORILLAS AND PRIUSES

In one of psychology's best known experiments, volunteers watch a video of two basketball teams—one wearing white shirts, the other black ones—who are passing around a basketball.[7] As they watch, the viewers have to count the number of times the white team passes the ball. About 25 seconds into the video, a person in a full-body gorilla costume walks straight through the action, traveling from right to left across the screen for a full 5 seconds, as the team members continue to pass the ball. Afterward, the viewers are asked to write down the number of passes they counted and then answer a series of additional questions that go something like this: Did you notice anything unusual about the video? Did you see anyone in the video besides the six basketball players? Did you, um, notice the giant gorilla?

Unbelievably, when psychologists tried this out on more than 200 people (back in the days before it became a viral YouTube video everyone had seen), nearly half of them—46 percent—completely missed the gorilla. After the experiment, when the researchers told them about the gorilla, many of them refused to believe they had missed something so obvious and demanded to view the video again. On this second viewing, now that they were looking for the gorilla, it was, of course, impossible to miss. So why did so many of them fail to see it the first time? Because they were so focused on counting passes, their neural filters had simply dumped the gorilla sighting right into their spam folder.

This experiment highlights what psychologists call "inattentional blindness," our frequent inability to see what is often right in front of us if we're not focusing directly on it. This aspect of human biology means that we can miss an astoundingly large number of things that might be considered "obvious." For instance, studies show that when people look away from a researcher for 30 seconds and then turn their attention back, many won't notice that the researcher is suddenly wearing a different color shirt. Other experiments have found that when pedestrians are stopped on the street and asked a question, a large number won't even notice if the person asking the question has quickly swapped places with someone else, so that they're now talking to a different person entirely.[8] In essence, we tend to miss what we're not looking for.

This selective perception is also why when we *are* looking for something, we see it everywhere. You've probably experienced this a million times. You hear a song once, and suddenly it seems it's always on the radio. You buy a new style of sneaker, and soon everyone at the gym is wearing the exact same pair. I remember the day I decided to buy a Toyota Prius, the streets suddenly began to overflow with them—every fourth car seemed to be a blue Prius (exactly the color I wanted to buy). Had the people in my town just that day decided to all go out and buy blue Priuses? Had the advertisers found out I was wavering and strategically inundated my environment with their product to seal my decision? Of course not. Nothing had changed but my focus.

Try this little experiment. Close your eyes and think of the color red. Really picture it in your mind's eye. Now open your eyes and look around your room. Is red popping out at you everywhere? Assuming elves didn't repaint your furniture while your eyes were closed, your heightened perception is due only to your change in focus. Repeated studies have shown that two people can view the same situation and actually see different things, depending on what they are expecting to see. It's not just that they come away with different interpretations of the same event, but that they have actually seen different things in their visual field.[9] For example, one study found that two people can look at the same picture of a friend and see two completely different expressions on that friend's face.[10] This not only affects our social relationships; if we are programmed to always read people negatively, it can hurt us at work, as well. Think of the consequences of reading a potential customer's expression as disinterest, when really it's satisfaction. Or reading a colleague's attitude as arrogance, when really it's helpfulness.

This is essentially what was going on with the two employees I overheard outside in Australia. Both aspects of the weather were there for them to experience in equal parts—the sunshine and the heat. The first man found the sunshine impossible to miss. The second man wasn't trying to be a curmudgeon—the unbearable heat was simply the only thing he could see.

While there are always different ways to see something, not all ways of seeing are created equal. As we know from people stuck in a Negative Tetris Effect, the consequences can be debilitating to both our happiness and our work performance. On the other hand, imagine a way of seeing that constantly picked up on the positives in every situation. That's the goal of a Positive Tetris Effect: Instead of creating a cognitive pattern that looks for negatives and blocks success, it trains our brains to scan the world for the opportunities and ideas that allow our success rate to grow.

THE POWER OF A POSITIVE TETRIS EFFECT

When our brains constantly scan for and focus on the positive, we profit from three of the most important tools available to us: happiness, gratitude, and optimism. The role happiness plays should be obvious—the more you pick up on the positive around you, the better you'll feel—and we've already seen the advantages to performance that brings. The second mechanism at work here is gratitude, because the more opportunities for positivity we see, the more grateful we become. Psychologist Robert Emmons, who has spent nearly his entire career studying gratitude, has found that few things in life are as integral to our well-being.[11] Countless other studies have shown that consistently grateful people are more energetic, emotionally intelligent, forgiving, and less likely to be depressed, anxious, or lonely. And it's not that people are only grateful *because* they are happier, either; gratitude has proven to be a significant *cause* of positive outcomes. When researchers pick random volunteers and train them to be more grateful over a period of a few weeks, they become happier and more optimistic, feel more socially connected, enjoy better quality sleep, and even experience fewer headaches than control groups.

The third driver of the Positive Tetris Effect is optimism. This instinctively makes sense; the more your brain picks up on the positive, the more you'll expect this trend to continue, and so the more optimistic you'll be. And optimism, it turns out, is a tremendously powerful predictor of work performance. Studies have shown that optimists set more goals (and more difficult goals) than pessimists, and put more effort into attaining those goals, stay more engaged in the face of difficulty, and rise above obstacles more easily.[12] Optimists also cope better in high stress situations and are better able to maintain high levels of well-being during times of hardship—all skills that are crucial to high performance in a demanding work environment.

As we saw briefly in the last chapter, expecting positive outcomes actually makes them more likely to arise. Few people have proven this more cleverly than researcher Richard Wiseman, who set out to discover why some of us seem to be consistently lucky, while others can't buy a break.[13] As you might have guessed, it turns out that there is no such thing—in a scientific sense, at least—as luck. The only difference (and it is a big one) is whether or not people *think* that they are lucky—in essence, whether they expect good or bad things to happen to them.

Wiseman asked volunteers to read through a newspaper and count how many photos were in it. The people who claimed to be lucky took mere seconds to accomplish this task, while the unlucky ones took an average of two minutes. Why? Well, on the second page of the newspaper a very large message read: "Stop counting, there are 43 photos in this newspaper." The answer, in short, was plain as day, but the unlucky people were far more likely to miss it, while the lucky people tended to see it. As an added bonus, half-way through the newspaper was another message that read, "Stop counting, tell the experimenter you have seen this and win $250."

The people who had claimed to be unlucky in life again looked right past this opportunity. Stuck in a Negative Tetris Effect, they were incapable of seeing what was so clear to others, and their performance (and wallets) suffered because of it. The extraordinary thing about Wiseman's study is that the *same* possibility for huge reward was latent in everyone's environment—it was just a matter of whether or not they picked up on it.

Think of the consequences this has on your career success, which is almost entirely predicated on your ability to spot and then capitalize on opportunities. In fact, 69 percent of high school and college students report that their career decisions depended on chance encounters.[14] The difference between people who capitalize on these chances and those who watch them pass by (or miss them entirely) is all a matter of focus. When someone is stuck in a Negative Tetris Effect, his brain is quite literally incapable of seeing these opportunities. But armed with positivity, the brain stays open to possibility. Psychologists call this "predictive encoding": Priming yourself to expect a favorable outcome actually encodes your brain to recognize the outcome when it does in fact arise.[15]

An executive I worked with once told me about a theater in his home town. Costumes were proving a big financial drain for the theater, since they were worn only once and were useless thereafter. Instead of lamenting this as a fixed cost of doing business, the owners reframed the situation and looked for possibility. First, they started renting out the costumes, creating a profitable side business. Then they donated money from their rentals to a local nonprofit organization that combats child abuse. Because they had stayed optimistic, they were able to both make brilliant use of the costumes and also grow a "double bottom line." They helped the community prosper while also increasing revenue for their theater.

Imagine a typical paper-pushing office. The objective reality of the physical place will always be the same: walls, carpet, stapler, computer. But, as with everything else, how we see that space is up to us. Some people will view the environment as constricting, confining, and depressing; others will see it as energizing and empowering. In other words, to some, it's an office; to others a prison cell (though hopefully you don't have bars on your office windows). Who do you think is more likely to thrive in these surroundings? Who will see the most opportunities for growth and success? Who will spot the ad in the newspaper that offers a free $250, or see how to turn an initial defeat into a profitable side business?

Now that we know how powerful a Positive Tetris Effect can be, we need to know how exactly we can train our brains to let in these messages that make us more adaptive, more creative, and more motivated—messages that allow us to spot and pounce on more opportunities at work and at play.

GETTING STUCK IN A POSITIVE TETRIS EFFECT

Just as it takes days of concentrated practice to master a video game, training your brain to notice more opportunities takes practice focusing on the positive. The best way to kick-start this is to start making a daily list of the good things in your job, your career, and your life. It may sound hokey, or ridiculously simple—and indeed the activity itself is simple—but over a decade of empirical studies has proven the profound effect it has on the way our brains are wired. When you write down a list of "three good things" that happened that day, your brain will be forced to scan the last 24 hours for potential positives—things that brought small or large laughs, feelings of accomplishment at work, a strengthened connection with family, a glimmer of hope for the future. In just five minutes a day, this trains the brain to become more skilled at noticing and focusing on possibilities for personal and professional growth, and seizing opportunities to act on them. At the same time, because we can only focus on so much at once, our brains push out those small annoyances and frustrations that used to loom large into the background, even out of our visual field entirely.

This exercise has staying power. One study found that participants who wrote down three good things each day for a week were happier and less depressed at the one-month, three-month, and six-month follow-ups.[16] More amazing: Even after stopping the exercise, they remained significantly happier and showed higher levels of optimism. The better they got at scanning the world for good things to write down, the more good things they saw, without even trying, wherever they looked. The items you write down each day don't need to be profound or complicated, only specific. You can mention the delicious take-out Thai food you had for dinner, your child's bear hug at the end of a long day, or the well-deserved acknowledgement from your boss at work.

A variation on the Three Good Things exercise is to write a short journal entry about a positive experience. We have long known that venting about hardships and suffering can provide welcome relief, but researchers Chad Burton and Laura King have found that journaling about *positive* experiences has at least an equally powerful effect. In one experiment, they instructed people to write about a positive experience for 20 minutes three times a week and then compared them to a control group who wrote about neutral topics.[17] Not only did the first group experience larger spikes in happiness, but three months later they even had fewer symptoms of illness.

Beyond all these benefits, you'll also notice that all the activities from the previous two chapters start coming to you more naturally. For instance, falling into a Positive Tetris Effect helps leaders give more frequent recognition and encouragement, which tips their teams above the Losada Line. It makes the meaning and purpose in your job more apparent, so that you can start connecting to your calling. It makes it easier to adopt an expressive and positive tone as you deliver task instructions, which primes your employees for enhanced creativity and problem solving. And it flat-out makes you happier, which means your own brain will be functioning at a higher level for more of the time.

PRACTICE, PRACTICE, PRACTICE

Of course, we can build this Tetris Effect only through consistency. As with any skill, the more we practice, the more easily and naturally it comes. Since the best way to ensure follow-through on a desired activity is to make it a habit (more about this in Principle 6), the key here is to ritualize the task. For example, pick the same time each day to write down your gratitude list, and keep the necessary items easily accessible and convenient. (A small steno pad and pen sit on my bedside table, specifically for this purpose.)

When I worked with employees at American Express, I encouraged them to set a Microsoft Outlook alert for 11 A.M. every day to remind themselves to write down their three good things. The bankers I worked with in Hong Kong preferred to write down their list every morning before they checked their e-mail. The CEOs I trained in Africa opted to say three gratitudes at the dinner table with their children each night. It doesn't matter when you do it, as long as you do it on a regular basis.

The more you involve others, the more the benefits multiply. When the CEOs in Africa brought the activity to their children, they not only discovered more things to be grateful about, but were also held more accountable for keeping up with the exercise. Several of the CEOs told me that whenever they'd had an especially terrible day at work and tried to skip writing down Three Good Things, their children actually refused to eat dinner until the exercise was completed. This kind of social support greatly increases the chance that these positive habits will stick. That's why I tell business leaders to do these exercises with their spouses as they fall asleep at night or over breakfast before they leave for work. A bonus: As they become more skilled at picking up on the positives all around them, they start to become better at seeing the things to be grateful for in their marriages as well. Furthermore, these exercises work as well with kindergartners as with college students, and as well with middle managers or small business owners as they do with captains of industry and Wall Street analysts. It's not your age, or what you do for a living; it's the training and consistency that count.

ROSE-TINTED GLASSES

Here's a common question I get when I discuss the virtues of a Positive Tetris Effect: "If I focus only on the good, won't I be blind to real problems? You can't run a business wearing rose-colored glasses."

In a sense, this is true. Looking at the world through a lens that completely filters out all negatives comes with its own problems. That's why I like to offer a slightly revised version of the metaphor: rose-tinted glasses. As the name implies, rose-tinted glasses let the really major problems into our field of vision, while still keeping our focus largely on the positive. So to this executive I would say, not only *can* you run a business wearing rose-tinted glasses, but you *should*. Science has shown that seeking out the positive has too many tangible advantages to be dismissed as mere cockeyed optimism or wishful thinking.

Still, to his question, can positivity be overdone? Absolutely. As it has become all too evident in recent years, irrational optimism is the reason market bubbles form —and inevitably burst. It causes us to buy houses we can't afford and to live above our means. It causes business leaders to sugarcoat the present and end up unprepared for the future. It can blind us to problems that need fixing, or areas that need improving (studies on "positive illusions" conclude that optimism becomes maladaptive when it causes us to grossly overestimate our current abilities).[18] There are also times when pessimism comes in handy—like when it stops us from making that foolish investment or risky career move, or from gambling with our health. Being critical can also be useful not just to individuals and businesses but to society as a whole, especially when it drives us to acknowledge inequalities and work to right them.

The key, then, is not to completely shut out all the bad, all the time, but to have a reasonable, realistic, healthy sense of optimism. The ideal mindset isn't heedless of risk, but it *does* give priority to the good. Not just because that makes us happier but because that is precisely what creates *more* good. Given the choice between seeing the world through rose-tinted glasses or always walking around under a rain cloud, the contest isn't even close. In business and in life, the reasonable optimist will win every time.

When we train our brains to adapt a Positive Tetris Effect, we're not just improving our chance at happiness, we're setting off a chain of events that helps us reap all the benefits of a positive brain. Focusing on the good isn't just about overcoming our inner grump to see the glass half full. It's about opening our minds to the ideas and opportunities that will help us be more productive, effective, and successful at work and in life. The possibilities, like the free $250, are there for everyone to see. Will you look right past them, or will you train your brain to see more?

FALLING UP

Capitalizing on the Downs to Build Upward Momentum

A s an undergraduate, I was often encouraged to sell my body. The Psychology Department was constantly offering money for willing research subjects; and since I was almost always short of funds, I was a willing guinea pig for experiments that ranged from mere humiliation to full-on trickery—everything from uncomfortable social encounters, to repeated MRIs, to grueling trials of mental and physical abilities. But the most memorable experiment of them all was a seemingly benign one called "Helping the Elderly."

The study was three hours long and promised to pay $20. To get things underway, two research assistants handed me a set of bike reflectors with Velcro straps and a pair of tight white biker shorts. One of the assistants said formally, "Please attach these reflectors to each of the joints on your body and put on the shorts. And oh, yes, we just ran out of white T shirts, so you'll have to go topless. Do you wish to proceed?"

For $20? They clearly underestimated me. A few minutes later, clad in reflective sensors covering my elbows, wrists, and knees, I emerged looking like a bare-chested robot. They then explained the study: The researchers were examining how the elderly fall to the ground, so that they could eventually help senior citizens avoid injuries. Of course, they couldn't actually ask the elderly to fall repeatedly for the study, so they recruited college students instead. Made perfect sense to me.

I was told to walk down a padded hallway in the dark while a video camera recorded the position of the reflectors on my joints. As I walked, one of four things would happen: (1) The floor would suddenly slide to the left, and I would crash onto the lightly padded walkway; (2) The floor would suddenly slide to the right, throwing off my balance and sending me crashing down to the left; (3) A cord attached to my right leg would be yanked out behind me, pitching me face first onto the walkway; and (4) If none of those things happened by the time I got to the end of the walkway, I was just supposed to throw myself to the ground. That last one sounded especially ludicrous—what kind of elderly person intentionally throws himself on the floor?

But 20 bucks was on the line, and so for the next hour I fell down once about every thirty seconds. At 120 falls, the research assistants emerged, giggled sheepishly, and admitted they had forgotten to put the video in the recorder. They would need to retape all the falls again. "Do you want to proceed?" Again I said yes.

Another 120 falls later, I was bruised, battered, and exhausted. With all the gear I had on, merely picking myself up off the mats took an enormous amount of energy, and the whole ordeal had taken a painful toll on my body. When I finally stumbled out into the hallway, the research assistants had been joined by a distinguished-looking professor, summoned to investigate a major irregularity: The experiment had never lasted this long.

The study, it turned out, had nothing to do with "helping the elderly." (Note to self: *Never* trust the name of a psych department study.) These researchers were actually studying motivation and resilience. They wanted to know: How much pain and discomfort could you put people through before they gave up? How much would a person withstand to get the reward he had set out to get? In my case, the answer was: a lot. The professor had come down to the hospital on a Saturday because I was the only one who had ever lasted the full three hours. As they stood there explaining all this to me, I couldn't help but wonder if I was supposed to feel stupid for withstanding all that abuse for a measly $20. But before I could say anything, the professor handed me ten crisp $20 bills. "It's the least we can do for putting you through that," he said. "The more subjects pick themselves up off the mats and keep going, the larger their reward. You've won the Grand Prize: $200."

That was nice of him. But more memorable than the generous prize were the lessons I learned about the nature of resilience—about picking ourselves up when we fall. Fast-forward a decade later, and I was reenacting a form of Helping the Elderly with tens of thousands of business leaders across the globe. In the midst of the greatest down economy of our time, executives felt the floor had dropped out from underneath them, investors felt like their foundation had violently shifted, and employees at all levels had found their legs yanked out by forces beyond their control. Every continent I traveled to, the refrain was the same: When I'm so exhausted from falling over and over again, how will I find the energy to pick myself up?

Back in my undergraduate guinea-pig days, I wouldn't have had a good answer for them, but this time I did: a strategy I first observed back in 2006 studying the most resilient of those Harvard students—Falling Up.

MAPPING THE WAY TO SUCCESS

The human brain is constantly creating and revising mental maps to help us navigate our way through this complex and ever-changing world—kind of like a tireless, overeager cartographer. This tendency has been wired in us through thousands of years of evolution: In order to survive, we must create physical maps of our environment, map out strategies for getting food and sex, and map out the possible effects of our actions. But these maps aren't just crucial to survival in the wilderness, they are vital to succeeding and thriving in the business world.

If you are talking to a client, for example, and trying to decide whether to lowball or highball an offer, your brain is unconsciously (and sometimes consciously) creating an event map with two possible paths and then trying to predict where those paths will lead: If you lowball, you might predict this path will lead to the client making a counteroffer, which will eventually take you to the final destination of an accepted bid. If you highball it, on the other hand, the path may lead to the client getting offended and ultimately taking his business elsewhere. All human decisions involve this kind of mental mapping: they start with an "I Am Here" point (the status quo), from which a variety of paths radiate outward, the number depending on the complexity of the decision, and the clarity of your thinking at the moment. The most successful decisions come when we are thinking clearly and creatively enough to recognize all the paths available to us, and accurately predict where that path will lead. The problem is that when we are stressed or in crisis, many people miss the most important path of all: the path up.

On every mental map after crisis or adversity, there are three mental paths. One that keeps circling around where you currently are (i.e., the negative event creates no change; you end where you start). Another mental path leads you toward further negative consequences (i.e., you are far worse off after the negative event; this path is why we are afraid of conflict and challenge). And one, which I call the Third Path, that leads us from failure or setback to a place where we are even stronger and more capable than before the fall. To be sure, finding that path in challenging times isn't easy. In a crisis, economic or otherwise, we tend to form incomplete mental maps, and ironically the path we have trouble seeing is often the most positive, productive one. In fact, when we feel helpless and hopeless, we stop believing such a path even exists—so we don't even bother to look for it. But this is the very path we *should* be looking for, because, as we'll see, our ability to find the Third Path is the difference between those who are crippled by failure and those who rise above it.

Study after study shows that if we are able to conceive of a failure as an opportunity for growth, we are all the more likely to experience that growth. Conversely, if we conceive of a fall as the worst thing in the world, it becomes just that. Jim Collins, author of *Good to Great,* reminds us that "we are not imprisoned by our circumstances, our setbacks, our history, our mistakes, or even staggering defeats along the way. We are freed by our choices."[1] By scanning our mental map for positive opportunities, and by rejecting the belief that every down in life leads us only further downward, we give ourselves the greatest power possible: the ability to move up not *despite* the setbacks, but *because* of them. In this chapter, you'll learn how.

POST-TRAUMATIC GROWTH

In today's society, it's all too easy to overlook the Third Path. One particularly salient example of this is the fact that when soldiers are heading to combat, psychologists commonly tell them they will return either "normal" or with Post-Traumatic Stress Disorder. What this does, in effect, is give these soldiers a mental map with only two paths—normalcy and psychic distress. Yet while PTSD is of course a well-documented and serious consequence of war (and while war can be so horrifying that returning "normal" might be a very attractive promise), another large body of research proves the existence of a third, far better path: Post-Traumatic Growth.

Bereavement, bone marrow transplantation, breast cancer, chronic illness, heart attack, military combat, natural disaster, physical assault, refugee displacement. If this reads like a random clip from an alphabetized nightmare list of the very worst things that can befall us, that's because it basically is. But it also happens to be a list of events that researchers have found to spur profound positive growth in many, many individuals.[2] Psychologists have termed this experience Adversarial Growth, or Post-Traumatic Growth, to distinguish it from the better-known term Post-Traumatic Stress. When I encountered this newer body of research for the first time, I was actually quite upset. Why had I not heard of it before? I felt like the world had been censoring research that was not only surprising, but could improve thousands of lives. And we're not just talking about a few fringe studies but many distinguished ones.

Over the last two decades, psychologist Richard Tedeschi and his colleagues have made the empirical study of Post-Traumatic Growth their mission. While Tedeschi admits that the idea itself is ancient—surely you've heard the maxim "what doesn't kill us makes us stronger"—he explains that "it has only been in the last 25 years or so that this phenomenon, the possibility of something good emerging from the struggle with something very difficult, has been the focus of systematic theorizing and empirical investigation."[3] Thanks to this study, today we can say for certain, not just anecdotally, that great suffering or trauma can actually lead to great positive change across a wide range of experiences. After the March 11, 2004, train bombings in Madrid, for example, psychologists found many residents experienced positive psychological growth.[4] So too do the majority of women diagnosed with breast cancer.[5] What kind of positive growth? Increases in spirituality, compassion for others, openness, and even, eventually, overall life satisfaction. After trauma, people also report enhanced personal strength and self-confidence, as well as a heightened appreciation for, and a greater intimacy in, their social relationships.[6]

Of course, this isn't true for everybody. So what distinguishes the people who find growth in these experiences from those who don't? There are a number of mechanisms involved, but not surprisingly, mindset takes center stage. People's ability to find the path up rests largely on how they conceive of the cards they have been dealt, so the strategies that most often lead to Adversarial Growth include positive reinterpretation of the situation or event, optimism, acceptance, and coping mechanisms that include focusing on the problem head-on (rather than trying to avoid or deny it). As one set of researchers explains, "it appears that it is not the type of event per se that influences posttraumatic growth, but rather the subjective experience of the event."[7] In other words, the people who can most successfully get themselves up off the mat are those who define themselves not by what has happened to them, but by what they can make out of what has happened. These are the people who actually use adversity to find the path forward. They speak not just of "bouncing back," but of "bouncing forward."[8]

"EUREKA, WE FAILED!"

While many of us, thankfully, live lives free of serious trauma, we all experience adversity of one kind or another at some point in our lives. Mistakes. Obstacles. Failure. Disappointment. Suffering. We have many words to describe the degrees of hardship that can befall us at any given moment in our personal or professional lives. And yet with every setback comes some opportunity for growth that we can teach ourselves to see and take advantage of. As my mentor Tal Ben-Shahar likes to say, "things do not necessarily happen for the best, but some people are able to make the best out of things that happen."

The most successful people see adversity not as a stumbling block, but as a stepping-stone to greatness. Indeed, early failure is often the fuel for the very ideas that eventually transform industries, make record profits, and reinvent careers. We've all heard the usual examples: Michael Jordan cut from his high school basketball team, Walt Disney fired by a newspaper editor for not being creative enough, the Beatles turned away by a record executive who told them that "guitar groups are on their way out." In fact, many of their winning mantras essentially describe the notion of falling up: "I've failed over and over again in my life," Jordan once said, "and that is why I succeed." Robert F. Kennedy said much the same: "Only those who dare to fail greatly can ever achieve greatly." And Thomas

Edison, too, once claimed that he had failed his way to success. For this very reason, many venture capitalists will only hire managers who have already experienced their share of business flops. A spotless résumé is not nearly as promising as one that showcases defeat and growth. So instead of putting "a wall around a failure as if it's radioactive," one consultant explains, companies should be having "failure parties."[9]

Coca-Cola lives this creed to great effect. In 2009, Coke's CEO actually started his annual investors meeting not by trumpeting the company's many successes, but by listing all of their failures. (Ever heard of OK Soda, Surge, or Choglit? Probably not.) The point of highlighting all these failures was to let the investors know that mistakes would sometimes be made and money would sometimes be lost, but that from these failures come valuable lessons—all of which have contributed to Coca-Cola's continuing triumphs.

Harvard Business Review points out that the smartest companies even commit errors on purpose, just to spur the kind of creative problem solving that leads to the most innovative ideas and solutions.[10] For example, back during Bell Telephone's heydey, the company usually required deposits from its "high-risk" customers, but it once purposely let 100,000 of these customers slide to see who would pay their bills on time regardless, and who would not. With this information, the company was able to design a far more efficient screening process—one that ended up adding millions of dollars in revenue. As the *Harvard Business* authors conclude, making mistakes like this is "a powerful way to accelerate learning and increase competitiveness."

It's for this reason that, however counterintuitive it may seem, psychologists actually recommend that we fail early and often. In his book *The Pursuit of Perfect*, Tal Ben-Shahar writes that "we can only learn to deal with failure by actually experiencing failure, by living through it. The earlier we face difficulties and drawbacks, the better prepared we are to deal with the inevitable obstacles along our path."[11] Studies have borne this out. In one experiment where 90 people went through a software training program, half were taught to prevent errors from occurring, while the other half were guided into mistakes during training.[12] And lo and behold, the group encouraged to make errors not only exhibited greater feelings of self-efficacy, but because they had learned to figure their own way out of mistakes, they were also far faster and more accurate in how they used the software later on.

HOW THE THIRD PATH GETS HIDDEN

Unfortunately, the path from failure to success is not always easy to spot. In the midst of crisis, we can get so stuck in the misery of the status quo that we forget another path is available. I saw this firsthand as the 2008 financial crisis swiftly and viciously pulled the floor out from under an entire workforce. One day in particular sticks out in my mind. I was in a Manhattan skyscraper, overlooking the void left seven years earlier by the September 11 attacks. That chilling memory was perhaps reason enough to feel qualms about speaking about the psychology of happiness to a group of senior vice presidents at a global credit card company. As I walked into the room and was hit by palpable despondency, these qualms only multiplied. Instead of the confident smiles and direct eye contact every speaker hopes to receive from an audience, I was met with ashen faces and utter silence. There was still about half an hour until my talk, and the employees were on a break from their morning meeting. Usually during breaks like this, everyone is typing furiously on a Blackberry while simultaneously gulping coffee and chatting with at least four people. But not this time.

The head of HR quickly pulled me aside and started speaking in anxious, hushed tones. He told me that the group had just moments before been informed of the company's planned response to the economic collapse, which included vast restructuring, drastic changes to job responsibilities, and massive layoffs. These people still had their jobs, he told me, but many would be losing valuable team members and colleagues, and nobody's career would be the same as it had been at daybreak. Before I could fully process the shifting of the ground, I realized a microphone was being attached to my shirt. Rarely have I dreaded talking about happiness, but this was one such moment.

Over the next few weeks and months, I paced the hallways of Fortune 500 firms in Hong Kong, Tokyo, Singapore, Sydney, London, and New York, waiting to speak hard on the heels of announcements that bonuses were being deep-sixed and workforces cut practically in half. At each company, I found more than a few managers and employees who were so completely frozen with fear they were unable to take any kind of action. Their mental maps seemed stuck on the grim present or, worse, focused only on paths that led further downward, to places like unemployment or bankruptcy.

One unhappy manager at a small manufacturing company in Seattle told me that while her team used to be famous for its lively meetings, she now found herself staring into "zombie eyes" and mute mouths. Another executive from a construction company in Johannesburg lamented that his usually extroverted sales force was avoiding client calls, not wanting to deliver more bad news. They couldn't see a positive future for those clients or for themselves, so why bother? At the headquarters of one global financial firm, I walked onto the catwalk above the expansive trading floor, famous for being the size of four football fields stacked back to back. Usually packed to the gills and vibrating with energy and activity, the giant room this time was wrapped in an ominous hush. People were walking around the empty desks with heads down, avoiding eye contact, and, as it seemed to me, avoiding work altogether.

Right when extra effort was most needed, the people I kept meeting seemed paralyzed, like they had given up. What was going on?

LEARNING HELPLESSNESS

To understand the psychology of failure and success in the modern business world, we need to step back briefly to the tail end of the Age of Aquarius. In the 1960s, Martin Seligman was not yet the founding father of positive psychology. He was only a lowly graduate student, studying the opposite of happiness in his university's laboratory.

Older researchers in Seligman's lab were doing some experiments with dogs, pairing noises, like a bell, with small shocks to see how the dogs would eventually react to the bell alone.[13] Then after this conditioning was complete, the researchers would put each dog in a "shuttlebox," a large box with two compartments, separated by a low wall. In one compartment, the dogs would get shocked, but on the other side they would be safe from shocks, and it was easy to jump over the wall. The researchers predicted that once the dogs heard the bell, they would immediately jump into the safe half of the box so they could avoid the shock they knew would follow. But that's not at all what happened.

As Seligman now tells the story, he remembers walking into the lab one day and overhearing the older researchers complaining. "It's the dogs," they lamented. "The dogs won't do anything. Something's wrong with them." Before the experiment started, the dogs had been able to jump over the barriers just fine, but this time they were just lying there. While the researchers contemplated what seemed to be a failed experiment, Seligman realized the value of what they had just stumbled upon: They had accidentally taught the dogs to be helpless. Earlier, the dogs had learned that once the bell rang, a shock was sure to follow, no matter what. So, now, in this new situation, they didn't try jumping to the safe half of the box because they believed there was nothing they could do to avoid the shock. Just like the workers at the Johannesburg construction company, they essentially figured, "why bother?"

After decades of studying human behavior, Seligman and his

colleagues found that the same patterns of helplessness that he saw in those dogs are incredibly common in humans. When we fail, or when life delivers us a shock, we can become so hopeless that we respond by simply giving up. The fact is that in our modern, often overstressed business world, cubicles are the new shuttleboxes, and workers the new dogs. In fact, one study shows just how closely we humans resemble our canine counterparts. Researchers took two groups of people into a room, turned on a loud noise, and then told them to figure out how to turn it off by pressing buttons on a panel.[14] The first group tried every combination of buttons, but nothing worked to stop the noise. (Another example of devious psychologists at work!) The second group, acting as a control, was given a panel of buttons that did successfully turn off the noise. Then both groups were given the same second task: They were put in a new room, the equivalent of a shuttlebox, and were once again treated to an obnoxious noise.

This time, both groups could easily stop the noise by simply moving a hand from one side to the other, just like the dogs could easily move to the other side of the box. The control group quickly figured this out and stopped the blare. But the group that had first been exposed to a noise they couldn't stop now just *let their hands lay there,* not even bothering to move them or try to make the noise stop. As one of the researchers said, "It was as if they'd learned they were helpless to turn off noise, so they didn't even try, even though everything else—the time and place, all that—had changed. They carried that noise-helplessness right through to the new experiment."[15]

ECONOMIC WHIPLASH

Shanghai is a city you can appreciate just for the sheer boomtown wonder of it all. As recently as the mid-1990s, much of this city, now home to 19 million people, was still farmland. But as foreign investment flowed into China and development took off, 20-story office buildings, once the city's highest, suddenly found themselves dwarfed by the 100-story behemoths that crowded the skyline, seeming to promise a prosperity that had no end in sight.

By the time I made my first trip to Shanghai, in the summer of 2008, that promise had been put on hold, not just in China but around the globe. Everywhere I went, from the 104th floor of the office building in the city's Pudong financial district to the New York Stock Exchange trading floor, I found people hijacked by stress. Unable to predict where the financial tsunami would head next, they were straitjacketed by despair and incapable of moving forward. I didn't fully understand what was keeping them so frozen in inaction, until a manager told me point-blank: "Market forces are out of my control. Share prices are out of my control. My bosses' decisions are out of my control. So there's nothing I can do. The waters feel like they're getting higher each day."

What I've realized from many companies I've spoken with over the past two years is that the meltdown of 2008 and its aftershocks had instilled a form of learned helplessness—a belief in the futility of our action—in many of the world's workers. But the problem is, when we eliminate any upward options from our mental maps, and worse, eliminate our motivation to search for them, we end up undermining our ability to tackle the challenge at hand.

And it doesn't end there. When people feel helpless in one area of life, they not only give up in that one area; they often "overlearn" the lesson and apply it to other situations. They become convinced that one dead-end path must be proof that all possible paths are dead ends. A setback at work might lead to despondency about one's relationship, or a rift with a friend might discourage us from trying to form bonds with our colleagues, and so on. When this happens, our helplessness spirals out of control, impeding our success in all areas of life. It's the very definition of pessimism and depression—an event map with all dead ends—and a surefire route to failure. We don't have to stretch far to see this negative cycle on a larger social scale—learned helplessness is endemic in inner city schools, prisons, and elsewhere. When people don't believe there is a way up, they have virtually no choice but to stay as down as they are.

FINDING THE PATH UP

You've probably heard the oft-told story of the two shoe salesmen who were sent to Africa in the early 1900s to assess opportunities. They wired separate telegrams back to their boss. One read: "Situation hopeless. They don't wear shoes." The other read: "Glorious opportunity! They don't have any shoes yet."

Odds are the same two salesmen would send back similar e-mails today if they were sent to Alaska to sell air conditioners or to the Gobi desert to sell swimsuits. The point, of course, is that when some people meet adversity, they simply stop looking for ways to turn failures into opportunities or negatives into positives. Others—the most successful among us—know that it's not the adversity itself, but what we do with it that determines our fate. Some will sit helpless, while others gather their wits, capitalize on their strengths, and forge ahead.

A TALE OF TWO BROKERS

Imagine two stockbrokers. For simplicity we'll call them Ben and Paul. Both are making high six-figure salaries, plus bonuses. Both have been in their positions for many years and expect to be in them many years more. And then comes the financial tsunami that sweeps them both away. Paul is devastated: His way of life is at stake (as is his special-order Mercedes). And every day brings worse news, a running invitation to sink deeper in despair. Ben, while initially just as upset, chooses to see the event as an opportunity to reevaluate his goals and pursue a new project. Similar backgrounds, almost identical professional experiences, very different outcomes.

We all know people who have reacted to adversity like Paul. But Ben's story is just as real. Ben Axler was an associate director in the investment banking division at Barclays when he was unexpectedly laid off.[16] Instead of feeling sorry for himself, he decided there was no time like the present to make the career move he'd been dreaming of, and he started a hedge fund. In short, Ben capitalized on his bad luck by turning it into an opportunity. And the opportunity turned out to be a good one; despite the down economy, he was able to sign up a whole slew of clients and ended up both happier, and better off financially than when he started, all because he was able to find the Third Path.

CRISIS AS CATALYST

Fortunately, just as personal crises can provide the foundation for positive individual growth, so can economic ones. They often propel companies to greater success, and many business juggernauts of the twentieth century—Hewlett-Packard and Texas Instruments among them—were actually launched during the Great Depression. Similarly, America's top companies have often used recessions to reevaluate and improve their business practices. As *Time* pointed out way back in 1958 (though its message is just as relevant today), "for every company that slims down its operation, another discovers new ways of doing things that should have been in effect for years but were overlooked during the boom."[17] Economic adversity forces companies to find creative ways to cut costs and inspires managers to get back in touch with the employees and operations on the ground floor. One company president admitted that going through a recession had actually proved invaluable: "We found all sorts of revisions we could make to improve our operation. Now these revisions work so well we wouldn't go back to the old way of doing things even if the recession ended tomorrow."[18] This may have been written over 50 years ago, but one look at how the most success-ful companies have pulled themselves up from the recent recession tells us that it holds just as true today.

The best leaders are the ones who show their true colors not during the banner years, but during such times of struggle. While a leader's natural reaction to financial crisis might be to lay low and wait for things to pick up, the *Wall Street Journal* stresses that this is the exact wrong approach; instead, managers should redouble their efforts, because "crises can be catalysts for creativity."[19] Leaders who become paralyzed by the obstacles in front of them miss this great opportunity. Helplessness will drive down not just their own performance but also employee well-being and their company's bot-tom line.

On the other hand, leaders who find themselves energized by challenge and motivated by failure reap all kinds of amazing re-wards. For example, when other leaders were struggling just to keep their companies afloat, Indra Nooyi, the CEO of PepsiCo, saw the recession as an opportunity to travel around the globe, boost-ing the spirits and trust of her employees in person. And this paid dividends: Not only did she strengthen the overall morale and per-formance of her company, but in 2009, *Fortune* voted her the most powerful woman in business.

The point is that when faced with obstacles or failure, succumb-ing to helplessness keeps us down on the mat, while looking for the path of opportunity helps us pick ourselves up. With this in mind, here are a few strategies for finding that Third Path in our careers and professional lives.

CHANGE YOUR COUNTERFACT

Consider the following scenario I have presented to business leaders in countries around the globe, always to the same effect. Imagine for a moment that you walk into a bank. There are 50 other people in the bank. A robber walks in and fires his weapon once. You are shot in the right arm.

Now if you were honestly describing this event to your friends and coworkers the next day, do you describe it as lucky or unlucky?

When I pose this same question to executives in my training sessions, the response is generally (and vociferously) divided about 70/30: 70 percent claim it is a supremely unfortunate event; the other 30 percent claim to have been very fortunate indeed. It's telling enough that the same event could inspire such different interpretations, but the real insight comes when I ask them to explain how they came to their decisions.

People who are in the unfortunate group say something like the following:

"I could have walked into any bank, at any time. This kind of thing almost never happens. How unlucky is it that I happened to be there? *And* that I was shot?!"

"There's a bullet in my arm; that's objectively unfortunate."

"I entered the bank perfectly healthy and I left in an ambulance. I don't know about you, Shawn, but that's not my idea of a good time."

One of my favorite responses came from a banker named Elsie with an impeccable British accent. "This is fundamentally inconvenient," she said dryly.

But my all-time favorite response, which I've actually heard more than once (and always from someone on Wall Street): "There were at least fifty other people in the bank. Surely someone deserved getting shot more than I did." (With a response like that, I'm not sure that's true.)

These people cannot understand how a typical bank errand turned gunshot wound could be construed as fortunate. But then they hear the other side's explanations of the same event:

"I could have been shot somewhere far worse than my arm. I could have died. I feel incredibly fortunate."

"It's amazing that nobody else got hurt. There were at least 50 other people in the bank, including children. It's unbelievably lucky that everybody lived to tell the tale."

Even though the responses differ dramatically, the point is that every brain in the room does the exact same thing. It *invents*—and that's an important word—a "counterfact." A counterfact is an alternate scenario our brains create to help us evaluate and make sense of what really happened.[20] Here's what I mean. The people who saw the outcome as unlucky imagined an alternate scenario of not having been shot at all; in comparison, their outcome seems very unfortunate. But the other group invented a very different alternate scenario: that they could have gotten shot in the head and died, or that many other people could have been hurt. Compared with that, surviving *is* very fortunate.

Here is the crucial part: Both the counterfacts are completely hypothetical. Because it's invented, we actually have the power in any given situation to consciously select a counterfact that makes us feel fortunate rather than helpless. And choosing a positive counterfact, besides simply making us feel better, sets ourselves up for the whole host of benefits to motivation and performance we now know accompanies a positive mindset. On the other hand, choosing a counterfact that makes us more fearful of the adversity actually makes it loom larger than it really is. For example, in one interesting study, researchers at the University of Virginia asked participants to stand on a skateboard at the top of a hill and estimate the slope of the hill below them.[21] The more frightened and uncomfortable the subject was standing on a skateboard, the higher and steeper the slope appeared. When we choose a counterfact that makes us feel worse, we are actually altering our reality, allowing the obstacle to exert far greater influence over us than it otherwise should.

CHANGE YOUR EXPLANATORY STYLE

Most professionals face daily setbacks, but the life of a salesman is, almost by definition, fraught with failure and rejection. In many businesses, only one in ten pitches leads to a sale, meaning that those salesmen experience rejection 90 percent of the time. This can get pretty demoralizing after a while, which helps to explain why there is such high turnover among life insurance salesmen. In the late 1980s, the turnover had gotten so bad at MetLife that half the new salesmen were quitting in year one, and only one in five remained by the fourth year. All told, the company was losing over $75 million a year in hiring costs alone.[22]

That's when MetLife hired Martin Seligman, who by then had moved on from studying learned helplessness in dogs and was now using these findings to explore how people bounce back from all kinds of adversity. Seligman had noticed that while most research subjects would indeed start to feel distressed and helpless after facing setback after setback, a consistent minority seemed immune. No matter what difficulty they faced, they always bounced right back. He soon discovered that they all shared a positive way of interpreting adversity—or what the researchers termed an optimistic "explanatory style."

Decades of subsequent study have since shown that explanatory style—how we choose to explain the nature of past events—has a crucial impact on our happiness and future success.[23] People with an optimistic explanatory style interpret adversity as being local and temporary (i.e., "It's not that bad, and it will get better.") while those with a pessimistic explanatory style see these events as more global and permanent (i.e., "It's really bad, and it's never going to change."). Their beliefs then directly affect their actions; the ones who believe the latter statement sink into helplessness and stop trying, while the ones who believe the former are spurred on to higher performance.

Virtually all avenues of success, we now know, are dictated by explanatory style. It predicts how well students do in high school, and even how well new recruits do at the U.S. Military Academy: First-year plebes with a more optimistic explanatory style perform better than test scores predict, and are less likely to drop out than their peers.[24] In the world of sports, studies of athletes ranging from collegiate swimmers to professional baseball players show that explanatory style predicts athletic performance.[25] It even predicts how well people recover after coronary bypass surgery.[26]

So when Seligman was brought on to help solve the problems the salespeople were having at MetLife, one of the first things he looked at was their explanatory style. And indeed, testing revealed that the agents with more optimistic styles sold 37 percent more insurance than those with pessimistic ones, and that the most optimistic agents actually sold fully 88 percent more than the most pessimistic ones. Furthermore, agents who were more optimistic were half as likely to quit as were the pessimists.

This was the answer MetLife was looking for. They decided to hire a special force of agents picked solely on the basis of explanatory style. And it paid off. The next year, these agents outsold their more pessimistic counterparts by 21 percent; during the second year, by 57 percent.

Aware it had struck gold, MetLife decided to completely overhaul its hiring practices from that day on. If would-be agents failed the regular industry test but scored well in an evaluation of explanatory style, MetLife hired them anyway. And if they passed the industry test but had a low score on explanatory style, the company rejected them, no matter how smart they seemed. The results: Within only a few years, MetLife's turnover had plummeted while its market share had increased by almost 50 percent.

LEARN YOUR ABCD'S

Of course, turning adversity into opportunity is a skill that comes more naturally to some people than others. Some people already have an optimistic explanatory style. They automatically imagine alternative scenarios that make them feel fortunate, interpret setbacks as short-lived and small in scope, and see inherent opportunity where others only see foreboding. Others don't have an optimistic explanatory style. Luckily, these techniques can be learned.

One way to help ourselves see the path from adversity to opportunity is to practice the ABCD model of interpretation: Adversity, Belief, Consequence, and Disputation.[27] Adversity is the event we can't change; it is what it is. Belief is our reaction to the event; why we thought it happened and what we think it means for the future. Is it a problem that is only temporary and local in nature or do we think it is permanent and pervasive? Are there ready solutions, or do we think it is unsolvable? If we believe the former—that is, if we see the adversity as short-term or as an opportunity for growth or appropriately confined to only part of our life—then we maximize the chance of a positive Consequence. But if the Belief has led us down a more pessimistic path, helplessness and inaction can bring negative Consequences. That's when it's time to put the D to work.

Disputation involves first telling ourselves that our belief is just that—a belief, not fact—and then challenging (or disputing) it. Psychologists recommend that we externalize this voice (i.e., pretend it's coming from someone else), so it's like we're actually arguing with another person. What is the evidence for this belief? Is it airtight? Would we let a friend get away with such reasoning? Or is the reasoning clearly specious once we step outside of ourselves and take a look? What are some other plausible interpretations of this event? What are some more adaptive reactions to it? Is there another counterfactual we can adopt instead?

And finally, if the adversity truly *is* bad, is it *as* bad as we first thought? This particular method is called decatastrophizing: taking time to show ourselves that while the adversity is real, it is perhaps not as catastrophic as we may have made it out to be. That may sound like a positive platitude stripped off of a Hallmark card, but the idea that things are never as bad as they seem is actually a fact based on our fundamental biology. Because thousands of years of evolution have made us so remarkably good at adapting to even the most extreme life circumstances, adversity never hits us quite as hard—or for quite as long—as we think it might.

For example, we might assume that a horrible injury would forever alter our ability to be happy, but in fact, after an initial adjustment and period of hardship, most victims of paralysis bounce back to just about the same level of happiness they experienced before.[28] Simply speaking, the human psyche is so much more resilient than we even realize. Which is why, when faced with a terrible prospect—for example, the end of a love affair or of a job—we overestimate how unhappy it will make us and for how long. We fall victim to "immune neglect," which means we consistently forget how good our psychological immune system is at helping us get over adversity.

Daniel Gilbert, author of *Stumbling on Happiness*, has performed a number of studies showing immune neglect in action.[29] College students overestimate how devastated they would feel at the end of a romantic relationship. Assistant professors predict that being denied tenure would lead to drastically lowered levels of happiness, when in fact professors denied tenure do not experience this at all. Adversities, no matter what they are, simply don't hit us as hard as we think they will. Just knowing this quirk of human psychology—that our fear of consequences is always worse than the consequences themselves—can help us move toward a more optimistic interpretation of the downs we will inevitably face.

So the next time you catch yourself feeling hopeless—or helpless—about some snag in your career, some frustration at your job, or some disappointment in your personal life, remember that there is always a Third Path upwards—your only task is to find it.

And above all, remember that success is not about never falling down or even simply about falling down and getting back up over and over like I did in the Helping the Elderly experiment. Success is about more than simple resilience. It's about *using* that downward momentum to propel ourselves in the opposite direction. It's about capitalizing on setbacks and adversity to become even happier, even more motivated, and even more successful. It's not falling down, it's falling up.

THE ZORRO CIRCLE

How Limiting Your Focus to Small, Manageable Goals Can Expand Your Sphere of Power

A ccording to legend, a masked hero named Zorro roamed what is now the southwestern United States, fighting for those who could not fight for themselves. Zorro was resolute, disciplined, and fearless, a combination that immortalized him as the popular hero of so many books, TV shows, and movies. Add to the mix his witty one-liners and effortless skill with women, and Zorro seems to embody too many irresistible qualities for any one man, even one played by Antonio Banderas.

But there is a lesser known chapter to Zorro's story. According to legend, Zorro was not always that swashbuckler able to swing from chandeliers and overpower ten men with the slash of his sword. At the beginning of the film *The Mask of Zorro*, we see him as the young and impetuous Alejandro, whose passion far exceeds his patience and discipline. His quest is to assail villains and right the injustices of the world, but he desires to do so immediately and spectacularly. The higher he flies, the farther he falls, until he soon feels out of control and utterly powerless. By the time the aging sword master Don Diego meets him, Alejandro is a broken man, a slave to drinking and despair. But Don Diego sees the young man's potential and takes him under his wing, promising Alejandro that mastery and triumph will come with "dedication and time." In the hidden cave that serves as Don Diego's lair, the elder sword master begins Alejandro's training by drawing a circle in the dirt. Hour after hour, Alejandro is forced to fight only within this small circle. As Don Diego wisely tells his protégé, "This circle will be your world. Your whole life. Until I tell you otherwise, there is nothing outside of it."

Once Alejandro masters control of this small circle, Don Diego allows him to slowly attempt greater and greater feats, which, one by one, he achieves. Soon he is swinging from ropes, besting his trainer in a sword fight, even performing a set of pushups over burning candles (not the most practical skill to hone, but cinematically impressive nonetheless). But none of these achievements would ever have been possible had he not first learned to master that small circle. Before that moment, Alejandro had no command over his emotions, no sense of his own skill, no real faith in his ability to accomplish a goal, and—worst of all—no feeling of control over his own fate. Only after he masters that first circle does he start to become Zorro, the legend.

CIRCLE OF CONTROL

The concept of the Zorro Circle is a powerful metaphor for how we can achieve our most ambitious goals in our jobs, our careers, and our personal lives. One of the biggest drivers of success is the belief that our behavior matters; that we have control over our future. Yet when our stresses and workloads seem to mount faster than our ability to keep up, feelings of control are often the first things to go, especially when we try to tackle too much at once. If, however, we first concentrate our efforts on small manageable goals, we regain the feeling of control so crucial to performance. By first limiting the scope of our efforts, then watching those efforts have the intended effect, we accumulate the resources, knowledge, and confidence to expand the circle, gradually conquering a larger and larger area. Don Diego didn't teach young Alejandro how to be a swashbuckling swordsman overnight. Zorro started small, then little by little mastered his ever-widening circle. His legendary success followed from there.

TENDING PLANTS AND CAREERS: THE IMPORTANCE OF CONTROL

Feeling that we are in control, that we are masters of our own fate at work and at home, is one of the strongest drivers of both well-being and performance. Among students, greater feelings of control lead not only to higher levels of happiness, but also to higher grades and more motivation to pursue the careers they really want. Similarly, employees who feel they have high levels of control at the office are better at their jobs and report more job satisfaction.[1] These benefits then ripple outward. A 2002 study of nearly 3,000 wage and salaried employees for the National Study of the Changing Workforce found that greater feelings of control at work predicted greater satisfaction in nearly every aspect of life: family, job, relationships, and so on.[2] People who felt in control at work also had lower levels of stress, work-family conflict, and job turnover.

Interestingly, psychologists have found that these kinds of gains in productivity, happiness, and health have less to do with how much control we actually have and more with how much control we *think* we have. Remember that how we experience the world is shaped largely by our mindset. Well, the most successful people, in work and in life, are those who have what psychologists call an "internal locus of control," the belief that their actions have a direct effect on their outcomes. People with an external locus, on the other hand, are more likely to see daily events as dictated by external forces.

It's easy to see why the former is more adaptive in work situations. If passed over for a promotion, for example, a person with an external locus of control might say, "The people here don't recognize talent; I never had a chance," and subsequently lose motivation.

After all, if we believe nothing we do matters, we fall prey to the insidious grip of learned helplessness I described in the last chapter. On the other hand, someone with an internal locus will look for what he or she might have done better, and then work to improve in that area. People with an external locus don't just duck the blame for failure, though; they also miss out on the credit for their successes, which can be equally maladaptive because it undermines both confidence and dedication. I once worked with a client who had such an external locus of control that no matter how many accolades she received, she always said that she just got lucky or that her boss had been easy on her. She never felt that her own actions had much impact on her achievements, and as a result she was never truly engaged or fulfilled by her work.

One of the best places to understand the effect of locus of control on performance is in the world of sports. Think about how the best athletes act in those ubiquitous post-game press conferences. Do they blame their losses on the sun for getting in their eyes, or the referee for making bad calls? Do they attribute wins to their horoscopes, or lucky streaks? No. When they win, they graciously accept the praise they receive and when they lose, they congratulate their opponent on a job well done. Believing that, for the most part, our actions determine our fates in life can only spur us to work harder; and when we see this hard work pay off, our belief in ourselves only grows stronger.

This is true in nearly every domain of life. Research has shown that people who believe that the power lies within their circle have higher academic achievement, greater career achievement, and are much happier at work.[3] An internal locus lowers job stress and turnover, and leads to higher motivation, organizational commitment, and task performance. "Internals," as they are sometimes called, have even stronger relationships—which makes sense given that studies show how much better they are at communicating, problem-solving, and working to achieve mutual goals. They are also more attentive listeners and more adept at social interactions—all qualities, incidentally, that predict success at work as well as at home.

Because feeling in control over our jobs and our lives reduces stress, it even affects our physical health. One sweeping study of 7,400 employees found that those who felt they had little control over deadlines imposed by other people had a 50 percent higher risk of coronary heart disease than their counterparts.[4] In fact, this effect was so staggering, researchers concluded that feeling a lack of control over pressure at work is *as great* a risk factor for heart disease as even high blood pressure.

But perhaps the most eye-opening example of how powerful the perception of control is doesn't come from the business world—it actually comes from the elderly. In one incredible study, researchers found that when they gave a group of nursing home residents more control over simple tasks in their daily lives—like putting them in charge of their own house plants—not only did their levels of happiness improve, but their mortality rate actually dropped in half.[5] It's hard to find a circle of control smaller than caring for a house plant, and yet feeling mastery over even that tiny task actually extended their lives.

LOSING CONTROL: THE DUELING BRAIN

Unfortunately, given how important it is to our success, we don't always feel in control. Some of us are inherently prone to an external locus, and the rest of us can fall into that mindset the second we feel overwhelmed by too many demands on our time, attention, and abilities. To fully understand how this happens, we need to take a closer look inside the brain.

As we go about our daily lives, our actions are often determined by the brain's two dueling components: our knee jerk–like emotional system (let's call him the Jerk) and our rational, cognitive system (let's call him the Thinker). The oldest part of the brain, evolutionarily speaking, is the Jerk, and it is based in the limbic (emotional) region, where the amygdala reigns supreme. Thousands of years ago, this knee-jerk system was necessary for our survival. Back then, we didn't have time to think logically when a saber-toothed tiger jumped out of the underbrush; instead, the Jerk readily leapt into action. The amygdala sounded the alarm, flooded our body with adrenaline and stress hormones, and sparked an immediate, innate reflex—a "fight or flight" response. It's thanks to the Jerk, really, that we are all sitting here ten thousand years later.

Today, fortunately, few saber-toothed tigers stalk our office parks. In the modern world, where life's problems are usually more complicated than flee or be eaten, the Jerk's reflexive responses can sometimes do more harm than good. In particular, when it comes to decision making, the Jerk often gets us in a lot of trouble. That's why, over thousands of years of evolution, we have also developed the Thinker, that rational system in the brain that resides mostly in the prefrontal cortex. This is what we use to think logically, draw conclusions from many pieces of information, and plan for the future. The Thinker's purpose is simple, but it reflects a huge evolutionary leap: *think, then react*.

Most of our daily challenges are better served by the Thinker, but unfortunately, when we're feeling stressed or out of control, the Jerk tends to take over. This isn't something that happens consciously. Instead, it's biological. When we're under pressure, the body starts to build up too much cortisol, the toxic chemical associated with stress. Once the stress has reached a critical point, even the smallest setback can trigger an amygdala response, essentially hitting the brain's panic button. When that happens, the Jerk overpowers the Thinker's defenses, spurring us into action without conscious thought. Instead of "think, then react," the Jerk responds with "fight or flight." We have become victims of what scientists call "emotional hijacking."

Over the past decade, researchers have been evaluating how this kind of emotional hijacking affects performance and decision making at work. In one study, psychologist Richard Davidson used his expertise in neuroscience to pinpoint why certain people were particularly resilient in the face of stress while others were so easily debilitated by it.[6] He put both groups in identical high-stress situations, like solving difficult math problems in a short amount of time or writing about the most upsetting moment of their lives, while he simultaneously tracked their brain function using functional Magnetic Resonance Imaging, or fMRI.

As each subject tackled the challenge at hand, Davidson watched both the rational and reflexive parts of the brain light up on the brain scan, dueling for supremacy. When he compared the patterns, he found that in the resilient individuals, the prefrontal cortex rapidly won over the limbic system; in other words, the Thinker took over almost immediately from the Jerk. The easily troubled group, on the other hand, exhibited a continuous rise in amygdala activity, which meant that the Jerk had hijacked the Thinker, overwhelming the brain's reasoning and coping capabilities, and making the distress much worse.

HIGHJACKED AT WORK

At this point you might be wondering, what does all this brain activity have to do with achieving our goals at work? Quite a lot, actually. Psychologist Daniel Goleman, author of the groundbreaking book *Emotional Intelligence,* has extensively studied the toll this emotional hijacking can take on our professional lives.[7] When small stresses pile up over time, as they so often do in the workplace, it only takes a minor annoyance or irritation to lose control; in other words, to let the Jerk into the driver's seat. When this hijacking occurs, we might lash out at a colleague or start to feel helpless and overwhelmed or suddenly lose all energy and motivation. As a result, our decision-making skills, productivity, and effectiveness plummet. This can have real consequences not just for individuals, but for entire teams of organizations. At one large company, researchers found that managers who felt the most swamped by job pressure ran teams with the worst performance and the lowest net profits.[8] A failing economy can be a powerful trigger for emotional hijacking, too. Neuroscientists have found that financial losses are actually processed in the same areas of the brain that respond to mortal danger.[9] In other words, we react to withering profits and a sinking retirement account the same way our ancestors did to a saber-toothed tiger.

Daniel Kahneman, the only psychologist to have ever won the Nobel Prize for Economics, has made enormous strides in our understanding of how the Dueling Brain affects decision making in business. Before he came onto the scene, the prevailing belief was that humans are rational decision makers—that we make financial and economic decisions based on a rational assessment of potential profits and losses. But Kahneman and his colleague Amos Tversky proved just how wrong this is.[10]

One classic experiment, known as the Ultimatum Game, goes like this: Researchers invite two people who do not know each other into the lab. One of them is given ten $1 bills and told to divide the money between himself and the other subject in any way he likes (he can keep all $10 for himself, he can split it $6 and $4, etc.). Then he gives the recipient an ultimatum: "Take the money or leave it." Here's the catch: If the recipient chooses to leave it, both people get nothing.

For traditional economists, this is fairly straightforward. A rational person will always take the deal, no matter how stingy. After all, even if it's only one dollar, that's still one more dollar than they came in with. But as it turns out, most recipients actually reject offers of $1 or even $2. Why? Because instead of rationally weighing their options, they allow their emotions—usually anger and annoyance at having been given a raw deal—to take over. This doesn't make rational sense, of course, because they're turning down a free $2 just to be spiteful. But it happens all the time. When neuroscientists investigate further, they find that the more active the limbic system is in the brain, the more likely the stingy offer will be rejected. As one researcher writes, "these findings suggest that when participants reject an unfair offer . . . it appears to be the product of a strong (seemingly negative) emotional response."[11]

I've seen the Jerk wreak havoc in companies all around the world. It is the reason shareholders buy high and sell low, even when they know they should do exactly the opposite. It is also the reason we fall prey to market bubbles, and the reason markets crash when those bubbles burst. As Jason Zweig points out in his book *Your Money and Your Brain,* "Everyone knows that panic selling is a bad idea—but a company that announces it earned 23 cents per share instead of 24 cents can lose $5 billion of market value in a minute-and-a-half."[12] When our brain hits the panic button, reason goes out the window and our wallets, our careers, and our bottom lines all suffer.

REGAINING CONTROL, ONE CIRCLE AT A TIME

So how do we reclaim control from the Jerk and put it back into the hands of the Thinker? The answer is the Zorro Circle. The first goal we need to conquer—or circle we need to draw—is self-awareness. Experiments show that when people are primed to feel high levels of distress, the quickest to recover are those who can identify how they are feeling and put those feelings into words. Brain scans show verbal information almost immediately diminishes the power of these negative emotions, improving well-being and enhancing decision-making skills.[13] So whether you do it by writing down feelings in a journal or talking to a trusted coworker or confidant, verbalizing the stress and helplessness you are feeling is the first step toward regaining control.

Once you've mastered the self-awareness circle, your next goal should be to identify which aspects of the situation you have control over and which you don't. When I worked with the Shanghai manager and his colleagues I mentioned in the last chapter, I asked them to write out all their stresses, daily challenges, and goals, then to separate them into two categories: things that they have control over and things they don't. Anyone can do this simple exercise on a piece of paper, an Excel spreadsheet, or even on a napkin over post-work martinis. The point is to tease apart the stresses that we have to let go of because they're out of our hands, while at the same time identifying the areas where our efforts will have a real impact, so that we can then focus our energy accordingly.

Once my trainees are armed with a list of what is indeed still within their control, I have them identify one small goal they know they can quickly accomplish. By narrowing their scope of action, and focusing their energy and efforts, the likelihood of success increases. Think of it this way: The best way to wash a car is to put a thumb over the hose's spout, so that only a fraction of the area is open. Why? Because this concentrates the water pressure, making the hose much more powerful. At work, the equivalent of this is concentrating your efforts on small areas where you know you can make a difference. By tackling one small challenge at a time—a narrow circle that slowly expands outward—we can relearn that our actions do have a direct effect on our outcomes, that we are largely the masters of our own fates. With an increasingly internal locus of control and a greater confidence in our abilities, we can then expand our efforts outward.

YOU CAN'T SPRINT YOUR WAY TO A MARATHON

At first, some perennial high achievers have a difficult time with this concept. Three years ago, I worked with a very busy vice president who wanted to stop running herself ragged at work—and start running marathons instead. She wasn't in the best shape of her life, as she hadn't been exercising at all because of her busy workload, but she believed that if she could manage a huge team across three continents, she could manage to run 26 miles. I'm no professional runner, but I feared her outsize ambition might get her in trouble. So I offered a few words of unsolicited advice: "If you haven't run a marathon before, perhaps you should start slowly by running laps around the track at the gym, then build up from there."

She didn't care for that idea. "Running laps?" she said. "You don't understand. I want to run a marathon in a month. I'll need to start long runs immediately." She bought sleek shoes, high-tech gear, and began running fiercely every morning before work. By the end of two weeks, she was racked by fatigue, crippled by shin splints, and frustrated that she hadn't yet managed to run more than five miles. So she gave up, 21 miles short of her goal. Unwilling to start with small circles, she had taken on too much at once, and failed. And she didn't feel good about it.

Unfortunately, when it comes to our work, we are often faced with unreasonable expectations—both those we set for ourselves and those others set for us. But when our goals are unrealizable, we run the risk of ending up like that overreaching marathoner—frustrated, dejected, and stuck. In today's results-obsessed workplace, it's no wonder we're impatient and overly ambitious. We want to be the top salesman or earn the highest bonus or have the biggest office—and we want it NOW. If we hire a new CEO, we're expected to be profitable the next quarter; if we hire a new head coach, we're expected to win the very next game. Our reality-TV culture, which tells us that change isn't worth making (or televising) unless it's immediate and Olympian in size, doesn't help either. We are taught to believe that total makeovers of house, body, and psyche are possible all in a 30-minute episode (minus commercials). But in the real world, this all-or-nothing mindset nearly guarantees failure. Furthermore, the feelings that result from frustrated attempts and overwhelming stressors hijack our brain, jumpstarting that vicious and insidious cycle of helplessness that puts our goals even further out of reach.

No matter what you may have heard from motivational speakers, coaches, and the like, reaching for the stars is a recipe for failure. In Part 1, I talked about pushing the limits of possibility. I do believe it's important to do this—just not all at once. That's why psychologists who specialize in goal-setting theory advocate setting goals of moderate difficulty—not so easy that we don't have to try, but not so difficult that we get discouraged and give up.[14] When the challenges we face are particularly challenging and the payoff remains far away, setting smaller, more manageable goals helps us build our confidence and celebrate our forward progress, and keeps us committed to the task at hand. As Harvard Business School professor Peter Bregman advises, "Don't write a book, write a page. . . . Don't expect to be a great manager in your first six months, just try to set expectations well."[15]

No matter how small the initial circle is, it can lead to big returns. In *The Talent Code,* Daniel Coyle discusses how the strategy of "finding and improving small problems" has helped businesses flourish.[16] The practice (often referred to as *kaizen,* which is Japanese for "continuous improvement") involves a focus on tiny, incremental changes—improving efficiency on a production line, for instance, by shifting a trash bin one foot to the left. As Coyle points out, each tiny fix can add up to over a million tiny fixes each year. With *kaizen,* in other words, companies use the Zorro Circle to transform incremental change into mammoth results.

PUTTING IT ALL TOGETHER

I once worked with the head copywriter of an advertising firm who found it difficult not to worry about the financial health of her company—how many clients account services was landing, what kind of designs the art department was producing, whether or not her boss would start laying people off. Once she realized that each of these things was well outside her control, and that worrying about them only led to heightened levels of stress, she was able to shift her focus toward fixing what was troubling her in her job, her workplace, and in many ways her life.

As with other clients, I had her make two lists—what she could control and what she couldn't. As often happens, she was surprised, I might say shocked, to see how much of her daily life fell into the former column. She managed a team of eight people, all talented copywriters who looked to her for instruction and guidance. She was in charge of leading the creative meetings that brainstormed ideas for each client. She may not have been a top executive, but every word the firm placed on a client's advertisement was in her hands.

So for her first Zorro Circle, we set the following goal: to improve only the copy that she herself wrote. Recommitting herself to this manageable goal not only helped her focus her energies on something she could handle; the best part was that, once her own performance improved, her circle of influence really did expand. The better her writing got, the harder her team worked to follow her example, and the team's improved performance soon raised the bar higher for other departments, which responded with renewed enthusiasm and creativity. Ironically, by recognizing that she had no control over the art department's designs, she indirectly influenced their designs after all. This gave her the confidence she needed to set her sights even higher, and pretty soon, her leadership was a great contributor to the company's overall performance.

PIZZA BOXES AND IN-BOXES

We often feel the most stress, or the most emotionally hijacked, when we stare into the void of our jam-packed to-do list, in-box, or desk top. One look at the towering pile of papers looming on our desk, or the 300 unread e-mails, and our feelings of control fly right out the window. As a freshman proctor, I advised more than my fair share of disorganized students, who ranged from the typically un-tidy to the pathologically messy. During my second year on the job, the fire department reported one of my students, a tennis player named Joey, because his room was so full of old pizza boxes, empty bottles, scattered newspapers, and falling towers of textbooks that it couldn't pass a fire code inspection. Not only was his room an incinerator waiting to happen, the fire inspector feared Joey might have trouble escaping his own room in the case of emergency (not to mention in the case of class).

Some messes can be appreciated as organized chaos, but Joey's disorder had crossed over from quirky to debilitating. On the one hand, he wanted to get his life in order; on the other, the idea of tackling this massive disaster felt completely overwhelming. So we drew a Zorro Circle, literally. I found a small patch of desk that had one stack of papers on it, and we traced a circle, only a foot in diam-eter, around it. "Let's clear it off," I told Joey, "and put each paper in its rightful place." Then, instead of moving on to the rest of the desk right away, I told him to spend the next day defending the newly clean patch against any threats to order. Given Joey's usual habits, even that was a difficult task (he admitted as much the next day), but it was manageable. And, once he had done it, he seemed genu-inely pleased. So the next day we chose another corner of his desk and applied the same rule. With each subsequent day came one more clutter-free circle—not to mention a greater sense of control and a strengthened commitment to the project. A mere two weeks later, the room was a spotless shadow of its former self. By estab-lishing small circles of success and gradually expanding outward,

Joey mastered the larger circle of his life. He was happy and so was the fire department.

A cluttered desk is fundamentally no different from a cluttered in-box—a problem that haunts too many modern workers. In both instances, the *things* of our lives have gained control over the *functionality* of our lives, and productivity suffers as a result. I had just given a talk to the employees of a large manufacturing company when one of the senior executives, Barry, invited me into his office. We weren't even inside the door when he began apologizing for the clutter; his office looked like a four-year-old had been playing "paper tornado." But Barry had an even bigger problem on his mind: his e-mail. He confessed that his in-box contained over 1400 messages, which had piled up over the last two months while he worked on an all-consuming project. Now that the project was over, he knew he had to start addressing the pileup, but the mere thought of it seemed to strike fear into his heart. I studied the problem over his shoulder as he scrolled through all his unread messages. Three minutes later, he was barely through a quarter of them. "I'll never dig out from under this mountain," he said, "I might as well contract a computer virus that just destroys my whole computer." His stress level was so high at this point that every new e-mail sent his body into a reflexive stress response. Just thinking about it made him feel nauseous. Not only did he want to avoid dealing with his e-mail, he was so overwhelmed by the situation, he didn't feel like doing any work at all.

I agreed to help. First, I told him, he needed to quell his growing anxiety. This in-box was not a saber-toothed tiger. It was a problem to be solved by planning and deliberate effort, not adrenaline-fueled panic. I could see he needed to talk about the problem, to put his feelings into words, in order to move the challenge from the emotional part of his brain to the problem-solving part. I reminded him that self-awareness was a swift antidote for emotional hijacking, and recommended that he keep a notebook nearby to jot down his thoughts whenever the stress seemed to be rising to the surface. Then we drew the next circle.

Dealing with two months' worth of unread e-mails was more than anyone could handle all at once, and Barry needed to see some progress right away. So I told him to forget everything that had been written before today and to respond only to each new e-mail as it came in. After three or four days of tackling only new e-mails, once he started to feel in command of the situation, he could go back through the e-mails of the day before and address those. And so he could proceed, tacking on one extra day at a time, until he slowly worked his way back to the beginning. I also told him he couldn't spend more than an hour each day on this task. Without a time limit, even small, incremental tasks can quickly escalate back into an overwhelming challenge with no end in sight.

Three weeks later, I received an e-mail from Barry. He proudly told me that if I responded immediately, I would be one of only five e-mails currently in his in-box. I was amazed. Furthermore, he had attached a picture of his spotless office, almost unrecognizable from the paper tornado I had first encountered. I wrote back that, assuming he hadn't subbed in a photo from an Office Depot ad, congratulations were in order. He had started with small, manageable steps forward, and now he was celebrating a giant success.

ZORRO GOES TO GOTHAM

As a native of the Southwest, Zorro never got to fight crime in New York City. But in a way, the same lessons that made Zorro a hero have helped make New York a safer city. In his book *The Tipping Point,* Malcolm Gladwell recounts how city officials battled a rising crime rate in the 1980s and '90s.[17] It was an overwhelming problem that no one quite knew how to fix—no matter how much money the city spent, no matter what the police did, they just couldn't seem to curb the dangerous trend. Finally, a small group of officials surprised everyone by adopting a radical new strategy, based on the now-famous Broken Windows Theory. First devised in 1982 by sociologists James Q. Wilson and George Kelling, the theory explains how small acts of vandalism can quickly balloon into widespread crime. As the theory has it, one broken window in an abandoned building will soon multiply into many broken windows, which will lead to graffiti, then muggings, then car thefts, and so on.

So the city officials decided to see whether this also worked in reverse. They started with the subway, immediately redirecting all their money and attention toward fixing the windows and cleaning up the graffiti, literally one car at a time. Understandably, city denizens were quite skeptical at first. As Gladwell explains, "Many subway advocates, at the time, told [them] not to worry about graffiti, to focus on the larger questions of crime and subway reliability, and it seemed like reasonable advice. Worrying about graffiti at a time when the entire system was close to collapse seems as pointless as scrubbing the decks of the Titanic as it headed toward the icebergs."

But despite the cries of these detractors, the city officials stuck to their plan, slowly expanding their efforts to include more and more subways lines, until all of the trains in the city were clean. And as their circles started to expand, so did their results. Before long, subway crime of all kinds—from fare beating to armed robberies—had dropped rapidly. Then they expanded their circle by cleaning up graffiti in the city at large, and amazingly, they soon saw crime fall across the board.

The point: Small successes can add up to major achievements. All it takes is drawing that first circle in the sand.

THE 20-SECOND RULE

How to Turn Bad Habits into Good Ones by Minimizing Barriers to Change

During one of the first trainings I ever gave on Wall Street, an impatient-looking man stood up in the back of the room and shouted over the heads of his fellow analysts. "Shawn, I know you're from Harvard and everything, but isn't this all a huge waste of time? Isn't positive psychology just common sense?"

I felt my heart drop into my stomach. I hadn't yet been in the consulting business long enough to know that being publicly challenged like this comes with the territory. Still, I gathered my wits and did my best to address the inquisitor head-on. I started by telling him that positive psychology draws on ideas from many esteemed sources ranging from ancient Greek philosophers, to hallowed religious traditions, to modern-day writers and thinkers. What's more, I went on, the principles and theories are then empirically tested and validated. So while some of the ideas espoused by positive psychology may very well be common sense, it's the science behind them that makes them unique and valuable. Clearly, though, this guy just wasn't buying it. He sat back down with a smug look, and I moved on to the next question, trying to accept the fact that you just can't win them all.

Not until after the session, as I sat with several of the analysts over lunch, did the significance of this encounter reveal itself. "Do you remember that guy who stood up during your talk?" one of them asked. I said that I very much did. Another analyst leaned in close. "That guy is the most unhappy person here. It's like a rain cloud follows over his head all the time. We can't put him on any teams because he's toxic."

This was a turning point for me. Here was someone who had dismissed most of what I had just been saying as too obvious to even discuss; yet apparently it wasn't obvious enough. I realized that he was the living embodiment of one of the greatest paradoxes of human behavior:

Common sense is not common action.

Would you be surprised if I told you that cigarettes are not a great source of vitamin C? Or that watching hours of reality television will not dramatically raise your IQ? Probably not. Similarly, we all know that we should exercise, sleep eight hours, eat healthier, and be kind to others. But does this common knowledge make doing these things any easier?

Of course not. Because in life, knowledge is only part of the battle. Without action, knowledge is often meaningless. As Aristotle put it, to be excellent we cannot simply think or feel excellent, we must act excellently. Yet the action required to follow through on what we know is often the hardest part. That's why even though doctors know better than anyone the importance of exercise and diet, 44 percent of them are overweight.[1] It's also why organizational gurus are often messy, religious leaders can be blasphemous, and why even some positive psychologists aren't happy all of the time. I work with countless business people who complain that every Monday they make the same resolutions to stop procrastinating or quit smoking, to keep up with their in-box, or start seeing their kids more; yet every Friday they find themselves wondering where the week went and what got in their way.

The fact of the matter is, positive habits are hard to keep, no matter how commonsensical they might be. Like most people, I wage this same battle every January 1, and by January 10, I'm right back where I started. In fact, the *New York Times* reports that a whopping 80 percent of us break our New Year's resolutions.[2] Even when we feel committed to positive change, sustaining it for any real length of time can seem nearly impossible. All too often our pledges go unfulfilled, and today's treadmill becomes tomorrow's clothing rack. If our brains have the capacity to change, as we now know they do, why is changing our behavior so hard, and how can we make it easier?

WE ARE "MERE BUNDLES OF HABITS"

During the years I spent working in Harvard's research lab, my workday started with a long ride up the elevator in William James Hall. The 15-story building has been home to Harvard's psychology department for decades, and it has housed more than its fair share of fascinating research—from B. F. Skinner and his famous box, to rambunctious bonobo monkeys and genetically engineered rodents. (All humanely treated, which is more than we can say for the graduate students.) The discoveries made by the building's namesake, though, might be its proudest heritage.

While his brother Henry was gaining worldwide fame as a novelist, William James was carving out his own niche in history with his breakthroughs in the field of psychology. Born a few years into the second half of the nineteenth century, James applied his training in medicine, philosophy, and psychology to his lifelong study of the human mind. He taught Harvard's first experimental psychology class in 1875 and by 1890 had published *Principles of Psychology*, a 1,200-page tour de force that became the precursor to the modern psychology textbook. As I tell my students every year, think of the poor undergraduates who took William James's class before you complain too loudly about this week's reading assignment.

In my mind, though, the greatest contribution William James

made to the field of psychology is one that was a full century ahead of his time. Humans, James said, are biologically prone to habit, and it is because we are "mere bundles of habits" that we are able to automatically perform many of our daily tasks—from brushing our teeth first thing in the morning to setting the alarm before climbing into bed at night.[3]

It is precisely because habits are so automatic that we rarely stop and think about the enormous role they play in shaping our behavior, and in fact our lives. After all, if we had to make a conscious choice about every little thing we did all day, we would likely be overwhelmed by breakfast. Take this morning as an example: I am guessing that you didn't wake up, walk into the bathroom, look quizzically into the mirror, and think to yourself, "Should I put on clothes today?" You didn't have to debate the pros and cons. You didn't have to call on your reserves of willpower. You just did it—the same way you probably combed your hair, gulped your coffee, locked your front door, and so on. And, excepting the exhibitionists in the reading public, you did not have to remind yourself all day to keep these clothes on. It was not a struggle. It didn't deplete your reserves of energy or brainpower. It was second nature, automatic, a habit.

None of this seems particularly groundbreaking to us today. But what William James concluded was indeed crucial to our understanding of behavioral change. Given our natural tendency to act out of habit, James surmised, couldn't the key to sustaining positive change be to turn each desired action into a habit, so that it would come automatically, without much effort, thought, or choice? As the Father of Modern Psychology so shrewdly advised, if we want to create lasting change, we should "make our nervous system our ally instead of our enemy."[4] Habits are like financial capital—forming one today is an investment that will automatically give out returns for years to come.

DAILY STROKES OF EFFORT

Of course, this is where the phrase "easier said than done" has particular relevance. Good habits may be the answer, but how do we create them in the first place? William James had a prescription for that, too. He called it "daily strokes of effort." This is hardly revelatory, basically a reworking of the old dictum "practice makes perfect." Still, he was on to something far more sophisticated than he could possibly have known at the time. "A tendency to act," he wrote, "only becomes effectively ingrained in us in proportion to the uninterrupted frequency with which the actions actually occur, and the brain 'grows' to their use."[5] In other words, habits form because our brain actually changes in response to frequent practice.

In fact, James had this exactly right, though it would take a hundred years before neuroscientists could explain why. Remember how we learned that the brain's structures and pathways are flexible and elastic? Well, it turns out that as we progress through our days learning new facts, completing new tasks, and having new conversations, our brains are constantly changing and rewiring to reflect these experiences. With apologies to the delicate nuances of neuroscience, here is what is happening in a nutshell: Within our brains are billions upon billions of neurons, interconnected in every which way to form a complex set of neural pathways. Electrical currents travel down these pathways, from neuron to neuron, delivering the messages that make up our every thought and action. The more we perform a particular action, the more connections form between the corresponding neurons. (This is the origin of the common phrase "cells that fire together, wire together.") The stronger this link, the faster the message can travel down the pathway. This is what makes the behavior seem second nature or automatic.

This is also how we become skilled at an activity with practice. For instance, the first time you try to juggle, the neural pathways involved are unused, and so the message travels slowly. The more time you spend juggling, the more these pathways get reinforced, so that on the eighth day of practice, the electrical currents are firing at a much more rapid pace. This is when you'll notice that juggling comes easier, requires less concentration, and that you can do it faster. Eventually, you can be listening to music, chewing gum, and having a conversation with someone else, all while those three oranges are flying through the air. Juggling has become automatic, a habit, cemented in your brain by a solid new network of neural pathways.

Given all that William James had right so many years ago, we should forgive him the one thing he got wrong. He believed, as did most scientists of his day, that this ability to create lasting brain change was exclusive to the young—essentially, the "you can't teach an old dog new tricks" school of thought. Thankfully, that's not the case. As you'll recall from the beginning of this book, scientists now know that the brain remains plastic and malleable well past the age of 20, through even our most senior years. That means that we have the power to create new habits and then reap the benefits whether we're 22 or 72.

THE GUITAR THAT WOULDN'T PLAY ITSELF

When I first learned about the science behind this phenomenon, I was eager to test it out. Could I really rewire my brain and create a new life habit by doing the same thing each day for a few weeks? It was time for an experiment, and the easiest way to do one was to make myself the subject.

I decided to take up the guitar once again, since I already owned one and knew that I enjoyed playing it. Because common wisdom has long proposed that it takes 21 days to make a habit, I decided to make a spreadsheet with 21 columns, tape it to my wall, and check off each day I played.[6] By the end of the three weeks, I felt confident that (a) I would have a grid full of 21 check marks, (b) daily guitar playing would have become an automatic, established part of my life, (c) my playing would improve, and (d) I would be happier for it.

Three weeks later, I pulled the grid down in disgust. Staring up at four check marks followed by a whole lot of empty boxes was more discouragement and embarrassment than I needed. I had failed my own experiment, and worse, I was no closer to telling potential dates that I was a musician. Worse still, I was shocked, depressed even, at how quick I had been to give up. A positive psychologist should be better at following his own advice! (Of course, the feelings of failure only deepen when you realize you're now a *depressed* positive psychologist.) The guitar was sitting in the closet, a mere 20 seconds away, but I couldn't make myself take it out and play it. What had gone wrong? It turns out that the telling words here are *make myself.* Without realizing it, I had been fighting the wrong battle—one I was bound to lose unless I changed my strategy.

WHY WILLPOWER IS NOT THE WAY

Tal Ben-Shahar loves to tell what he calls "the story of the chocolate cake." Back home in Israel, Tal's mother was famous for her delicious chocolate cake. One afternoon, when Tal and his friends arrived home from school, she pulled one out of the oven and offered everyone a slice. Tal refused, citing his strict training regimen for the National Squash Championships. So he sat and watched enviously as his friends devoured their mouthwatering snack; then they all went back to their homework. Hours later, Tal returned to the fridge to examine the cake. It still looked delicious. But no, he thought, he would stay strong. Another hour passed, another check on the cake. Yup, still there. Soon, it was all he could think about. Finally, in the middle of the night when everyone else was sleeping, Tal crept down to the kitchen and devoured the *entire* remaining cake. Every last bite.

Anyone who has ever tried to maintain a strict diet has

experienced this failure of willpower. We deny and deny ourselves until all of a sudden we can't take it anymore, and the floodgates break. Five successful days of carrot sticks and tofu wedges are followed by a pizza binge or a feast fit for five. As any dietician will tell you, relying on willpower to completely avoid unhealthy food nearly guarantees relapse; that's why people who crash diet are more likely to regain weight than people who eat healthily but don't deny themselves—and why only 20 percent of dieters are able to keep off the lost weight for any extended length of time.[7] The more we attempt to "stay strong," the harder we eventually fall—usually right into a tub of Ben & Jerry's.

The point is that whether it's a strict diet, a New Year's resolution, or an attempt at daily guitar practice, the reason so many of us have trouble sustaining change is because we try to rely on willpower. We think we can go from 0 to 60 in an instant, changing or overturning ingrained life habits through the sheer force of will. Tal thought telling himself he was on a diet would be enough to keep him away from his mother's chocolate cake. I thought telling myself to follow some spreadsheet would discipline me enough to practice the guitar. Well, that worked . . . for four days. Then I went back to regularly scheduled programming.

WILLPOWER GETS A WORKOUT

The reason willpower is so ineffective at sustaining change is that the more we use it, the more worn-out it gets. You may know this intuitively, but it took renowned researcher Roy Baumeister hundreds of chocolate chip cookies and a lot of disgruntled research subjects to prove it as fact.

In one of many studies on the subject of willpower, Baumeister and his colleagues invited college students into their lab, instructing them not to eat anything for at least three hours prior to the experiment.[8] Then he split them into three groups. Group 1 was given a plate of chocolate chip cookies, which they were told not to eat, as well as a healthy plate of radishes which they were welcome to eat to their heart's content. Group 2 was presented with the same two plates of cookies and radishes, but they were told they could eat off whichever plate they liked. Group 3 was given no food at all. After enduring these situations for a significant length of time, the three groups were then given a set of "simple" geometric puzzles to solve. Note the quotes around *simple*. In truth, this was another one of psychology's favorite tools: the unsolvable puzzle.

As I learned the hard way through my Help the Elderly experience, psychology researchers love using impossible games to see how long participants will persevere at a task. In this case, individuals in Groups 2 and 3 long outlasted those in Group 1, who quickly threw up their hands in defeat. Why? Because the students who had to use every ounce of their willpower to avoid eating the enticing chocolate chip cookies didn't have the willpower or mental energy left to struggle with a complex puzzle—even though avoiding cookies and persisting on a puzzle are seemingly completely unrelated.

Studies have replicated this finding with a huge range of tasks designed to tap willpower.[9] In one, people were asked to watch a humorous film and suppress their laughter, then solve difficult anagrams. In another, they were instructed to write about a day in the life of an obese person without using any stereotypes, then were told to suppress a specific thought ("don't think about a white bear"). And indeed, no matter what the tasks were, they always performed significantly worse on the second than the first. If they had resisted laughter for ten minutes, they couldn't persist on an anagram. If they had suppressed stereotypes, they couldn't avoid thinking about a white bear. And so on.

The point of these experiments was to show that no matter how unrelated the tasks were, they all seemed to be tapping the same fuel source. As the researchers wrote, "many widely different forms of self-control draw on a common resource, or *self-control strength,* which is quite limited and hence can be depleted readily."[10] Put another way, our willpower weakens the more we use it.

Unfortunately, we face a steady stream of tasks that deplete our willpower every single day. Whether it's avoiding the dessert table at the company lunch, staying focused on a computer spreadsheet for hours on end, or sitting still through a three-hour meeting, our willpower is consistently being put to the test. So it's no wonder, really, that we so easily give in to our old habits, to the easiest and most comfortable path, as we progress through the day. This invisible pull toward the path of least resistance can dictate more of our lives than we realize, creating an impassible barrier to change and positive growth.

THE PATH OF LEAST RESISTANCE

As Cathy sits tethered to her desk on Tuesday, she daydreams about the upcoming Saturday and all its possibilities. She wants to go biking on the trail by her house, join in a pickup soccer game at the local park, and see that Matisse exhibit at the museum. She might even dive into that pile of books she has been wanting to read. Like all of us, Cathy has a number of hobbies and activities that engage her interests and strengths, energize her days, and make her happy. And yet, when her free Saturday actually does roll around, where does she end up? Conspicuously not on her bike or at the soccer field, and certainly not at that art exhibit everybody was raving about—it's 20 minutes away! Her remote control, on the other hand, is within very easy reach, and Bravo happens to be airing a *Top Chef* marathon. Four hours later, Cathy has sunk deeper and deeper into the couch, unable to shake a listless sense of disappointment. She had better plans for the afternoon, and she wonders what happened to them.

What happened to Cathy was something that happens to all of

us at one time or another. Inactivity is simply the easiest option. Unfortunately, we don't enjoy it nearly as much as we think we do. In general, Americans actually find free time more difficult to enjoy than work.[11] If that sounds ridiculous, consider this: For the most part, our jobs require us to use our skills, engage our minds, and pursue our goals—all things that have been shown to contribute to happiness. Of course, leisure activities can do this too, but because they're not required of us—because there is no "leisure boss" leaning over our shoulder on Sunday mornings telling us we'd better be at the art museum by 9 A.M. sharp—we often find it difficult to muster the energy necessary to kick-start them. So we follow the path of least resistance, and that path inevitably leads us to the couch and the television. And because we are "mere bundles of habit," the more often we succumb to this path, the more difficult it becomes to change directions.

Unfortunately, though these types of "passive leisure," like watching TV and trolling around on Facebook, might be easier and more convenient than biking or looking at art or playing soccer, they don't offer the same rewards. Studies show that these activities are enjoyable and engaging for only about 30 minutes, then they start sapping our energy, creating what psychologists call "psychic entropy"—that listless, apathetic feeling Cathy experienced.

On the other hand, "active leisure" like hobbies, games, and sports enhance our concentration, engagement, motivation, and sense of enjoyment. Studies have found that American teenagers are two and half times more likely to experience elevated enjoyment when engaged in a hobby than when watching TV, and three times more likely when playing a sport. And yet here's the paradox: These same teenagers spend *four times* as many hours watching TV as they do engaging in sports or hobbies. So what gives? Or, as psychologist Mihaly Csikszentmihalyi put it more eloquently, "Why would we spend four times more time doing something that has less than half the chance of making us feel good?"[12]

The answer is that we are drawn—powerfully, magnetically—to

those things that are easy, convenient, and habitual, and it is incredibly difficult to overcome this inertia. Active leisure *is* more enjoyable, but it almost always requires more initial effort—getting the bike out of the garage, driving to the museum, tuning the guitar, and so on. Csikszentmihalyi calls this "activation energy." In physics, activation energy is the initial spark needed to catalyze a reaction. The same energy, both physical and mental, is needed of people to overcome inertia and kick-start a positive habit. Otherwise, human nature takes us down the path of least resistance time and time again.

AN OFFER YOU CAN'T REFUSE

As you might imagine, advertisers and marketers make their living on the path of least resistance. Ever bought something with a mail-in rebate? Did you actually mail it in? Didn't think so. That's why companies offer them. This is also why magazines send us a free five-week subscription, then automatically start deducting money from our account in the sixth week. Sure, we can refuse the offer, as long as we mail back that little card saying, "No thank you, I would like to cancel my subscription." Unfortunately, that requires just too much activation energy, and the gimmick pays off for the magazine.

In the world of marketing, the term is "opt-out"—a genius invention, really, that takes supreme advantage of human psychology. Opt-out marketing is when people are added to mailing lists without ever consciously consenting, so that if they want to stop the barrage of promotional e-mails, they must actively unsubscribe themselves. To "unsubscribe" requires finding the tiny link at the bottom of the e-mail, then clicking through one or two more websites before finally arriving at the desired destination. The company is betting, often successfully, that this process involves far more energy and effort than most people are willing to expend.

Martin Lindstrom, a marketing expert who uses neuroscience to explore the psychology of our consumer habits, points out that phone companies are special benefactors of this strategy.[13] There is almost always a better monthly plan available than the one the phone comes with, but we usually stick with the default because it's just too difficult to do the research and then even more difficult to switch plans. One especially fascinating study Lindstrom did on the famous Nokia ringtone, perhaps the most ubiquitous four-note sound in the world, revealed the powerful pull that the path of least resistance has on us. By using fMRI technology to analyze people's brains during exposure to the sound, he found a nearly universal negative emotional response. And yet amazingly, 80 million Nokia users have it as their ringtone. Why would they keep the ring that grates on their ears and sends them into an emotional tailspin every time they get a call? Because it's the default option. And whether we're aware or it or not, default options are everywhere, shaping our choices and our behavior in all areas of our lives.

At the grocery store, we buy more food off shelves that directly meet our eye and less off those that require us to look up or kneel down.[14] Every retailer knows this, and you can be sure they exploit it by putting the most expensive brands at eye level. Online advertisers now conduct market research with sophisticated eye-tracking machines, determined to develop the perfect place for a banner ad on a website, the place that we will see without expending any additional energy.[15] In clothing stores, too, everything is set up to capitalize on our gravitation to the default path. As Lindstrom points out, we're more likely to buy an item of clothing if we can give it a "sensory test run" by touching the fabric, so the most expensive clothes are set at the perfect height for such an experience. Try this out the next time you enter a store. When your hands are at your side, each table of clothes sits almost exactly at your fingertips, begging to be grabbed.

In the workplace, the path of least resistance is especially maladaptive, luring us into a whole host of bad habits that breed procrastination and undercut productivity. I often encounter this problem in my own professional life, but I had to travel all the way to Hong Kong for the gravity of the situation to really hit home.

THE PATH TO DISTRACTION

It was the second day of the training session I was giving at a large technology company in Hong Kong, a city so electric it makes Times Square look like Topeka. I had found some time to work privately with Ted, one of the lead managers on the marketing team, who was struggling to keep up with his workload. No matter how much he worked, he always felt behind, and he had to keep extending his hours to keep up with it all. "I don't do anything except work now," Ted confessed, "and it's still not enough."

I told him that he wasn't alone. I hear this same story, almost word for word, no matter what country I'm in or who I'm talking with. Regardless of our job description, we never seem to have enough time to get everything done. Eight-hour workdays turn into 12- and 14-hour ones, and still we feel behind. How can this be? Why do we have so much trouble being productive? After listening to Ted describe, from start to finish, how he went about his day, two important answers suddenly clicked into place: (1) Ted was working all the time, and (2) Ted was almost never working.

When Ted arrives at 7 A.M., the first thing he does is open his Internet browser. His home page is CNN, so he starts reading up on the day's breaking news. His intent is to scan the major headlines and move on, but invariably, he ends up clicking through the other links that catch his eye. Then without even thinking about it, he opens two different websites where he checks his stocks and investments to see how they fared overnight.

Next, he checks his e-mail, which will continue to stay open throughout the day, alerting him every time he receives new messages. Once he wades through his in-box, clicks on a couple more links and attachments, and fires back a few responses, he's ready to get to work. Sort of. Turns out, Ted generally gets about 30 minutes of real work done before he takes a quick coffee break. Then he sits back down at his computer, where he can't help but notice that his home page has a whole new batch of headlines to scan. And what's this? Ten new e-mails? He'd better read them. Then he checks his stocks, again, just to be sure financial Armageddon hasn't kicked in. Finally, Ted refocuses and gets into a groove writing a new marketing plan . . . which lasts for about 10 minutes until his concentration is broken again by the arrival of new e-mail. To quote Kurt Vonnegut, "and so it goes."

Does this sound at all familiar? After a few quick calculations, we concluded that Ted probably checks his stocks three times an hour, his e-mail five times an hour, and news websites about once an hour. And that's actually quite typical. The American Management Association reports that employees spend an average of 107 minutes on e-mail a day.[16] A group of London workers I spoke with admitted that they checked stocks about 4 or 5 times an hour; that's 35 times a day. And I suspect that if most office workers tallied up all the minutes they spent each day on blogs, social networking sites, Amazon.com, and so forth, it would paint a very alarming picture indeed. No wonder it's so hard to get anything done!

And that's not even the worst of it. The actual time we give to these distractions is part of the problem, but the larger issue is that our attention hits a wall each time we stray. Research shows that the average employee gets interrupted from their work every 11 minutes, and on each occasion experiences a loss of concentration and flow that takes almost as many minutes to recover from.[17] Yet in today's world, it's just too easy for us to be tempted. As a *New York Times* article put it, "distracting oneself used to consist of sharpening a half-dozen pencils or lighting a cigarette. Today, there is a universe of diversions to buy, hear, watch and forward, which makes focusing on a task all the more challenging."[18]

As Ted and I worked to find ways to minimize the distractions,

I had an epiphany: It's not the sheer number and volume of distractions that gets us into trouble; it's the ease of access to them. Think about it. If you want to check your stocks, do you have to sit there and watch a stock ticker run through the whole alphabet? Of course not. You can program a website to update you on the ones you're interested in and give you regular updates. If you want to read the latest political news or some commentary on the hot new movie, do you have to troll through all the dozens of sites and blogs to find one on the desired subject? No way. You can set up an RSS feed for your favorite blog topics and have them delivered right to your in-box. Similarly, you can get all your favorite sports news, celebrity gossip, restaurant reviews, and everything else e-mailed right to you. Technology may make it easier for us to save time, but it also makes it a whole lot easier for us to waste it. In short, distraction, always just one click away, has become the path of least resistance.

REDIRECTING THE PATH:
THE 20-SECOND RULE

In allowing himself to be swept along this path, Ted had become ensnared in a series of very bad habits. In his case, these all involved procrastination, which got me thinking: Could the psychological mechanisms that were derailing Ted's productivity also explain why I had failed to follow my regimen of guitar playing? Had the path of least resistance led me astray? I thought back to that initial experiment. I had kept my guitar tucked away in the closet, out of sight and out of reach. It wasn't far out of the way, of course (my apartment isn't that big), but just those 20 seconds of extra effort it took to walk to the closet and pull out the guitar had proved to be a major deterrent. I had tried to overcome this barrier with willpower, but after only four days, my reserves were completely dried up. If I couldn't use self-control to ingrain the habit, at least not for an extended period, I now wondered: What if I could eliminate the amount of activation energy it took to get started?

Clearly, it was time for another experiment. I took the guitar out of the closet, bought a $2 guitar stand, and set it up in the middle of my living room. Nothing had changed except that now instead of being 20 seconds away, the guitar was in immediate reach. Three weeks later, I looked up at a habit grid with 21 proud check marks.

What I had done here, essentially, was put the *desired* behavior on the path of least resistance, so it actually took less energy and effort to pick up and practice the guitar than to avoid it. I like to refer to this as the 20-Second Rule, because lowering the barrier to change by just 20 seconds was all it took to help me form a new life habit. In truth, it often takes more than 20 seconds to make a difference—and sometimes it can take much less—but the strategy itself is universally applicable: Lower the activation energy for habits you want to adopt, and raise it for habits you want to avoid. The more we can lower or even eliminate the activation energy for our desired actions, the more we enhance our ability to jump-start positive change.

SIRENS & SLURPEES

This is not a new idea—but it is a really good one. Remember the scene from Homer's *Odyssey* where Odysseus tries to guide his ship past the dangerous Sirens, those beauties with voices so seductive they could lure any man to certain death? Odysseus knows he will be powerless to resist their call, so he tells his men to tie him to the ship's mast, ensuring that they will sail safely by. Because he knows willpower will fail him, he puts enough activation energy in between him and the path of temptation.

More than two thousand years later, and in only a slightly different cultural context, the main character in the movie *Confessions of a Shopaholic* freezes her credit cards in blocks of ice to physically stop herself from an impulsive buy. Sounds silly, but putting ten minutes of hair-drying and chiseling in between her and her AmEx was enough to stall her troubling habit. Sure, this may be an exaggeration (from Hollywood, how surprising), but financial advisors actually do recommend that people who can't resist the siren song of a sale leave their credit cards at home in a desk drawer, safely out of reach.

Luckily, shopping isn't one of my big weaknesses, but watching too much television used to be. According to a quick Google search, the average American watches five to seven hours of television a day. At one point, I was watching about three hours a day, which was of course decreasing my productivity and time with my real-life friends. I wanted to watch less television, but every time I'd come home from work, I would be tired from teaching, and it was so easy to sit down on the couch and press the "on" button on the remote control. So I decided to do another experiment on myself. This time, I determined to play the same trick my brain had played upon me when I didn't play the guitar. I took the batteries out of the remote control, took my stopwatch, and walked the batteries exactly 20 seconds away and left them in a drawer in my bedroom. Would that be enough to cure me of my TV habit?

The next few nights when I got home from work, I plopped down on the couch and pressed the "on" button on the remote—usually repeatedly—forgetting that I had moved the batteries. Then, frustrated, I thought to myself, "I hate that I do these experiments." But sure enough, the energy and effort required to retrieve the batteries—or even to walk across the room and turn the TV on manually—was enough to do the trick. Soon I found myself reaching for a book I had purposefully placed on the couch, or the guitar that now sat on a stand right by the couch, or even the laptop, now positioned in easy reach, on which I was writing this manuscript. As the days passed, the urge to watch TV waned, and the new activities became more habitual. Eventually, I even found myself doing things that required far more activation energy than retrieving batteries, like going out to play pickup basketball or meeting friends for dinner. And I felt much more energized, productive, and happy for it.

By adding 20 seconds to my day, I gained back three hours.

The 20-Second Rule is an especially crucial ally in our quest for healthier eating habits. Researchers have found that they can cut cafeteria ice cream consumption in half by simply closing the lid of an ice cream cooler.[19] And that when people are required to wait in another, separate line to purchase chips and candy, far fewer will do so.[20] In essence, the more effort it takes us to obtain unhealthy food, the less we'll eat of it, and vice versa. This is why nutritionists recommend that we prepare healthy snacks in advance so that we can simply pull them out of the refrigerator, and why they recommend that when we do eat junk foods, we take out a small portion, then put the rest of the bag away, well out of our reach. In his book *Mindless Eating*, Brian Wansink writes about a friend of his who couldn't resist stopping at 7-Eleven to get a Slurpee on his way home from work each day.[21] Finally, "he decided that if he couldn't keep his car from driving into 7-Eleven, he would take a different route home, zigzagging around the temptation." Our best weapon in the battle against bad habits—be they Slurpees, *Seinfeld* reruns, or distractions at work—is simply to make it harder for ourselves to succumb to them.

Clever minds have come up with some creative ways to put barriers between ourselves and our vices. For instance, in an increasing number of U.S. states, compulsive gamblers can request that the government put them on a list that actually makes it illegal for them to enter casinos or collect any gambling earnings. Some cell phone carriers offer a service to prevent imbibers from "drunk dialing" by blocking all outgoing calls (except 911) after a certain hour on weekends. The Google e-mail client Gmail offers a similarly amusing but effective option that requires someone to solve a series of math problems before they can send an e-mail late at night, thereby protecting employees who have downed a bottle of wine from e-mailing their bosses a misspelled list of grievances.

Governments, too, have found a way to use the 20-Second Rule in service of the greater public good. For example, polls show that the number of people willing to be organ donors is quite high, but that most are deterred by the long process of filling out the right forms to do so. In response, some countries have switched to an opt-out program, which automatically enrolls all citizens as donors.[22] Anyone is free to withdraw their name, of course, but when staying on the list becomes the default option, most people will do so. This really works; when Spain switched to opt-out, the number of donated organs immediately doubled.

Before I stumbled upon the 20-Second Rule, I'm not sure I could have done much more to help Ted in Hong Kong than diagnose his paradoxical problem: He was working almost all the time, yet almost never working. But once I realized why he was having so much trouble staying focused, I decided it was time to see how this strategy could take office distractions off the path of least resistance.

SAVE TIME BY ADDING TIME

The first step is a seemingly counterintuitive one—disable many of the shortcuts that were originally designed to "save time" at the office. For example, I encouraged Ted to keep his e-mail program closed while he worked, so it would no longer send jarring alerts whenever he received new mail. Any time he wanted to check e-mail, he'd have to actively open the program and wait for it to load. While this reduced involuntary interruptions, it was still too easy for him to click on the little Outlook icon whenever his mind wandered, so to protect against habitual checking, we made it even more difficult. We disabled the automatic login and password for the account, took the shortcut off the computer desktop, then hid the application icon in an empty folder, buried in another empty folder, buried in another empty folder. Essentially, we created the electronic version of Russian stacking dolls. As he told me one day at the office, only half jokingly, it was now "a total pain in the ass" to check e-mail.

"Now we're getting somewhere," I replied.

We did the same for his other distractions, disabling his stock widget, changing his home page from CNN to a blank search page, and even turning off his computer's ability to process cookies so it couldn't "remember" the stocks and websites he usually checked. Every additional button he was required to click, even every additional address he was required to type into a web browser, raised the barrier to procrastination and improved his chances of remaining on task. I pointed out that he still had complete freedom to do what he wanted; just like in an opt-out program, his choice had not been taken away at all. The only thing that had changed was the default, which was now set to productivity, instead of to distraction.

That first day in Hong Kong, Ted was not only skeptical, but a little annoyed with me. It seemed to him (and to the other executives on whom I had inflicted similar miseries) that I was only making their busy lives more difficult. Who was I to disable their cookies? (I don't even know what cookies are!) But a few days later, once they realized how much more work they were getting done (and in less time), they had come around.

SLEEP IN YOUR GYM CLOTHES

The 20-Second Rule isn't just about altering the time it takes to do things. Limiting the choices we have to make can also help lower the barrier to positive change. You may recall how Roy Baumeister's willpower studies showed that self-control is a limited resource that gets weakened with overuse. Well, these same researchers have discovered that too much choice similarly saps our reserves.

Their studies showed that with every additional choice people are asked to make, their physical stamina, ability to perform numerical calculations, persistence in the face of failure, and overall focus drop dramatically.[23] And these don't have to be difficult decisions either—the questions are more "chocolate or vanilla?" than they are *Sophie's Choice*. Yet every one of these innocuous choices depletes our energy a little further, until we just don't have enough to continue with the positive habit we're trying to adopt.

One of the life habits I wanted to create was exercising in the morning. I knew from numerous research studies that exercise in the morning raises your performance on cognitive tasks and gives your brain a "win" to start a cascade effect of positive emotions. But information is not transformation, because every morning I would wake and ask myself, Do I want to exercise? And my brain would reply, No I do not.

If you've ever tried to start up the habit of early-morning exercise, you have probably encountered how easy it is to get derailed by too much choice. Each morning after the alarm clock sounds, the inner monologue goes something like this: Should I hit the snooze button or get up immediately? What should I wear to work out this morning? Should I go for a run or go to the gym? Should I go to the nearby gym that's more crowded or the quieter gym that's slightly farther away? What kind of cardio should I do when I get there? Should I lift weights? Should I go to kickboxing class or maybe yoga? And by that point you're so exhausted by all the options, you've fallen back asleep. At least that's what would happen to me. So I decided to decrease the number of choices I would have to make in order to get myself to the gym.

Each night before I went to sleep, I wrote out a plan for where I would exercise in the morning and what parts of my body I would focus on. Then, I put my sneakers right by my bed. Finally—and most important—I just went to sleep in my gym clothes. (And my mom wonders why I'm not married yet.)

But the clothes were clean, and I had essentially decreased the activation energy enough so that when I woke up the next morning, all I had to do was roll off my bed, put my feet (which already had socks on them) into my shoes, and I was out the door. The decisions that seemed too daunting in my groggy morning state had been decided for me, ahead of time. And it worked. Eliminating the choices and reducing the activation energy made getting up and going to the gym the default mode. As a result, once I ingrained a lifetime positive habit of morning exercise, I now don't have to sleep in my gym clothes anymore.

Subsequently, in talking to athletes and nonathletes worldwide, I hear the same from both: Something weird happens in the human brain when you put your athletic shoes on—you start to think it is easier to just go work out now than to "take all this stuff back off again." In reality, it's easier to take off the shoes, but your brain, once it has tipped toward a habit, will naturally keep rolling in that direction, following the path of perceived least resistance.

This isn't just about getting yourself to exercise. Think of the positive changes you want to make at your job, and figure out what it would mean to "just get your shoes on" at work. The less energy it takes to kick-start a positive habit, the more likely that habit will stick.

SET RULES OF ENGAGEMENT

Whether you're trying to change your habits at work or at home, the key to reducing choice is setting and following a few simple rules. Psychologists call these kinds of rules "second-order decisions," because they are essentially decisions about when to make decisions, like deciding ahead of time when, where, and how I was going to work out in the morning.

Of course, this technique isn't just good for decisions like whether to use the treadmill or StairMaster. In his brilliant book *The Paradox of Choice*, Barry Schwartz explains how setting rules in advance can free us from the constant barrage of willpower-depleting choices that make a real difference in our lives.[24] If we make a rule to never drive a car when we've had more than one drink, for example, we eliminate the stress and uncertainty of trying to make a judgment call every time we aren't sure if we're too drunk to drive (which probably means we are). At work, setting rules to reduce the volume of choice can be incredibly effective. For example, if we set rules to only check our e-mail once per hour, or to only have one coffee break per morning, we are less likely to succumb in the moment, which helps these rules to become habits we stick to by default.

Rules are especially helpful during the first few days of a behavior-changing venture, when it's easier to stray off course. Gradually, as the desired action becomes more habitual, we can become more flexible. For instance, you won't often hear an experienced chef say, "I make it a rule to always follow the recipe exactly as it is," because some of the best dishes are made through creative experimentation in the kitchen. But for a beginning cook like me, this rule is entirely necessary. Since I don't know enough about cooking to know *how* to be spontaneous, straying from the rules could lead to disaster, or to a dozen tuna-fish brownies.

I once worked with an account executive named Joseph, who needed rules at work the same way I need rules in the kitchen. He was a pretty reserved, somber individual—in dress and manner he reminded me of one of those seventeenth-century New England preachers. That was just on the surface, though. Deep down, Joseph desperately wanted to capitalize on the Happiness Advantage by spreading positivity to his team, but acting upbeat and openly encouraging his employees just didn't come naturally to him. Each morning, he would set out to be more positive but always found himself quickly falling back into his default mode. He admitted to me that when he attempted positive interaction during team meetings, he would get overwhelmed by choices like: What should I say that's encouraging? To whom? When should I say it? How much praise should I give? Paralyzed by indecision, he'd end up saying nothing at all, and the meeting would end with Joseph once again silently lamenting another missed opportunity. All these decisions had required too much activation energy. We needed to set some rules to make this easier.

The first rule was this: Every day, before he walked through the conference room doors, he had to think of one employee he could thank for something. Then, the second rule was: Before he started the meeting and anything else could get in the way, he had to publicly thank that person. A simple sentence would do, and then he could move on to the rest of the meeting as planned, without the myriad choices hanging over his head.

A month later, I happened to be back at the company for a training session when I ran into Joseph in the hallway. No one would have described him as ebullient, but he certainly appeared happier and warmer than before. He told me that our daily rule had made it far easier for him to follow through on his goal, and he was enjoying the benefits of increased positivity in the workplace. In fact, two weeks into his new ritual, he found himself wanting to say a *second* positive comment to someone later on in the meeting, even though he had already reached his goal. Now he could relax the rules, confident the new habit was firmly in place.

IT'S ALL IN THE SHOES

This book is full of ways we can capitalize on the Happiness Advantage. But without actually putting those strategies into action, they remain useless, like a set of expensive tools that sit locked behind a glass case. The key to their use—to permanent, positive change—is to create habits that automatically pay dividends, without continued concerted effort or extensive reserves of willpower. The key to creating these habits is ritual, repeated practice, until the actions become ingrained in your brain's neural chemistry. And the key to daily practice is to put your desired actions as close to the path of least resistance as humanly possible. Identify the activation energy—the time, the choices, the mental and physical effort they require—and then reduce it. If you can cut the activation energy for those habits that lead to success, even by as little as 20 seconds at a time, it won't be long before you start reaping their benefits. The first step metaphorically—and sometimes literally—is just to get your shoes on.

SOCIAL INVESTMENT

Why Social Support Is Your Single Greatest Asset

was 18 years old, lost in a burning building, and blind. As I fumbled through the flames, it occurred to me: Maybe I shouldn't have volunteered for this.

It was my senior year of high school, and I was coming to the tail end of my 90 hours of volunteer firefighter training in my hometown of Waco, Texas. The final test before completing the training was called the Fire Maze, an exercise in which the veteran firefighters would put us newbies through our first, real-life, full-scale fire. Weighed down with flame-repellent suits, oxygen tanks, and dread, we were led to an empty farm silo called the Smoke Tank. The firefighters opened the metal door to reveal a giant room filled with an intricate wooden maze, with walls ten feet high and combustibles like old tires and pieces of wood littering the floor. Before we even had time to take in the whole scene, the veteran firefighters put torches to the wood, and the entire maze lit up in flames.

The Texas sun had already heated the day to nearly 100 degrees, but that seemed cool compared to the furnace blast now racing through the building. We picked up our masks, only to find that they had been completely covered in black paint—to replicate how hard it is to see in a real fire, our instructors said. I looked out at the growing blaze in front of us; this "fake" fire seemed plenty real to me. I put on my mask. I couldn't see a thing.

The firefighters yelled our instructions over the roar of the flames:

There is a dummy trapped in the middle of the maze.

Your goal is to rescue him as quickly as possible. In a real fire in a strange home, it is exceedingly easy to get lost and disoriented. The only way to avoid this is to keep in constant contact with the wall.

You will enter the building in teams of two, holding on to each other, so one of you can hold onto the wall, while the other sweeps the floor for the dummy.

This task would be nearly impossible alone, but working with a partner, it can be done fairly easily.

The firefighters assured us that the whole task should take only seven to ten minutes, but that we had a whole hour of oxygen in our tanks just in case. An alarm bell would alert us when we were down to our final five minutes of air, giving us plenty of time to exit safely. Finally, the firefighters reminded us again of our human lifelines—our partners. In a fire, it might seem counterintuitive to hold on to your teammate, but that was the best way of getting out alive.

The veterans flung open the door, and we crawled headfirst into the inferno. I started gulping oxygen, and I could feel my partner grip my jacket at the wrist and hear him breathing just as hard. We started timidly feeling our way through the smoke. He went first, keeping a hand on the wall, while I held onto him with one hand and used the other to feel along the floor for the dummy. About ten minutes into the maze, everything seemed to be going fine, except for the fact that we couldn't see and felt moments away from heat stroke. But we still hadn't found the dummy.

That's when I heard the bell. Surrounded by flames and smoke, blind, and crawling around on my knees, I tried to make sense of what was happening. Why was the alarm on my partner's air tank going off? There had to be at least 45 minutes of oxygen left, yet the bell meant he only had five minutes of air to go. Must be some kind of mistake, I thought.

Then *my* bell went off.

Veteran firefighters would have remained calm. We panicked. Our ability to reason vanished. I unthinkingly let go of my partner, and then he let go of the wall, which meant the worst: We were both alone, and we had both lost the way back out. Disoriented and frightened, we flailed blindly in opposite directions, groping the air and calling each other's name. But I couldn't hear him over the roar of the fire and was sure he couldn't hear me either. As the minutes ticked by, I began to feel increasingly helpless and scared. I crawled around frantically, sure that my oxygen supply was rapidly running out.

Finally, after what seemed like an eternity, I felt the heat recede as a pair of strong arms dragged me out of the maze into safety. As I gulped in the fresh air, the veterans revealed several things. First, everything that had gone wrong had been part of the training; the bells on the tanks were set to go off early, raising the false alarm that we were out of air. Second, when the firefighters went in after us, they had found me crawling around in circles at a dead end, and my partner 20 feet away, equally lost and doing more or less the same. Third, there had been no dummy. As the firefighters like to say at the end of training every year: The only dummies in the fire are the newbies. And they always have to be saved.

At the time, I remember thinking that this was a particularly cruel trick. But years later, I'm impressed at how memorably the Fire Maze training instilled in me the lesson that is at the heart of Principle 7—that when we encounter an unexpected challenge or threat, the only way to save ourselves is to hold on tight to the people around us and not let go.

THE MISTAKE WE MAKE

This principle is just as true in the modern workplace as it is in the fiery smoke tank. In the midst of challenges and stress at work, nothing is more crucial to our success than holding on to the people around us. Yet when the alarm bells at work go off, all too often we become blind to this reality and try to go it alone; and as a result we end up like I did, circling helplessly at some dead-end corner until we run out of air.

I have seen too many businessmen and -women fall prey to this miscalculation. I can remember hearing the trading bell ring at the end of one particularly vicious day in November of 2008. The Dow was way down; countless sums of money had been lost. I watched as swarms of traders loosened their ties and walked dejectedly off the floor. But what struck me was that they didn't retreat to the stronghold of their teams as they normally did after a day of trading. They all walked off silent and alone.

These were smart, capable people with MBAs from some of the world's leading institutions, yet in a situation that required them to be firing on all cylinders, they were actively undercutting themselves. At the very time that they needed one another most, they were forgoing their most valuable resource: their social support. Time and again during those perilous months, I saw companies jettison team trainings and social "perks," ignoring plummeting team morale in favor of things deemed more "important." But in fact, nothing was more important than what they were letting go of.

We don't have to go to the brink of a collapsing economy to understand how easy it is to retreat into our own shells at the moment we need to be reaching out to others the most. We've all been there some time or another. A daunting project gets dropped on our desk, and we get consumed with worry that we'll fail to meet the demands. Is there enough time to get it all done? What will happen if we don't? As the deadline looms and the pressure mounts, we start eating lunch at our desks, working late, coming in on weekends. Soon, we're "focused liked a laser" (or so we tell ourselves), which means no face time with direct reports, no casual hallway chats, no time even for nonessential calls with clients. Even our e-mails are more brusque and impersonal. As for time with family and friends, well, these things are the first to go when we're in crisis mode. But even though we're giving work our undivided attention, our productivity is declining, and as the deadline nears, our goal seems to be slipping further and further out of reach. And so we hunker down, shut off our cell phones, retreat into the bunker of ourselves and double-lock the door.

One of two things usually happens at this juncture. Either we falter and fail to finish the project, or we power through and get it done, then immediately get rewarded with another challenging project, though we now have zero oxygen left in our tank. Either way, we're not only miserable, dejected, and overwhelmed, but lost in a dead end, unable to perform—and all alone.

The most successful people take the exact opposite approach. Instead of turning inward, they actually hold tighter to their social support. Instead of divesting, they invest. Not only are these people happier, but they are more productive, engaged, energetic, and resilient. They know that their social relationships are the single greatest investment they can make in the Happiness Advantage.

INVESTING IN THE HAPPINESS ADVANTAGE

One of the longest-running psychological studies of all time—the Harvard Men study followed 268 men from their entrance into college in the late 1930s all the way through the present day.[1] From this wealth of data, scientists have been able to identify the life circumstances and personal characteristics that distinguished the happiest, fullest lives from the least successful ones. In the summer of 2009, George Vaillant, the psychologist who has directed this study for the last 40 years, told the *Atlantic Monthly* that he could sum up the findings in one word: "love—full stop." Could it really be so simple? Vaillant wrote his own follow-up article that analyzed the data in great detail, and his conclusions proved the same: that there are "70 years of evidence that our relationships with other people matter, and matter more than anything else in the world."[2]

This study's findings have been duplicated time and again. In their book *Happiness,* psychologists Ed Diener and Robert Biswas-Diener review the massive amount of cross-cultural research that has been conducted on happiness over the last few decades, and they conclude that, "like food and air, we seem to need social relationships to thrive."[3] That's because when we have a community of people we can count on—spouse, family, friends, colleagues—we multiply our emotional, intellectual, and physical resources. We bounce back from setbacks faster, accomplish more, and feel a greater sense of purpose. Furthermore, the effect on our happiness, and therefore on our ability to profit from the Happiness Advantage, is both immediate and long-lasting. First, social interactions jolt us with positivity in the moment; then, each of these single connections strengthens a relationship over time, which raises our happiness baseline permanently. So when a colleague stops you in the hallway at work to say hello and ask about your day, the brief interaction actually sparks a continual upward spiral of happiness and its inherent rewards.

Positive outliers already know this to be true—indeed, it's what makes them positive outliers. In a study appropriately titled "Very Happy People," researchers sought out the characteristics of the happiest 10 percent among us.[4] Do they all live in warm climates? Are they all wealthy? Are they all physically fit? Turns out, there was one—and *only* one—characteristic that distinguished the happiest 10 percent from everybody else: the strength of their social relationships. My empirical study of well-being among 1,600 Harvard undergraduates found a similar result—social support was a far greater predictor of happiness than any other factor, more than GPA, family income, SAT scores, age, gender, or race. In fact, the correlation between social support and happiness was 0.7. This may not sound like a big number, but for researchers it's huge—most psychology findings are considered significant when they hit 0.3. The point is, the more social support you have, the happier you are. And as we know, the happier you are, the more advantages you accrue in nearly every domain of life.

SURVIVING AND THRIVING WITH SOCIAL INVESTMENT

Our need for social support isn't just in our heads. Evolutionary psychologists explain that the innate need to affiliate and form social bonds has been literally wired into our biology.[5] When we make a positive social connection, the pleasure-inducing hormone oxytocin is released into our bloodstream, immediately reducing anxiety and improving concentration and focus. Each social connection also bolsters our cardiovascular, neuroendocrine, and immune systems, so that the more connections we make over time, the better we function.

We have such a biological need for social support, our bodies can literally malfunction without it.[6] For instance, lack of social contact can add 30 points to an adult's blood pressure reading.[7] In his seminal book *Loneliness*, University of Chicago psychologist John Cacioppo compiled more than thirty years' worth of research to convincingly show that a dearth of social connections is actually just as deadly as certain diseases.[8] Naturally, it causes psychological harm as well; it shouldn't surprise you that a national survey of 24,000 workers found that men and women with few social ties were two to three times more likely to suffer from major depression than people with strong social bonds.[9]

When we enjoy strong social support, on the other hand, we can accomplish impressive feats of resilience, and even extend the length of our lives. One study found that people who received emotional support during the six months after a heart attack were three times more likely to survive.[10] Another found that participating in a breast cancer support group actually doubled women's life expectancy post surgery.[11] In fact, researchers have found that social support has as much effect on life expectancy as smoking, high blood pressure, obesity, and regular physical activity.[12] As one set of doctors put it, "When launching a life raft, the prudent survivalist will not toss food overboard while retaining the deck furniture. If somebody must jettison a part of life, time with a mate should be last on the list: He needs that connection to live."[13] When set adrift, it seems, those of us who hold on to our raftmates, not just our rafts, are the ones who will stay afloat.

SOCIAL CAPITAL AS STRESS RELIEF

The same strategy—hold onto others—is just as crucial for our survival as we navigate the daily stresses of the working world. Studies show that each positive interaction employees have during the course of the work day actually helps return the cardiovascular system back to resting levels (a benefit often termed "work recovery"), and that over the long haul, employees with more of these interactions become protected from the negative effects of job strain. Each connection also lowers levels of cortisol, a hormone related to stress, which helps employees recover faster from work-related stress and makes them better prepared to handle it in the future.[14] Furthermore, studies have found that people with strong relationships are less likely to perceive situations as stressful in the first place.[15] So in essence, investing in social connections means that you'll find it easier to interpret adversity as a path to growth and opportunity; and when you *do* have to experience the stress, you'll bounce back from it faster and better protected against its long-term negative effects.

In the volatile world of work, this ability to manage stress, both physically and psychologically, is a significant competitive advantage. For one, it has been found to greatly reduce a company's health care costs and rate of absenteeism. But perhaps more important, it directly impacts individual performance. Researchers have found that the "physiological resourcefulness" that employees gain from positive social interactions provides a foundation for workplace engagement—employees can work for longer hours, with increased focus, and under more difficult conditions.[16] For instance, when AT&T was suffering massive layoffs and internal turmoil after being split into three separate companies, one senior leader working daily in the trenches noticed that certain employees were faring better under the pressure than others.[17] As he commented to Harvard professor Daniel Goleman, "The pain is not being felt everywhere. In a lot of the tech units where people work in tight teams, and where they find great meaning in what they do together, they're fairly impervious to the turmoil." Why? Because individuals who invest in their social support systems are simply better equipped to thrive in even the most difficult circumstances, while those who withdraw from the people around them effectively cut off every line of protection they have available, at the very moment they need them most.

To fully understand the importance of this distinction and the consequences it has for our future success, let's take a quick trip to the gridiron.

ALL I NEED TO KNOW I LEARNED FROM THE NATIONAL FOOTBALL LEAGUE

In the world of American football, a few positions get virtually all the attention: quarterbacks, wide receivers, and star running backs. They're the ones who grab most of the headlines, and their paychecks and fame are testament to their importance. But another group of football players is equally highly paid and perhaps even more valued—the offensive line—and yet very few people know who they are or what they do. Almost no fans walk around wearing their jerseys, but they should.

When a football team lines up on the field, the quarterback stands behind a line of five oversized human beings crouched down on the turf. This is the offensive line. Just inches away from them awaits the opposing team, ready to pounce. At the sound of the whistle, massive, muscled bodies come flying forward, using every ounce of their weight and strength to rush the quarterback and smash him to the ground. The offensive line is the only thing standing between the quarterback and this charging mass of humanity. They don't score touchdowns, they don't kick field goals. They only have one job—protect the quarterback—but it is the most important job on the football field. After all, you can't win a football game if the quarterback is flat on his back before he ever has time to throw.

When Hall of Fame quarterback Joe Montana first had the privilege of playing behind a really superb offensive line, he excelled like never before. As Michael Lewis writes in the book *The Blind Side*, Montana played "like a kid who'd been given the answers to the test in advance."[18] After the game, Montana told reporters, "I'd never seen us execute like that. . . . That's why it didn't look tough for us. But it was. Our line was stopping them, and when I got that time, things became easy." Everyone credited Joe Montana, but he credited his offensive line.

Even though most of us live far removed from the football field, we each have our own version of an offensive line: our spouses, our families, and our friends. Surrounded by these people, big challenges feel more manageable and small challenges don't even register on the radar. Just as the offensive line protects a quarterback from a particularly brutal sack, our social support prevents stress from knocking us down and getting in the way of our achieving our goals. And just as the offensive line helped Montana throw a touchdown that would have been otherwise impossible, our social ties help us capitalize on our own particular strengths—to accomplish more in our work and in our lives.

These benefits aren't confined to the short-term, either. In a longitudinal study of men over the age of 50, those with a high rate of stressful life experiences suffered from a far higher rate of mortality over the next seven years.[19] But the same study found that this higher rate of mortality held true for everyone *except* the men who said they had high levels of emotional support. Like a quarterback who has been protected from sacks his whole career, a lifetime of strong social relationships provides crucial protection against the dangerous effects of stress. We can't always stop the 350-pound linemen flying at us, but we can ALL invest in a strong offensive line. And that can make all the difference.

THEY EXCEL WITH A LITTLE HELP FROM THEIR FRIENDS

Unfortunately, not everyone makes this investment. Often, the misguided urge to turn inward starts even before we enter the working world. You'll recall that as an officer of Harvard, I spent twelve years living in a dorm with undergraduates. While this afforded me many unique life experiences I wouldn't recommend, like going twelve years eating all my meals on trays, one of the best parts of being in the trenches was having the chance to see the different strategies these 18 to 22 year olds devised to help them find their way through the maze of Harvard. Though every one of these students was exceptional in one way or another, when it came to handling the inevitable stresses of such a challenging and competitive environment, year after year I noticed that certain students had a significant leg up while others, despite all their intelligence and efforts, seemed to sabotage their own forward progress.

Two freshman in particular stand out in my memory: Amanda and Brittney. They were roommates. Both had spirited personalities, and both made friends quickly and effortlessly that first September.

But as midterms approached, their paths began to diverge. As the pressure mounted, Amanda found a secluded cubicle in the library and spent most of her days and nights there. She started skipping our dorm study breaks—she didn't have time for frivolous activities like sharing snacks and stories with her classmates. Once an active member of our dorm's Ultimate Frisbee team, she stopped coming to practices and games. When I finally caught up with her one day in the dining hall, as she was taking her lunch to go—most likely back to the library—she admitted that she was just too stressed to focus on anything else but her schoolwork. "My friends will understand," she said. It wasn't her friends I was worried about.

Meanwhile, Brittney was flourishing. She wasn't oblivious to the challenges or pressures, and she wasn't working any less hard than Amanda. But instead of quarantining herself in a cubicle, she was organizing study groups. For her "Magic of Numbers" class (note: course title not made up), she e-mailed a group of six friends and had each person write a summary of one week's readings, then they convened at lunch a few times a week to share their work. I remember I once stumbled on one of these sessions, only to find them talking about *The Simpsons*. "I thought this was a math study group?" I asked in mock exasperation. One young man looked up at me, then pointed at Brittney. "We were ordered to make time for small talk," he said. When I checked in with her at a study break a few weeks later—where she was taking ten minutes off from homework to join our Oreo-eating contest—Brittney just shrugged her shoulders. "It's a lot of work. But, I don't know, I guess it's just nice to know we're all pulling an all-nighter together."

I won't belabor the point here. But let's just say that by January, one of these students had succumbed to the pressure and stress and was wishing she could transfer to someplace less competitive. The other was happy, well-adjusted, and performing exceptionally in her courses. While Amanda and Brittney are real people, they also represent the choices each of us has when faced with adversity.

Many business leaders I encounter believe, just as Amanda did, that the road to success is one they have to travel alone, but this simply isn't the case. The most successful people I've worked with know that even in an extraordinarily competitive environment, we are more equipped to handle challenges and obstacles when we pool the resources of those around us and capitalize on even the smallest moments we spend interacting with others. Every time Brittney had lunch or a study session with her friends, she wasn't just having a good time—she was decreasing her stress level, priming her brain for high performance, and capitalizing on the ideas, energy, and motivation that social support provides. While Amanda was divesting from her network and floundering as a result, Brittney was investing in something that continually paid dividends. Just as social support is a prescription for happiness and an antidote to stress, it is also a prime contributor of achievement in the workplace.

INVESTING IN HIGH PERFORMANCE

We learned in Principle 5, the Zorro Circle, that those of us who believe we have control over the outcome of our fates have a huge advantage in work and in life. This fact can't be denied. But it also doesn't mean we have to exist in a vacuum or that our success hinges on our efforts alone. Remember the 70-year-long Harvard Men Study? Researchers found that social bonds weren't just predictive of overall happiness, but also of eventual career achievement, occupational success, and income.[20]

This truth is sometimes still difficult for many of us to accept, given how deep the ethic of individualism runs in our culture (after all, reading Ralph Waldo Emerson's essay *Self-Reliance* is practically an American rite of passage). We are particularly independent-minded when it comes to assigning credit for achievements. Stanford psychologist Carol Dweck likes to illustrate the folly of this belief by asking her students to describe how they picture history's greatest minds at work.[21] When you think of Thomas Edison, she asks them, what do you see?

"He's standing in a white coat in a lab-type room," comes the average reply. "He's leaning over a light bulb. Suddenly, it works!"

"Is he alone?" Dweck asks.

"Yes. He's kind of a reclusive guy who likes to tinker on his own."

As Dweck relishes in pointing out, this couldn't be further from the truth. Edison actually thrived in group settings, and when he invented the light bulb, he did so with the help of 30 assistants. Edison was actually a social creative, not a lone wolf! And when it comes to society's most innovative thinkers, so often assumed to be eccentric, solitary geniuses, he was not the exception to the rule.

We have all heard the popular maxim "two heads are better than one," but the benefits of social interaction in the workplace go far beyond group brainstorming. Having people we can count on for support in the office—even having people we can talk to about last night's *Lost* episode—actually fuels individual innovation, creativity, and productivity. For instance, one study of 212 employees found that social connections at work predicted more individual learning behavior, which means that the more socially connected employees felt, the more they took the time to figure out ways to improve their own efficiency, or their own skill set.[22]

Perhaps most important, social connections motivate. When over a thousand highly successful professional men and women were interviewed as they approached retirement and asked what had motivated them the most, throughout their careers, overwhelmingly they placed work friendships above both financial gain and individual status.[23] In *Good to Great,* Jim Collins illuminated a similar truth: "The people we interviewed from good-to-great companies clearly loved what they did largely because they loved who they did it with."[24]

The better we feel about these workplace relationships, the more effective we will be. For example, a study of over 350 employees in 60 business units at a financial services company found that the greatest predictor of a team's achievement was how the members felt about one another.[25] This is especially important for managers because, while they often have little control over the backgrounds or skill sets of employees placed on their teams, they do have control over the level of interaction and rapport. Studies show that the more team members are encouraged to socialize and interact face-to-face, the more engaged they feel, the more energy they have, and the longer they can stay focused on a task.[26] In short, the more the team members invest in their social cohesion, the better the results of their work.

HIGH-QUALITY CONNECTIONS

To make a difference to work performance and job satisfaction, social contact need not always be deep to be effective. Organizational psychologists have found that even brief encounters can form "high-quality connections," which fuel openness, energy, and authenticity among coworkers, and in turn lead to a whole host of measurable, tangible gains in performance. Jane Dutton, a psychologist who specializes in this subject at the University of Michigan Business School, explains that "any point of contact with another person can potentially be a high-quality connection. One conversation, one e-mail exchange, one moment of connecting in a meeting can infuse both participants with a greater sense of vitality, giving them a bounce in their steps and a greater capacity to act."[27]

Again, this isn't just in the interest of having a fun and friendly workplace (though that is an important bonus). Each one of these social connections pays dividends. At IBM, for example, when MIT researchers spent an entire year following 2,600 employees, observing their social ties, even using mathematical formulas to analyze the size and scope of their address books and buddy lists, they found that the more socially connected the IBM employees were, the better they performed.[28] They could even quantify the difference: On average, every e-mail contact was worth an added $948 in revenue. There in black and white is the power of social investment. And IBM wisely decided to capitalize on it by starting a program at its Cambridge, Massachusetts, office to facilitate the introductions of employees who didn't yet know one another.

Google is perhaps the most famous example of a company that truly understands the importance of social connections. This isn't just lip service—Google reflects this understanding in their practices. Not only do company cafeterias stay open well past the hours of the traditional workday, making it easy for employees to dine together as much as possible, Google employees have access to on-site day care and are even encouraged to make time to visit their kids throughout the day.

UPS is another successful company that has invested in social capital. Every day in cities and towns around the country, you can find three or four local UPS trucks parked together as their drivers sit nearby eating lunch.[29] They swap stories, information, and misplaced packages. Given that this practice takes the drivers off their scheduled routes, and takes more time than a solitary lunch would, many people are surprised that the UPS brass, so obsessed with efficiency, would encourage the practice. But they do. They know that this social interaction pays out in the long run, not just for the individual drivers, but for the organization as a whole.

Other companies, like Southwest Airlines, Domino's Pizza, and The Limited, have set up programs that foster social investment, literally, by allowing employees to donate money to colleagues confronted with medical and financial emergencies.[30] The result is that the employees involved (and even those who aren't, but simply know the program is there) feel a greater commitment to one another, and also to the company as a whole. At one Fortune 500 retail organization, a manager shared his reaction to their Employee Support Foundation: "I have a sense of pride in the company. . . .

I think it's good to give and, you know, it definitely makes me feel . . . that I'm working for a company that shares in some of my sensibilities and cares about people." These feelings then translate into real dividends, including lower absenteeism and turnover rates, and increased employee motivation and engagement.

GLUE GUYS

Of course, sweeping corporate policies like these aren't always necessary; small differences can have just as much of an impact. Once on a visit to the London offices of financial giant UBS, I learned it was a weekly tradition for the traders to gather around a beer cart on Friday afternoon. A few years ago, the dean of Harvard Law School had similar ideas about improving the quality of life for her overstressed law students. She set up coffee stations between classrooms and a volleyball court in the yard, so that students could find ways to socialize, even if just for a few minutes, between grueling classes.

Sadly, these policies are often the first to go when companies find themselves in financial straits—another example of our tendency to divest when the going gets tough. UBS recently suspended its weekly beer cart because of budget constraints, but, thanks to the cohesive culture the tradition had helped create, it lived on. When I last visited the office, employees couldn't wait to tell me about how two managers had dipped into their own lightened pockets to buy beer for their teams. They knew that preserving this ritual would go a long way toward boosting morale, especially during that difficult time. If the mood of their employees when I visited was any indication, it worked.

The people who actively invest in their relationships are the heart and soul of a thriving organization, the force that drives their teams forward. In sports, these people are called "glue guys." As the *Wall Street Journal* has explained, this type of player "quietly holds winning teams together. . . . Statisticians don't buy that they exist, but psychologists do. And players and managers swear by them."[31] Given that a baseball team spends a minimum of 81 games a year on the road, playing *and* living together, the importance of getting along shouldn't be too surprising. In the high-stakes environment of professional sports, teams can disintegrate in a hurry under the pressure. Glue guys keep players stuck together at those tough moments when it is most tempting to let go.

THE VERTICAL COUPLE

In one of my favorite episodes of the wickedly satirical sitcom *The Office*, Stanley, a grumpy employee with no patience for his bumbling boss's antics, has been ordered by his doctor to wear a heart monitor to work. He's recently had some heart trouble, and the monitor will warn him if his heart rate rises to a dangerous level. Enter Michael Scott, poster child for disastrously inept bosses everywhere. Every time Michael wanders within two feet of Stanley, the heart monitor goes off, and the closer Michael gets, the louder and more uncontrollably it beeps. Mere proximity to his incompetent and irritating boss causes Stanley's heart rate to skyrocket.

Of course, this is a plot of a television show, but it's actually not as removed from reality as it sounds. Back in the real world, a team of British researchers decided to follow a group of employees who worked for two different supervisors on alternate days—one they had good rapport with, and one they didn't.[32] In other words, a boss they loved and a Michael Scott. And indeed, on the days the dreaded boss worked, their average blood pressure shot up. A longer, 15-year study even found that employees who had a difficult relationship with their boss were 30 percent more likely to suffer from coronary heart disease.[33] It seems a bad relationship with your boss can be as bad for you as a steady diet of fried foods—and not nearly as much fun.

Of all the social ties we have at work, the boss/employee relationship, what Daniel Goleman has cleverly termed a "vertical couple," is the single most important social bond you can cultivate at work. Studies have found that the strength of the bond between manager and employee is the prime predictor of both daily productivity and the length of time people stay at their jobs. Gallup, which has spent decades studying the practices of the world's leading organizations, estimates that U.S. companies lose $360 billion each year due to lost productivity from employees who have poor relationships with their supervisor.[34] It is no wonder the vertical couple could have such a profound effect on company performance, given that, as Goleman says, it is "a basic unit of organizational life, something akin to human molecules that interact to form the latticework of relationship that *is* the organization."[35]

So when this relationship is strong, companies reap the rewards. Those MIT researchers found that employees with strong ties to their manager brought in more money than those with only weak ties—besting the company average by $588 of revenue each month. And in a study astonishingly large in scope, when Gallup asked ten million employees around the world if they could agree or disagree with the following statement: "My supervisor, or someone at work, seems to care about me as a person," those who agreed were found to be more productive, contributed more to profits, and were significantly more likely to stay with their company long-term.[36]

The best leaders already know this, and they go out of their way to make employees feel cared for. When a fire destroyed the Malden Mills factory in a small town in Massachusetts, CEO Aaron Feuerstein announced that he would continue to pay the salaries of all 3,000 workers who were suddenly without a job. In their book *In Good Company*, Don Cohen and Laurence Prusak discuss how much this one action shocked the American public. Feuerstein was heralded as a selfless hero, even invited to the White House. But as the authors point out, "that the public and the business world would consider Feuerstein's action so extraordinary and apparently 'unbusinesslike' suggests that many people do not yet understand the value of social capital in organizations. . . . the money he spent was an investment in the future of his business."[37]

It is clearly in the best interest of everyone involved—the boss, the employee, and the organization as a whole—to prioritize relationships. Unfortunately, in today's harried and fast-paced workplace, far too few leaders put in the time required to forge strong bonds with either their colleagues or their employees. It certainly doesn't require paying everyone's salary—all it takes, we have seen, is a commitment to frequent and positive social interaction. And yet a recent poll found that 90 percent of respondents believed workplace incivility was a serious problem.[38] Many leaders simply refuse to put in the effort, and the reasons are many and varied: not enough hours in the day, a fear of undermining their authority by getting too close to those they manage, a perpetual crisis-mode mindset (The woods are on fire! The sky is falling!), and even the simple belief that work is for work, not friendship. And yet the more they ignore the power of social investment, they more they undermine both their company's performance and their own.

APPRECIATING ASSETS

Financial planners tell us that the surest way to grow our stock portfolios is to keep reinvesting the dividends. So it is with our social portfolios as well. Not only do we need to invest in new relationships, we should always be reinvesting in our current relationships because, like our stocks, social support networks grow stronger the longer they are held. Fortunately, there is a whole host of techniques we can use to aid us in this endeavor.

Every time you cross the office threshold, you have an opportunity to form or strengthen a high-quality connection. When traveling down busy corridors, greet colleagues you cross paths with, and remember to look them in the eye. This isn't just for show; neuroscience has revealed that when we make eye contact with someone, it actually sends a signal to the brain that triggers empathy and rapport. Ask interested questions, schedule face-to-face meetings, and initiate conversations that aren't always task-oriented. A popular manager at a top 100 law firm once told me that he set out to learn one new thing about a co-worker each day, which he would then reference in later conversations. The social capital he invested in each day paid out in increasingly large ways as his employees felt more connected to both him and the firm. Of course, this does take effort on the front end. In an interview with *Fast Company*, one CEO and former head of a venture capital firm acknowledged that "to maximize the value that one gets from a relationship, one has to give a great deal. I spend a fair amount of my time making introductions, providing referrals, providing connections, and generally engaging with the breadth of the community to benefit the business and personal lives of others."[39]

We all know that an important part of maintaining a social bond is being there, both physically and emotionally, when someone is in need. But an interesting new body of research suggests that how we support people during *good* times, more than bad times, affects the quality of a relationship. Sharing upbeat news with someone is called "capitalization," and it helps multiply the benefits of the positive event as well as strengthen the bond between the two people involved.[40] The key to gaining these benefits is *how* you respond to someone's good news.

Shelly Gable, a leading psychologist at the University of California, has found that there are four different types of responses we can give to someone's good news, and only one of them contributes positively to the relationship.[41] The winning response is both active and constructive; it offers enthusiastic support, as well as specific comments and follow-up questions. ("That's wonderful! I'm glad your boss noticed how hard you've been working. When does your promotion go into effect?") Interestingly, her research shows passive responses to good news ("That's nice.") can be just as harmful to the relationship as blatantly negative ones ("*You* got the promotion? I'm surprised they didn't give it to Sally, she seems more suited to the job.") Ouch. Perhaps the most destructive, though, is ignoring the news entirely. ("Have you seen my keys?") Gable's studies have shown that active-constructive responding enhances relationship commitment and satisfaction, and fuels the degree to which people feel understood, validated, and cared for during a discussion—all of which contribute to the Happiness Advantage.

BUILDING A SOCIALLY INVESTED TEAM

If you're a leader, you not only have the power to strengthen your own connections, but to foster a work environment that values, instead of hinders, social investment. For example, when new hires enter an organization, leaders can take the time to introduce them to everyone, even—and especially—people in other departments with whom they might not be working directly. In fact, why stop there; existing employees, too, should do all they can to meet others in far-flung corners of the organization. That's why some companies have long-term employees spend one day learning the ropes of a different department; after all, the more chances for employees to meet one another, the more chances they have to forge high-quality connections. And the more buy-in from Human Resources, the more effective this strategy becomes.

So if you're in a leadership position in your company (or even if you're not!), simply introducing two employees who don't know each other is probably the easiest and fastest way to invest in social dividends. To be even more effective, the introductions should go beyond just name, department, and job description. Mike Morrison, vice president and dean of the University of Toyota, likes to ask employees: "What's on the other side of your card?" In other words, the front of your business card may read "Managing Director," but you may better identify with "big picture thinker" or "educator" or "calm under fire." This kind of information—or even a few simple details like where a person lives, what his or her favorite hobby is—cuts through the red tape to get somewhere more meaningful, and it can more immediately and effectively forge a connection between two people.

It is important to note that building strong social capital does not require that all colleagues become best friends or even that everyone like one another all the time—this would be impossible. But what does matter is that there be mutual respect and authenticity. Coercing employees into awkward icebreakers or forced bonding activities, like making everyone at a meeting share something about their private lives, only breeds disconnection and mistrust.[42] Better that these moments happen organically—which they will if the environment is right. The best leaders give their employees the space and time to let moments of social connection develop on their own.[43] So the more physical spaces available to publicly commune, the better. When a CEO of one company saw that some of the best social connections—people laughing, swapping stories about their weekend, bouncing ideas off one another—were taking place on the stairwells, he actually expanded the stairways and put coffee machines on the landings to encourage this practice.

Time for team lunches and after-hours socialization is also crucial. Even the classically boring meeting, says Jane Dutton, can be designed in a way to foster high-quality connections. Meeting practices that encourage member contribution and active listening foster group commitment. One of the best managing directors I know makes his meetings Blackberry-free, so that all eyes are on one another at all times. He is an example of a leader Dutton would call "relationally attentive."[44] The more attentive we are to the relationship dynamics of our teams, the better.

If our goal is to foster team cohesion, the language we use matters. Remember the difference in group cooperation when a task was termed the "community game" instead of the "Wall Street game"? We can promote social connection at work just by using language that implies a common purpose and interdependence. Dutton also recommends that we work on being present, both physically and mentally.[45] That means when someone walks into your office to talk, don't stare at your computer screen. When someone calls you on the phone, don't keep typing that e-mail. An accountant once told me that the minute he heard a clicking keyboard on the other end of the phone call, he knew his boss was disengaged. Forging a connection requires active listening—giving someone your full attention and also allowing them to have their say. As Dutton explains, "many people listen as if waiting for an opportunity to make their own point." Instead, focus on the speaker and their opinion, and then ask interested questions to learn more.

The leaders most committed to social investment also get moving, quite literally. The best way to form more connections at work is to get out from behind the desk. This idea of "managing by walking around" was popularized in the 1980s by leadership expert Tom Peters, who learned about the practice from the leaders of Hewlett–Packard. (Peters even gave it an acronym—MBWA—to signify its importance.) MBWA allows managers to get to know employees, share good news and best practices, hear concerns, offer solutions, and deliver encouragement. Jim Kelly, CEO of UPS, is one famous practitioner. "I don't even know the phone numbers of the people on our management committee," he has said, "because I never pick up the phone if they're in the office. We just walk into each other's offices when we need to talk."[46] Twenty-five years after first discussing its role in organizational success, Tom Peters says, MBWA is as important as ever, and still woefully underused.[47]

Connecting with employees face-to-face also provides a perfect opportunity to put into practice a recommendation we talked about earlier in the book—frequent recognition and feedback. Not only can it raise a team above the Losada Line, but delivering specific and authentic praise for a job well done also strengthens the connection between two people. This is why I often ask managers to write an e-mail of praise or thanks to a friend, family member, or colleague each morning before they start their day's work—not just because it contributes to their own happiness, but because it very literally cements a relationship. Whether the "thank you" is for years of emotional support or for one day of help around the office, expressions of gratitude at work have been proven to strengthen both personal and professional bonds.[48]

In fact, studies have shown that gratitude sparks an upward spiral of relationship growth where each individual feels motivated to strengthen the bond.[49] It also predicts feelings of integration and cooperation within a larger group, which means that the more gratitude one employee expresses toward another employee, the more social cohesion they feel among the whole team. In other words, gratitude can fuel your own identity as a "glue guy."

LESSONS FROM A FIRE MAZE

As I saw when the economy crumbled, sometimes it takes a crisis to teach us the importance of social investment. In a front-page story on this phenomenon, the *Washington Post* reported a marked increase in carpooling and community bonding once the recession hit; people even started holding "yardwork parties" where neighbors could swap lawnmowers and landscaping advice.[50] As one man noted, "People are helping each other and getting back together. You're not the lone ranger anymore." Even the executives I work with—people who only months before the recession had been inward-looking, personal-results-driven, and intent on going it alone—started espousing and practicing cooperation and teamwork in those dark days after the collapse. Workaholics with suddenly less on their plate started coming home earlier to spend more time with their children and spouses. Formally individualistic managers started leaving the comfort of their offices and making the rounds, cubicle to cubicle. They may have been left no other choice at first, and they might backslide once the economy goes on the upswing again, but many have told me that being forced to reexamine their way of life (and work) has ended up being the best thing that could have happened to them.

In an ideal world, of course, it shouldn't take a crisis to bring this point home, especially given the wealth of evidence showing that our relationships are the greatest predictor of both happiness and high performance. So even though our basic instincts might tell us to turn inward, positive psychology knows better. When caught in a fire, holding on to others is the best chance we have for successfully finding our way out of the maze. And in everyday life, both at work and at home, our social support can prove the difference between succumbing to the cult of the average and achieving our fullest potential.

PART 3

THE RIPPLE EFFECT

. . .

SPREADING THE HAPPINESS ADVANTAGE
AT WORK, AT HOME, AND BEYOND

■ ■ ■

A couple of months ago, I spoke to a group of CEOs and their spouses in Hong Kong. Afterward, over drinks at a reception, a very self-assured if slightly tipsy CEO shook my hand warmly and said, "Thank you, Shawn. That research was brilliant and rings so true." He then leaned in and whispered conspiratorially, "I already do most of it, but my wife really needed to hear it."

His stage whisper was loud enough for everyone in line to hear, and as he gestured to his wife standing 15 feet away, I recognized her as one of the first people I had talked to that evening. I smiled and whispered back equally loudly and conspiratorially, "Thank you, sir. She said the same thing about you."

I relate this story not as an example of how to stir up trouble in a perfect stranger's marriage, but to show that no matter where I am in the world, most people think this research is useful for them, but even more useful for all the people around them. The person we have the greatest power to change is ourselves. But while the seven principles must start at the individual level, they by no means end there. To conclude this book, I want to talk about how making these changes in ourselves can impact those around us.

Once we start capitalizing on the Happiness Advantage in our own lives, the positive changes quickly ripple out. This is why positive psychology is so powerful. Using all seven principles *together* sparks an upward spiral of happiness and success, so that the benefits quickly become multiplicative. Then the positive effects begin to ripple outward, increasing the happiness of everyone around you, changing the way your colleagues work, and eventually shaping your entire organization.

SPIRALING UPWARD

This whole process starts with your brain. As we saw in Principle 6, your thoughts and actions are constantly shaping and reshaping the neural pathways in the brain. This means that the more you practice the exercises outlined in this book, and the more you shift your mindset toward the positive, the more you cement these habits for the long haul. And as your brain becomes more adept at one habit, it improves your ability to capitalize on another. That's because these principles don't work in isolation. I've presented them as seven distinct principles for the purpose of clarity, but as you may have already noticed, they are inextricably linked, and using several in concert with one another only enhances their collective power.

For instance, the Tetris Effect fuels Falling Up, because training ourselves to scan the world for the positive can help us reinterpret failures as opportunities for growth. And Social Investment can help us in our quest to master the 20-Second Rule, since strong social support holds us accountable to new habits. Of course, we can also use the 20-Second Rule to improve our Social Investment by decreasing the activation energy required to form high-quality connections at work. And the more high-quality connections we form, the more likely we are to see our work as a calling instead of just a job, which in turn fuels the Happiness Advantage. So on and so on. The effects of one principle become the trigger for another, so that they become far more than just the sum of their parts. Together, they can take us farther than any one could on its own.

RIPPLING OUTWARD

The benefits don't stop there. The more we capitalize on the Happiness Advantage ourselves, the more we can impact the lives of those around us. Extraordinarily, recent research exploring the role of social networks in shaping human behavior has proven that much of our behavior is literally contagious; that our habits, attitudes, and actions spread through a complicated web of connections to infect those around us. In their groundbreaking book *Connected,* Nicholas Christakis and James Fowler draw on years of research to show how our actions are constantly cascading and bouncing off each other in every which way and direction.[1] "Ties do not extend outward in straight lines like spokes on a wheel," they write. "Instead, these paths double back on themselves and spiral around like a tangled pile of spaghetti, weaving in and out of other paths that rarely ever leave the plate."

This theory holds that our attitudes and behaviors don't only infect the people we interact with directly—like our colleagues, friends, and families—but that each individual's influence actually appears to extend to people within three degrees. So when you use these principles to make positive changes in your own life, you are unconsciously shaping the behavior of an incredible number of people. As James Fowler explains it, "I know that I'm not just having an impact on my son, I'm potentially having an impact on my son's best friend's mother."[2] This influence adds up; Fowler and Christakis estimate that there are nearly 1,000 people within three degrees of most of us. This is a true ripple effect—by trying to make ourselves happier and more successful, we actually have the ability to improve the lives of 1,000 people around us.

At this point, this might seem a little far-fetched. To begin to understand why our behavior is so infectious, and our influence so powerful, we need to first take a look at one of my favorite experiments.

SMILES IN THE BRAIN

I begin most of my lectures by asking the audience to break up into pairs. Then I say something like the following:

> *Over the course of your life, you have excelled in part because of your impressive self-discipline. You have used it to study so you could pass the classes you needed to, apply to the schools and jobs you needed to, and be successful enough that you are in this room to hear this lecture today. I want you to take all of that self-discipline you've been cultivating for the past couple decades to do the following. For the next seven seconds, no matter what your partner says or does, I want to you to show absolutely no emotional reaction. Do not get angry, sad, or frustrated, and do not smile or laugh. Go completely blank. Show no emotion, no matter what.*

I then ask each Person #2 to simply look their partner in the eyes and smile at them genuinely. I have done this experiment hundreds of times in corporate settings across the world, with everyone from nervous newbies to cantankerous lifers. The result is always the same. Virtually no one can refrain from returning their partner's smile, and most break into laughter almost immediately. It doesn't matter if I do this experiment during a week of massive layoffs or on a day when the stock market has plunged 600 points, I still see the same involuntary explosion of smiles. Even in parts of the world where smiling is less of a social norm, 80 to 85 percent of the participants cannot stop themselves from smiling.

If you think about this, it's really pretty incredible. After all, if these people have the self-discipline and focus to work 10- to 16-hour days, lead global teams, and manage multimillion dollar projects, surely they can handle a task as simple as controlling their facial expression for a mere seven seconds, right? But the fact is, they can't. Because something is going on in their brains that they aren't even consciously aware of. This mysterious force is the foundation of the ripple effect.

MIRROR MIRROR ON THE WALL

One Friday evening this past February, I landed in Australia, exhausted but excited about my very first adventure Down Under. That weekend, I intended to visit the Opera House, Koala Park, and the Harbour Bridge before Monday rolled around and I was due in downtown Sydney to run an executive training session. But first I headed down to the hotel lobby to engage in one of my favorite business-trip rituals: find a local bar, watch local sports, listen to locals talk. I was lucky enough to grab a stool just as an important rugby match was about to start on TV. Soon, a boisterous crowd had gathered around to watch.

The match was hardly underway before one of the rugby players got decked—hard. Midstride, with ball in hand, he'd taken a swift elbow to the face that pitched him backward in a way I thought physically impossible for someone with bones. The entire bar erupted into an audible groan. I saw the man to my right put his hands to his face, in the exact spot the rugby player had been hit. Then I noticed the guy sitting next to him had just done the same. And then I realized, amazingly, I had done it, too.

Now, we were at a bar in Sydney, while the game was at a stadium in Brisbane, several hundred miles away. None of us was on the rugby pitch, nor had any of us been assaulted by an errant elbow. Yet we had all responded physically, involuntarily (and quite dramatically), as though we ourselves had been hit.

What happened at that Australian sports bar is exactly the same thing that happens when I do the Smile Experiment. But only in the last decade have scientists finally had the technology to peer inside our brains and uncover the reason behind it. What they found were something called mirror neurons: specialized brain cells that can actually sense and then mimic the feelings, actions, and physical sensations of another person.[3] Let's say a person is pricked by a needle. The neurons in the pain center of his or her brain will immediately light up, which should come as no surprise. But what *is* a surprise is that when that same person sees someone *else* receive a needle prick, this same set of neurons lights up, just as though he himself had been pricked. In other words, he actually feels a hint of the pain of a needle prick, even though he himself hasn't been touched. If this sounds incredible, believe me when I tell you it has been replicated in countless other experiments involving sensations that range from pain to fear to happiness to disgust.

In fact, I bet you've even experienced this in your daily life. Have you ever been watching someone play golf on TV and catch yourself involuntarily moving in the direction of his swing? Obviously, your conscious brain knows that you are sitting on the couch eating potato chips, but another small part of your brain—the part where the mirror neurons reside—thinks you are out on that green. (Incidentally, this is one reason athletes watch training videos and play video games; because even without physical practice, the effects of practice get wired into their brains.) Then, because mirror neurons are often right next to motor neurons in the brain, copied feelings often lead to copied actions—suddenly you are moving like you're swinging a golf club without even knowing it. This is why smiles become contagious and why babies automatically mimic the funny faces their parents make. And it's why watching someone get elbowed in the face in Brisbane immediately caused a barful of rugby fans in Sydney to reach toward their own faces in agony.

YOUR COLLEAGUES ARE CONTAGIOUS

This phenomenon isn't exclusive to physical sensations or actions—thanks to these same mirror neurons, our emotions, too, are enormously contagious. As we pass through the day, our brains are constantly processing the feelings of the people around us, taking note of the inflection in someone's voice, the look behind their eyes, the stoop of their shoulders. In fact, the amygdala can read and identify an emotion in another person's face within 33 milliseconds, and then just as quickly prime us to feel the same.[4] In addition to this subconscious process, people also consciously assess the mood of those around them and act accordingly. Both processes together make it possible for emotions to jump from person to person in an instant. In fact, studies have shown that when three strangers meet in a room, the most emotionally expressive person transmits his or her mood to the others within just two minutes.[5]

Unfortunately, the power of emotional contagion means that overt negativity can infect a group of people almost instantly. Daniel Goleman couldn't have said it better: "Like secondhand smoke, the leakage of emotions can make a bystander an innocent casualty of someone else's toxic state."[6] This means that when we feel anxious or adopt an overtly negative mindset, these feelings will start to seep into every interaction we have, whether we like it or not. You may have noticed that when your boss walks into a meeting in a palpably bad mood, within just minutes it will have spread to the entire room. And the effects ripple out from there, as each worker returns back to his or her own office, spreading that negativity to everyone in his or her path. If just two minutes can have such an impact, imagine the effects of sharing a work environment with an overtly negative person for two weeks, or two years. In fact, emotions are so shared, organizational psychologists have found that each workplace develops its own group emotion, or "group affective tone," which over time creates shared "emotion norms" that are proliferated and reinforced by the behavior, both verbal and nonverbal, of the employees.[7] We have all encountered office environments that suffer from toxic emotion norms, and now we also know that their bottom-line results suffer because of it.

SPREADING THE HAPPINESS ADVANTAGE

Luckily, positive emotions are also contagious, which makes them a powerful tool in our quest for high performance in the workplace. Positive emotional contagion starts when people subconsciously mimic the body language, tone of voice, and facial expressions of those around them. Amazing as it might sound, once people mimic the physical behaviors tied to these emotions, it causes them to feel the emotion themselves. Smiling, for instance, tricks your brain into thinking you're happy, so it starts producing the neurochemicals that actually do make you happy. (Scientists call this the facial feedback hypothesis, and it is the basis of the recommendation "fake it till you make it." While authentic positivity will always trump its faux counterpart, there is significant evidence that changing your behavior first—even your facial expression and posture—can dictate emotional change.)[8]

So the happier everyone is around you, the happier you will become. This is why we laugh more at a funny movie when we're in a theater full of laughing people (and similarly why television sitcoms use a laugh track). Likewise, the happier we are at work, the more positivity we transmit to our colleagues, teammates, and clients, which can eventually tip the emotion of an entire work team.

Few people have illuminated this domino effect more perfectly than Yale psychologist Sigal Barsade, who conducted a study where he assigned volunteers a group task and then secretly instructed one member of the group to be overtly positive.[9] He then videotaped the proceedings, tracked the emotions of each individual team member before and after the session, and assessed both individual and group performance on the task itself. The results were remarkable: When the positive team member entered the meeting, his mood became instantly contagious, traveling around the room and infecting those around him. Furthermore, this positive mood improved each individual team member's performance, as well as their ability to accomplish the task as a group. The teams where one person sparked positive emotional contagion experienced less group conflict, more cooperation, and—most important—greater overall performance on the task at hand. So just one positive team member—one person using the Happiness Advantage—can affect both the individual attitudes and performance of those around him, as well as the dynamic and accomplishments of the group as a whole.

Of course, some people have a more powerful effect on a group's emotional tone than others. For starters, the more genuinely expressive someone is, the more their mindset and feelings spread.[10] But if openly expressing positivity doesn't come naturally to you, there are other ways your own positive habits can become contagious. For instance, the stronger your social connections, the more influence you wield. You may have noticed that when you spend time with a close friend, you feel in tune with each other. This is because the neural activity in your brain's emotional center is actually mirroring his or hers—and vice versa—and soon you fall into sync, like two pianos playing the same song. When you walk down the hallway together, your arms and legs even swing in sync. You two are in rapport, the basis of positive social connection and a major conduit for spreading the Happiness Advantage. Rapport demands our full attention, our warmth, and our coordinated responsiveness.[11] In return, we feel a resonance that not only increases our happiness, but actually makes us more successful and productive. Workers in rapport think more creatively and efficiently, and teams in rapport perform at higher levels—their thoughts are attuned and their brains are in effect working as one.

The more socially invested we are, the more chances we have at attaining this level of rapport, which in turn makes our own behavior more contagious. So when we model the type of mindset and habits that fuel high performance, we are in effect instilling these very mindsets and habits in our colleagues, friends, and loved ones. One study of Dartmouth College students by economist Bruce Sacerdote illustrates how powerful this influence is.[12] He found that when students with low grade-point averages simply began room-ing with higher-scoring students, their grade-point averages in-creased. These students, according to the researchers, "appeared to infect each other with good and bad study habits—such that a roommate with a high grade-point average would drag upward the G.P.A. of his lower-scoring roommate."

One way to build rapport, and therefore extend this influence, is with eye contact. Studies show that rapport strengthens between two people when they lock eyes, proving that the old business wis-dom about always looking people in the eye is actually scientifically sound advice.[13] This is also why couples so often say to each other, "Look at me when I'm talking to you," and why orgasms are stronger when we look into our partner's eyes. Eye contact tells our mirror neurons to fire, and when they do, the result is better performance, whether we're in the boardroom or in the bedroom.

The power to spark positive emotional contagion multiplies if you are in a leadership position. Studies have found that when lead-ers are in a positive mood, their employees are more likely to be in a positive mood themselves, to exhibit prosocial helping behaviors toward one another, and to coordinate tasks more efficiently and with less effort.[14] Sit around an unsmiling or anxious boss for too long, and you too will start to feel sad or stressed, regardless of how you felt originally. Whereas if your boss is using the seven princi-ples to increase his own positivity, your mere proximity to him will allow you to start to feel the benefits. And not just of greater hap-piness, but of all the advantages that come cascading along with it. As we now know, people in positive moods are better able to think creatively and logically, and to engage in complex problem solving, even be better negotiators. It is no surprise then that CEOs who are rated high on scales of positive expression are more likely to have employees who report being happy, and who describe their work-place as a climate conducive to performance.[15] Similar studies of sports teams have found not only that one happy player was enough to infect the mood of the entire team, but also that the happier the team was, the better they played.[16] So without even actively trying to change the way you lead, using these seven principles to increase your own level of positivity will start to change the group dynamics—and performance—of your whole team.

What this means is that leading by example is no longer an empty mantra. Practicing the seven principles in your own life can actually become your most effective leadership tool, without your even knowing it. Take an executive who has been writing down a gratitude list each night before he goes to sleep. As he leads his team's morning meeting, he's now in a mindset that allows him to spot more opportunities to be positive, which might compel him to praise the work of one of his direct reports. This in turn (a) primes the recipient's brain with positive emotions, which helps him think more creatively and efficiently; (b) gives him a sense of having achieved a goal, however small, and thus the confidence to go after bigger and bigger ones; and c) provides the spark that builds a high-quality connection between the executive and his employee, and cements the social cohesion and organizational commitment of the whole group. All of this ensures that each person in that room will spread positivity to their own reports, and so on and so on, until each person—and the organization as a whole—profits from it. Thus, what started as a personal, at-home exercise for one member of management trickles down to impact everyone at every level of the organization.

EVERY BIG WAVE STARTS SMALL

It has been said that a single butterfly flapping its wings can create a hurricane halfway around the world. As this theory, known as the Butterfly Effect, goes, the flap of a butterfly's wings may be one tiny motion, but it creates a slight gust of wind that eventually picks up greater and greater speed and power. In other words, one very small change can trigger a cascade of bigger ones.

Each one of us is like that butterfly. And each tiny move toward a more positive mindset can send ripples of positivity through our organizations, our families, and our communities. Remember in Part 1, we talked about how we can never really know the true extent of our potential? Well, the ripple effect is the perfect example of how there are no real discernible limits to our influence and our power.

When you capitalize on the Happiness Advantage, you are doing far more than improving your own well-being and performance; the more you profit from the principles in this book, the more everyone around you profits. In Principle 1, we talked about the Copernican revolution underway in the field of psychology, and how, just as Copernicus discovered that the earth actually orbits the sun, recent advances in positive psychology and neuroscience have taught us that success actually revolves around happiness, not the other way around. Well, as it turns out, and as you've seen in this chapter, this finding is even more revolutionary than we could have ever imagined. Because we now also know that it's not just our own individual success that orbits around our happiness. By making changes within ourselves, we can actually bring the benefits of the Happiness Advantage to our teams, our organizations, and everyone around us.

NOTES

■ ■ ■

DISCOVERING THE HAPPINESS ADVANTAGE

1 Kaplan, K. A. (January 12, 2004). College faces mental health crisis. *The Harvard Crimson*.

2 U.S. Job Satisfaction at lowest level in two decades. (January 5, 2010). *The Conference Board*.

3 Seligman, M.E.P. (2002). *Authentic Happiness*. New York: Free Press, at 117.

THE HAPPINESS ADVANTAGE AT WORK

1 Lyubomirsky, S., King, L., & Diener, E. (2005). The benefits of frequent positive affect: Does happiness lead to success? *Psychological Bulletin, 131*, 803–855.

2 For a comprehensive overview of this research, see Peterson, T. D., & Peterson, E. W. (2009). *Yale Journal of Health Policy, Law, and Ethics, 9*, 357–434.

CHANGE IS POSSIBLE

1 Nudo, R. J., Milliken, G. W., Jenkins, W. M., & Merzenich, M. M. (1996). Use-dependent alterations of movement representations in primary motor cortex of adult squirrel monkeys. *Journal of Neuroscience, 16*, 785–807.

2 Maguire, E., Gadian, D., Johnsrude, I., Good, C., Ashburner, J., Frackowiak, S., & Frith, C. (2000). Navigation-related structural change in the hippocampi of taxi drivers. *Proceedings of the National Academy of Sciences, USA, 97*(8), 4398–4403.

3 The story of Roger is my own, based on the series of studies neuroscientist Alvaro Pascual-Leone conducted on people learning braille. See Doidge, N. (2007). *The Brain That Changes Itself*. New York: Penguin, at 198–200.

4 For two eminently readable books on the history and science behind neuroplasticity, I recommend Doidge, N. (2007). *The Brain That Changes Itself*.

New York: Penguin, and Schwartz, J. M., & Begley, S. (2003). *The Mind and the Brain: Neuroplasticity and the Power of Mental Force.* New York: Harper Perennial.

PRINCIPLE #1: THE HAPPINESS ADVANTAGE

1 It should be noted that I am not claiming happiness to be the center of everything, merely a major cause of success. As for what the center of everything is, I'll leave that to philosophers and theologians smarter than I. Or rather to each individual reader.

2 Diener, E., & Biswas-Diener, R. (2008). *Happiness: Unlocking the Mysteries of Psychological Wealth.* Malden, MA: Wiley-Blackwell, at 4.

3 For an empirical study on these three distinct routes to happiness, see: Peterson, C., Park, N., & Seligman, M.E.P. (2005). Orientations to happiness and life satisfaction: The full life versus the empty life. *Journal of Happiness Studies, 6,* 25–41.

4 Peterson, C. (2006). *A Primer in Positive Psychology.* New York: Oxford University Press, at 79.

5 Fredrickson, B. (2009). *Positivity.* New York: Crown Publishers, at 39.

6 Lyubomirsky, S., King, L., & Diener, E. (2005). The benefits of frequent positive affect: Does happiness lead to success? *Psychological Bulletin, 131,* 803–855.

7 Lyubomirsky, S., King, L., & Diener, E. (2005). The benefits of frequent positive affect: Does happiness lead to success? *Psychological Bulletin, 131,* 803–855, at 834.

8 Staw, B., Sutton, R., & Pelled, L. (1994). Employee positive emotion and favorable outcomes at the workplace. *Organization Science, 5,* 51–71.

9 Diener, E., Nickerson, C., Lucas, R. E., & Sandvik, E. (2002). Dispositional affect and job outcomes. *Social Indicators Research,* 229–259.

10 Danner, D., Snowdon, D., & Friesen, W. (2001). Positive emotions in early life and longevity: Findings from the nun study. *Journal of Personality and Social Psychology, 80,* 804–813.

11 Seligman, M.E.P. (2002). *Authentic Happiness.* New York: Free Press, at 4.

12 Gallup-Healthways Well-Being Index. (2008). As referenced in: Associated Press. (June 18, 2008). Poll: Unhappy workers take more sick days.

13 Cohen, S., Doyle, W. J., Turner, R. B., Alper, C. M., & Skoner, D. P. (2003). Emotional style and susceptibility to the common cold. *Psychosomatic Medicine, 65,* 652–657.

14 Fredrickson, B. L. (1998). What good are positive emotions? *Review of General Psychology, 2,* 300–319; Fredrickson, B. L. (2001). The role of positive emotions in positive psychology: The broaden-and-build theory of positive emotions. *American Psychologist, 56,* 218–226.

15 Fredrickson, B. L., & Branigan, C. (2005). Positive emotions broaden the scope of attention and thought-action repertoires. *Cognition and Emotion, 19,* 313–332.

16 Schmitz, T. W., De Rosa, E., & Anderson, A. K. (2009). Opposing influences of affective state valence on visual cortical encoding. *Journal of Neuroscience, 29,* 7199–7207.

17 Gallagher, W. (2009). *Rapt.* New York: Penguin, at 36.

18 Master, J. C., Barden, R. C., & Ford, M. E. (1979). Affective states, expressive behavior, and learning in children. *Journal of Personality and Social Psychology, 37,* 380–90.

19 Bryan, T., & Bryan, J. (1991). Positive mood and math performance. *Journal of Learning Disabilities, 24,* 490–494.

20 Kopelman, S., Rosette, A. S., & Thompson, L. (2006). The three faces of Eve: Strategic displays of positive, negative, and neutral emotions in negotiations. *Organizational Behavior and Human Decision Processes, 99,* 81–101.

21 Estrada, C. A., Isen, A. M., & Young, M. J. (1997). Positive affect facilitates integration of information and decreases anchoring in reasoning among physicians. *Organizational Behavior and Human Decision Processes, 72,* 117–135.

22 Fredrickson, B. L., Mancuso, R. A., Branigan, C., & Tugade, M. M. (2000). The undoing effect of positive emotions, *Motivation and Emotion. 24,* 237–258.

23 Fredrickson, B. L. (2001). The role of positive emotions in positive psychology: The broaden-and-build theory of positive emotions. *American Psychologist, 56,* 218–226, at 222.

24 Lyubomirsky, S., Sheldon, K., & Schade, D. (2005). Pursuing happiness: the architecture of sustainable change. *Review of General Psychology, 9,* 111–131.

25 Winter, A. (May, 2009). The science of happiness. *The Sun Magazine.*

26 Lyubomirsky, S. (2007). *The How of Happiness.* New York: Penguin, at 70.

27 Shapiro, S. L., Schwartz, G.E.R., & Santerre, C. (2005). Meditation and positive psychology. In Snyder, C. R., & Lopez, S. J. (Eds.), *Handbook of Positive Psychology* (pp. 632–645). New York: Oxford University Press.

28 (April 3, 2006). Just the expectation of a mirthful laughter experience boosts endorphins 27 percent, HGH, 87 percent. *American Physiological Society.* Retrieved at www.physorg.com/news63293074.html.

29 Post, S. G. (2005). Altruism, happiness, and health: It's good to be good. *International Journal of Behavioral Medicine, 12,* 66–77; Schwartz et al. (2003). Altruistic social interest behaviors are associated with better mental health. *Psychosomatic Medicine, 65,* 778–785.

30 Lyubomirsky, S. (2007). *The How of Happiness.* New York: Penguin, at 127–129.

31 Keller, M. C., Fredrickson, B. L., et al. (2005). A warm heart and a clear head: The contingent effects of mood and weather on cognition. *Psychological Science, 16,* 724–731.

31 Gerber, G. L., Gross, et al. (1980). The "main-streaming" of America: Violence

profile no. 11. *Journal of Communication, 30*, 10–29. As cited in Barbara Fredrickson's *Positivity*, at 173.

32 Babyak, M., Blumenthal, J., Herman, S., Khatri, P., Doraiswamy, P., Moore, K., Craighead, W., Baldewicz, T., & Krishnan, K. (2000). Exercise treatment for major depression: Maintenance of therapeutic benefit at ten months. *Psychosomatic Medicine, 62*, 633–638.

33 Frank, R. H. (2000). *Luxury Fever.* New York: Princeton University Press.

34 Landau, E. (February 10, 2009). Study: Experiences make us happier than possessions. *CNN.com* Retrieved at www.cnn.com. For a more in-depth discussion of the psychological benefits of experiences over material goods, see the article: Van Boven, L., & Gilovich, T. (2003). To do or to have? That is the question. *Journal of Personality and Social Psychology, 85*(6), 1193–1202.

35 Dunn, E., Aknin, L. B., & Norton, M. I. (2008). Spending money on others promotes happiness. *Science, 319*, 1697–1688.

36 *See* VIA Signature Strengths Assessment, University of Pennsylvania website, www.authentichappiness.sas.upenn.edu/testcenter.aspx.

37 Seligman, M.E.P., Steen, T. A., Park, N., & Peterson, C. (2005). Positive psychology progress: Empirical validation of interventions. *American Psychologist, 60*, 410–421.

38 Loehr, J., & Schwartz, T. (2003). *The Power of Full Engagement: Managing Energy, Not Time, Is the Key to Performance and Personal Renewal.* New York: Free Press, at 65.

39 Connelly, J. (2002). All together now. *Gallup Management Journal, 2*, 12–18.

40 Greenberg, M. H., & Arakawa, D. (2006). Optimistic managers and their influence on productivity and employee engagement in a technology organization. As cited in: Robison, J. (May 10, 2007). The business benefits of positive leadership. *Gallup Management Journal.*

41 For more on what best motivates us, see: Deci, E. L. (1996). *Why We Do What We Do.* New York: Penguin.

42 Kjerulf, A. (2006). *Happy Hour Is 9 to 5.* Lulu Publishing.

43 Conley, J. (2007). *Peak: How Great Companies Get Their Mojo From Maslow.* New York: Jossey-Bass.

44 Barsade, S. G.(2002). The ripple effect: Emotional contagion and its influence on group behavior. *Administrative Science Quarterly; 47*, 644–675.

45 Bachman, W. (1988). Nice guys finish first: A SYMLOG analysis of U.S. Naval commands. In: Polley, R. B. et al. (Eds.) *The SYMLOG Practitioner: Applications of Small Group Research.* New York: Praeger. As cited in Goleman, D. (1998). *Working with Emotional Intelligence.* New York: Bantam, at 188.

46 Losada, M. (1999). The complex dynamics of high performance teams. *Mathematical and Computer Modeling, 30*, 179–192; Losada, M., & Heaphy, E. (2004). The role of positivity and connectivity in the performance of business teams: A

nonlinear dynamics model. *American Behavioral Scientist, 47*(6), 740–765; Fredrickson, B. L., & Losada, M. (2005). Positive affect and the complex dynamics of human flourishing. *American Psychologist, 60*(7), 678–686. For more on Losada's fascinating work and his collaboration with Barbara Fredrickson, see Fredrickson's book *Positivity,* 120–138.

47 Losada, M. (December 9, 2008). Work teams and the Losada Line: New results. *Positive Psychology News Daily.* Retrieved at http://positivepsychologynews. com/news/guest-author/200812091298.

PRINCIPLE #2: THE FULCRUM AND THE LEVER

1 Langer, E. (2009). *Counterclockwise: Mindful Health and the Power of Possibility.* New York: Ballantine.

2 Blakeslee, S. (October 13, 1998). Placebos prove so powerful even experts are surprised. *New York Times.*

3 Blakeslee, S. (October 13, 1998). Placebos prove so powerful even experts are surprised. *New York Times.*

4 Blakeslee, S. (October 13, 1998). Placebos prove so powerful even experts are surprised. *New York Times.*

5 Crum, A. J., & Langer, E. J. (2007). Mindset matters: Exercise and the placebo effect. *Psychological Science, 18*(2), 165–171.

6 Saks, A. M. (1995). Longitudinal field investigation of the moderating and mediating effects of self-efficacy on the relationship between training and newcomer adjustment. *Journal of Applied Psychology, 80*(2), 211–225.

7 Shih, M., Pittinsky, T., & Ambady, N. (1999). Stereotype susceptibility: Identity salience and shifts in quantitative performance. *Psychological Science, 10,* 80–83.

8 Dillon, S. (January 22, 2009). Study sees an Obama effect as lifting black test-takers. *New York Times.*

9 Dweck, C. S. (2006). *Mindset: The New Psychology of Success.* New York: Ballantine, at 7.

10 Blackwell, L. S., Trzesnieswki, K. H., & Dweck, C. S. (2007). Implicit theories of intelligence predict achievement across an adolescent transition: A longitudinal study and an intervention. *Child Development, 78*(1), 246–263.

11 Dweck, C. S. (2006). *Mindset: The New Psychology of Success.* New York: Ballantine, at 17.

12 Lyubomirsky, S., Sheldon, K., & Schade, D. (2005). Pursuing happiness: The architecture of sustainable change. *Review of General Psychology, 9,* 111–31.

13 Lyubomirsky, S. (2007). *The How of Happiness.* New York: Penguin, at 15.

14 Wrzesniewski, A., McCauley, C., Rozin, P., & Schwartz, B. (1997). Jobs, careers, and callings: People's relations to their work. *Journal of Research in Personality, 31,* 21–33.

NOTES

15 For more on job crafting, see: Wrzesniewski, A., & Dutton, J. (2001). Crafting a job: Revisioning employees as active crafters of their work. *Academy of Management Review, 26*(2), 179–201.

16 Wrzesniewski, A. (2003). Finding positive meaning in work. In Cameron, K. S., Dutton, J. E., & Quinn, R. E. (Eds.), *Positive Organizational Scholarship: Foundations of a New Discipline,* (pp. 296–308). San Francisco: Berrett-Koehler, at 304.

17 Conley, J. (2007). *Peak: How Great Companies Get Their Mojo from Maslow.* New York: Jossey-Bass, at 98.

18 Haslam, S. A., Salvatore, J., Kessler, T., & Reicher, S. D. (March 4, 2008). How stereotyping yourself contributes to your success (or failure). *Scientific American Mind.*

19 Liberman, V., Samuels, S. M., & Ross, L. (2004). The name of the game: Predictive power of reputations versus situational labels in determining prisoners' dilemma game moves. *Personality and Social Psychology Bulletin, 30,* 1175–1185.

20 Rosenthal, R., & Jacobson, L. (1968). *Pygmalion in the Classroom: Teacher Expectation and Pupils' Intellectual Development.* New York: Holt, Rinehart and Winston.

PRINCIPLE #3: THE TETRIS EFFECT

1 Stickgold, R., Malia, A., Maguire, D., Roddenberry, D., & O'Connor, M. (2000). Replaying the game: Hypnagogic images in normals and amnesics. *Science, 290,* 350–353.

2 Earling, A. (March 21–28, 1996). The Tetris effect: Do computer games fry your brain? *Philadelphia City Paper.*

3 Eaton, W. W., Anthony, J., Mandel, W., & Garrision, R. (1990). Occupations and the prevalence of major depressive disorder. *Journal of Occupational Medicine, 32,* 1079–1087.

4 Benjamin, G.A.H., Kaszniak, A., Sales, B., & Shanfield, S. B. (1986). The role of legal education in producing psychological distress among law students and lawyers. *American Bar Foundation Research Journal,* 225–252. For a full literature review on law student distress, see Peterson, T. D., & Peterson, E. W. (2009). *Yale Journal of Health Policy, Law, and Ethics, 9,* 357–434.

5 Peterson, T. D., & Peterson, E. W. (2009). *Yale Journal of Health Policy, Law, and Ethics, 9,* 357–434.

6 For a more in-depth discussion of the science of attention, see Gallagher, W. (2009). *Rapt: Attention and the Focused Life.* New York: Penguin.

7 Simons, D. J., & Chabris, C. F. (1999). Gorillas in our midst: Sustained inattentional blindness for dynamic events. *Perception, 28,* 1059–1074.

8 Many studies have been done about our tendency toward "change blindness."

One example: Simons, D. J., & Levin D. T. (1998). Failure to detect changes to people in a real-world interaction. *Psychonomic Bulletin and Review, 5,* 644–649.

9   Massad, C. M., Hubbard, M., & Newtson, D. (1979). Selective perception of events. *Journal of Experimental Social Psychology, 15*(6), 513–532.

10 Halberstadt, J., Winkielman, P., Niedenthal, P. M., & Dalle, N. (2009). Emotional conception: How embodied emotion concepts guide perception and facial action. *Psychological Science, 20,* 1254–1261.

11 Emmons, R. A. (2007). *Thanks! How the New Science of Gratitude Can Make You Happier.* New York: Houghton Mifflin.

12 For a sampling of the extensive scientific literature on optimism, see: Carver, C. S., & Scheier, M. F. (2005). Optimism. In Snyder, C. R., & Lopez, S. J. (Eds.), *Handbook of Positive Psychology* (pp. 632–645). New York: Oxford University Press; Scheier, M. F., Weintraub, J. K., & Carver, C. S. (1986). Coping with stress: Divergent strategies of optimists and pessimists. *Journal of Personality and Social Psychology, 51,* 1257–1264.

13 Wiseman, R. (2003). The luck factor. *The Skeptical Inquirer, 27,* 1–5.

14 Bright, J. F., Pryor, R. G. L., & Harpham, L. (2005). The role of chance events in career decision making. *Journal of Vocational Behavior, 66,* 561–576.

15 Schneider, L. (October 7, 2009). Life decisions & career paths—Leave it all to chance? *Huffington Post.* In his article, Schneider cites Colleen Seifert, a psych professor at the University of Michigan and an expert on predictive coding. For more on this phenomenon, see: Seifert, C., & Patalano, A. L. (2001). Opportunism in memory: Preparing for chance encounters. *Current Directions in Psychological Science, 10,* 198–201.

16 Seligman, M.E.P., Steen, T. A., Park, N., & Peterson, C. (2005). Positive psychology progress: Empirical validation of interventions. *American Psychologist, 60,* 410–421.

17 Burton, C., & King, L. (2004). The health benefits of writing about intensely positive experiences. *Journal of Research in Personality, 38,* 150–163.

18 Taylor, S. E. (1988). *Positive Illusions.* New York: Basic.

PRINCIPLE #4: FALLING UP

1   Collins, J. (2009). *How the Mighty Fall.* New York: HarperCollins, at 120.

2   For a review, see: Linley, P. A., & Joseph, S. (2004). Positive change following trauma and adversity: A review. *Journal of Traumatic Stress, 17*(1), 11–21. Here is a sampling of studies that support the list given in this chapter: Bereavement (Davis, Nolen-Hoeksema, & Larson, 1998), Bone marrow transplantation (Fromm, Andrykowski, & Hunt, 1996), Breast cancer (Cordova, Cunningham, Carlson, and Andrykowski, 2001; Weiss, 2002), Chronic illness (Abraido-Lanza, Guier, & Colon, 1998), Heart attack (Affleck, Tennen, Croog, & Levine,

1987), Military combat (Fontana & Rosenheck, 1998; Schnurr, Rosenberg, and Friedman, 1993), Natural disaster (McMillen, Smith, & Fisher, 1997), Physical assault (Snape, 1997), Refugee displacement following war (Powell, Rosner, Butollo, Tedeschi, & Calhoun, 2003).

3 Tedeschi, R. G., Calhoun, L. G., & Cann, A. (2007). Evaluating resource gain: Understanding and misunderstanding posttraumatic growth. *Applied Psychology: An International Review, 56* (3), 396–406, at 396.

4 Val, E. B., & Linley, P. A. (2006). Posttraumatic growth, positive changes, and negative changes in Madrid residents following the March 11, 2004, Madrid train bombings. *Journal of Loss and Trauma, 11,* 409–424.

5 Weiss, T. (2002). Posttraumatic growth in women with breast cancer and their husbands: An intersubjective validation study. *Journal of Psychosocial Oncology, 20,* 65–80.

6 Linley, P. A., & Joseph, S. (2004). Positive change following trauma and adversity: A review. *Journal of Traumatic Stress, 17*(1), 11–21.

7 Val, E. B., & Linley, P. A. (2006). Posttraumatic growth, positive changes, and negative changes in Madrid residents following the March 11, 2004, Madrid train bombings. *Journal of Loss and Trauma, 11,* 409–424, at 410.

8 Walsh, F. (2002). Bouncing forward: Resilience in the aftermath of September 11. *Family Processes, 41,* 34–36, at 35.

9 McGregor, J. (July 10, 2006). How failure breeds success. *BusinessWeek.* The subheading I chose for this chapter, "Eureka We Failed!" is a quote from this issue of *BusinessWeek,* which carried that headline on its cover.

10 Schoemaker, P.J.H., & Gunther, R. E. (June, 2006). Wisdom of deliberate mistakes. *Harvard Business Review.*

11 Ben-Shahar, T. (2009). *The Pursuit of Perfect.* New York: McGraw-Hill, at 22.

12 Lorenzet, S. J., Salas, E., & Tannenbaum, S. I. (2005). Benefiting from mistakes: The impact of guided errors on learning, performance, and self-efficacy. *Human Resource Development Quarterly, 16,* 301–322.

13 Seligman, M.E.P. (1991). *Learned Optimism.* New York: Knopf, at 19–21.

14 Hiroto, D. S. (1974). Locus of control and learned helplessness. *Journal of Experimental Psychology, 102,* 187–193.

15 As described by Martin Seligman in *Learned Optimism,* at 29.

16 Dickler, J. (October 9, 2009). Wall St. casualties: Where are they now? www.cnn.com.

17 (June 9, 1958). Recession Benefits. *Time Magazine.*

18 (June 9, 1958). Recession Benefits. *Time Magazine.*

19 Chakravorti, B. (March 18, 2009). How to innovate in a downturn. *The Wall Street Journal.*

20 Richard Wiseman is perhaps the leading proponent of this strategy, something

he calls "counterfactual thinking." For a more in-depth discussion of the concept and how you can put it to use, check out his 2003 book *The Luck Factor* (New York: Miramax).

21 Stefanucci, J. K., Proffitt, D. R., Clore, G. L., & Parekh, N. (2008). Skating down a steeper slope: Fear influences the perception of geographical slant. *Perception, 37*, 321–323.

22 For the whole MetLife story, see Seligman, M.E.P. (1991). *Learned Optimism.* New York: Knopf, at 97–106.

23 See for example: Peterson, C., & Barrett, L. C. (1987). Explanatory style and academic performance among university freshmen. *Journal of Personality and Social Psychology, 53,* 603–607; Nolen-Hoeksema, S., Girgus, J., & Seligman, M.E.P. (1986). Learned helplessness in children: A longitudinal study of depression, achievement, and explanatory style, *Journal of Personality and Social Psychology, 51,* 435–442. Seligman, M.E.P., & Schulman, P. (1986). Explanatory style as a predictor of productivity and quitting among life insurance sales agents. *Journal of Personality and Social Psychology, 50,* 832–838.

24 Seligman, M.E.P. (1991). *Learned Optimism.* New York: Knopf, at 152–153.

25 Seligman, M.E.P., Nolen-Hoeksema, S., Thornton, N., & Thornton, K. M. (1990). Explanatory style as a mechanism of disappointing athletic performance. *Psychological Science, 1,* 143–146. For a more extensive discussion of explanatory style and athletic performance, see Seligman's book *Learned Optimism,* pp. 155–166.

26 Scheier, M. F. et al. (1989). Dispositional optimism and recovery from coronary artery bypass surgery: The beneficial effects on physical and psychological well-being. *Journal of Personality and Social Psychology, 57,* 1024–1040.

27 This ABCD model has a long and rich history, starting with Albert Ellis, father of cognitive therapy, then adapted by Martin Seligman (see *Learned Optimism* and *Authentic Happiness*) and also put to great use by Karen Reivich and Andrew Shatte in their excellent book *The Resilience Factor.*

28 Diener, E., Lucas, R. E., & Scollon, C. N. (2006). Beyond the hedonic treadmill: Revising the adaptation theory of well-being. *American Psychologist, 61,* 305–314.

29 Gilbert, D. T., Wilson, T. D., Pinel, E. C., Blumberg, S. J., & Wheatley, T. P. (1998). Immune neglect: A source of durability bias in affective forecasting. *Journal of Personality and Social Psychology, 75*(3), 617–638.

PRINCIPLE #5: THE ZORRO CIRCLE

1 See for example: Sparr, J. L., & Sonnentag, S. (2008). Feedback environment and well-being at work: The mediating role of personal control and feelings of helplessness. *European Journal of Work and Organizational Psychology* 17(3), 388–412; Spector, P. (2002). Employee control and occupational stress. *Current Directions in Psychological Science,* 11(4).

2 Thompson, C. A., & Prottas, D. J. (2005). Relationships among organizational family support, job autonomy, perceived control, and employee well-being. *Journal of Occupational Health Psychology, 10*(4), 100–118.

3 For studies on the importance of control, see for example: Findley, M. J., & Cooper, H. M. (1983). Locus of control and academic achievement: A literature review. *Journal of Personality and Social Psychology, 44*(2), 419–427; Shepherd, S., Fitch, T. J., Owen, D., & Marshall, J. L. (2006). Locus of Control and Academic Achievement in High School Students. *Psychological Reports, 98*(2), 318–322; Carden, R., Bryant, C., & Moss, R. (2004). Locus of Control, Test Anxiety, Academic Procrastination, and Achievement Among College Students. *Psychological Reports, 95*(2), 581–582. Ng, T. W. H. (2006). Locus of control at work: A meta-analysis. *Journal of Organizational Behavior, 27*(8), 1057–1087. Spector, Paul E. et al. (2002). Locus of control and well-being at work: How generalizable are Western findings? *Academy of Management Journal, 45*(2), 453–466. Lefcourt, H. M., Holmes, J. G., Ware, E. E., & Saleh, W. E. (1986). Marital locus of control and marital problem solving. *Journal of Personality and Social Psychology, 51*(1), 161–169. Lefcourt, H. M., Martin, R. A., Fick, C. M., & Saleh, W. E. (1985). Locus of control for affiliation and behavior in social interactions. *Journal of Personality and Social Psychology, 48*(3), 755–759.

4 Syme, L., & Balfour, J. (1997). Explaining inequalities in coronary heart disease. *The Lancet, 350*, 231–232.

5 Rodin. J., & Langer, E. J. (1977). Long-term effects of a control-relevant intervention with the institutionalized aged. *Journal of Personality and Social Psychology, 35*(12), 897–902.

6 Goleman, D. (1998). *Working with Emotional Intelligence.* New York: Bantam, at 77.

7 Goleman, D. (1998). *Working with Emotional Intelligence.* New York: Bantam, at 75.

8 Lusch, R. F., & Serpkenci, R. (1990). Personal differences, job tension, job outcomes, and store performance: A study of retail managers. *Journal of Marketing, 54*, 85–101.

9 Zweig, J. (2007). *Your Money and Your Brain: How the New Science of Neuroeconomics Can Help Make You Rich.* New York: Simon and Schuster.

10 See for example: Kahneman, D., & Tversky, A. (1979). Prospect theory: An analysis of decisions under risk. *Econometrica, 47*, 313–327; Kahneman, D., & Tversky, A. (1984). Choices, values and frames. *American Psychologist, 39*, 341–350.

11 Cassidy, J. (September 18, 2006). Mind games. *The New Yorker;* Cohen, J. D. (2005). The vulcanization of the human brain: A neural perspective on interactions between Cognition and Emotion. *Journal of Economic Perspectives, 19*(4), 3–24.

12 Zweig, J. (2007). *Your Money and Your Brain: How the New Science of Neuroeconomics Can Help Make You Rich.* New York: Simon and Schuster, at 3.

13 Zweig, J. (2007). *Your Money and Your Brain: How the New Science of Neuroeconomics Can Help Make You Rich.* New York: Simon and Schuster, at 172.

14 See for example: Locke, E. A. (2002). Setting goals for life and happiness. In Snyder, C. R., & Lopez, S. J. (Eds.), *Handbook of Positive Psychology* (pp. 299–312). New York: Oxford University Press.

15 Bregman, P. (September 1, 2009). How to escape perfectionism. *How We Work Blog.* Retrieved at www.HarvardBusiness.org.

16 Coyle, D. (2009). *The Talent Code.* New York: Bantam Books, at 211.

17 Gladwell, M. (2000). *The Tipping Point.* New York: Little, Brown and Company, at 139–146.

PRINCIPLE #6: THE 20-SECOND RULE

1 Kalb, C. (October 13, 2008). Drop that corn dog, doctor. *Newsweek.*

2 Parker-Pope, T. (December 31, 2007). Will your resolutions last until February? *New York Times.* Citing a study by FranklinCovey of 15,000 people.

3 James, W. (1899). *Talks To Teachers On Psychology and To Students On Some of Life's Ideals.* (Harvard University Press, 1983), at 48.

4 James, W. (1892). *Psychology: Briefer Course.* (Harvard University Press, 1984), at 133.

5 James, W. (1892). *Psychology: Briefer Course.* (Harvard University Press, 1984), at 136.

6 While the popular belief is that it takes anywhere from 21 to 30 days to make a habit, there has been little empirical testing on this subject; obviously, actual length of time depends on both the person and the action. Recently, Phillipa Lally and her colleagues at the University College London conducted a study that found the average number of days 96 volunteers needed to turn an action (for instance, going for a 15-minute run every day) into an automatic habit was 66, though people ranged greatly, from 18 to 254 days. The study's most reassuring news was that skipping one day did not derail eventual habit formation, which should encourage us not to abandon our progress should we get slightly off track. Lally, P., van Jaarsveld, C.H.M., Potts, H.W.W., & Wardle, J. (2009). How are habits formed: Modeling habit formation in the real world. *European Journal of Social Psychology* (in press).

7 "The National Weight Control Registry estimates that only 20 percent of dieters successfully keep off lost weight for more than a year." Ansel, K. (2009). Is your diet making you gain? Retrieved at www.health.msn.com.

8 Baumeister, R. F., Bratslavsky, E., Muraven, M., & Tice, D. M. (1998). Ego

depletion: Is the active self a limited resource? *Journal of Personality and Social Psychology,* 74(5), 1252–1265.

9 See for example: Baumeister, R. F., Vohs, K. D., & Tice, D. M. (2007). The strength model of self-control. *Current Directions in Psychological Science, 16*(6), 351–355: Gailliot, M., Plang, E., Butz, D., & Baumeister, R. (2007). Increasing self-regulatory strength can reduce the depleting effect of suppressing stereotypes. *Personality and Social Psychology Bulletin, 33,* 281–294. While self-regulation tires after repeated use, the good news is that, like a muscle, it can be strengthened over time with practice. So for instance, while willpower is not useful to sustain a restrictive diet, especially if someone has already experienced control-depleting tasks throughout the day, prolonged commitment to a task that requires self-regulation, like a two-month exercise program, can actually improve self-regulation. See Oaten, M., & Cheng, K. (2006). Longitudinal gains in self-regulation from regular physical exercise. *The British Psychological Society, 11,* 717–733; Oaten, M., & Cheng, K. (2007). Improvements in self-control from financial monitoring. *Journal of Economic Psychology, 28,* 487–501.

10 Muraven, M., & Baumeister, R. (2000). Self-regulation and depletion of limited resources: Does self-control resemble a muscle? *Psychological Bulletin, 126,* 247–259.

11 Csikszentmihalyi, M. (1997). *Finding Flow: The Psychology of Engagement in Everyday Life.* New York: Basic Books, at 65.

12 Csikszentmihalyi, M. (1997). *Finding Flow: The Psychology of Engagement in Everyday Life.* New York: Basic, at 67.

13 Lindstrom, M. (2008). *Buyology.* New York: Broadway Business, at 99.

14 For more information on fascinating studies like this one, see Thaler, R. H., & Sunstein, C. (2008). *Nudge: Improving Decisions About Health, Wealth, and Happiness.* New York: Penguin.

15 Barnes, B. (July 26, 2009). Lab watches web surfers to see which ads work. *New York Times.*

16 Leyden, J. (June 23, 2003). One in five U.S. firms has sacked workers for e-mail abuse. Retrieved at www.theregister.co.uk.

17 Thompson, C. (October 16, 2005). Meet the life hackers. *New York Times.* Citing a study performed at the University of California-Irvine.

18 Hafner, K. (February 10, 2005). You there, at the computer: Pay attention. *New York Times.*

19 Meyers, A. W., Stunkard, A. J., & Coll, M. (1980). Food accessibility and food choice. *Archives of General Psychiatry, 37,* 1133–1135. For more in depth descriptions of this study and the one cited above it, as well as many more like them, see Brian Wansink's brilliant book *Mindless Eating,* especially pages 78–88.

20 Meiselman, H. L., Hedderley, D., Staddon, S. L., Pierson, B. J., & Symonds, C. R.

(1994). Effect of effort on meal selection and meal acceptability in a student cafeteria. *Appetite, 23*, 43–5.

21 Wansink, B. (2006). *Mindless Eating: Why we eat more than we think*. New York: Bantam, at 82.

22 Hawkes, N. (July 18, 2007). Everyone must be an organ donor unless they opt out, says Chief Medical Officer. Retrieved at www.timesonine.co.uk.

23 Vohs, K. D., et al. (2008). Making choices impairs subsequent self-control: A limited-resource account of decision making, self-regulation, and active initiative. *Journal of Personality and Social Psychology, 94*(5), 883–898.

24 Schwartz, B. (2004). *The Paradox of Choice*. New York: Harper Perennial, at 113.

PRINCIPLE #7: SOCIAL INVESTMENT

1 Shenk, J. W. (June 2009). What makes us happy? *The Atlantic Monthly*.

2 Valliant, G. (July 16, 2009). Yes, I stand by my words, "Happiness equals love—full stop." *Positive Psychology News Daily*. Retrieved at http://positive psychologynews.com/news/george-valient/200907163163.

3 Diener, E., & Biswas-Diener, R. (2008). *Happiness. Unlocking the Mysteries of Psychological Wealth*. Malden, MA: Wiley-Blackwell, at 66.

4 Diener, E., & Seligman, M. (2002). Very happy people. *Psychological Science, 13*, 81–84.

5 For a thorough explanation of our innate need to bond with others, see: Baumeister, R. F., & Leary, M. R. (1995). The need to belong: Desire for interpersonal attachments as a fundamental human motivation. *Psychological Bulletin, 117*(3), 497–529.

6 For a particularly eloquent and in-depth discussion of the biological importance of social contact, see: Lewis, T., Amini, F., & Lannon, R. (2001). *A General Theory of Love*. New York: Vintage. For an empirical example of how lack of social contact leads to decreased immune function, see: Cohen, S., Doyle, W., Skoner, D., Rabin, B., & Gwaltney, J. (1997). Social ties and susceptibility to the common cold. *Journal of the American Medical Association, 277*, 1940–1944.

7 Hawkley, L. C., Masi, C. M., Berry, J. D., & Cacioppo, J. T. (2006). Loneliness is a unique predictor of age-related differences in systolic blood pressure. *Psychology and Aging, 21*(1), 152–164.

8 Cacioppo, J. T. (2008). *Loneliness: Human Nature and the Need for Social Connection*. New York: W.W. Norton and Company.

9 Blackmore, E. R., et al. (2007). Major depressive episodes and work stress: Results from a national population survey. *American Journal of Public Health, 97*(11), 2088–2093.

10 Berkman, L. F., Leo-Summers, L., & Horwitz, R. I. (1992). Emotional support and survival after myocardial infarction. A prospective-population-based study of the elderly. *Annals of Internal Medicine, 117*, 1003–9.

11 Spiegel, D., Bloom, J., Kraemer, H., & Gottheil, E. (1989). Effect of psychosocial treatment on survival of patients with metastatic breast cancer. *The Lancet, 2,* 888–891.

12 House, J., Landis, K., & Umberson, D. (1988). Social relationships and health. *Science, 241,* 540–544.

13 Lewis, T., Amini, F., & Lannon, R. (2001). *A General Theory of Love.* New York: Vintage, at 206.

14 Heaphy, E., & Dutton, J. E. (2008). Positive social interactions and the human body at work: Linking organizations and physiology. *Academy of Management Review, 33,* 137–162; Theorell, T., Orth-Gomér, K., & Eneroth, P. (1990). Slow-reacting immunoglobin in relation to social support and changes in job strain: A preliminary note. *Psychosomatic Medicine, 52,* 511–516.

15 Carlson, D. S., & Perrewe, P. L. (1999).The role of social support in the stressor-strain relationship: An examination of work-family conflict. *Journal of Management 25,* (4), 513–540.

16 Heaphy, E., & Dutton, J. E. (2008). Positive social interactions and the human body at work: Linking organizations and physiology. *Academy of Management Review, 33,* 137–162

17 Goleman, D. (1998). *Working with Emotional Intelligence.* New York: Bantam, at 217–218.

18 Lewis, M. (2006). *The Blind Side.* New York: W. W. Norton, at 111.

19 Rosengren, A., Orth-Gomer, K., Wedel, H., & Wilhelmsen, L. (1993). Stressful life events, social support, and mortality in men born in 1933. *British Medical Journal, 307,* 1102–1105.

20 Vaillant, G. (July 16, 2009). Yes, I stand by my words, "Happiness equals love—full stop." *Positive Psychology News Daily.* Retrieved at http://positive psychologynews.com/news/george-vaillant/200907163163

21 Dweck, C. S. (2006). *Mindset: The New Psychology of Success.* New York: Ballantine, at 55.

22 Carmeli, A., Brueller, D., & Dutton, J. E. (2009). Learning behaviours in the workplace: The role of high-quality interpersonal relationships and psychological safety. *Systems Research and Behavioral Science, 26,* 81–98.

23 Holahan, C. K., & Sears, R. R. (1995). *The Gifted Group in Later Maturity.* Palo Alto, Calif.: Stanford University Press.

24 Collins, J. (2001). *Good to Great: Why Some Companies Make the Leap . . . And Others Don't.* New York: HarperBusiness.

25 Campion, M. A., Papper, E. M., & Medsker, G. J. (1996). Relations between work team characteristics and effectiveness: A replication and extension. *Personnel Psychology, 49,* 429–452.

26 Heaphy, E., & Dutton, J. E. (2008). Positive social interactions and the human

body at work: Linking organizations and physiology. *Academy of Management Review, 33*(1), 137–162.

27 Dutton, J. (2003). *Energize Your Workplace: How to Create and Sustain High-Quality Connections at Work.* San Francisco: Jossey-Bass, at 2.

28 Baker, S. (April 8, 2009). Putting a price on social connections. *BusinessWeek.*

29 Cohen, D., & Prusak, L. (2001). *In Good Company: How Social Capital Makes Organizations Work.* Boston: Harvard Business School Press, at 95–97.

30 Grant, A. M., Dutton, J. E., & Rosso, B. D. (2008). Giving commitment: Employee support programs and the prosocial sensemaking process. *Academy of Management Journal, 51,* 898–918.

31 Everson, D. (July 16, 2009). Baseball's winning glue guys. *The Wall Street Journal.*

32 Wagner, N., Feldman, G., & Hussy, T. (2003). The effect of ambulatory blood pressure of working under favourably and unfavourably perceived supervisors. *Occupational Environmental Medicine, 60,* 468–474.

33 Bradberry, T. (January 30, 2009). A bad boss can send you to an early grave. *Philanthropy Journal.* Retrieved at www.philanthropyjournal.org.

34 Bradberry, T. (January 30, 2009). A bad boss can send you to an early grave. *Philanthropy Journal.* Retrieved at www.philanthropyjournal.org.

35 Goleman, D. (1998). *Working with Emotional Intelligence.* New York: Bantam, at 215.

36 Buckingham, M., & Coffman, C. (1999). *First, Break All the Rules.* New York: Simon and Schuster.

37 Cohen, D., & Prusak, L. (2001). *In Good Company: How Social Capital Makes Organizations Work.* Boston: Harvard Business School Press, at 24–25.

38 Pearson, C. M., Andersson, L. M., and Porath, C. L. (2000). Assessing and attacking workplace incivility. *Organizational Dynamics,* 123–137.

39 Pattison, K. (September 8, 2008). The social capital investment strategy. *Fast Company.*

40 Gable, S. L., Reis, H. T., Impett, E., & Asher, E. R. (2004). What do you do when things go right? The intrapersonal and interpersonal benefits of sharing positive events. *Journal of Personality and Social Psychology, 87,* 228–245.

41 Gable, S. L., Gonzaga, G. C., & Strachman, A. (2006). Will you be there for me when things go right? Supportive responses to positive event disclosures. *Journal of Personality and Social Psychology, 91,* 904–917.

42 Cohen, D., & Prusak, L. (2001). *In Good Company: How Social Capital Makes Organizations Work.* Boston: Harvard Business School Press.

43 Authors Cohen and Prusak discuss how leaders can invest in the "space and time to connect" in their book *In Good Company.* See specifically pp. 81–101.

44 Dutton, J. E. (2003) *Energize Your Workplace: How to Create and Sustain High-Quality Connections.* San Francisco: Wiley, at 161.

45 Dutton, J. E. (Winter 2003). Fostering high-quality connections. *Stanford Social Innovation Review*.

46 Cohen, D., & Prusak, L. (2001). *In Good Company: How Social Capital Makes Organizations Work*. Boston: Harvard Business School Press, at 22.

47 Peters, T. (September 16, 2005). MBWA after all these years. *Dispatches from the New World of Work*. Retrieved at www.tompeters.com/dispatches/008106.php.

48 Lyubomirsky, S. (2007). *The How of Happiness*. New York: Penguin Books, at 97–100.

49 Algoe, S. B., Haidt, J., & Gable, S. L. (2008). Beyond reciprocity: Gratitude and relationships in everyday life. *Emotion, 8*, 425–429.

50 Trejos, N. (July 17, 2009). Recession lesson: Share and swap replaces grab and buy. *Washington Post*.

SPREADING THE HAPPINESS ADVANTAGE AT WORK, AT HOME, AND BEYOND

1 Christakis, N. A., & Fowler, J. (2009). *Connected*. New York: Little, Brown and Company.

2 Thompson, C. (September 10, 2009). Are your friends making you fat? *New York Times*.

3 A pioneer in the field of neuroscience has recently authored a book that does an enviable job of explaining the complex science behind mirror neurons and how they relate to empathy: Iacoboni, M. (2008). *Mirroring People*. New York: Picador.

4 Goleman, D. (2006). *Social Intelligence*. New York: Bantam, at 65.

5 Friedman, H., & Riggio, R. (1981). Effect of individual differences in nonverbal expressiveness on transmission of emotion. *Journal of Nonverbal Behavior, 6*, 96–104.

6 Goleman, D. (2006). *Social Intelligence*. New York: Bantam, at 14.

7 Kelly, J. R., and Barsade, S. G (2001). Mood and emotions in small groups and work teams. *Organizational Behavior and Human Decision Processes, 86*, 99–130.

8 Zajonc, R. B., Murphy, S. T., & Inglehart, M. (1989). Feeling and facial efference: Implications for the vascular theory of emotion. *Psychological Review, 96*, 395–416.

9 Barsade S. G. (2002). The ripple effect: Emotional contagion and its influence on group behavior. *Administrative Science Quarterly, 47*, 644-675.

10 Friedman, H., & Riggio, R. (1981). Effect of individual differences in nonverbal expressiveness on transmission of emotion. *Journal of Nonverbal Behavior, 6*, 96–104.

11 Goleman, D. (2006). *Social Intelligence*. New York: Bantam, at 29–37.

12 Thompson, C. (September 10, 2009). Are your friends making you fat? *New York Times*.

13 Goleman, D. (2006). *Social Intelligence*. New York: Bantam, at 30. Goleman is citing Bavelas, J. B., et al., (1986). I *show* how you feel: Motor mimicry as a communicative act. *Journal of Social and Personality Psychology, 50*, 322–29.

14 George, J. M., & Bettenhausen, K. (1990). Understanding prosocial behavior, sales performance, and turnover: A group level analysis in a service context. *Journal of Applied Psychology, 75*, 698–709; Sy, T., Cote, S., & Saavedra, R. (2005). The contagious leader: Impact of the leader's mood on the mood of group members, group affective tone, and group processes. *Journal of Applied Psychology, 90*, 295–305.

15 Lyubomirsky, S., King, L. A., & Diener, E. (2005). The benefits of frequent positive affect: Does happiness lead to success? *Psychological Bulletin, 131*, 803–855.

16 Totterdell, P. (2000). Catching moods and hitting runs: Mood linkage and subjective performance in professional sports teams. *Journal of Applied Psychology, 85*, 848–859.

INDEX

. . .

ABOUT THE AUTHOR

■ ■ ■

SHAWN ACHOR is one of the world's leading experts on human potential, having researched and lectured in forty-two countries working to bridge the gap between the science of happiness and performance in our everyday lives. Trained by some of the pioneers in the field of positive psychology, he served as the head teaching fellow to help design and teach the famed "happiness" course, the most popular at Harvard at the time. He now serves as the founder and CEO of Aspirant, a research and consulting firm that uses positive psychology to enhance individual achievement and cultivate a more productive workplace. Achor's lectures on the science of happiness and human potential have received attention in the *New York Times*, *Boston Globe*, and *Wall Street Journal* and on CNN and NPR. Shawn Achor lives in Cambridge, Massachusetts.

ed) stocks." Evolution itself, in other words, has been forced into a new trajectory.

2. SPONTANEOUS DECARBONIZATION?

The Commission's coronation of the Anthropocene coincides with growing scientific controversy over the 4th Assessment Report issued last year by the Intergovernmental Panel on Climate Change (IPCC). The IPCC is mandated to establish scientific baselines for international efforts to mitigate global warming, but some of the most prominent researchers in the field are now challenging its reference scenarios as overly optimistic, even pie-in-the-sky thinking.

The current scenarios were adopted by the IPCC in 2000 to model future global emissions based on different "storylines" about population growth, as well as technological and economic development. Some of the panel's major scenarios are well-known to policymakers and greenhouse activists, but few outside the research community have actually read or understood the fine print, particularly the IPCC's confidence that greater energy efficiency will be an "automatic" byproduct of future economic development. Indeed, all the scenarios, even the "business as usual" variants, assume that at least 60 percent of future carbon reduction will occur independently of greenhouse mitigation measures.

The panel, in effect, has bet the ranch, or rather the planet, on unplanned, market-driven progress toward a post-carbon world economy, a transition that implicitly requires wealth generated from higher energy prices ultimately finding its way to new technologies and renewable energy. (The International Energy Agency recently estimated that it would cost $45 trillion to halve greenhouse gas emissions by 2050.) Kyoto-type accords and carbon markets are designed—almost as an analog to Keynesian "pump-priming"—to bridge the shortfall between spontaneous decarbonization and the emissions targets required by each scenario. Serendipitously, this reduces the costs of mitigating global warming to levels that align with what seems, at least theoretically, to be politically possible, as expounded in the British *Stern Review on the Economics of Climate Change* of 2006 and other such reports.

Critics argue, however, that this represents a heroic leap of faith that radically understates the economic costs, technological hurdles, and social changes required to tame the growth of greenhouse gases. European carbon emissions, for example, are still rising (dramatically in some sectors), despite the European Union's much praised adoption of a cap-and-trade system in 2005. Likewise there has been little evidence in recent years of the automatic progress in energy efficiency that is the *sine qua non* of the IPCC scenarios. Although *The Economist* characteristically begs to differ, most energy researchers believe that, since 2000, energy intensity has actually risen; that is, global carbon dioxide emissions have kept pace with, or even grown marginally faster than, energy use.

Coal production, especially, is undergoing a dramatic renaissance, as the nineteenth century has returned to haunt the twenty-first century. Hundreds of thousands of miners are now working under conditions that would have appalled Charles Dickens, extracting the dirty mineral that allows China to open two new coal-fueled power stations every week. Meanwhile, the total consumption of fossil fuels is predicted to increase at least 55 percent over the next generation, with international oil exports doubling in volume.

The United Nations Development Program, which has made its own study of sustainable energy goals, warns that it will require "a 50 percent cut in greenhouse gas emissions worldwide by 2050 against 1990 levels" to keep humanity outside the red zone of runaway warming (usually defined as a greater than two degrees centigrade increase this century). Yet the International Energy Agency predicts that, in all likelihood, such emissions will actually increase in this period by nearly 100 percent—enough greenhouse gas to propel us past several critical tipping points.

Even while higher energy prices are pushing SUVs towards extinction and attracting more venture capital to renewable energy, they are also opening the Pandora's box of the crudest of crude oil production from Canadian tar sands and Venezuelan heavy oil. As one British scientist has warned, the very last thing we should wish for (under the false slogan of "energy independence") is new frontiers in hydrocarbon production that advance "humankind's ability to accelerate global warming" and slow the urgent transition to "non-carbon or closed-carbon energy cycles."

FIN-DU-MONDE BOOM

What confidence should we place in the capacity of markets to reallocate investment from old to new energy or, say, from arms expenditures to sustainable agriculture? We are propagandized incessantly (especially on public television) about how giant companies like Chevron, Pfizer Inc., and Archer Daniels Midland are hard at work saving the planet by plowing profits back into the kinds of research and exploration that will ensure low-carbon fuels, new vaccines, and more drought-resistant crops.

As the current ethanol-from-corn boom, which has diverted 100 million tons of grain from human diets mainly to American car engines, so appallingly demonstrates, "biofuel" may be a euphemism for subsidies to the rich and starvation for the poor. Likewise "clean coal," despite a vigorous endorsement from then-Senator Barack Obama (who also champions ethanol), is, at present, simply a huge deception: a $40 million advertising and lobbying campaign for a hypothetical technology that *Business Week* has characterized as "being decades away from commercial viability."

Moreover, there are disturbing signs that energy companies and utilities are reneging on their public commitments to the development of carbon-capture and alternative-energy technologies. The Bush administration's "marquee demonstration project," FutureGen, was scrapped this year after the coal industry refused to pay its share of the public-private "partnership"; similarly, most U.S. private-sector carbon-sequestration initiatives have recently been cancelled. In the United Kingdom, meanwhile, Shell has just pulled out of the world's largest wind-energy project, the London Array. Despite heroic levels of advertising, energy corporations, like pharmaceutical companies, prefer to overgraze the commons, while letting taxes, not profits, pay for whatever urgent, long-overdue research is actually undertaken.

On the other hand, the spoils from high energy prices continue to gush into real estate, skyscrapers, and financial assets. Whether or not we are actually at the summit of Hubbert's Peak—that peak oil moment—whether or not the oil-price bubble finally bursts, what we are probably witnessing is the largest transfer of wealth in modern history.

An eminent Wall Street oracle, McKinsey Global Institute, predicts that if crude oil prices remain above $100 per barrel—they are, at the moment, approaching $140 a barrel—the six countries of the Gulf Cooperation Council alone will "reap a cumulative windfall of almost $9 trillion by 2020." As in the 1970s, Saudi Arabia and its Gulf neighbors, whose total gross domestic product has almost doubled in just three years, are awash in liquidity: $2.4 trillion in banks and sovereign wealth funds according to a recent estimate by *The Economist*. Regardless of price trends, the International Energy Agency predicts, "more and more oil will come from fewer and fewer countries, primarily the Middle East members of OPEC [The Organization of the Petroleum Exporting Countries]."

Dubai, which has little oil income of its own, has become the regional financial hub for this vast pool of wealth, with ambitions to eventually compete with Wall Street and the city of London. During the first oil shock in the 1970s, much of OPEC's surplus was recycled through military purchases in the United States and Europe, or parked in foreign banks to become the "subprime" loans that eventually devastated Latin America. In the wake of the attacks of 9/11, the Gulf states became far more cautious about entrusting their wealth to countries like the United States governed by religious fanatics. This time around, they are using "sovereign wealth funds" to achieve a more active ownership in foreign financial institutions, while investing fabulous amounts of oil revenue to transform Arabia's sands into hyperbolic cities, shopping paradises, and private islands for British rock stars and Russian gangsters.

Two years ago, when oil prices were less than half of the current level, *The Financial Times* estimated that planned new construction in Saudi Arabia and the emirates already exceeded $1 trillion. Today, it may be closer to $1.5 trillion—considerably more than the total value of world trade in agricultural products. Most of the Gulf city-states are building hallucinatory skylines—and, among them, Dubai is the unquestionable superstar. In a little more than a decade, it has erected 500 skyscrapers, and currently leases one-quarter of all the high-rise cranes in the world.

This super-charged Gulf boom, which celebrity architect Rem Koolhaas claims is "reconfiguring the world," has led Dubai developers to proclaim the advent of a "supreme lifestyle" represented by seven-star hotels and private islands. Not surprisingly, then, the United Arab Emirates and its neighbors have the biggest per capita ecological footprints on the planet. Meanwhile, the rightful owners of Arab oil wealth, the masses crammed into the angry tenements of Baghdad, Cairo, Amman, and Khartoum, have little more to show for it than a trickle-down of oil-field jobs and Saudi-subsidized *madrassas*. While guests enjoy the $5,000 per night rooms in Burj Al-Arab, Dubai's celebrated sail-shaped hotel, working-class Cairenes riot in the streets over the unaffordable price of bread.

CAN MARKETS ENFRANCHISE THE POOR?

Emissions optimists, of course, will smile at all the gloom-and-doom and evoke the coming miracle of carbon trading. What they discount is the real possibility that a sprawling carbon-offset market may emerge, just as predicted, yet produce only minimal improvement in the global carbon balance-sheet as long as there is no mechanism for enforcing real net reductions in fossil fuel use.

In popular discussions of emissions-rights trading systems it is common to mistake the smokestacks for the trees. For example, the wealthy oil enclave of Abu Dhabi (the senior partner of Dubai in the

United Arab Emirates) loudly brags that it has planted more than 130 million trees—each of which does its duty in absorbing carbon dioxide from the atmosphere. But this same artificial forest in the desert also consumes huge quantities of irrigation water produced or recycled from expensive desalination plants. The trees may allow Sheik Khalifa bin Zayed to wear a halo at international meetings, but the rude fact is that they are an energy-intensive beauty strip, like most of so-called green capitalism.

And, while we're at it, let's just ask: What if the buying and selling of carbon credits and pollution offsets fails to turn down the thermostat? What exactly will motivate governments and global industries then to join hands in a crusade to reduce emissions through regulation and taxation?

Kyoto-type climate diplomacy assumes that all the major actors, once they have accepted the science in the IPCC reports, will recognize an overriding common interest in gaining control over the runaway greenhouse effect. But global warming is not *War of the Worlds*, where invading Martians are dedicated to annihilating all of humanity without distinction. Climate change, instead, will initially produce dramatically unequal impacts across regions and social classes, reinforcing, rather than diminishing, geopolitical inequality and conflict.

As the United Nations Development Programme emphasized in its report last year, global warming is, above all, a threat to the poor and the unborn, the "two constituencies with little or no political voice."

Coordinated global action on their behalf thus presupposes either their revolutionary empowerment (a scenario not considered by the IPCC) or the transmutation of the self-interest of rich countries and classes into an enlightened "solidarity" without precedent in history. From a rational-actor perspective, the latter outcome only seems realistic if it can be shown that privileged groups possess no preferential "exit" option; that internationalist public opinion drives policymaking in key countries; and that greenhouse gas mitigation could be achieved without major sacrifices in upscale Northern Hemispheric standards of living—none of which seems highly likely.

And what if growing environmental and social turbulence, instead of galvanizing heroic innovation and international cooperation, simply drive elite publics into even more frenzied attempts to wall themselves off from the rest of humanity? Global mitigation, in this unexplored but not improbable scenario, would be tacitly abandoned (as, to some extent, it already has been) in favor of accelerated investment in selective adaptation for Earth's first-class passengers. We're talking here of the prospect of creating green and gated oases of permanent affluence on an otherwise stricken planet.

Of course, there will still be treaties, carbon credits, famine relief, humanitarian acrobatics, and perhaps the full-scale conversion of some European cities and small countries to alternative energy. But the shift to low, or zero, emission lifestyles would be almost unimaginably expensive. (In Britain, it currently costs $200,000 more to build a zero carbon, "level 6" eco-home than a standard unit of the same area.) And this will certainly become even more unimaginable after, perhaps, 2030, when the convergent impacts of climate change, peak oil, peak water, and an additional 1.5 billion people on the planet may begin to seriously throttle growth.

THE NORTH'S ECOLOGICAL DEBT

The real question is this: Will rich counties *ever* mobilize the political will and economic resources to actually achieve IPCC targets or, for that matter, to help poorer countries adapt to the inevitable, already "committed" quotient of warming now working its way through the slow circulation of the world ocean?

To be more vivid: Will the electorates of the wealthy nations shed their current bigotry and walled borders to admit refugees from predicted epicenters of drought and desertification like the Maghreb, Mexico, Ethiopia, and Pakistan? Will Americans, the most miserly people, when measured by per capita foreign aid, be willing to tax themselves to help relocate the millions likely to be flooded out of densely settled, mega-delta regions like Bangladesh?

Market-oriented optimists, once again, will point to carbon offset programs like the Clean Development Mechanism which, they claim, will allow green capital to flow to the Third World. Most of the Third World, however, probably prefers for the First World to acknowledge the environmental mess it has created and take responsibility for cleaning it up. They rightly rail against the notion that the greatest burden of adjustment to the Anthropocene epoch should fall on those who have contributed least to carbon emissions and drawn the slightest benefits from 200 years of industrialization.

In a sobering study recently published in the *Proceedings of the [U.S.] National Academy of Science*, a research team has attempted to calculate the environmental costs of economic globalization since 1961, as expressed in deforestation, climate change, overfishing, ozone depletion, mangrove conversion, and agricultural expansion. After making adjustments for relative cost burdens, they found that the richest countries by their activities had generated 42 percent of environmental degradation across the world, while shouldering only 3 percent of the resulting costs.

The radicals of the South will rightly point to another debt as well. For thirty years, cities in the developing world have grown at breakneck speed without any equivalent public investment in infrastructure services, housing, or public health. In large part, this has been the result of foreign debts contracted by dictators, payments enforced by the International Monetary Fund, and public sectors wrecked by the World Bank's "structural adjustment" agreements.

This planetary deficit of opportunity and social justice is well caught by the fact that more than one billion people, according to UN Habitat, currently live in slums and that their number is expected to double by 2030. An equal number, or more, forage in the so-called informal sector (a first-world euphemism for mass unemployment). Sheer demographic momentum, meanwhile, will increase the world's urban population by 3 billion people over the next 40 years (90 percent of them in poor cities), and no one—absolutely no one—has a clue how a planet of slums, with growing food and energy crises, will accommodate their biological survival, much less their inevitable aspirations to basic happiness and dignity.

If this seems unduly apocalyptic, consider that most climate models project impacts that will uncannily reinforce the present geography of inequality. One of the pioneer analysts of the economics of global warming, Petersen Institute fellow William R. Cline, recently published a country-by-country study of the likely effects of climate change on agriculture by the later decades of this century. Even in the most optimistic simulations, the agricultural systems of Pakistan (-20 percent of current farm output) and Northwestern India (-30 percent) are likely devastated, along with much of the Middle East, the Maghreb, the Sahel belt, Southern Africa, and the Caribbean and Mexico. Twenty-nine developing countries will lose 20 percent or more of their current farm output to global warming, while agriculture in the already rich north is likely to receive, on average, an 8 percent boost.

In light of such studies, the current ruthless competition between energy and food markets, amplified by international speculation in commodities and agricultural land, is only a modest portent of the chaos that could soon grow exponentially from the convergence of resource depletion, intractable inequality, and climate change. The real danger is that human solidarity itself, like a West Antarctic ice shelf, will suddenly fracture and shatter into a thousand shards.

Of course the people don't want war... But after all, it is the leaders of the country who determine the policy, and it's always a simple matter to drag the people along... All you have to do is tell them they are being attacked, and denounce the pacifists for lack of patriotism and exposing the country to danger. It works the same in any country.

—Hermann Goering, at the Nuremberg Trials, 1946.

INTRODUCTION

Over the years, my family has bought three or four little books on how to lead the greenest life possible. We've all seen those well-intentioned pamphlets at the checkout counters of bookstores and grocery stores: *Fifty Ways to Save the Planet*; *Going Totally Green*; *Making a Difference*; and so on. While they may pale these days considering the enormity of the environmental crisis, we nonetheless still take the advice to heart, choosing low-energy light bulbs, installing low-flush toilets, turning down the thermostat, refusing to warm up the car's engine for extended periods, and on and on. Every little bit helps, as the experts tell us, and, besides, we need to feel that we are doing something. But no list in any of those books addresses the largest single source of pollution in this country and in the world: the United States military—in particular, the military in its most ferocious and stepped-up mode—namely, the military at war.

In a nation like ours, where military might trumps diplomatic finesse, the supreme irony may be that the planet, and not human beings, will provide the most stringent corrective to political overreaching. The earth can no longer absorb the punishment of war, especially on a scale and with a ferocity that only the wealthiest, most powerful country in the world—no, in history—knows how to deliver. While the United States military directed its "Operation Iraqi Freedom" solely against the Iraqis, no one—not a single citizen in any part of the globe—has escaped its fallout. When we declare war on a foreign nation, we now also declare war on the Earth, on the soil and plants and animals, the water and wind and people, in the most far-reaching and deeply infecting ways. A bomb dropped on Iraq explodes around the world. We have no way of containing the fallout. Technology fails miserably here. War insinuates itself, like an aberrant gene and, left unchecked, has the capacity for destroying the Earth's complex and sometimes fragile system.

So we can act like honorable and conscientious citizens, conserving all the energy we can. We can feel good about all those glossy magazine ads from Shell and Exxon Mobil telling us how their companies now treasure the environment, producing their fuels in the cleanest ways possible. We can fall for Detroit's latest news, too, convincing us of a revolutionary breakthrough in fuel efficiency: 300 horsepower cars that get still 30 or 32 miles per gallon on the highway. But that's just insanity wearing a green disguise. None of those advertised boasts and claims really matter. They still cling to fossil fuels and further our campaign to kill off everything on the planet with our addictive need. But, even if those claims did make a slight difference, even if we could slow down global warming, ultimately it would not matter. For, in the background, lurking and ever-present, a giant vampire silently sucks out of the Earth all the oil it possibly can, and no one stops it. And so here's the awful truth: even if every person, every automobile, and every factory suddenly emitted zero emissions, the Earth would still be headed head first and at full speed toward total disaster for one major reason. The military—that voracious vampire—produces enough greenhouse gases, by itself, to place the entire globe, with all its inhabitants large and small, in the most immanent danger of extinction.

As we contemplate America in the opening years of the twenty-first century, then, let us reconsider George Washington's farewell warning that "overgrown military establishments...under any form of government, are inauspicious to liberty, and are to be regarded as particularly hostile to republican liberty." Today, our own military has grown beyond an institution hostile to liberty and has wrapped its arms of death around life itself. And, from all the available evidence, it will not let go. Unlike most animals, the military has no surrender mechanism. Unless we all summon the strength to confront the military—no easy task—it will continue to work its evil.

I write as a citizen, not a politician; as a layman, not a scientist; as an outsider from the academy, not an insider from the Pentagon. Most of the information that I present here us deliberately withheld from the general public, made intentionally obscure, folded inside arcane reports, or hidden on hard-to-find governmental websites by the Department of Defense (DoD), or the Pentagon, or the General Accounting Office. Researching the military is like trying to uncover the truth in the former Soviet Union. Governments always conduct a good deal of their business in clandestine ways. The Bush administration, however, enjoyed the well-earned reputation as particularly deceptive, tight-lipped, secretive, and downright hostile to the most routine questions and probes—and especially over things that appeared so obviously illegal, like spying on citizens through wiretapping telephone calls and intercepting international e-mail messages, all without the legally required warrants. We will see how eager the Obama administration will be to reveal its inner workings. Transparency was one of the goals of Obama's campaign, and he repeated that mantra over and over again.

About the most critical and freighted issue, like declaring war on another nation, the Bush administration broadcasted the boldest of lies, announcing to the American public that Saddam Hussein possessed weapons of mass destruction, and that unless we took military action the world faced the horror of evaporating in a mushroom cloud. Bush, Cheney, and their assorted neo-conservative hawks met in secret directly following the attack of 9/11, determining ways it could circumvent the Geneva Convention, holding indefinitely anyone the President desired without leveling charges or granting judicial review.

Bush invoked executive privilege, extending it, oddly enough, to his Vice President, who argued, strangely, that he was not part of the executive branch; the Department of Justice seemed bent on destroying records, like e-mail messages that circulated between key members of the department; and the CIA deliberately destroyed videotaped interrogations of Guantanamo detainees that purportedly showed evidence of torture, including simulated drowning, or what has come to be known, in the most neutered language, as if it were a summer pastime, "water boarding." All the while, the Bush administration complained about the opaqueness inside those nations that Bush placed on the Axis of Evil, nations like Iran, Iraq, and North Korea.

The Bush administration's level of arrogance and secretiveness stood terribly at odds with a growing number of citizens who wanted to know what was going on, who wanted to know, as precisely as possible, what acts the government committed, both in this country and around the world, in their name. Perhaps the liberation movements of the sixties and seventies encouraged such an inquiring spirit. Perhaps the Internet, too, has helped to foster a climate of snooping. And, then, of course, breaking the government's stranglehold on secrecy enjoys the precedent of one of the most monumental, revealing, and politicizing leaks in history: Daniel Ellsberg's dissemination, in 1971, of 7,000 pages of top-secret information on the conduct of the war in Vietnam, that the *New York Times* published as *The Pentagon Papers.*

Whatever the reason, people now believe strongly that it is their right to have more and more of the facts. Citizens demand disclosure. Even the most apolitical of people now demand their republic back. Millions of Americans, some who had never in their lives gone to the polls, voted for Barack Obama for just that reason. For eight long years, the Bush administration held the citizens of this country hostage to fear and war and the threat of foreign invasion and attack, compounded by the additional threat of the immigration of millions of so-called "illegal aliens" from Mexico and Latin America. We might do well to pay attention, once more, to that one particular part of Washington's warning to his countrymen: "Overgrown military establishments…are inauspicious to liberty."

But before we rejoice too soon in the new administration, recall that, directly before the election, Obama sounded very much like the old administration when he announced that he would probably need to send two more battalions into the foothills of Afghanistan. Bin Laden is still the prize; victory is still the illusion. War is still the way. The impulse toward war transcends parties: Republicans defend their war in Iraq; Democrats defend Kosovo. Saddam Hussein is a tyrant and practiced genocide on the Kurds. Slobodan Milosovic is a tyrant and practiced genocide on the Albanians. The names change, the nations shift, but the war drums reverberate with their same incessant and insistent beat. And almost everyone listens—conservatives and liberals—and almost everyone responds.

Both Democratic and Republican senators and representatives authorized the use of force in Iraq on October 11, 2002. Yes, some brave voices voted no—156 in all (23 senators and 133 representatives). I applaud those 156 souls, but how is it that millions upon millions of ordinary citizens could see through the trumped-up intelligence reports and stepped-up speeches, and took to the streets marching and demonstrating and shouting No to the war? War holds a certain fascination for politicians, as if it were the highest achievement of their careers, in the name of keeping democracy intact. The so-called "Last Great War" seems to color every decision to invade the next country on the enemies list, allowing the latest round of politicians, once again, to stand tall to save the world from out-and-out tyranny.

The war in Iraq has produced an odd series of books. Academics and journalists have written far fewer of the usual books on the strategy and history of the Iraq War, and many more on the chicanery, clandestine meetings, and outright secrecy of the Bush White House in the pursuit of that war. The titles rolled out of the old-line New

York publishing houses and from independent presses in the thousands. An awful lot in Washington was rotten; you could smell it everywhere. And the smell, I am afraid, lingers. And the revelations keep coming.

We recently found out, for instance, that even the highly guarded and highly secret Guantanamo Prison, perched on forty-five acres in the foothills of Cuba, contains somewhere within its boundaries—or maybe even outside its borders—an internal and even more secret prison that goes by the name Camp 7, which supposedly held fifteen "high value detainees." The existence of the prison within a prison became known only on December 8, 2007, from declassified notes belonging to a battery of attorneys who had come to represent other prisoners. Guards routinely gave tours of Guantanamo to reporters and visiting dignitaries, but they allowed no one to see Camp 7. Secretary of Defense Robert Gates declared it off limits and will not even say who has responsibility for its oversight.[1]

"Not everybody, even those with the Joint Task Force, has access or even knowledge of where Camp 7 is," Army Colonel Bruce Vargo told an AP reporter. Colonel Vargo served as commander of the military's Joint Detention Group at Guantanamo, and he is quick to point out that he had absolutely no responsibility for Camp 7.[2] This dodge turns out to be quite convenient, for if no one has direct responsibility for the camp then no one can be held responsible for the tortures that purportedly took place within its stone walls—no one, of course, but a handful of low level soldiers, who the Bush administration tagged as the really "bad apples," and who managed with their actions to spoil the entire bushel. A bipartisan senate report released on December 11, 2008, concludes something different: "the physical and mental abuse of detainees in Iraq, Afghanistan, and Guantanamo Bay, Cuba, was the direct result of Bush administration detention policies and should not be dismissed as he work of bad guards or interrogators."[3]

More and more Americans now want to know the price of supposedly opening freedom's door for other people in other countries. And, if our own government refuses to tell us, other countries no longer stay mum, but now feel comfortable in delivering the awful news. We have engendered such ill will around the world that our former colonial subjects feel a great sense of power and relief in tattling on the world's great big bully. And they speak out now quite readily.

Who are they? Well, Chalmers Johnson lists the countries in his book, *Blowback: The Cost and Consequences of American Empire.* Johnson reaches back some fifty years—of course, our aggression has gone on for much longer—and his list covers a great deal of the world:

> The American people may not know what is done in their name, but those on the receiving end surely do—including the people of Iran (1953), Guatemala (1954), Cuba (1959 to the present), Congo (1960), Brazil (1964), Indonesia (1965), Vietnam (1961–73), Laos (1961–73), Cambodia (1961–73), Greece (1967–74), Chile (1974), Afghanistan (1979 to the present), El Salvador, Guatemala, Nicaragua (1980s), and Iraq (1991 to the present), to name only the most obvious cases.[4]

Once our military moves into a place, it does not leave. We advertise our role as peace keeping, or border patrolling, or as some other euphemistic kind of undertaking, but the evidence leads a person to conclude only one thing: having visited, having occupied, the United States Armed Forces do not ever leave. "Nation building" (or in the case of Iraq, "nation re-building") always turns out to be an episode in colonizing and crippling the other.

To try to get to the truth, I rely on my own digging—in military manuals, government and anti-government websites, in reference books, exposés, and in an increasing number of leaked memos. I also rely heavily on the work of a dedicated and dogged cadre of inspired citizens, who have managed to mine important data from the most varied and, at times, the most unlikely of sources, and who have published their findings on blogs and websites and i-newsletters. The country owes a great deal of thanks to that motley band of Insurgents of the Internet. In many cases, they have put the major newspapers (and the majority of the most prominent politicians) in this country to shame.[5]

And then, of course, we must give our thanks and praise to those brave journalists who, against efforts to censure and frighten them, continue to report from the Middle East, in general. A few independent photographers traveled to Iraq before the beginning of Shock and Awe, and made Americans familiar with ordinary Iraqi men, women, and children trying to cope with impending death. And, over the years, we have had bloggers, who, at great risk to their own lives, continued to send reports from Baghdad and, most impressive, continued to send them from outside the fortified boundaries of the so-called Green Zone, from remote and dangerous villages.

Finding answers for virtually any question about the military, in general, or the war in Iraq, in particular, is not easy. Finding exact answers is next to impossible. Even for what one might think are the most basic of questions—how many civilians have we killed in this war?—one comes up against a great degree of uncertainty. For instance, only in January 2008, did we get a report from the World Health Organization (WHO), with the help of the Iraqi government, setting the number of Iraqi civilians killed in the war at what seems the ridiculously low figure of 151,000. These numbers count only the first three years of the war, but we had to wait six years to get even that data.[6] The Associated Press makes the point that many people risked their lives going door to door, in villages across the country, to conduct their interviews. At least one statistician from the WHO lost his life in the process.

Epidemiologists at the Bloomberg School of Public Health at Johns Hopkins University, along with a team of Iraqi physicians, conduced a national cross-sectional cluster sample survey of mortality in Iraq in 2003. Their study concluded that the number of "excess Iraqi deaths as a consequence of war" had reached 655,000. They published their results in the British medical journal *The Lancet* in October 2006. According to the study's authors, between May 2003 and June 2008, 50 percent of Iraqi children under fifteen years of age were killed by coalition air strikes.

The website *Unknown News* set the number of deaths at over 688,000, as of December 10, 2008. And the well-respected British group, Opinion Research Business Survey, calculated the number of civilian deaths, as of October 2006, at a low of 733,158 to a high of 1,446,063. The website *Information Clearing House*, which has done a remarkable job reporting the news all through the war in Iraq, lists, as of January 2009, the civilian death count at 1,297,997.

Because it adheres to a strict policy of not keeping tally of civilian deaths, we will not learn the number from the United States military. Or, as General Tommy Franks so eloquently put it, when asked about civilian deaths in Iraq: "We don't do body counts." Franks' line is true, except, of course, when it comes to Americans. In fact, we know the exact number of deaths and casualties for American GIs, as well as the death counts for all the members of the coalition forces.

All of which means, in the end, that we will probably never learn the answer to what should be, certainly, one of the most crucial and fundamental questions: In pursuing our wars in Iraq and Afghanistan, how many civilians have we killed? I do not expect to know their names, but I do expect to know the number. That we do not know the answer to that question—and yet do know the precise figures for the stock market each and every day, for the dollar amount of the bank bailouts—says a great deal, I believe, about the arrogance and disregard that all wars engender for all living things. It speaks loudly to the way we first denigrate, say, Iraqis into rag-heads, jihadis, sand-niggers, camel-jockeys—into the enemy—making it so much easier, finally, to toss them into that gross and euphemistic category, civilian body counts.

I believe every American, like it or not, should know that horrific death number, but once more, the truth passes us by. I have come to know intimately the meaning of that phrase my parents threw at me when I was a kid and they wanted to keep me in the dark. "That's a military secret," they would say to me. If that did not work, they resorted to saying, "You're much too young" or "I'll tell you when you're older." Well, now I am older, and here again I have that awful feeling that my elders find it much too dangerous—much too compromising and revealing—to let me in on the truth.

The military keeps almost every fact under wraps, and will not give up much. The blind man's scramble to uncover the truth devolves into an insidious and stupid chain of reactions. Publish what you have gleaned from some Internet source on the conduct of the war, for instance, and military experts will quickly pounce and promote you on every right-wing blog as a know-nothing idiot, or worse yet, a traitor. Even those who support the military less passionately rule out any chance for cooperative work. They generally hold to a tough-guy's attitude of American might and right that precludes any prospect for such a communal effort. That's just the way it is, buddy, so love it or leave it.

On conservative blogs, one finds much the same attitude. Just try to figure out what's going on. I dare you! And that spirit can take an even nastier turn once the blogger detects even the slightest criticism of the United States military. The Pentagon has become one massive secret order: the Masonic Lodge of American culture. Only those who have been carefully screened—for the right color, the right schools, the right family and friends, the right political leanings—can gain entrance. And those who know the secret language and learn the secret handshake keep their information oh so well guarded.

To determine even something as straightforward as the exact number of Americans in uniform, on active duty, in Iraq, turns out to be confusing and complicated. The so-called "surge" muddied the issue even more, what with various stop-orders and early-rotation orders in place, shortened training-periods, National Guard call-ups, along with requests by field generals for thousands more Military Police and support battalions. To say nothing of civilian contractors, most of whom assume their jobs superbly well-armed, well-armored, and ready to declare as the enemy anything that moves or mouths off. Some critics point out that even the Pentagon, itself, may not be able to provide precise numbers or answers for some of the questions I raise in this essay.

Who, then, does know the answers, one immediately asks? As odd as it may seem, the Pentagon may be just too huge, too segmented and secretive for any one person to know—from the field commanders, on up through the generals, to the Secretary of Defense himself. And the top man, the commander-in-chief, well, the last one seemed thoroughly indifferent to details, facts, and especially to analysis. Reading tired him. A cluttered desk bothered him. A welter of details confused him. Complexity baffled. He called himself consistent and the decider; critics called him stubborn and the bumbler.

For all those reasons, I intend this piece as an *essay*, in the word's original sense—a "trial," an "attempt," and an "excursion," in trying to frame the right questions and trying to root around for the correct answers. Montaigne in the late-sixteenth century invented the genre we call the essay. To remind him of the method of thinking and writing peculiar to the form, he wore a medallion around his neck. On one side of it he had inscribed, "What do I know?," and on the other a question mark. In that tradition, I ask you to think of this essay as a protracted question mark, and to consider that question mark as a hook, with which I want to corral a good many people into pondering something that they may not have thought of before: the crisis of the military and pollution.

I admit at the outset that I have a rough but informed answer to my central question: How much does the military contribute to worldwide pollution and thus to global warming? But, even without precise answers, I can report that the numbers, in terms of greenhouse gases, stagger the imagination. Should I have a more precise answer? I think so, if for no other reason than that—besides the fact that, as a taxpayer, I, along with hundreds of millions of other Americans, help pay the enormous bill for our military adventures—the stakes are so incredibly high, which is no less than the continuing life of the planet itself. As little as ten years ago, that phrase, "the life of the planet," might have sounded like hyperbole. Today, because of the immanent crisis of global warming, those words have taken on a remarkably frightening reality. In a very real way, then, I am suggesting that the military holds our fate in its vise-like grip.

Is it possible for any average citizen to get hold of that kind of precision? I do not think so, not without a room full of experts on matters military, political, climatological, scientific, and strategic. I hope that at some time such a meeting of informed people might in fact take place, so that the truth might be uncovered and made public. For even my limited research leads me to believe that we cannot as a people endure on this planet while still having the option of full-scale war to fall back on. We must eliminate the possibility of war—for us, and, as I hope to show, for the rest of the developing countries, like China, India, and Russia, as well.

I need to add one final comment about my research. After living in this country for more than fifty years, and after reading enough American history, one develops a nose for the truth. It is not hard to acquire. One learns to sniff out the villains. They may change their names over time, but their functions remain precisely the same. Doctor Martin Luther King Jr. could smell that foul odor better than most folks. Of course, a black person knows the truth of the nation in a way and in a degree that no white person ever could. More than forty years ago, on August 16, 1967, just a few short months before his assassination, King delivered a talk entitled "Where Do We Go From Here?" In that talk, in which King castigates America for bombing the people of Vietnam, he spoke the magic word that would lead anyone to understand the goal and desire of American capital. He uttered the tiny word "oil." From that word, *oil*, he pointed out, flows our domestic and foreign policy. Here is King, then, in 1967 (notice that, over those forty years, little if anything has changed):

> I want to say to you as I move to my conclusion, as we talk about Where do we go from here, that we honestly face the fact that the movement must address itself to the question of restructuring the whole of American society. There are forty million poor people here. And one day we must ask the question, Why are there forty million poor people in America? And when you begin to ask that question,

you are raising questions about the economic system, about a broader distribution of wealth. When you ask that question, you begin to question the capitalistic economy. And I'm simply saying that more and more, we've got to begin to ask questions about the whole society. We are called upon to help the discouraged beggars in life's marketplace. But one day we must come to see that an edifice which produces beggars needs restructuring. It means that questions must be raised. You see, my friends, when you deal with this, you begin to ask the question, Who owns the oil?[7]

"Who owns the oil?" I find it interesting that King did not give his audience an outright answer to that question. Did he, however, ask the right question? Asking the right question can, at times, be more important than answering an irrelevant question. I am fairly certain that, without uttering the exact words, he did in fact answer the question, because, as I said, only four short months later, an assassin's bullet silenced him. So King left it to us, to each one of us, to answer the question, which should lead us, of course, to think not just about oil, but also about control and power, imperial might, and the perpetuation of that might at any cost, including full-scale war. To try to answer the question is to understand why this country consumes so much oil, and oil's importance in maintaining a late-capital economy.

Thinking about oil, one quickly runs across the association between "national security" and something called "energy security," two concepts linked more than sixty years ago by President Roosevelt. In 1945, Roosevelt agreed to protect the Saudi Royal Family in exchange for access to oil. President Carter solidified the agreement, saying very firmly in his 1980 State of the Union address that any attempt to cut that flow to the United States would be corrected "by any means necessary, including military force." To show that he meant business President Carter created the Rapid Deployment Joint Task Force, designed to deliver military strikes in the area of the Persian Gulf. Ronald Reagan prepared for a much more powerful military attack in the region by turning the Joint Task Force into a full-scale combat organization known as the U.S. Central Command (CENTCOM). Michael T. Klare, Professor of Peace and World Security Studies, Hampshire College, says that the US military "has come to serve as a global oil protection service, guarding pipelines, refineries, and loading facilities in the Middle East and elsewhere."[8]

In this context, remember that upon their arrival in Baghdad, US troops immediately seized and protected the Oil Ministry Headquarters, while turning their backs on looting in the schools, hospitals, and museums. The supreme irony hits one smack in the face: the very real possibility that we are fighting this seemingly endless war in Iraq—destroying the people, their will, their heritage, history, and the very land they live off of—so that we can procure more and more oil. To reach that goal of more oil, the military consumes enormous amounts of fuel and, in turn, spews into the atmosphere more and more greenhouse gases, along with other more lethal kinds of pollution. Such a self-defeating strategy ranks up there on the stupidity scale with the 50s nuclear deterrent policy that went by the apt acronym, MAD, Mutually Assured Deterrence, in which each side tried to stockpile as many nuclear missiles as possible. To start a war was to end the world, the argument went, making for an even crazier and endless scramble for each side to acquire more and more weapons of mass destruction.

And so with King's magic word in mind, let me return to the problem at hand, troop levels, attempting to address that question now with some specificity. In August 2006, President Bush reported that the number of troops in Iraq hovered somewhere between 140,000 and 160,000. Five months later, on January 10, 2007, Bush as commander-in-chief announced his new strategy: to supplement what he now said were the approximately 130,000 troops in Iraq with an additional 21,500. His projected supplement finally exceeded 35,000, with another 12,000 National Guard soldiers, deployed in June 2007, on top of that number.[9] That totals roughly 177,000 GIs, but who really knows what the actual number was, or what it finally turned out to be? General David Petraeus, the top military-commander in Iraq during the surge, promised the American people that they would know the exact figure by the end of May 2007. That date came and went, and Petraeus never revealed the magic number. Add to that 177,000, the troops in what the Pentagon commonly refers to as the "War Theater"—that is, Iraq and its neighboring countries—and that number increases by perhaps another 100,000, to a whopping 277,000.[10] On the campaign trail, even John McCain, a stout military man, could not get correct the number of troops in Iraq, setting the number around 130,000, or what he called pre-surge levels. Obama tried to correct him, but muffed it, as well, opting for the figure of 155,000 troops.[11]

That's the number of troops in Iraq. What about all our men and women in uniform? What's that number? The Congressional Research Service, quoting the Department of Defense's Contingency Tracking System, put the total deployment well past that figure—at 260,000.[12] Chalmers Johnson argues for a much higher total number. He gets there by first taking up the number of military bases. Citing the DoD's Base Structure Report, which itemizes and domestic military real estate, Johnson points out that, for the fiscal year ending 2003, the Pentagon owned or rented 702 bases in about 130 foreign countries. (Johnson also points out that the military, as he emphasizes it, "HAS another 6,000 bases in the United States and its territories.")[13]

These numbers, as large as they may appear, do not, as Johnson makes clear, include the bases that American forces currently occupy globally. The Base Report, for instance, does not mention garrisons in Kosovo, Afghanistan, Iraq, Israel, Kuwait, Kyrgyzstan, Qatar, and Uzbekistan. Johnson reaches this astonishing conclusion: "If there was an honest count, the actual size of our military empire would probably top 1,000 different bases in other people's countries, but no one—possibly even the Pentagon—knows the exact number for sure, although it has been distinctly on the rise in recent years."[14] Johnson rightly calls these bases America's colonies.

Indeed, for fiscal 2005, Johnson fixes the figure for overseas bases at 737, in the same number of foreign countries. (For fiscal 2007, the number rose to 823 overseas bases, and 86 in our territories.) Johnson maintains that, to determine the exact number of troops and equipment, we must add in the more than 500,000 soldiers, dependents, technicians, and civilian contractors, along with their rolling and flying stock that the United States has stationed at those bases in those foreign countries. According to Base Structure Report for 2005, the actual number of US military personnel—including those in the states—worldwide amounts to the following: 1,840,062 on active duty, supported by 473,306 DoD civil service employees, and 203,327 local hires. The actual number of personnel on active duty, including Afghanistan, in 2008 and 2009 easily exceeds the Pentagon's stated number of 1.4 or 1.5 million, to 2.5 million or perhaps even more.[15]

According to the Pentagon, our overseas bases contain 32,337 barracks, hangars, hospitals, and other buildings, which it owns, and another 16,527 that it leases or rents. The military occupies 687,347 acres overseas, and 29,819,492 acres worldwide—a total of some 30 million acres—making the Pentagon the world's largest landlord. To give some comparison here about those numbers, the Arctic Refuge began in 1923 with the United States Navy establishing Petroleum Reserve No. 4 in Northwest Alaska to ensure a continuing supply of oil for national security needs. The area totaled 23 million acres, 7 million acres less than what the military currently dominates overseas. Yellowstone Park has a bit over 2 million acres; Yosemite Park a little over 760,000 acres.

In the middle of his analysis of our military bases overseas, Chalmers Johnson adds this wonderfully wry observation: "Interestingly enough, the thirty-eight large and medium-sized American facilities spread around the globe in 2005—mostly air and naval bases for our bombers and fleets—almost exactly equals Britain's thirty-six naval bases and army garrisons at its imperial zenith in 1898. The Roman Empire at its height in 117 AD required thirty-seven major bases to police its realm from Britannia to Egypt, from Hispania to Armenia. Perhaps the optimum number of major citadels and fortresses for an imperialist aspiring to dominate the world is somewhere between thirty-five and forty." America is well situated to take over—everything.[16] Of course, these bases manufacture their own heavy amounts of pollution, a subject I take up in a later section of this essay.

But here, as with nearly every other subject that has to do with the military, the phrase "the bottom line," empties itself of any real meaning, for the military knows no bottom line. Try as hard as one might, a person cannot find a solid baseline for virtually any military subject, because in great part such certainty, as I mentioned earlier, does not exist. How much fuel does the military consume? No one knows for certain. Ten experts provide ten different answers; accounting practices within the branches of the military vary. The same levels of uncertainty hold for subjects like the numbers of vehicles, amount of munitions, and, as we have seen, for the heart of the military, the number of troops themselves.

And so when we say "the military" or "our sons and daughters in uniform" or "those in harm's way," these phrases point to no reality with any specificity. We pay for a military, but we have no idea of its size or scope or composition. We do not even know the places where they are stationed. As taxpayers, we own stock in a nefarious corporation that cooks its books until they are well done. When they get audited, they typically tell the auditors to go to hell.

Chalmers Johnson makes the point over and over again that the Pentagon itself may not know the answers to many of the questions I have raised so far. We would not allow such behavior in any other field or, dare I say, in any other profession. But then again it is exactly this kind of profligate waste and lack of accountability that has led to other recent disasters in this country, like the feeble attempt at restoring the lower wards in New Orleans following Hurricane Katrina, the greed in the unregulated financial markets, and the lost and forgotten people on our streets and behind bars in our jails and prisons. Very few people, if any, know the numbers of those homeless or those living in severe poverty in this country. But even if few people know, some people must care. And that number must grow. And hence this book.

I
POLLUTION: A SNAPSHOT

One question, and one question only, drives this essay: how much does the United States military add each year to worldwide pollution? To say it in a more pointed way: how much does the military contribute to that most dire and most imminent of crises, global warming? I am particularly interested in this question whenever the military ratchets up its presence, and that of course means the present moment, for, during times of war, the military's use of fossil fuel radically increases. In 1940, for example, the armed forces accounted for one percent of the nation's total energy consumption. Five years later, as World War II got underway, that number increased to twenty-nine percent.[17] And we have in the recent past declared war against at least two countries. We have tallied nearly eight years of war in Afghanistan, and six years in Iraq. That translates into nearly fourteen compound years of shooting, firing, dropping, exploding, and incinerating.

I have devoted the first part of this essay to the invasion, decimation, and subsequent occupation of Iraq. That was the war that at least captured the attention of some Americans for some time, which is to say for a time events in Iraq made the front page of a few of the country's major newspapers. Adding Afghanistan onto what I have found obviously increases the numbers, particularly toward the middle months of 2008 and into 2009, when the Taliban stepped up its attacks in and around Kabul. I also limit myself to the United States military. I could have easily picked the Israeli military or the Russian military, but I live in this country. Its actions represent me; I aim at making change here. So I first want to determine just how much damage America has visited on the planet these past six years since "Shock and Awe" began at 10:15, the evening of March 19, 2003, when, according to some sources, 1,700 aircraft—bombers, fighters, and other warships—flew roughly 1,400 strike sorties on critical targets, and fired 504 cruise missiles, directly into the heart of Baghdad.[18]

Those are the raw numbers and, as we know only too well, numbers make abstract the gruesome reality of maiming and killing human beings. Here's a personal, graphic account of that first night from a reporter embedded with the 332nd Air Expeditionary Wing. Notice how, even in an eyewitness account, the writer cannot escape the tyranny of numbers. After describing the gore and the stench, the impulse kicks in to list. Even the word decimation has the idea of number buried in the word—"to kill every tenth person":

> The attack crafts are flying low altitude missions in support of the ground troops now penetrating Iraq, carrying a 30mm Gatling gun that's capable of destroying enemy tanks by firing at the rate of 3,900 rounds per minute and dropping up to 16,000 pounds of bombs.
>
> On Friday evening, the first night of the so-called "shock and awe" phase of the war, 150 sorties from this base alone had been planned. But additional Iraqi missile launches and ground intelligence increased that effort to 250 sorties. By late Friday night, 2,000 coalition-wide sorties struck 1,000 different targets. For this base's part, the 250 sorties were the biggest launch it has executed for the duration of Operation Southern Watch and Operation Iraqi Freedom, but a bigger night was expected Saturday.

"Every airplane was associated with the 'shock and awe' posture across the entire field," said 332nd Wing Commander Col. Cesar Rodriguez. "North, south, east, and west, airpower sorties were delivered to generate the total 'shock and awe' and to continue to isolate the regime from its field of forces."

As Marines continued to battle in Basra, ground troops called in intelligence to the squadron operations center here, and a series of close-air-support sorties of A-10s, British Harriers, marine F-18s and F-16s responded.[19]

I am thrown back on the same basic urge, left to wonder just how many total rounds those planes actually fired. No one is telling: the numbers for munitions constitute one of the most carefully guarded and elusive of all military secrets. A spokesman for USCENTAF (United States Central Command, Air Force), in an e-mail response from a reporter to that very question—How many rounds did the military fire?—makes the point quite emphatically: "WE DO NOT REPORT CANNON ROUNDS." That spokesman's superior, Lt. Col. Jon Kennedy, followed that message with another, perhaps even testier one: "Glad to see you appreciate the tremendous efforts [my subordinate] has already expended on you. Trust me, it's probably much more significant than the relentless pursuit of the number of cannon rounds."[20] Whatever the number, it has to astronomic, and, for reasons I will talk about momentarily, absolutely lethal.

Some numbers the military does let us in on. From March 19 to April 9, 2003, for instance, according to the Air Force's own website, "the Air Force [flew] more than 30,000 sorties, including 12,000 strike sorties, and dropped more than 21,300 munitions, 70 percent of which were precision-guided."[21] Before the start of the war, Harlan Ullman, one of the authors of the military strategy originally known as "rapid dominance" and which later became known as "shock and awe," told a CBS reporter what he hoped for in those first two days. He said he expected the United States military to deliver eight hundred Tomahawk cruise missiles—one every four minutes, day and night, for the first forty-eight hours. Those 800 cruise missiles—each one weighing close to 3,000 pounds—add up to a whopping total of 1,200 tons, or 2,400,000 pounds of explosives![22]

How can we possibly fathom that number—2,400,000 pounds of explosives? And what does that term actually mean that we use so easily and with such facility—an explosive? What actually explodes? What lives? Who dies? Certainly, no one really knows like Iraqi families, who carry out their lives, or try to, directly beneath bombs that fall on their homes, or in the midst of IEDs (Improvised Explosive Devices) that blow up in their markets or mosques or schools. And for those who survive, many of them maimed and wounded, what kinds of chemicals do they find themselves breathing? What sort of poisoned water do they find themselves drinking? How much contaminated produce do they find themselves eating?

To answer these questions, we must consider more than greenhouse gases and the wholesale polluting of the atmosphere. We must concentrate on the earth itself, the grit and dirt upon which people walk, on which kids play, and in which farmers grow their fruits and vegetables. We have to think about two of the mightiest and most sacred rivers of the world—the Tigris and the Euphrates—and the fish that swim in them, or used to. And so I choose to look at the pollution of the land, the animals, the rivers, lakes, and the oceans, by the United States military.

Mesopotamia holds the distinction as one of the birthplaces of literacy in the world. In what we now call modern Iraq, archeologists uncovered a series of Sumerian tablets, incised with pictographs that date from around 3500 BCE. If only for that reason, historians have named the area "the cradle of civilization." Over the centuries, as one might imagine, the country has assembled hundreds of thousands of manuscripts and books. In the National Library of Iraq, the equivalent of our Library of Congress, over 500,000 printed books and serials went up in flames during the first weeks of the invasion; the Library considered 5,000 of those as rare. Iraq's National Archives, which contained documents dating from the Ottoman period, received heavy bombing damage the first weeks of the war, and lost a good deal of its contents. The Al-Awqaf Library, part of the Ministry of Religious Affairs, lost over 5,000 Islamic manuscripts to bombing and looting.[23]

According to one newspaper account, "many irreplaceable documents, photographs, maps and books—some centuries old—were either destroyed in the fighting or were stolen in the rampant looting that followed. A vital part of Iraq's culture seems to have disappeared forever."[24] The director-general of the library, Saad Iskander, lamented that the "library lost 60 percent of our state records and documents—they were either burned or damaged by water." He went to say that the Americans wiped out a big part of Iraqi culture in just the first few days of their occupation.[25]

I do not know how to count such destruction of centuries of manuscripts, books, and religious artifacts, in my calculation of pollution. Does the near wholesale eradication of a culture's founding heritage, literacy itself, along with its documents constitute a form of pollution, or at the very least, a form of severe and certain fallout? Do we have any category in the imagination for the wholesale eradication of a nation's history? What would we call such a monstrous act at such a base level? Does the destruction of the heart of literacy have repercussions on how other peoples in other countries now look at the idea of literacy? How could anyone possibly look at such acts squarely and deliberately and say no, this is all necessary if we are to win the hearts and minds of the people. A tyrant lived here and we are doing it for the people's own good, and someday they will come to see just that and thank us all. Here is another instance of that twisted logic of war where we use up oil to secure it. In our bombing, we destroy the Iraqis and their country in order to save them from their awful fate. This is utter madness.

Besides the birthplace of literacy, for many historians, Mesopotamia also serves as the place where agriculture began some thirteen centuries ago, and hence its name, the Fertile Crescent. Recall, the US invasion of Iraq started in the spring of 2003, on March 19th. Evidence suggests that military planners picked the time of the invasion with some heightened sense of perverted care. At that same time, the middle of March, Iraqi farmers typically harvest their barley and wheat fields in the Tigris River valley and plant their vegetables in the south. As Jeffrey St. Clair, one of the editors of *CounterPunch*, points out, in both 1991 and in 2003, "US bombing raids targeted cattle feed lots, poultry farms, fertilizer warehouses, pumping stations, irrigation systems, duel depots and pesticide factories—the very infrastructure of Iraqi agriculture." (Jeffrey St. Clair, "The Rat in the Grain—Dahn Amstutz and the Looting of Iraqi Agriculture, *CounterPunch*, July 4, 2003. See also Daniel Stone, "The Assault on Iraqi Agriculture—US Agribusiness Targets the Fertile Crescent, *Coastal Post*, August 2006.) In the spring of 2003, Americans made it impossible for farmers to harvest their grain before it rotted in the fields. St. Clair describes the fallout of our bombing as the slow starvation of a people: "The banks, which provide credit and cash, have been looted, irrigation systems destroyed, road travel restricted, markets closed, warehouses and grain silos pillaged…Iraqi farmers need more than eight million gallons of diesel fuel to power combines and harvesters. But most of the fuel depots were incinerated by US bombing strikes."

Again, I am at a loss to name this kind of pollution, where the fuel goes up in flames, and the population finds itself crippled by starvation. But in Iraq even this kind of pollution stands beside the point. For we have to confront more than ordinary pollution—if such a phrase is not in itself a contradiction—or even more than extraordinary pollution, and turn to the most grossly shocking form of pollution—radiation poisoning. A report from the United Nations Environment Program, dated 2004, estimates that at least four million pounds of low-level but radioactive dust, the residue from spent munitions made with depleted uranium, now covers a good portion of the deserts and cities of Iraq. Which means that a good deal of that country now hums with low-level radiation. How could that have happened? Or, to say it another way, how did we allow that to happen? In this country, why do we have to uncover this kind of horrendous information from blogs and websites rather than from the major newspapers, which, in their rush to support the war, either neglected or refused outright to cover such unspeakable acts?[26]

II
HOW MUCH FUEL?

I begin this part of the story with the combat vehicles, planes, and helicopters, and then only with a selection of them. The vital statistics for almost all armament—their type and number—remain highly classified. By one count, the United States Armed Forces currently commands the deserts and the neighborhoods of Iraq with about 30,000 vehicles.[27] According to its own figures, the DoD inventory of fleet vehicles worldwide—including passenger cars, buses, light trucks, and so on—totals 187,493, 13 percent of which it houses overseas.[28] The Army and Marine Corps own and operate their own tactical wheeled vehicles, such as 140,000 High-Mobility Multipurpose Wheeled Vehicles (the HMMWV, or HUMVEE). The Army also operates over 4,000 combat vehicles and several hundred fixed wing aircraft. Except for eighty nuclear submarines and aircraft carriers, the entire military fleet runs on oil.[29]

Armor often means the difference between living and dying, and so the Army relies on heavily armored machines like the HMMWV (M1114) and its seventeen variations, including the Guardian Armored Security Vehicle M1117 (popular with MPs), the Cougar HEV Armored Truck, the LAV (light armored vehicle), the ICV (infantry carrier vehicle), the Stryker troop carrier, the High Mobility

Multi-Purpose Wheeled Vehicle M1151, the Bradley Fighting Vehicle, the M-1 Abrams tank, and a behemoth called the Mine-Resistant Ambush-Protective vehicle, a thirty-ton armored bus for ferrying VIPs, and popularly known as the Rhino Runner. Military brass covet the Rhino Runner, for it holds the distinction as the most heavily armored, safest vehicle ever manufactured.[30]

I list here but a few of the vehicles in the Army's inventory. The military uses scores of other, more obscure tracked- and wheeled-vehicles as well. As you can imagine, such armored vehicles do not sit lightly on the ground. A United Nations Environment Program report about the first Gulf War points to the damage inflicted by seventy-ton tanks like the M-1 Abrams on the ecology of the desert: "Approximately fifty percent of Kuwait's land area has had its fragile soil surface destroyed as scores of tanks moved out of that country each day and headed for Iraq." Once the surface of the desert has broken apart, the report goes on, the wind has an easier job of eroding even more land mass.[31]

The military—the Army, Navy, and Air Force—leads the world, of course, in its wide range of flying machines, including fixed-wing attack jets, transport planes, helicopters, stealth bombers, and much more. Based on data provided by CENTAF, I count forty-three different types of fighter planes, eleven different kinds of attack planes, thirteen kinds of bombers, sixteen kinds of cargo planes, and nine different kinds of helicopters—all told, ninety-two different kinds of aircraft.[32]

Military brass also operates its own private airline, known as the Air Mobility Command or AMC. The Pentagon prefers to keep these planes, for the most part, off the record. The AMC consists of a fleet of long-range C-17 Globemasters, C-5 Galaxies, C-141 Starlifters, KC-135 Stratotankers, KC-10 Extenders, and C-9 Nightingales. As an additional perk, for generals and admirals, the military has on hand, for their private use, seventy-one Lear jets, thirteen Gulfstream IIIs, and seventeen Cessna Citation luxury jets.

These armored vehicles, planes, and luxury planes consume close to two million reported gallons of oil every day. As I have said, we are using up at an alarming rate the very commodity we have sworn to protect.[33] For Doctor King, recall, oil constitutes the full-time business of America in general. It should make sense to us, then, that the business of the military, both in times of peace and war, likewise, has to be oil itself. In the end, the United States must have access to as much oil as possible—it would love to own it all—to maintain its position as the most prosperous nation in the world. Indeed, since capitalism requires an ever-expanding market, the country must have more and more oil each year. The nation's appetite grows in concert with the market.

Of the Army's top ten gas-guzzlers, only the M-1 Abrams tank and the Apache helicopter are combat vehicles. As for the rest, ironically, the military needs most of these fuel-famished vehicles—along with a good number of its troops—for re-supplying its vast fleet of fuel-dependent combat vehicles and fighter planes. These support, or non-tactical, vehicles consume over half the fuel in the battlefield.[34] Fuel constitutes the lifeblood of these vehicles, and they require it in astonishing amounts, consume it with astonishing speed, and demand it with astonishing rapidity. To complicate things even more, the military currently uses fourteen different kinds of fuel products, from gasoline and diesel to a range of highly toxic jet fuels, either kerosene or naphtha-derived. Jet fuel—JP-8—accounts for more than fifty percent of total DoD fuel consumption.[35]

No wonder, then, that *The Energy Bulletin*, a clearing house for information regarding the peak global energy supply, for May 2007, can list the following astonishing facts:

> The US military is the largest consumer of energy in the world.... The DoD's total primary energy consumption in fiscal year 2006 was 1 quadrillion Btu [1,000,000,000,000,000]. It corresponds to only 1 percent of total energy consumption in USA. For those of you who think this is not much...Nigeria, with a population of more than 140 million, consumes as much energy as the US military. The DoD

per capita consumption (524 trillion Btu) is 10 times more than per capita energy consumption than China, or 30 times more than that of Africa.

The Energy Bulletin bases its numbers on a total of 1.4 million active duty military and civilian personnel.[36]

- The Pentagon is the largest single consumer of petroleum in the world, using enough oil in one year to run all of the transit systems in the United States for the next fourteen to twenty-two years. It is not, of course, just that our own military consumes inconceivable amounts of gasoline. The military also consumes one quarter of the world's jet fuel. A class at the University of Wisconsin, "Iraq and Our Energy Future," taught by Professor Zoltan Grossman, uncovered the following shocking bits of data: The world's militaries combined are responsible for an astonishing two-thirds of the ozone-depleting, greenhouse gas, chlorofluorocarbon, or CFC-113, released into the atmosphere. CFCs are highly persistent and highly toxic, and at one moment tore a hole in the ozone layer as large, in terms of square miles, as the Arctic itself. The Army and Air Force use CFC-113 as a cleaning solvent for tanks and airplanes. Doctor Helen Caldicott, the physician and anti-nuclear activist who started Physicians for Social Responsibility, believes the problem extends far beyond simple cleaning solvents. She indicts the military for releasing chlorofluorocarbons into the atmosphere during the process of enriching uranium for munitions.[37]

The one thing we do know with some certainty about the military is that fuel accounts for more than three-quarters of the Department of Defense's energy consumption. According to *The Energy Bulletin*, the Defense Energy Support Center (DESC), the agency charged with procuring all fuel products for all branches of the military, "purchases more light refined petroleum product that any other single organization or country in the world."[38] It should thus come as no surprise that the military also ranks as the largest single polluter of any single agency or organization in the world. Only three countries consume more oil per capita than the Department of Defense: Gibraltar, Netherland Antilles, and Singapore.[39] For just the first three weeks of combat in Iraq, the Army calculated that its branch alone would require more than 40 million gallons of fuel, an amount equivalent to the total gasoline used by all Allied Forces combined during the four years of World War I.[40] Or the amount of fuel that approximately 80,000 people burn through in an entire year's worth of driving.

For fiscal year 1999, the DESC spent its yearly budget of 3.5 billion dollars for 110 million barrels of petroleum products. That represents such a colossal amount of fuel, I feel compelled to let the DESC boast about its own numbers: "That's enough fuel for 1,000 cars to drive around the world 4,620 times—or 115.5 trillion miles." But, as staggering as that figure might sound, the DoD outdid itself in fiscal 2004. That year, the DESC almost doubled its purchases—by that time, we had two wars to support—spending 8.5 billion dollars for 144 million barrels of petroleum product. Since each barrel yields about 19.5 gallons of fuel, 144 million barrels of petroleum product equals nearly 2.8 billion gallons of gasoline![41]

The United States Department of Transportation Statistical Records Office places the number of vehicles registered in this country at 62 million. According to the EPA, the average driver goes through 500 gallons of fuel a year, which means that sixty-two million vehicles, collectively, consume approximately 31 billion gallons of fuel for the year. The DoD's 2.8 billion gallons of fuel would keep almost ten percent of those vehicles, 5.6 million of them, running for the entire year.

The DESC's 144 million barrels of oil for the year averages out to about 395,000 barrels per day, almost as much as the daily energy consumption of Greece.[42] But those numbers do not, in the end, mean very much. While researching any military subject presents enormous difficulties for the layperson, the most convoluted and messy one surely must be fuel. Several major factors make it impossible to uncover actual numbers for fuel consumption, so that the number of barrels a day that the military uses—a number deliberately well hidden—has to be a good deal higher than the reported 395,000 barrels a day—much closer to 500,000 barrels per day, and, as I want to show, probably much higher than that—in fact, nearly triple that figure, to one million barrels a day or more.

To begin, the DoD provides no official accounting for the amount of oil the military consumes in garrisons and bases abroad. And that figure may be substantial. Tom Cutler, former head of NATO's Petroleum Planning Committee, says that as much as "one-third of US military consumption occurs outside US territorial boundaries." The Pentagon does not count that fuel in its published figure of 144 million barrels. If Cutler is anywhere near accurate, we need to add at least another 45 or 50 million barrels per year to the total, or around 150,000 barrels a day. That would immediately raise the daily military consumption to around 550,000 barrels a day.

There's more. None of the official Pentagon figures include fuel that the military obtains at no cost overseas. And, again, that number may be fairly substantial. Kuwait has been the largest supplier of such fuel, providing US troops with free fuel from the start of the Gulf War in 2003. According to an article in *Agence France-Presse*, for March 17, 2000, "Kuwait supplied the United States military with fuel at no cost." But after two years, the Kuwaitis began to rethink their on-going largesse and, when America ousted Saddam Hussein, they decided that they should get paid for their fuel.[43] The London-based pan-Arab newspaper, *Al-Hayat*, reported that, in March 2005, the Kuwaiti government demanded a payment of 500 million dollars for the fuel it had supplied to the US Army from March 2003 to fall 2005. The Emirate had settled on a preferential price for the United States of twenty-one dollars a barrel.

No matter the discount, then Secretary of Defense, Donald Rumsfeld, wrote an indignant letter back to Kuwaiti's energy minister, Sheik Ahmed Fahd Al Ahmed Sabah. Rumsfeld made it clear that Washington had liberated the Emirate from Iraqi occupation in 1991 and now, because Kuwait enjoys a fiscal surplus, he saw no need for Kuwait to demand any payment for a single drop of that fuel.[44]

If the Kuwaiti numbers are anywhere near correct—and Rumsfeld never disputes those figures in his letter—we need to add an additional 75,000 barrels a day to our running total of 550,000 barrels.[45] The number then grows from the official 395,000 or 400,000 barrels a day, to roughly 625,000 barrels a day, already an increase of over 50 percent. No military source has revealed whether Kuwait is continuing to supply that free fuel or not, or even if it now supplies fuel at a cost, and how much it supplies. One can only wonder. And the chase for answers and accuracy goes on.

For the DoD's numbers also omit fuel consumed by independent contractors, by leased and privatized facilities, and by all the rented and leased fleet vehicles. What shall we add for all those extras to the stated number? Conservatively, perhaps, another 100,000 or 150,000 barrels a day? That would now bring us to 725,000 or more barrels a day. Given that each barrel yields 19.5 gallons, all the branches of the military consume on the order of 14.5 million gallons of fuel every day. At this point, its fuel consumption would rank it with the daily use of nations like Singapore, Australia, Thailand, and the Netherlands. (Australia has a population of 20.5 million people, the Netherlands 26.6 million and Thailand 61.5 million people. Remember, the military has a stated 1.4 or 1.5 million soldiers on active duty.) And I have not yet included the most significant and probably largest omission that prevents anyone from finding out the military's total number of barrels.

The Pentagon employs a different accounting practice for the fuel that the Navy uses when it operates in international waters, adding yet another level of murkiness to an already opaque problem. Indeed, no one outside the Pentagon, and maybe no one *inside* the Pentagon, can say with any certainty just how much fuel the Navy actually uses. (Some critics of military fuel efficiency say that the Navy's figures may even be higher than the largest consumer of fuel of all the armed services: the Air Force.) For the Pentagon places the fuel it designates for consumption in international waters—that which the Navy primarily uses in its ships on the open seas—in a separate category called International Bunker Fuel.

International Bunker Fuel—or more accurately called Bunker Oil—remains totally off the record, ghost stuff, as unidentified as the prisoners the United States keeps confined at Guantanamo Bay. I should note that even in the case of civilian commercial shipping, for the purposes of greenhouse emissions inventories, the United States subtracts data about International Bunker Fuel from its national totals. How large, then, is the military Bunker number? Who knows? My figure for the military of 725,000 or more barrels a day, which at the outset may have sounded extreme, could, in fact, turn out to be a quite conservative estimate. The final number might run as high as one million barrels a day, or close to half a billion barrels a year. I settle on that figure of one million as a safe, and even conservative, number.

Again, using the figure of 19.5 gallons of fuel that each barrel of oil yields, at a million barrels a day, the military would wind up using close to 20 million gallons of fuel each and every day. If that indeed turns out to be the case, the United States military would then rank in fuel consumption with countries like Indonesia, Iran, and Spain. Only fourteen countries, including the United States, would exceed those military numbers. It is truly an astonishing accomplishment, especially when one considers, once again, that the military has only about 1.5 million troops on active duty, and Iran has a population of 66 million, Indonesia a whopping 235 million.

The military is thus consuming fossil fuel out of proportion to nations 200 times its size. We have been doing this steadily for years and years. Surely, we do not think that the rest of the world does not notice. We should not be surprised that our country inspires deep feelings of envy, hatred, and even outright aggression. The former president told us that the extremists hate our democratic way of life. I think they hate our imperial way of life.

In the end, however, no military official, and no independent scholar seems to know the answer to what would seem like two straightforward questions: How much fuel are we, American citizens, purchasing to keep the armed services running at full speed, and thus to keep 300 million Americans safe and secure? And, two, how much are we paying for that fuel? (Of course I am asking, how much greenhouse gases are we willing to pump into the atmosphere, around the world, for that so-called protection?) As for the first question, the most honest conclusion may come from one critical observer, who has followed the intricacies of military fuel consumption very closely, for a fairly long time: "The reality is that even the U.S. Department of Defense (DoD) does not know precisely where and how much energy it consumes."[46]

And for the second, but related, question—"How much do Americans pay for that fuel?"—we can say quite generally that military fuel does not come cheap. In 2002, at something called the Tactical Wheeled Vehicles Conference, General Paul Kern, head of the Army Materiel command, revealed that the actual cost of fuel, depending on how it got delivered, could range anywhere from a low of 1 dollar to a high of 400 dollars per gallon. The average, he allowed, hovered around an astonishing 300 dollars a gallon.[47]

III
"BIGGER, FASTER, AND MORE SOPHISTICATED WEAPONS": FUEL EFFICIENCY

Military vehicles have utterly no respect for CAFE (Corporate Average Fuel Economy) standards, or fuel standards of any kind. After all, we are at war; fuel economy is a luxury. But war or not, military vehicles exist in a world apart from conservation of any kind. One hears talk these days from military planners about the desire for more fuel-efficient vehicles and the need for alternative fuels. Think about what that actually means: a cleaner, more efficient way of killing human beings. As if moving from the single shot rifle to an automatic made for a better society. How bizarre to think about installing "an environmentally sensitive culture" inside the military. We might then boast to the Iraqis: Notice how little fuel we consumed to destroy your homeland. The reasoning is absurd.

The topic is, finally, of little real concern for the Pentagon. Indeed, the military refers to fuel consumption in terms of "gallons per mile," "gallons per minute," and "barrels per hour." One quickly realizes that military "assets," as the Pentagon likes to call its rolling arsenal, have to operate in a world all their own, free of restraints of any kind—both in the fuel they consume and the pollutants they exhaust. For example, the High Mobility Multi-Purpose Wheeled Vehicle, the Humvee, gets four miles per gallon. But that's amazingly fuel efficient compared with the stalwart of all the fighting vehicles, the M-1 Abrams tank, which, according to the military's own spec sheets, gets .2 miles per gallon, or, stated another way, requires five gallons of fuel to cover a single mile. Just firing up the tank's turbine requires ten gallons of fuel. During battle, over ideal terrain, the Abrams can go through roughly 7 barrels, or 252 gallons—usually of JP-8 jet fuel— each and every hour (a barrel of oil yields more gallons of diesel and jet fuel than it does of regular gasoline). It takes nearly 500,000 gallons a day to supply an armored division of 348 tanks. The Army tries to keep its entire inventory of Abrams tanks up and running in Iraq—all 1,838 of them.

The Army's principle flying machine, the Apache helicopter, blows through fuel at an astonishing rate. Powered by two General Electric gas-turbine engines, each rated at 1,890-horsepower, the Apache gets about one-half mile to the gallon. Just 1 pair of Apache battalions in a single night's raid will consume about 60,000 gallons of jet fuel.[48]

Feeding the appetites of these voracious machines, with gasoline or diesel orkerosene, requires intricate logistical planning and support from some 2,000 trucks, a battery of computers, another 20,000 GIs, and, according to an Associated Press article for September 2007, as many as 180,000 workers under federal contracts, perhaps more contract workers, in fact, than soldiers.[49] Over thirty private security companies operate in Iraq, including the major ones like Blackwater USA, Triple Canopy; Kellogg, Brown & Root; DynCorp International; and the Vinnell Corporation. The largest of them, however, is not even American, but British, named the Aegis Defense Services. The Department of Defense awarded Aegis with the largest security catch up to that time, May 2004—"a massive $293 million, three-year contract."[50]

Many of the contract workers—especially those employed by Blackwater—served formerly as military Special Forces troops, such as Navy Seals and the Army's Delta Force. The Seals conduct their operations guided by the philosophy of "spray and pray"—shoot first and hope to God that you have hit the right target—a credo that seems to underlie a good deal of the behavior of the mercenaries working for Blackwater USA. The company's CEO, Erik Prince, left a career appointment in the Seals to start what is now a billion-dollar federal contracting firm, Blackwater USA. After the uproar over some of his men who "sprayed" to death seventeen innocent Iraqis on September 16, 2007 in Baghdad, the *Wall Street Journal* reported that Erik Prince no longer cared about the security business. He intended, instead, to expand into a "full spectrum" defense contractor, the *Journal* went on, offering "one-stop shopping" for anything and everything the military might need, from unmanned planes to tanks and ammunition.[51]

The Navy uses an enormous amount of that fuel. The Navy's battleships consume sixty-eight barrels per hour. No match for its nonnuclear aircraft carriers, which burn approximately 134 barrels per hour.[52] Rear Admiral Eugene Carroll, Jr., retired from the US Navy and now part of the Center for Defense Information, a think-tank based in Washington, DC, served as the commander of the carrier the *USS Independence*. Talking about his ship, Carroll provided a picture of the staggering amounts of fuel that those huge vessels require. Keep in mind that the Independence weighs 81,000 tons fully loaded, and stretches almost 3.5 football fields in length. The ship gets its power from four 70,000 shp steam turbines.

In 1991, Admiral Carroll boasted that,

> while stationed off the coast of Vietnam, the ship [*USS Independence*] consumed 100,000 gallons of fuel a day. Every four days the *Independence* took on a million gallons of new fuel—half of which went to supply the carrier's jet aircraft. Steaming to the Persian Gulf in fourteen days, the Independence would consume more than two million gallons of fuel. Simply "standing by" in the Gulf, the carrier must still consume oil at a voracious pace in order to purify 380,000 gallons of fresh water daily and produce enough electricity to power the equivalent of a city of 40,000 people.

While the Navy decommissioned the forty-year-old *Independence* at the end of September 1998, Carroll's testimony offers some evidence of the almost unimaginable appetites of the Navy's huge aircraft carriers.[53]

According to the US Navy Official Website, as of November 2007, the Navy had 335,000 personnel on active duty, an inventory of 4,000 airplanes and helicopters, and most important, 285 combat and support ships.[54] The DoD keeps classified the number and kinds of vessels stationed in the Gulf. But, we do know that President Bush ordered the *USS Stennis* and the *USS Ronald Reagan* to the Gulf in January 2007 as part of the surge. He also sent a "strike group," led by the nuclear aircraft carrier the *USS Eisenhower*, along with a cruiser, a destroyer, a frigate, a submarine escort, and a supply ship.

Already sitting in the Gulf were ten other "Carrier Task Forces" built around the aircraft carriers *Kitty Hawk, Constellation, Enterprise, John F. Kennedy, Chester W. Nimitz, Carl Vinson, Theodore Roosevelt, George Washington, Harry S. Truman,* and the *Abraham Lincoln.*"[55] On the subject of naval build-up, Chalmers Johnson reports that "to dominate the oceans and seas of the world, we are creating some thirteen naval task forces built around aircraft carriers whose names sum up our military heritage—*Kitty Hawk, Constellation, Enterprise, John F. Kennedy, Nimitz, Dwight D. Eisenhower, Carl Vinson, Theodore Roosevelt, Abraham Lincoln, George Washington, John C. Stennis, S. Truman,* and *Ronald Reagan.*"

The *USS Abraham Lincoln*—familiar to us as the ship on whose deck President Bush declared to the nation, on May 2, 2003, his famous (or infamous) phrase, "Mission Accomplished"—remains in service, but the military keeps classified all the numbers about its fuel consumption. The *USS Lincoln* helped deliver the opening salvos and air strikes in Operation Iraqi Freedom. From March 2003 until mid-April of that same year, during its deployment in the Gulf, the Navy launched 16,500 sorties from its deck, and fired 1.6 million pounds of ordnance from its guns.[56]

Of all the branches, the Air Force, by every account, uses the most fuel.[57] In 2006, for instance, the Air Force consumed nearly half of the DoD supply, 2.6 billion gallons of jet fuel, the same amount of fuel US planes consumed during World War II from December 1941 to August 1945.[58] Any of the Air Force's large helicopters—the Sea Stallion, Super Stallion, Sea Dragon, or Pave Low III—suck up five gallons every mile. But that's nothing compared with the fighter planes. The F-4 Phantom Fighter uses 40 barrels of fuel per hour, or more than 1,600 gallons, each and every hour.[59] At peak thrust, the F-15 uses about 25 gallons per minute, or 1,580 gallons per hour; the F-16 Fighter Jet uses a bit more, 28 gallons per minute or 1,680 gallons per hour—as much fuel in that 1 hour as in 3 years of driving for the average American!

Tom Cutler, whom we met earlier as head of NATO's Petroleum Advisory Committee, writing in the *Armed Forces Journal International* (Spring 2004) points out, that to reach supersonic speeds, a pilot must turn on the plane's afterburners, which can triple a jet's speed and increase fuel consumption twenty times. With its afterburners kicked in, for example, "the F-15 torches fuel at the astounding rate off 4 gallons per second—14,400 gallons per hour. And as the military opts for bigger, faster, and more sophisticated weapons, fuel efficiency continues to plummet."[60]

As astounding and shocking as that figure may sound—14,400 gallons an hour—the principle gas hog award goes to the B-52 Stratocruiser, which has 8 jet engines, and zips through an astonishing 86 barrels of fuel, or roughly 3,334 gallons per hour. That's with no afterburners. That number represents the plane's standard fuel use, hour after hour. Imagine: 500 gallons per minute! In just ten of those minutes, the B-52 gulps down the same amount of fuel that the average driver consumes over one year of driving.[61]

To keep the B-52 or the F-111 in the air for extended periods of time requires in-flight re-fueling. According to Janet Ginsberg, of *Business Week* magazine, the Air Force—the military's largest consumer, at two billion gallons a year—spends most of its fuel-delivery budget refueling planes in the air, at a cost of $17.50 per gallon....Fuel efficiency has never been a military priority, largely because the Pentagon's accounting system considers fuel purchase costs separately from delivery costs. That may have played a role in a 1997 decision by the Air Force not to install more efficient engines in the B-52H bomber.[62]

The B-52H Bomber, the plane to which Ginsberg refers, is nicknamed the Stratofortress by the military. While it holds an enormous 47,975 gallons of fuel, it still requires mid-air refueling. That's the job of the aerial refueling tankers, the KC-135 Stratotanker and the larger KC-10 Extender, which carries twice as much fuel as the Stratotanker—about 356,000 pounds, or close to 60,000 gallons. The Air Force owns both of these flying gas stations. It also owns 94 of those B-52H long-range bombers. Using EPA standards for yearly automobile fuel consumption, the amount of fuel that the KC-10 carries would keep the average family car—which uses, you will recall, on average about 500 gallons a year—running for approximately 118 years—in other words, a couple of lifetimes of driving.

The Pentagon makes public very few statistics about the B-52H and F-117 Stealth fighter planes, except to boast that the B-52H can carry 16 of the 2000-pound laser-guided bombs or 80 of the 500-pound laser-guided bombs. It is remarkable that we even know that the Stealth fighters exist. The number and kinds of vehicles, and planes housed at those 860 American bases in foreign countries, also remain a mystery. We can assume, with confidence, however, that those bases run through a considerable number of barrels of fuel.

20miles

100GAL.

20miles **1**GAL.

IV
HOW MUCH POLLUTION?
AN AWFUL LOT

While we may not know the exact figures for military pollution, we can, nonetheless, reach an approximate figure. We do know, with a greater degree of certainty, the numbers for America's civilian fuel consumption. I use that number here as a baseline to help us understand the magnitude of the military's demands on fossil fuels. The United States leads the world in oil consumption, using approximately 20.6 million barrels of oil daily.[63] (Forty percent of that oil—roughly 9.1 million barrels—Americans devote to one use only: powering their motor vehicles.) The petroleum industry's publication, *The Alaska Pipeline*, offers this revealing statistic: "Americans use more oil for their motor vehicles than the total combined amounts used by Russia, Canada, the United Kingdom and France."

But an even more shocking statistic is that, while the United States represents about five percent of the world population—about 330 million people—it consumes a quarter of the world's oil. Daily oil consumption for the entire world totals about 82 million barrels a day. Five percent of that figure—America's percentage of the world population—would mean that America should consume a little more than 4 million barrels a day, which would drop us from the number one slot, down to the third most thirsty country in the world, just slightly behind Japan, a nation that, with 127 million people, currently consumes 5.6 million barrels of oil each day.

China, with a population more than four times that of the United States, now ranks second to the United States in oil consumption, even though it uses about a third less, around 6.5 million barrels a day. (I have more to say about the economic aspirations of China and its potential fuel use later.) Russia, with a population of 142 million—that is, with half the population of the United States—uses one-tenth as much as we do, 2.5 million barrels per day. Canada, with a population of just over 33 million people, uses a little over 2 million barrels of oil a day, but consumes fuel at roughly the same per capita rate as the United States.

One way of understanding those 20-plus million barrels of oil that Americans consume each day is to convert them into something more understandable, like gallons of fuel. Each barrel of oil ends up yielding approximately 19.5 gallons of fuel. In this country, then, each and every day, roughly 400 million gallons of fuel disappear, seemingly without a trace, out the tailpipe of some vehicle or out the smokestack of some machine or factory. As wild as it sounds, each gallon of gasoline, which weighs about six pounds, more than triples its weight when it burns, ending up in the atmosphere as some 19.4 pounds of carbon. Which is to say that each gallon of gasoline produces over three times its weight in deadly gases that help seal the fate of the planet. According to the last census numbers, America has 100 million households. Each household, then, on average, consumes 4 gallons of gasoline a day, and is responsible for polluting the atmosphere with almost eighty pounds of carbon every day, just from the burning of fossil fuel. That does not include electricity and natural gas, which we must add to the total pollution numbers, as well.

As of April 2007, as I mentioned before, the military counted a little over 1.4 million people on active duty—the actual number may be much higher—which amounts to something like .005 percent of the total civilian population. If the military used fuel in the same proportion as the entire civilian population in the United States, then we could expect it to consume about 100,000 barrels of oil per day. We know it consumes at least something in the order of ten times that figure.[64]

Keep in mind that the US civilian population already consumes fuel at a rate dramatically out of all proportion to the population of the country—staggeringly greater than almost every other country in the world. Which says, of course, to a large part of the world—particularly to its poorest people—that America gobbles up the world's treasures with an appetite so monstrously greedy that it has absolutely no regard for the rest of the world. Knowing the way America gluts itself on fuel, here is an informative comparison: Each man, woman and child in this country consumes on average 1.3 gallons per day. Now comes the shocker: for 2007, each deployed soldier consumed almost 12 times the civilian amount, about 15 gallons of fuel a day. (In Vietnam, the figure reached 9 gallons a day for each soldier; in Operation Desert Storm that number rose slightly, to 10 gallons for each soldier.)[65]

The only way I know how to make military pollution in any way tangible in this essay is through numbers, but, as with almost every other military subject, the Department of Defense provides little or no data for its many thousands of vehicles. On top of that, while the great majority of vehicles burn gasoline, others use diesel, and still others use one form or another of jet fuel. In addition, a utility vehicle like the Abrams Tank can burn whatever is available, making it even more difficult to determine exact CO_2 numbers. With those caveats in mind, I forge ahead. I base my calculations of CO_2 pollution on the United States Environmental Protection Agency's fact sheet EPA420-F-05-003, dated February 2005, on greenhouse gas emissions from passenger vehicles. According to the EPA, each gallon of gasoline produces 19.4 pounds of CO_2; each gallon of diesel produces 22.2 pounds of CO_2. The average passenger vehicle, the EPA estimates, travels a total of 12,000 miles per year, and, at speeds not exceeding sixty miles per hour, gets 23.9 miles per gallon. In the process, that vehicle consumes approximately 500 gallons of gasoline, and emits a little over 10,000 pounds (5.5 metric tons) of the green-house gas, carbon dioxide.

If we think about these numbers in terms of pollution, the entire country pumps into the atmosphere a staggering 8 billion pounds of greenhouse gases each and every day, which translates into 4 million tons daily. If I use the figure that I have calculated as more nearly the correct one for the military, 1 million barrels of oil a day, then the combined armed forces sends into the atmosphere about 400 million pounds of greenhouse gases a day, or 200,000 tons. That totals 146 billion pounds a year—or 73 million tons of carbon a year. The military's pollution represents an additional five percent that we must factor into this country's total pollution number. So, instead of the United States producing twenty-five percent of the world's pollution—already a shockingly high number—this country sends aloft a bit more than thirty percent of the world's greenhouse gases.

But here's something perhaps even more shocking and insidious than the military's raw numbers: As alarming as those numbers might seem, few if any citizens have ever seen them, or will ever see them. Raw data about the military's fuel consumption simply do not factor into the 400 million gallons of fuel that the country consumes each and every day; and they do not figure into any of the pollution figures that this country makes public. Military numbers remain off of any official reports, secret and out of sight. They appear nowhere public. It is like having another, albeit smaller, shadow country located right within our borders, but over which, it would appear, we have absolutely no control and about which, it would also appear, we can do absolutely nothing.

And I am talking here only about the most obvious form of pollution, that which comes from the burning of fossil fuels: greenhouse gases. The building of military bases consumes a great deal of fuel, especially those the size of our major military installations in Baghdad, and of our mega-air base in Balad, where the "daily air traffic pile-ups," according to Nick Turse, resemble those "one might see over Chicago's O'Hare."[66] As of the end of 2005, the US occupied

106 separate bases in Iraq, ranging in size from the gigantic Camp Victory complex near Baghdad's International Airport, which houses command headquarters, to a few small outposts.[67]

Summer temperatures in Iraq can soar to 110 or 120 degrees and things begin heating up as early as April, which presents particular problems. The military employs huge and complicated air conditioning systems for cooling water so it can be drunk, for cooling command centers to make them habitable, and for cooling sophisticated computers to make them operable. Some GIs are lucky enough to have air-conditioned tents. To keep planes flying in such intense heat requires even more complicated and sophisticated systems of air conditioning. The Air Force employs something called the "multi-man intermittent cooling system"—"a large air-conditioning unit equipped with ten long hoses to pump cool air into the chemical warfare suits worn by runway workers."[68] A great deal of fuel goes to running small and large generators in Iraq to keep air conditioners running at top speed twenty-four hours a day for months on end. We can only guess at the CO_2 emissions, and other pollutants, produced by such massive and complicated air conditioning systems.

Exploding bombs and cluster bombs, cannon rounds, napalm, and depleted uranium, all represent other and, in many cases, even more horrendous and deadly kinds of pollution, some forms of which persist in the atmosphere and in the earth and in human beings seemingly forever. This list does not include small arms rounds, and here the estimated numbers, once again, turn out to be staggering. For instance, for one year alone, the military estimates that it will need 1.5 billion rounds of small ammunition for their M-16 rifles. The Army now purportedly manufactures what it calls "green ammo," which has tungsten instead of lead cores in its 5.56 mm bullets.[69] Army officials add, however, that the change will improve the kill rate since the new ammunition allows for more accurate firing. Or, as one Army official put it: "Don't let 'environmentally friendly' fool you: The new rounds proved slightly more accurate than the lead versions during testing."[70]

One of the ironies of war is that, while we can calculate the pollution created by the explosion of bombs and the destruction of the infrastructure, we also have to calculate the pollution created—the fuel consumed—in rebuilding those destroyed buildings and institutions. To make thing worse, targeted bombing involves blowing up highly volatile and extremely strategic sites like fuel and weapons depots, power plants, fertilizer plants, and chemical plants, releasing much more toxic waste into the atmosphere, obviously, than do residences and normal factories.

But, once again, bear in mind that no source I can find knows, with any degree of certainty, anything approximating an exact number for the military's fuel consumption—and no military official seems willing, or perhaps even able, to reveal that magic number. Even the Energy Information Administration, listed by the federal government as the Official Energy Statistics for the United States Government, carries the following, thoroughly understated warning: "Estimating, even roughly, the quantity of oil consumed for overseas military operations is an uncertain procedure."

In addition, we should also realize that the numbers I present here reflect only the most basic of greenhouse emissions—carbon. As I want to show in the course of this essay, the military's ability to pollute the environment extends far beyond the most common greenhouse gas, CO_2. In fact, in the twisted world of war, CO_2 may represent the most benign of the military pollutants. As I intend to show, the armed forces pumps into the ecological system more lethal, and much more long-lasting toxins in the course of its normal daily operations.

In a year, the average driver, as I have said, produces what seems like nothing compared with the military, a mere 10 thousand pounds. The military pollution for one year equals that which some 14.6 million cars produce driving for an entire year. And, the military has been pumping at least this much additional CO_2, probably close to 146 billion pounds of carbon—73,000 tons—into the atmosphere in Iraq, every year, for the past six years, and in Afghanistan every year, for the past seven-plus years. And, as I have also said, this represents only the pollutants most familiar to the average person—namely carbon. Other fuels that the military employs complicate my figures on total pollution.

For instance, Bunker Oil pollutes more viciously than other fuels. Even the petroleum industry itself refers to Bunker Oil as "dirty fuel." One can easily see the reason for that designation: After they complete the process of refining the oil, refiners produce Bunker Fuel from the thick sludge that remains literally at the bottom of the barrel. Environmentalists describe Bunker Fuel as more than 1,000 times dirtier than the diesel fuel that trucks and buses burn. Bunker spills in the ocean, in places like Alaska and California, have created environmental nightmares, killing not just birds and fish, but plant and coral life on the ocean floor.[71] Because of its potential to kill off marine life so ferociously, environmental groups in California, and other states, have called for its ban, at least within coastal waters.

Bunker Oil contains a higher concentration of sulfur than other diesel fuels, and so pollutes not just by leaving behind CO_2, but SO_2 (sulfur dioxide), as well. The two gases in combination form a thicker layer in the atmosphere and hold the sun's heat in more tenaciously, and thus do more damage to the environment than any one of the gases in isolation. In actuality, then, the military may not only be consuming two or three times more fuel than the DoD's stated 350,000 barrels per day, or even higher, but it may also may be polluting the earth more intensely and more perniciously than anyone knows or can discover.

Ships pollute beyond merely using Bunker Oil. Besides spreading the ocean surface with its own CO_2, SO_2, and residual oil, sea-going vessels create something called "Ship Tracks" that tail off, like vapor trails, in the atmosphere and have the potential for changing the microstructure of marine stratiform clouds. Made up of sulfur dioxide, nitrous oxide, and water molecules from both diesel-powered and steam-turbine powered ships, these long-lived clouds, according to some studies, help to intensify the greenhouse effect, once again, by locking in place the CO_2 in the atmosphere.

The military is now using more and more of the high-powered and highly toxic JP-8 jet fuel for many of its vehicles. According to environmentalists like George Monbiot, aircraft represent the fastest and most pernicious growing source of carbon dioxide emissions. Monbiot makes the point that aviation fuel has something called a "radiative forcing ratio of around 2.7." What this means, he explains, is that, because of the added nitrous oxide, soot, sulfur dioxide and water particles, "the total warming effect of aircraft emissions is 2.7 times as great as the effect of the carbon dioxide alone. The water vapor they produce forms ice crystals in the upper troposphere which trap the earth's heat."[72]

But we must proceed with caution here, for the truth is that scientists do not understand the full effects on the atmosphere of gases emitted by airplanes, which is to say that airplanes may prove even more destructive to the atmosphere than anyone knows or guesses. The Oak Ridge National Laboratory claims that "current emissions measurement methodology is not suitable for ultra fine particles that are the dominant species in the aircraft exhaust. The fate and transport of the precursor gases and the ultra fine particles in the reactive plume of aircraft exhaust are not well understood at the present."[73]

Some things, however, are fairly certain. For instance, several studies have pointed out the serious health risks to GIs from contamination by JP-8. One of those studies reached the following conclusion: "JP-8 is less volatile than its predecessor on skin and clothing which may result in prolonged exposure. The slowly evaporating JP-8 fuel tends to linger on exposed personnel during their interaction with their previously unexposed colleagues."[74] Another study, undertaken by the Department of Microbiology and Immunology, in 1997, at the University of Arizona, Tucson, reports that chronic exposure to jet fuel can adversely affect liver function, result in emotional dysfunction, cause abnormal electroencephalograms, shorten attention span, and decrease sensorimotor speed. Exposure to JP-8 can further compromise the immune system, causing alterations so profound and long-lasting, the study goes on to warn, that they can result in "an increased likelihood of development and/or progression of cancer, as well as autoimmune diseases."[75] The DoD has paid no attention to the report, advising only that GIs handling the fuel over long periods of time wear gloves.

And, once again, we must ask about carbon from those planes. Kerosene—jet fuel—puts considerably more carbon per gallon into the atmosphere than gasoline or diesel. The environmental action group World Changing calculates that "a 5,000 mile flight...puts out a ton and half of CO_2 *for every person on the plane*" (italics theirs).[76] Serious environmentalists are starting to talk about a total ban on air travel as a possible result of carbon overload. If a Boeing 747-100, say, holds roughly 450 passengers, the carbon output for a flight from New York to Los Angeles totals almost 1,350,000 pounds, or 675 tons. At altitude, airplanes spew not only carbon dioxide, but also nitrous oxide, sulfur dioxide, soot, and water vapor, a combination that may triple their total warming effect on the climate—the radiative effect that Monbiot and others warn us against. For that reason, some climate scientists refer to flying as "carbon overload." (Supersonic aircraft create pollution 5.4 times more corrosive to the environment than conventional aircraft.)

Trying to calculate CO_2 pollution for military flying is once again one of those instances of trying to make informed estimates. For one thing, if we consider the Stealth F-117, we know next to nothing about its fuel consumption. We do know, however, that sorties for that plane at the beginning of the Iraq War lasted 1.6 hours. Flying out of some distant bases raised the average sortie time to 5.4 hours, with some sorties lasting up to 7 hours—refueling accomplished in the air. There were 42 F-117s, each flying over 1,300 combat sorties. Using an average of 5 hours per sortie, at 619 miles per hour, time in the air for just this type of plane comes to 190,827,000 miles, resulting in an astonishing 26 million tons of carbon. To get some idea of the magnitude of that number, it would take a fully loaded Boeing

747-100, flying from Los Angeles to New York, 328,165 trips to produce that same amount of pollution. On average, 40 flights leave from LAX for JFK daily, so those 328,165 trips, in commercial terms, would take 8,204 days, or almost 23 years. Sixty other kinds of planes flew sorties over Iraq. The total amount of carbon dioxide that went into the atmosphere is not just high—but goes totally unreported.

A draft report prepared by the Bush administration for the United Nations, released in March 2007 (but due one year earlier, in January 2006), estimates that for the United States the emissions of greenhouse gases will rise from 7.7 billion tons in 2000 to 9.2 billion tons in 2020—an increase of 19.5 percent. James Connaughton, Chairman of the White House Counsel on Environmental Quality, the office responsible for the report, points out that the biggest source of the gases, about 84 percent, results from the burning of fossil fuels, chiefly oil, coal, and natural gas.[77] Since the report includes no category for the military, it remains entirely silent on the amount of greenhouse gases that the military has pumped into the atmosphere, twenty-four hours a day, every day, for the past six years in Iraq, and for the past seven-plus years in Afghanistan, and in other places that we hear nothing about. With over 800 of those bases overseas, we cannot know about them all. But we occasionally hear about some of them when the local people decide they have had enough and want the military off their land.

Those military bases, of course, contribute their own toxins to worldwide pollution. Remember, we really do not know the figures for the military's fuel consumption overseas. But we do know that the military cannot operate without enormous amounts of it and thus cannot operate without polluting everything it touches. The military locates the overwhelming majority of its bases in places where people are poor, with little time and legal expertise to face the formidable bureaucracy of the United States military. Of course, it turns out that those who protest against and petition the military are mainly poor people of color, a combination that does not generally make for success, particularly against such a commanding giant like the United States military.

Most overseas military base agreements with the so-called host country were signed well before the world had the environmental awareness it has now, and so contain, at best, vague environmental provisions, if any. The military has compounded the problem because it keeps few records on the exact amounts of toxic materials and explosives it has used, and no records about exact locations where they used them. In addition, the United States affords no legislative environmental protection for our foreign bases. And finally the Pentagon spends virtually nothing cleaning up toxins overseas.[78]

The public record at times comes clear, but usually after the military vacates a base for bigger quarters. For example, only after the Pentagon closed the Subic Naval Station and the Clark Air Force Base in the Philippines, in 1992, did the Filipino people discover that the military had been dumping tons of toxic material into the ground and into the rivers and streams, and had buried barrels of it in uncontrolled landfills, having not released this data to the Philippine government itself. When Mount Pinatubo erupted, in 1991, 20,000 people found themselves homeless. The US military relocated most of those people onto the grounds of their former facility. The people dug wells and planted crops—"unaware that the ground water they drank and bathed in, the soil their rice and sweet potatoes grew in, the creeks and ponds they fished in were contaminated by toxic substances dumped during a half century of U.S. tenure."[79] The water alone held a range of contaminants, including heavy metals, pesticides, acids, degreasing solvents, and old munitions. Health workers began keeping track of a sudden rise in "spontaneous abortions, stillbirths, and birth defects; kidney, skin, and nervous system disorders; cancers, and other conditions that can be caused by exacerbated exposure to chemical intoxicants."[80]

Satchell goes on to say that Philippine doctors and government officials, abetted by the independent studies of health and pollution experts from the West, now believe that hundreds or more residents were poisoned by heavy metals like lead and mercury; degreasing solvents, used oil, pesticides, acids, asbestos, and old munitions. Today, Satchell says, "the Pentagon acknowledges polluting major overseas bases but insists that the United States isn't obligated to clean them up." In response to a Philippine senator asking for help cleaning up the site in 2000, then US Defense Deputy Undersecretary Sherri Goodman responded: "Our laws do not permit us to spend funds for the purposes you have requested."

The discoveries in the Philippines put local people on alert. Some of them protested—valiantly and bravely—to oust the US military from their lands. Farmers in both Japan and South Korea protested the contamination of their fields by the military exploding live rounds where they raise their crops.[81] In several locations in Germany, at about the same time as the discovery in the Philippines, workers discovered that industrial solvents, firefighting foams, and waste had converged to destroy their delicate ecosystems.[82]

And we have even witnessed one great and decisive victory on the Puerto Rican island of Vieques in the North Atlantic. For several decades, the Navy used the island as a practice site to train bomber pilots, using live rounds. In 1999, two bombs purportedly went astray and killed a civilian guard. In 2001, the people of Vieques voted in a referendum to throw the military off its island. The referendum passed; and in 2003 the Navy withdrew.

But that's just part of the story. What the Navy left behind tells a much harsher and vicious tale. Consider the following statement from James Porter, Professor of Ecology at the University of Georgia, on April 17, 2001, in support of the Vieques referendum:

> Our ecological investigations on Vieques show destruction to coral reefs from bombing activity there. In addition, we discovered the existence of thousands of barrels and compressed gas cylinders sunk onto the coral reefs of Vieques. We have now demonstrated that those toxic substances are leaking from the underwater bombs, and that this toxic material is now found in living marine organisms on

the reef. The containers are rusting and are fragile, but some are still intact.

This sensitive area lies within the bombing impact area, with the consequence that even so called "green" munitions can break them open. The risks posed to human and environmental health by any further disruption of this site are unacceptable.[83]

Kathryn McCarrey wrote the principle book on the struggle on Vieques Island; it is aptly titled *Military Power and Popular Protest*. She tells how the Navy has used the eastern end of the island for bombing exercises since the 1940s. According to the Navy itself, they bombed the island over that period approximately 180 days a year: "In 1998, the last year before protest interrupted maneuvers, the Navy dropped twenty-three thousand bombs on the island, the majority of which contained live explosives." The most serious destruction to the island has occurred at the live-impact range, but all 14,000 acres and its waters at the eastern tip of the island have been used for live firing practice, amphibious landing sites, and toxic waste dumps. Coral reefs and sea grass beds have been seriously compromised from bombing, sedimentation, and chemical dumping. Groundwater has been contaminated by nitrates. Heavy metals have contaminated the live-impact range; studies have shown that those metals have entered the food chain. McCaffrey concludes her section on pollution with this grim news: "Of particular concern are revelations that the navy has fired depleted uranium munitions on the range and the particular dangers and risks that poses for the civilian population."[84]

None of this, as I have said, is part of the public record. And that the military hides all its data about pollution—both in magnitude and in kind—makes us everyday citizens into fools and dupes. Public service announcements, advertisements, politicians, and celebrities, all with the best of intentions, urge every American to recycle and reuse. Be responsible, they shout. In one way or another, they tell us that it is up to each one of us to turn aside the horrible effects of global warming, and that the cumulative effects of each small action add up. Every paper product carries the friendly reminder to dispose of waste and to recycle properly. Those in charge make us feel that the crisis rests solely with us—that such a crisis remains in our hands to fix or to fumble. But the military numbers reveal a different, perverse truth.

Even if every person in America decided to stop driving today, and even if every polluting factory in the country voluntarily shut down its operations right now, the land and the animals and the water and the air—those things that we generally occlude by referring to them as the environment—would still face a most serious assault. And, ironically, that greatest single assault on the environment, on all of us around the globe, comes from one agency, that one agency in business to protect us from our enemies, the Armed Forces of the United States.

The terrorists have attacked our country. Unwittingly, perhaps, we gave them permission. They turn out to be our own military. We can't hear the bombs blasting, or the guns rattling—all of that takes place at a pleasantly far distance. But we're breathing in the fallout; we're drinking up the fallout. We, too, are collateral damage. We, too, are victims of friendly fire. We all live on an island that resembles, more or less, Vieques.

It's time to turn the equation around. Global warming is not just *our* problem—*my* problem—but, more than that, it is also the *military's* problem, our government's serious and continuing problem. The latest statements from the Obama administration seem to place our military in Afghanistan in a combat mission for a very long time. Even with the SOFA agreement in place, no one knows how many troops will remain in Iraq in their so-called peace-keeping mission, removed from the towns and villages and billeted at their various sprawling bases around Iraq. We have built the largest and most expensive embassy in the world, in Iraq—700 million dollars, with 26 hardened buildings, on 104 acres, just five acres shy of Vatican City. Citizens look like patron saints of the environment compared with the rampant destruction that the military causes.

Research into the military and war brings one face to face with the most heart-wrenching fallout that one could ever imagine. I end this section with one particularly painful example. According to a report by researchers at Portland State University in Oregon, released in the summer of 2007, male veterans of the wars in the Middle East are twice as likely to commit suicide as their civilian male counterparts. Once again, this is hard data to hunt down, for the Pentagon employs no comprehensive system for tracking suicides of veterans of the Iraq and Afghanistan wars. The Department of Veterans Affairs tallies the number of those suicides, but only if the veteran has already received his or her discharge from the military. The Associated Press reported on October 31, 2007 that, according to the Department of Veterans Affairs, from the start of the war in Afghanistan, in 2001, to the end of 2005, 283 soldiers who had served and been discharged committed suicide. The report further indicated that the suicide rate for the Army in 2006 had risen to 17.3 per 100,000 troops, the highest level in 26 years.[85]

How do we count these victims of the war? Into what if any category should we place them? I know that I cannot strictly attribute their deaths to pollution, but at least one writer, Penny Coleman, in her book *Flashback: Post-Traumatic Stress Disorder, Suicide, and the Lessons of War*, connects some of those suicides, at least, to untreated Post-Traumatic Stress Disorder (PTSD), the source of which trauma, she argues, comes from the military's use of defoliants in Gulf War I and perhaps Gulf War II. But who knows why they took their own lives? No one seems willing to carry out any extensive research on military suicides. And so we are left to wonder. Their deaths definitely constitute fallout from this war, only a different kind, and a different order, from those felled by ordnance and munitions and various kinds of poisons.

The father of one suicide victim refers to his son, who served two tours in Iraq, as "KBA": Killed Because of Action. That man's son is gone, as completely and thoroughly as any young man who had been blown up by an IED on a road in Iraq. We will have to search hard, however, to find that young man counted in any war statistic, or to locate him in any recognizable category. But he has certainly disappeared from his father's life—and his mother's life, and possibly his brother and sister's life, and from twenty or thirty or a hundred other lives. Whatever the case, the indelible fact remains that the father and mother grieve deeply and continuously over the unspeakable loss of their son. Such pain does not dissipate easily or quickly, or even ever. Walt Whitman, who tended the wounded and the dying on the battlefields of the Civil War, describes those matters of the grieving heart and how the grief knows no boundaries:

> *The living remain'd and suffer'd, the*
> *mother suffer'd,*
> *And the wife and the child, and the*
> *musing comrade suffer'd,*
> *And the armies that remain'd suffer'd.*

In November 2005, *CBS News* reviewed data on suicide rates among returning GIs from the Middle East in all fifty states. What they uncovered prompted them to call their findings on suicides an epidemic: In 2005, there were at least 6,256 suicides among those who served in the armed forces. The highest rates occur in veterans aged twenty to twenty-four, all of whom CBS points out, joined and served during the "war on terror." This rate exceeds by two to four times the rate for the same age group in the civilian population. Over 4,000 GIs have lost their lives to the so-called insurgents in Iraq. A good many more GIs—fifty percent more—lose their lives to the pounding psychological horrors of having to fight a war, of having to kill, from seeing others killed, or from exposure to defoliants or depleted uranium. Degrading others into the enemy, degrades one's own self in the process. So these young men and women die, not in battle with the enemy, but with themselves. In an act of grisly irony, the GI turns into an enemy, as well, and kills himself or herself.

Where, then, do we actually locate the war? Who or what is the enemy? What counts as pollution and fallout—even death?

I need to make one last point here. The more the public becomes aware of the troubles GIs face when they return, the more problems it seems to make for the returning veterans. The Associated Press reports on a government study that purports to show that employers are reluctant to hire returning GIs and that, when they do find jobs, GIs get paid less than their civilian counterparts: "Strained by war, recently discharged veterans are having a harder time finding civilian jobs and are more likely to earn lower wages for years, partly because of employer concerns about their mental health and overall skills." The study, done in late 2007, found that 18 percent of the veterans who looked for jobs within one to three years of their discharge were still unemployed. One out of every four who did find jobs earned less than 22,000 dollars per year.[86]

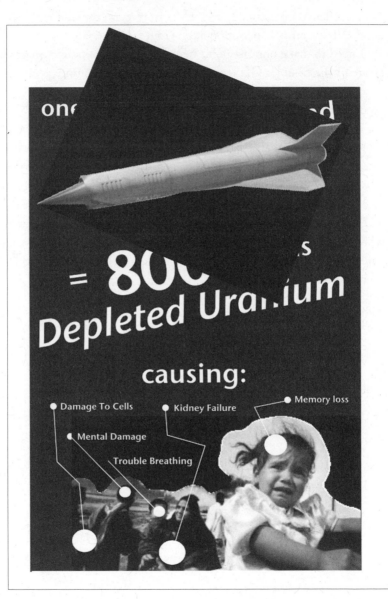

V
DEPLETED URANIUM

Ll this talk about pollution, however, may fade into just so many numbers in the face of one sobering fact: that a good deal of the country of Iraq, both its deserts and cities, hums with radioactivity.[87] For, since 1991, the US has been manufacturing "just about all [of its] bullets, tank shells, missiles, dumb bombs, smart bombs, and 500- and 2,000-pound bombs, and everything else engineered to help our side in the war of Us against Them, [with] depleted uranium in it. Lots of depleted uranium. A single cruise missile, which weighs 3,000 pounds, carries within its casing 800 pounds of depleted uranium."[88] Recall that the Air Force dropped 800 of those bombs in just the first two days of the war. The math: 800 bombs multiplied by 800 pounds of depleted uranium equal 640,000 pounds, or 320 tons of radioactive waste dumped on that country *in just the first two days of devastation.*[89]

The Pentagon and United Nations Environment Program estimate that in March and April of 2003, alone, United States and British forces in Iraq used somewhere between 1,100 and 2,200 tons of armor-piercing shells containing depleted uranium. Dan Fahey, a representative of the veterans advocacy group, Swords to Ploughshares, who served in the Persian Gulf War in 1991, says that the United States and Britain released in one year alone—2003—100 to 200 tons of depleted uranium. That's a total of roughly 40,000 pounds of deadly depleted uranium.[90] No wonder, then, that the *London Sunday Times* reported, in February 2006, that a few days after "Shock and Awe" began, radiation detectors in Britain recorded a four-fold spike in air-borne uranium. One can only imagine what that spike might have registered closer to ground zero, directly over the city of Baghdad and its environs. A few concerned scientists have provided at least a clue.

One such clue comes from Doctor Ahmad Hardan, scientific advisor to the World Health Organization, who says that the use of depleted uranium "has caused a health crisis that has affected almost a third of a million people. DU has a half-life of 4.7 billion years— that means thousands and thousands of Iraqi children will suffer for tens of thousands of years to come. This is what I call terrorism."[91] The rate of malignancies in children in Basra has quadrupled since the last Gulf War.

As a physician, Hardan conducted most of his research in the south of Iraq, especially in Basra, and because children remain particularly vulnerable to radiation, his predictions for the children of Iraq read like some kind of science fiction nightmare. Over the next two years, he says, he expects to see a significant rise in diseases of children's eyes: "cataracts, anophthalmia, microphthalmia, corneal opacities, and coloboma of the iris." He also foresees fetal deformations, sterility in both sexes, increases in miscarriages, and increases in premature births (and deaths). But most gruesome, perhaps, are his predictions for congenital malformations, additional abnormal organs, hydrocephaly, anencephaly, and delayed growth.[92]

I ask again: How is it possible that such a crucial story never took over the front page of every major newspaper in this country, and never appeared on every major news channel in this country? Why is it that such significant information appeared first only on out-of-the-way internet sites, and has only recently, eighteen years after the first Gulf War and eight years into the second gulf war, begun to appear in some newspapers? While the Pentagon does not deny using depleted uranium, various military spokesmen have repeatedly insisted that its toxicity remains at safe levels for GIs.

In the first Gulf War, Operation Enduring Freedom, the military limited its use of depleted uranium to desert areas. In 2003, in Operation Iraqi Freedom, Pentagon strategists lifted all such restrictions, leaving the military free to use Depleted Uranium indiscriminately near and in heavily populated areas. Larry Johnson, a reporter for the *Seattle Post-Intelligencer*, wrote in 2002, that "DU shell holes in the vehicles along the Highway of Death [in Iraq] are 1,000 times more radioactive than background radiation, according to Geiger counter readings ..." He added that "one destroyed tank near Baghdad was 1,400 times more radioactive than normal background radiation. Another was 1,500 times more radioactive than background."[93]

Depleted uranium is essentially U-238, the isotope that remains after the fissionable isotope, U-235, has been extracted from uranium ore. To use U-235 for nuclear reactors, it must be enriched to three percent. Enriching it further to ninety percent makes it suitable for use in nuclear warheads, which scientists call "weapons grade" uranium. Enrichment thus "depletes" the natural uranium of its isotopic fraction of U-235.[94] We should more accurately call the uranium recycled for use in munitions "dirty depleted uranium," or "uranium plus," because it contains additional highly-toxic elements, like plutonium. According to the reporter Robert James Parsons, who has followed the subject for some time, "1.6 kilograms of plutonium can kill 8 billion people."[95]

For decades, the military viewed depleted uranium as mere waste. And, because depleted uranium continues to emit radioactivity over its 4.5 billion year half-life, the military struggled to find ways to dispose of what Project Censored estimates as the 750,000 tons (1.5 billion pounds!) of radioactive waste that the military generates annually, "more than the five largest chemical companies in the US combined. This pollution occurs globally as the US maintains bases in dozens of countries."[96] By turning nuclear waste into weapons, the

Pentagon offered proof of true Yankee ingenuity. On the one hand, the Pentagon had found a solution to a huge storage problem and, on the other, it had created a new and powerful, highly useful category of weaponry. And the solution came with a bonus for arms manufacturers, for the military could offer all their nuclear waste to them free of charge. Up to that point, arms makers had to use the non-radioactive alternative, tungsten, as a penetrator, most of which they mined in China, and that proved very expensive.

Scientists classify depleted uranium as a pyrophoric, a substance that ignites at a velocity tremendous enough to create a literal firestorm, burning at unimaginably high temperatures, anywhere from 3,000–5,000° centigrade, or 5,432–9,032° degrees Fahrenheit. Such intense heat enables a missile or shell to penetrate the hardest of armor, carbonizing everything it touches, resulting in a profusion of millions and millions of tiny particles—in effect, an overwhelming fallout of radioactive dust—consisting of a uranium oxide aerosol that contaminates whatever surface on which it finally settles. Wind can also carry these small particles considerable distances. Most of the dust particles measure less than 1.5 microns, small enough for Iraqi men, women and especially small children, to take into their systems—through their pores, their mouths, and most destructively through their nostrils, a most deadly source of internal radiation. Just through the simple act of breathing, the population of Iraq, in the most literal sense, unwittingly poisons itself every day.[97]

To make matters even worse, the intense heat transforms those tiny particles into a stone-like hardness, turning them into insoluble pellets, and so making it a near impossibility for the body to excrete. Those pellets may account for the many kinds of illnesses that Iraqis, especially children, now experience. Larry Johnson, the investigative reporter from the *Seattle Post-Intelligencer*, tells us that, nine years after the first Gulf War, military doctors were still detecting depleted uranium in urine samples in fourteen out of twenty-seven British, Canadian, and United States veterans. Physicians also diagnosed every one of those returning veterans as suffering from typical Gulf War

Syndrome ailments. Some clinicians think that a connection might thus exist between depleted uranium and the onset of so-called Gulf War Syndrome.[98] The root cause of Post Traumatic Stress Disorder might lie in something other than emotional or psychic trauma. In some cases, PTSD may indeed have a deep physical cause.

Arthur Bernklau, executive director of Veterans for Constitutional Law, in New York, harbors no doubt about the connection between depleted uranium and Gulf War Syndrome. Writing in the *Preventive Psychiatry E-Newsletter*, he blames depleted uranium for the death of 11,000 Gulf War soldiers: "Of the 580,400 soldiers who served in Gulf War I, 11,000 now are dead. By the year 2000, there were 325,000 on permanent medical disability. More than a decade later, more than half (56 percent) who served in Gulf War I have permanent medical problems. The disability rate for veterans of the world wars of the last century was 5 percent, rising to 10 percent in Vietnam." Bernklau goes on to say that "the long-term effect of DU is a virtual death sentence."[99]

Marion Fulk, a former nuclear physicist from the Lawrence Livermore Nuclear Weapons Lab, who also worked on the Manhattan Project, interprets the new and rapid malignancies in the soldiers (from the second Gulf War) as "spectacular—and a matter of concern." Fulk concludes: "While this important story appeared in a Washington newspaper and the wire services, it did not receive national exposure—a compelling sign that the American public is being kept in the dark about the terrible effects of this terrible weapon."[100]

Depleted uranium exhibits a particular affinity for the bones, kidneys, and sexual organs, which can produce severe chromosomal damage, difficult if not impossible to detect.[101] It turns out, then, that United States military not only has killed perhaps hundreds of thousands of Iraqi men, women, and children, but that its long-range policy carries the added horror of destroying future generations, as well. This country manufactures those weapons; we must see this policy as deliberate.

To put it bluntly, this country has managed to implement a thoroughgoing system for total eradication—what the entomologist E.O. Wilson and others refer to, with a word that does not appear in the first edition of the *Oxford English Dictionary*, as *omnicide*—the destruction of all life, human and animal and vegetable, through the corrosive actions of human beings. The war in Iraq may have fallen off the front page, and the number of suicide bombers may have decreased, but the destruction of all life forms continues. And the killing continues in great part through the slow but steady and continual radioactive poisoning of the entire Iraqi population. Even after our troops leave the country, our presence will linger, in the most pernicious, insidious, and ghostly way. We might all well ask the question here: How does radiation contribute to global warming?

Human beings are not the only victims of this unspeakable poisoning through exposure to uranium. Plants and animals also absorb the radioactive particles, making uranium a permanent part of the food chain. Once in the soil, a report by the United Nations Environmental Program concludes, depleted uranium pollutes the groundwater by increasing uranium levels one hundred fold.[102] Scientists have gathered a good portion of the data about deaths from radiation in Iraq from the first Gulf War. According to an article in *The Lancet*, a leading medical journal, mortality rates among Iraqi children have increased sharply, along with cancer rates: "As many as 500 children a day are dying in Iraq." The report notes that the "death rate for Iraqi children under 5 years of age increased from 2.3 percent in 1989 to 16.6 percent in 1993.[103] The United Nations Children's Fund, UNICEF, reported that "mortality of children under five more than doubled to 131 per 1,000 live births from 1994 to 1999. Cases of lymphoblastic leukemia have more than quadrupled, with other cancers also increasing at an alarming rate."[104]

The Save the Children Foundation and the National Center for Health Statistics have released the latest studies, in May 2007, of infant mortality rates around the world. While the rate in the United States has remained fairly constant over the past two decades, the rate in Iraq is, to use the word from the report, soaring: "In the years since 1990, Iraq has seen its child mortality rate soar by 125 percent, the highest increase of any country in the world."

Adult males show the highest increases in cancers of the lung, bladder, bronchus, skin, and stomach. Adult females experience the highest increases in breast and bladder cancer, and Non-Hodgkin Lymphoma. Congenital malformations have also increased, as Ahmad Hardan predicted, as have diseases of the immune system.[105] In 1999, a United Nations sub-commission considered depleted uranium dangerous enough to call for its ban worldwide; and in November 2006 the European Union made its fourth plea for a moratorium on such weapons.[106]

We do have some data for Gulf War II, and they repeat what we know from the first Gulf War. Nearly half of the soldiers in a unit recently returned from Iraq developed malignant growths—eight malignancies out of twenty soldiers. Commenting on those numbers, Marion Fulk attributes what he calls those "quick malignancies" to the particular effect of depleted uranium. According to some medical experts, such abnormalities provide "critical evidence" that the source must be depleted uranium weapons.[107]

One might wonder just what those malignancies mean? Are they just surface evidence of some deeper, more profound damage to the system? Robert C. Koehler, of the Tribune Media Services, in Chicago, summarizes what others have reported: "DU dust does more than wreak havoc on the immune systems of those who breathe it or touch it; the substance also alters one's genetic code. The Pentagon's response to such charges is denial, denial, denial. And the American media is [sic] its moral co-conspirator."[108]

So, what do the malignancies mean? Nothing good, I would think, particularly when one considers a photo essay that *Life* magazine ran four years after the conclusion to the first Gulf War. The piece, which they bravely titled "Tiny Victims of Desert Storm," featured photographs of numerous cases of birth defects or immune-system problems in infants conceived or born by families of returning veterans.

The article concluded that "of the 400 such vets who answered [Don Riegle's Senate Banking] Committee inquiries, a startling 15 percent reported defects of immune-system problems in children conceived after the war."[109] It may be of some interest to note here that the Department of Veterans Affairs, along with all the other kinds of traumas and deaths it refuses to tally, keeps no records of birth defects that occur in families of veterans.

Imagine a good portion of the country of Iraq, then, covered with a fine film of the highly toxic U-238 isotope. I can assign no number to this kind of pollution; it registers on no known scale. So difficult to fathom, the idea barely registers in the ordinary person's imagination. The United States military refuses to allocate any money for its clean-up and, unlike Britain, refuses to disclose the grid coordinates where it has used the radioactive munition.[110] The United States has prevented Iraq from importing equipment to clean up the radioactive dust.

I quote here from Mark Gaffney's incisive work on the military's use of depleted uranium in the first Gulf War to give some graphic sense of the weapon's ability to utterly devastate a battlefield, not just for the moment, but also for millennia to come:

> When a ten-pound uranium shell slices through a target vehicle it sheds a part of its mass, causing a firestorm of burning and non-burning uranium fragments. These, in turn, cause catastrophic secondary fires and explosions. In war footage of Desert Storm the flaming DU shells can be seen arcing like tracers across the night sky. The slender rounds are solid DU—no explosive charge is needed. Each has a plastic outer casing known as a sabot, which centers the round in the bore and which falls away after the shell exits the gun tube. The war footage is graphic. It shows that targeted Iraqi vehicles stood no chance. Pity the poor Iraqi soldiers who came under DU attack. Very few lived to tell about it. Within seconds, most were charred beyond recognition in an incendiary fireball. US military jargon even coined a new term, "crispy critters," to describe the grisly Iraqi corpses of war.[111]

In 2002, at the Armed Forces Radiobiology Research Institute, in Bethesda, Maryland, researchers found that even though the alpha radiation from depleted uranium may be relatively low, breathing in depleted uranium as a metal can damage a person's DNA and create carcinogenic lesions in the cells that make up the bones.[112] To give some idea of the potency of depleted uranium, US troops or Iraqis breathing-in no more than a gram is equivalent to receiving an x-ray every few minutes over the course of their shortened lives.[113]

Diane Henshel, an Associate Professor of Public and Environmental Affairs at Indiana University and the co-author of an article in *Nature*, in Spring 2003, on the effects of depleted uranium, warns: "[The Iraqi people] will have increased problems with changes in behavior, and increasing problems with their kidneys. And at high enough levels you will start to see effects on their sperm count... There are studies that indicate that birth defects are increasing in the areas of high depleted uranium concentration of the Gulf War...A whole host of heavy metals that are used in weapons in small concentrations, of which not much is known, but they are going to end up in the soil, in the air, in the water of people in any war-torn area in Iraq."[114]

It is near impossible to imagine the willful eradication of the future of a civilization, but Iraqis are undergoing exactly that horrific experience. And it is we, as citizens of this country, who are responsible for such terrible crimes against humanity. All that death and desecration has been done in our name, and we are permitting it to happen. Although the information has been difficult to uncover, it is now there, apparent and obvious. National Public Radio has acknowledged its use on its news program, *Science Friday*. We cannot anymore fall back on the excuse of ignorance. Radiation poisoning is taking place in our name. It is making a hell out of children's lives. I am not naïve enough to think we can shut down such an insidious practice, or horrors even worse, without shutting down the entire operation, without eliminating war. But, I do know that they must be shut down.

With more than thirty percent of the GIs returning from Iraq diagnosed with Post-Traumatic Stress Disorder, or some kind of brain damage, disorientation, or depression, one does not have to be a medical expert to safely conclude that, in at least a portion of those cases, as I have suggested earlier, exposure to depleted uranium has caused those GIs to suffer from something we defuse with the generalized name, Gulf War Syndrome. Rather than an evil promulgated by the Pentagon itself, such naming turns things around and makes it the GI's problem.[115] All of which should give us pause about the rising incidence of bizarre illnesses and strange forms of cancers in the Iraqi population itself, as well as in our own returning veterans. It should also make us re-think the high incidence of suicides in returning veterans from Iraq.

I return once again to Mark Gaffney for a conclusion. To frame it, I remind us that the Bush administration issued repeated warnings over its eight-year term that

> so-called Islamo-Fascists have the ability, and what's more the desire, to attack us with radiological weapons. However, the evidence makes it clear, as Gaffney points out, that our leaders have done it on a greater scale. America's use of DU weapons has already caused the deaths of hundreds of times more Iraqi and Afghani civilians, including women and children, than died in the 9/11 attack. Moreover, it is likely that the DU particles already released into the environment, given their insidious effects and 4.5 billion year half-life, will go on killing innocent people for a very long time; indeed, perhaps for the rest of human history, essentially for all of time. In short, our leaders have permanently fouled our nest, surely the ultimate atrocity. They cannot plead ignorance....The toxic effects of DU were understood even at the time of the Manhattan Project.[116]

PERCHLORATE

A HIGHLY TOXIC EXPLOSIVE INGREDIENT

CAN:

- INHIBIT THYROID FUNCTION

- CAUSE BIRTH DEFECTS

- LOWER IQs

- EXPOSE INFANTS AND CHILDREN TO HIGHLY SERIOUS HEALTH DEFECTS

AND IS FOUND IN EXCESSIVE AMOUNTS IN:

- 93% OF LETTUCE AND MILK TESTED NATIONALLY

- 97% OF BREAST MILK SAMPLES TAKEN RANDOMLY FROM AROUND THE U.S.

VI
BOMBS AWAY, ALL DAY

W ho knows how many million pounds of depleted uranium the United States visited on all forms of life in the city of Baghdad on that first moonless night alone—March 19, 2003—of "Shock and Awe?" We may never know, but I count thirty-six different kinds of bombs that the military currently uses, from precision-guided missiles to unguided munitions, and an array of cluster bombs, most of them containing some amount of depleted uranium in their nose cones.[117] Writing in the *New Yorker* in late 2005, Seymour Hersh maintained that just one single Marine aircraft wing dropped more than 500,000 tons of bombs in Iraq from March to November 2003.[118] That's one billion pounds of horror, several hundred million pounds of which consisted of radioactive waste that showered the city.

Some military experts think Hersh got his facts wrong, even though Hersh claims he got his data from a Marine website. Whatever the case, according to CENTAF's own numbers, from March 19, 2003 to November of that same year, the military launched 19,040 guided missiles; 8,885 unguided missiles; dropped 23,836 unguided cluster bombs; 44,954 unguided Rockeye cluster bombs; and 165,236 WCMD cluster bombs. Who knows what the tonnage totals? But given the numbers we do know something about, we can conclude that the decimation must have been enormous, in terms of buildings leveled, human beings killed, and psyches forever decimated.[119]

Nick Turse, who has been researching the air war on Iraq from its inception, points out that the military is especially cagey about statistics for aerial bombing. He says, however, that Air Force officers acknowledge that United States and coalition aircraft dropped at least 111,000 pounds of bombs in 2006—55 tons of munitions. That figure does not include guided missiles, unguided rockets, or cannon rounds. It also does not include the bombing done by the Marine Corps or by armed helicopters.[120]

In its arsenal, the Pentagon boasts of several major bombs. The first is the laser-guided GBU-28 (Guided Bomb Unit) "Dense-Metal Penetrator," more commonly called the Bunker Buster, developed by the Raytheon Corporation. This is a weapon that, according to some accounts (again, as with most things military, numbers differ here), weighs upwards of 4,700 pounds with a 4,400-pound penetrating warhead.[121] Designed to penetrate multi-layered hardened targets or structures buried deep beneath the earth, the bomb explodes underground, the weight of the bedrock pressing down on it compounding the bomb's explosive energy. "The resulting seismic shock wave could crush an underground bunker—or the internal organs of anyone caught in the 'overpressure' from a blast wave twenty-times stronger than the bomb blast itself."[122]

A reporter for the *Le Monde diplomatique*, Robert James Parsons, reveals that the military affectionately (and secretly) refers to the GBU as the Great Big Uranium, since the bomb contains an explosive charge of depleted uranium weighing as much as 1.5 metric tons. Parsons goes on to say that the "GBU 'dirty bomb' eclipses any terrorist's fantasy—one-and-a-half metric tons of aerosolized particles capable of causing genetic mutations and death for the next four billion years."[123]

According to statistics from CENTAF, the most frequently used bomb in Iraq in 2006 was the smaller GBU-12, again a laser-guided general purpose bomb weighing a mere 500 pounds. Again, Nick

Turse, in "Bombs Over Baghdad," points out that "in addition to 95 GBU-12s 'expended,' 67 satellite-guided, 500-pound GBU-38s and 15 GBU-31/32 munitions were dropped on Iraqi targets in 2006, according to Air Force figures."

These weapons are followed by a series of what are called Fuel Air Explosive weapons—or thermobaric weapons, ranging in size from 100 pounds to 500 pounds. Fueled by ethylene oxide, upon impact these bombs produce an aerosol cloud or mist, which instantaneously detonates, releasing a shock wave so powerful that it blows into bits anything—buildings, trees, rocks, animals, and, of course, people— over an astonishing 50,000 square feet area.

The Pentagon lists another major bomb, the BLU-82B, or what the military playfully refers to as "Big Blue 82," or "The Daisy Cutter." The military dropped these Daisy Cutters out of the back of C-130 transport planes in Afghanistan to seal cave entrances in Tora Bora. Weighing 7.5 tons (15,000 pounds), the bomb contains a warhead filled with 12,600 pounds of GSX, a gelled-slurry explosive, which on impact creates a concussive effect greater than the Bunker Buster, rupturing ear drums and internal organs, and, as the huge firebomb sucks all the oxygen out of a wide area, killing every living thing either through incineration or asphyxiation, or both. An embedded reporter provides a description of a Daisy Cutter attack: "The sound split the air. It was like a thunderclap directly overhead at the height of a ferocious storm. I could see the massive oily black cloud of the explosion as it rolled across the hillside, a mixture of thick smoke, chunks of earth and debris."[124]

Perhaps the most insidious munitions in the military arsenal are the cluster bombs, the CBU-87B and the BLU-97B. Dropped from an aircraft, a 2000-pound cluster bomb releases 202 bomblets at a preset altitude, which float down on tiny parachutes and detonate upon hitting the ground. Those bomblets have the capacity to spray an area 400 feet by 800 feet with molten steel slugs designed to penetrate armor and to kill every living thing in its vicinity. An officer on the aircraft carrier the *USS Carl Vinson*, in his own understated way, describes the effect of a behemoth bomb, especially on human beings: "A 2000-pound bomb, no matter where you drop it, is a significant emotional event for anyone within a square mile."[125] One stands in a kind of stupefied awe at such an instrument of killing, that, from as far as one mile away, can create something the military refers to as "a significant emotional event."

Cluster munitions have a high failure rate, making them more lethal than ordinary bombs. After they explode, cluster munitions leave on the ground many of their small, undetonated bomblets, which go off whenever a person or animal or child happens to touch one, or accidentally brushes against one.[126] Most munitions have a failure rate of 3 percent. The Pentagon ascribes a "conservative dud rate" of 5 percent to its cluster munitions. Human Rights Watch reports a failure rate for cluster munitions as high as thirty percent.[127] Given the killing nature of military hardware, that high failure rate seems deliberate, an integral part of the design of cluster bombs, makes them function more like landmines than ordinary bombs.

Thus, cluster bombs behave somewhat like Depleted Uranium, releasing their allotment of death over a long period of time, turning grazing fields and agricultural plots and picnic spots into places of fright and fear, where, at any moment, ordinary unsuspecting Iraqis can unexpectedly find themselves blown into bits. Marc Galasco, the senior military analyst at Human Rights Watch, abhors the military's use of cluster bombs, more even than its willingness to use weapons loaded with depleted uranium: "The single greatest risk civilians face with regard to a current weapon is that is in use."[128] Galasco wants to see them outlawed, and wants the United States to lead the way.

Reports on the air war rarely make the news, and when they do appear, they mainly repeat military propaganda and announcements about air strikes. Thus, many of the details and most of the numbers about the air war in Iraq remain secret. Few if any news agencies report on cluster munitions. That's why the Mennonite Central Committee—which has studied cluster bombs for more than thirty years—filed a Freedom of Information Act request for disclosure of the military's use of cluster bombs since the end of major combat operations in Iraq. In its response to the Mennonites, the Air Force confirmed that "63 CBU-87 cluster bombs were dropped in Iraq between May 1, 2003 and August 1, 2006. These 12,726 BLU-97 bomblets...dropped since May 2003 do not include, according to statistics provided by Human Rights Watch, almost two million cluster sub-munitions used by coalition forces in Iraq in March and April 2003."[129]

Air Force officials acknowledge that the US and coalition aircraft dropped at least 111,000 pounds of other types of bombs in Iraq in 2006. This does not include guided or unguided missiles, unguided rockets, or cannon rounds. It also does not include the munitions expended by the Marine Corps and other coalition fixed-wing aircraft or any Marine helicopter gun ships. Finally, the figure does not include any munitions fired by the helicopters operated by the private contractors carrying out their mercenary work in Iraq.[130]

No military official seems willing to talk about the exact number of cannon rounds fired by helicopters. Colonel Robert A. Fitzgerald, the Marine Corps' head of aviation plans and policy, did, however, speak in general terms about the subject in *National Defense Magazine*, early in 2007. He said that, in 2006, "Marine rotary-wing aircraft flew more than 60,000 combat flight hours, and fixed-wing platforms completed 31,000. They dropped 80 tons of bombs and fired 80 missiles, 3,532 rockets and more than 2 million rounds of smaller ammunition." I am assuming, by the magnitude of the numbers, that Colonel Fitzgerald did not limit his remarks to Iraq.[131]

All of the military's missiles and bombs derive their percussive impact from a mixture of 80 percent TNT mixed with 20 percent of atomized aluminum powder—a fire intensifier, which works by increasing the speed at which the explosive reaches its maximum pressure. The entire lethal mixture is known as tritonal. Over 647 pounds of tritonal, for instance, provide the explosive force for the 4,700-pound Bunker Buster.[132]

The largest bomb, an air to surface missile, which goes by the designation GBU-43B, or more affectionately as MOAB, the Mother Of All Bombs, carries 21,600 pounds (over 10 tons) of TNT mixed with aluminum powder. The MOAB is the largest-ever, satellite-guided, air-delivered bomb in history. The MOAB's destructive force so terrified Iraqi troops in the first Gulf War that they referred to its effect in a most portentous image: "steel rain."[133]

Aluminum powder can be very toxic, causing a potentially serious lung disease, pulmonary fibrosis, which in severe cases, can lead to a drawn-out painful death. Some studies have suggested a connection between exposure to high concentrations of aluminum dust with Alzheimer's disease and other neurological disorders. While the International Agency for Research on Cancer has determined that prolonged exposure to aluminum flake is carcinogenic to humans, the Pentagon argues that aluminum dust carries no long-term health risks and thus refuses to undertake any studies.[134]

In fact, after persuading Congress to exempt the military from the nation's wildlife protection laws, the Pentagon is now pushing its "Readiness and Range Preservation Initiative," which seeks immunity from three important and fundamental federal laws: the Clean Air Act, the Resource Conservation and Recovery Act, and the Superfund Law. Which is to say that the Pentagon seeks to exempt itself from laws regulating air quality, hazardous waste, and toxic cleanup, in spite of the fact that it offers no evidence to support its claim that existing statutes hinder military readiness. Karen Wayland, legislative director at the Natural Resources Defense Council, takes offense at the Pentagon's reasoning: "The Pentagon's push for blanket exemptions from federal health and pollution cleanup safeguards makes a mockery of national defense. Using national security to sacrifice our nation's environmental security will endanger our health, leaving us less safe."[135]

Before these bombs can explode, they have to arrive at their targets. For that they need fuel. Which, quite obviously, produces even more pollution. The Department of Defense holds the distinction as the single largest polluter in the United States, not only, as I pointed out earlier, because of its consumption of fuel and discharge of explosives. The DoD also holds the distinction as pollution champ because of its manufacture of solid rocket fuel, which uses a highly toxic explosive ingredient called perchlorate, and which has leaked in varying amounts from military bases and defense and aerospace plants in over twenty-two cities in this country. The DoD program for cleaning up perchlorate includes 28,000 currently or formerly contaminated sites in every state and territory, as well as locations in other countries.

The United States Centers for Disease Control concluded that percholorate has severely contaminated this nation's food and water supply, including much of the lower Colorado River. The National Academy of Sciences (NAS), in its report of the human health hazards of perchlorate, found excessive amounts of the chemical in ninety-three percent of lettuce and milk it tested.[136] In samples of breast milk taken randomly from around the US, ninety-seven percent of women tested positive for perchlorates—an example, in this country, of the poisoning that we can attribute to military waste coursing through the very heart of the food chain.[137]

The NAS determined that perchlorates are roughly ten times more toxic to humans than the DoD has been claiming, and can inhibit thyroid function by limiting its uptake of iodide. Continual disruption of the thyroid gland can cause birth defects, lower IQs, and expose infants and young children to highly serious health risks. Of course, when all those rockets explode in Iraq they release, among numerous other pollutants, that very same, highly toxic perchlorate. I can find no agency that has tested for the presence of perchlorate in the water supply in any place in Iraq, in the milk of Iraqi mothers, or in the blood streams of Iraqi adults or children.

Closely related to the toxic effects of aluminum powder and perchlorate is the military's quite shocking use of its new version of napalm. The British newspaper, *The Independent*, reported on August 10, 2003, that "American pilots dropped the controversial incendiary agent napalm on Iraqi troops during the initial advance on Baghdad.

The attacks caused massive fireballs that obliterated several Iraqi positions." The same article also pointed to its use in March and April of 2003, "when dozens of napalm bombs were dropped near bridges over the Saddam Canal and the Tigris River, south of Baghdad." A reporter from the *Sydney Morning Herald*, Lindsay Murdoch, bore witness to one of those fire bombings: "Safwan Hill went up in a huge fireball and the observation post was obliterated. 'I pity anyone who is in there,' a Marine sergeant said. 'We told them to surrender.'" The United States Department of Defense denied the use of napalm during Operation Iraqi Freedom, insisting that "we completed destruction of our last batch of napalm on 4 April, 2001."

Technically, the Department of Defense spoke the truth. The United States did not drop napalm, which consists of a mixture of fuel and a polystyrene-like gel that causes it to stick to people's skin as it burns, and proves nearly impossible to remove or to extinguish. Napalm derives its name from a formula of naphthalene combined with palmitate. Incendiary munitions kill, in a most ruthlessly painful way, by immolation and, because they emit a large amount of carbon dioxide, by asphyxiation, as well.[138] A 1980 United Nations convention banned the use of napalm against civilian targets. The United States, which did not sign the treaty, is one of the few nations that uses napalm, which it employed most notably in Vietnam, and which has come down to us in that one well-known and vivid photograph of a young girl running down a dirt trail, her flesh burning off her body.

The Pentagon based its denial, it turns out, on a technicality. The United States military currently employs an incendiary weapon called the Mk-77 Mod 5 Firebomb, which is identical to the earlier and standard Mk-77 napalm weapon—Napalm B—but instead of using gasoline and benzene as fuel, the new edition uses a kerosene-based jet fuel, reformulated using a smaller concentration of benzene. These new and improved incendiary weapons each weigh about 510 pounds and consist of 44 pounds of the polystyrene-like gel and 63 gallons of jet fuel. In a strange twist of language, the military claims that the new napalm is less harmful to the environment. I assume military leaders do not include human beings in the environment category. Aside from carbon dioxide, which the Clinton administration had classified as a pollutant, the Pentagon remains mum about the possible pollutants from napalm. In fact, the Bush administration has removed CO_2 from its classification as a pollutant, providing a boon to both the manufacturers of automobiles and munitions.

What the Pentagon does not say is that the addition of oxidizers to the new formula makes the goo even more lethal than the old napalm, by making it harder to remove from the flesh. And so, even though this incendiary weapon attaches to the flesh and burns and burns, because of its recast formula, the military insists that no one should rightfully call this improved horror napalm. That name, the official version of napalm, and the gruesome photographs associated with its use, have already been taken. This new weapon will, of course, generate its own images of terror.

Thus, General Tommy Franks would make George Orwell proud. The former Commander of CENTCOM traffics in the best (or worst) of Newspeak. In an early report that the military had used napalm in Tora Bora, Afghanistan, in the pursuit of Osama Bin Laden, General Franks responded, "We're not using—we're not using the old napalm in Tora Bora." Again, General Franks spoke the truth—up to a very limited point. Yes, the military did not use the old napalm, but he neglected to add that the Army was using the newer version of napalm. John Pike, Director of the military studies group *GlobalSecurity.org*, reaches the following reasonable conclusion: "You can call it something other than napalm but it is still napalm. It has been reformulated in the sense that they [the US military] now use a different petroleum distillate, but that is it. The US is the only country that has used napalm for a long time. I am not aware of any other country that uses it."

Tommy Franks aside, Marine Corps fighter pilots and commanders, who have returned from Iraq, admitted to dropping dozens of firebombs on bridges over the Saddam Canal and the Tigris River.

"We bombed both those [bridge] approaches," Colonel Randolph Alles said in an interview. Alles commanded Marine Air Group 11, during the initial invasion, and offered this brief, cryptic statement: "Unfortunately, there were people there because you could see them in the cockpit videos. There were Iraqi soldiers there. It's no great way to die."[139] "Most of the world understands that napalm and incendiaries are a horrible, horrible weapon," says Robert Musil, Director of the group Physicians for Social Responsibility. "It takes up an awful lot of medical resources. It creates horrible wounds." Musil went on to say that the Pentagon's insistence on different kinds of napalm indeed make the discussion "Orwellian. They do not want the public to know. It's a lie."

How many of those new firebombs did we drop? According to a letter from the UK Minister of Defense to former Labour MP Alice Mahon, the 1st Marine Expeditionary Force "used a total of 30 MK 77 weapons in Iraq between 31 March and 2 April 2003."[140] Lindsay Murdoch, the reporter from the *Sydney Herald*, who traveled with a Marine unit those first few days of "Shock and Awe," offers the following devastating account of the Marines' seemingly indiscriminate use of the new napalm: "Marine Cobra helicopter gun ships firing Hellfire missiles swept in low from the south. Then the Marine howitzers, with a range of 30 kilometers, opened a sustained barrage over the next eight hours. They were supported by US Navy aircraft which dropped 40,000 pounds of explosives and napalm, a US officer told the *Herald*."[141]

We already know napalm's brutal effect—or whatever we choose to call this most recent firebomb—on human beings. Incendiaries give off large amounts of carbon monoxide as they ignite, causing people to pass out and burn. What is the effect on the environment of tens of thousands of pounds of burning jet fuel and benzene—on the water supply, the vegetation, the air, on the probably thousands of frightened and disoriented animals? Who knows? What we have here is just one more of those incalculable costs of waging war against a so-called vicious enemy, who will stop at nothing to kill us all off.

The cost, in money or in lives or in pollution, simply does not seem to matter to those in authority. Killing is paramount. The means, no matter how brutal, always justify that one end. Under such conditions, it is difficult to take seriously a category called collateral damage. The overwhelming majority of the destruction and devastation—to both buildings and humans—is absolutely direct and deliberate.

One more controversial weapon, also banned by several international treaties, is white phosphorous. The military is not supposed to use WP, as they call it, on human targets, only as a way of illuminating the nighttime battlefield. But the Pentagon admitted to using WP as an incendiary weapon in 2004 in its assault on Fallujah. Colonel Barry Venable said that white phosphorous he had ordered was used to dislodge the enemy from its entrenched positions. A documentary made by the Italian television broadcast system, RAI, and titled *Fallujah, The Hidden Massacre*, made the case that Iraqi civilians, including women and children, had died of burns caused by WP during that same Fallujah assault. Military spokesmen have denied its use. Three artillerymen, who took part in the battle of Fallujah, wrote an article in *Field Artillery* magazine in the March/April 2005 issue in which they say the following: "WP proved to be an effective and versatile weapon. We used it for screening missions…and, later in the fight, as a potent psychological weapon against insurgents in trench lines and spider holes…We fired 'shake and bake' missions at the insurgents using WP to flush them out and high explosive shells to take them out." ["US Forces Used 'Chemical Weapons' in Iraq" *The Independent*, 16 Nov. 2005

On contact with the skin, white phosphorous burns at a fairly high temperature and proves almost impossible to extinguish. Water only speeds up the burning process. Doctors typically cut out the phosphorous from the skin. Once it enters the skin, it can cause severe damage to the heart, lungs, and kidneys, and eventually can prove fatal. The EPA has classified it as a serious air pollutant. Inhaling its heavy smoke can also prove dangerous, and in some cases, can cause bone deterioration. A University of Maryland study, conducted in

1982, reported on the deaths each year of thousands of ducks, geese, and swans at Eagle Falls, Alaska. They died from water contaminated by white phosphorous that leeched from several local military bases.

We have stepped behind the pollution numbers here to examine the military's means of killing. In many of the instances—maybe in all—the means reveal even more horror than their possible results. How can we ever again call ourselves a nation of concerned citizens? The atrocities at Abu Ghraib, almost all but forgotten now, divert our attention from the larger, ongoing, and invisible horror, that is, from the war itself and, perhaps more important, from the engineers who devise and direct those wars in Iraq and Afghanistan.

VII
THE FATE OF THE EARTH

I f, as some war critics say, the United States invaded Iraq to secure its oil, thus, in the logic of war, reducing our dependence on foreign oil, I have tried to show in this essay that, in trying to achieve that goal, the United States has certainly consumed and spilled and burned a tremendous amount of that precious stuff. Martin Luther King got it right forty years ago, and it is just as right today. America also triggered a release of greenhouse gases of crisis proportions. It should come as no surprise that invasions prompt retaliations, what Chalmers Johnson calls "blowback." And so, when Iraqi troops moved out of Kuwait at the end of Gulf War I in 1991, they set fire to Kuwait's oil fields. (If it's that precious, sabotage dictates, then destroy it.) Oil accounts for 95 percent of Kuwait's export earnings.

The Iraqis set ablaze more than 600 wells, many of them burning continuously for 9 months or more. It amounted to between 5 and 6 million barrels of oil that went up in smoke, along with 70–100 million cubic meters of natural gas. Smoke clouds covered an enormous 10,000 square miles, blocking out the sun, and reducing temperatures by 18° Fahrenheit. A thousand people died of acrid smoke inhalation. The fires released some 300 million tons of CO_2 into the atmosphere. That's 600 billion pounds of greenhouse gases! The fires also released sulfur dioxide, nitrous oxide, hydrogen sulfide, hydro-carbons, and soot. (Soot translates as solid particles embedded in tar.) About 60 million barrels of oil leaked into the ground, poisoning 40 percent of the groundwater. Another 6 million barrels (120 million gallons of fuel) also leaked into the sea, causing the largest oil slick ever recorded, destroying large portions of the local fish, bird, and mammal population.[142] Prawn fishing ended forever.[143]

One thing at least seems clear. No American president can afford to have Congress ratify the Kyoto Accords and still wage the kind of carbon-assault for which the United States has become famous. Today's brand of warfare, especially, just relies too heavily on staggering amounts of oil; it produces too much greenhouse gas to ever willingly constrain itself with any kind of treaty. The military can brook limits of no kind whatsoever. It cannot even withstand scrutiny of any kind. The Pentagon conducts its business behind very thick and very closed doors. It writes its own rules and either follows them or violates them, depending on the situation. And so the beat goes on. Very few people in positions of authority, both in and out of government, have the temerity to criticize even the smallest part of military operations. Patriotism will not allow it. Standards of good citizenship will not permit it. Tradition forbids it.

For fiscal 2009, George Bush proposed, for the Pentagon, an 8 percent increase of 36 billion dollars, on top of the 624.6 billion dollars already in the defense spending for 2008. On June 30, 2008, Bush signed legislation for an additional 162 billion dollars, to pay for the wars in Iraq and Afghanistan, and hailed the vote as a rare bipartisan move, as if, finally, government was working. That legislation brings the amount Congress has voted since the war on Iraq began to more than 650 billion dollars, not counting the 200 billion dollars for the war in Afghanistan.[144] That amounts to roughly 110 billion dollars for each of the 6 years we have been in Iraq, or 9 billion dollars each year. That's just for Iraq. In 2007, the Pentagon spent 17 billion dollars. The Nobel economist Joseph E. Stiglitz suggests that with all costs factored into the cost of the war—including medical treatment for returning vets—Iraq will cost us all, finally, at least 2 and maybe even 3 trillion dollars to produce the kind of devastation—human and otherwise—that I have tried to document in this essay.[145]

And yet, if we can believe the results of some Gallup polls, conducted during the week of June 6, 2007, Americans seem to trust the military three times as much as they trust the President of the United States, and five times more than their elected representatives in Congress. The poll asked a sample of people to respond to the following statement: "I am going to read you a list of institutions in American society. Please tell me how much confidence you have in each one: a great deal, quite a lot, or very little." The results: 39 percent of the people said they had a "great deal" of trust in the military; 23 percent said they had a great deal of trust in the police; 14 percent in the supreme court; 12 percent in the President; 7 percent in the criminal justice system; and, at the bottom of the list, just 4 percent of the people had a great deal of trust in Congress. Another 30 percent said they had "quite a lot" of trust in the military. That's 69 percent of the people asked, then, that had a great deal or a quite a lot of trust in the military. What do they actually trust? The Bush Administration had people so scared, it appears, they felt that they had to believe in the military. They had no other choice. And since most Americans pay no direct sacrifice for that huge military, or for the wars, they simply want it. They think they need it to keep them safe and secure. It's like wanting to be an atheist, but wondering, my god, what if?! And so, no matter all the protests on the streets, and all the posturing in Congress, after six years of what many people agree is the worst and most grotesque mistake in the history of this country, the military rolls on and on in Iraq—in a different form and different configuration, perhaps—but it continues its monstrous presence on some of the largest US military bases in the world.

Such public compliance helps feed the beast. The military's gigantic maw opens wide to consume more and more fuel, using up more and more money, all the while wasting more and more lives, and helping to destroy the environment at a rapid clip. A great many citizens believed that a Senate with even a slight majority of Democrats could put a stop to the war. But, the war continues—supported by a continuing round of debates and discussions that give the appearance of honest and sincere argument, followed always by another round of funding. And Obama picks up the chant, promising in his tenure to kill Osama Bin Laden, as if that would put an end to anything significant. And, as we know, Obama has pledged to send two more battalions into Afghanistan and made that one of the first orders of business on his first full day in office. And, we have not heard his plans for Pakistan—not yet.

As I said, some so-called Green Hawks now take the position that the military must support the environmental revolution, developing, for instance, a more energy-efficient fighting machine, or working on synthetic fuels that pollute much less. But, to repeat, that's just so the armed forces can move faster over longer stretches of terrain, allowing combat units to decimate even more land, to wipe out even more plants and animals and humans, at a much faster rate. But, then, PR is of utmost importance. And so, even James Woolsey, the former director of the CIA and a devout Iraqi hawk, has learned to look like an environmentalist. He now drives a Toyota Prius, with two more hybrids on order. He admits to making a geopolitical point, not an environmental one: Let us not be so dependent on the Muslim theocracies for our oil, he proudly declares.[146]

In an attempt not just to be greener but kinder and gentler, the Air Force Research Laboratory has been working on new munitions it calls the Dense Inert Metal Explosive (DIME). The Air Force developed the new device in response to complaints that bombing in urban areas creates civilian casualties, more commonly known as collateral damage. DIMEs are 250-pound bombs that, instead of using metal casings, use a carbon fiber that turn into dust rather than showering a wide area with dangerous fragments. Filled with explosives mixed with a heavy-metal tungsten alloy, the DIME bomb explodes into billions of pieces of super-heated micro shrapnel—an incredibly destructive blast in a small area, or what the military calls "focused lethality."

DIME munitions carry horrific side effects. Several studies have shown that shrapnel of HMTA (heavy metal tungsten alloy) has caused cancer in laboratory rats. I know the usual comment that rats are not people, but, in this case, all ninety-two rats implanted with tungsten alloy contracted a rare cancer called rhabdomyosarcoma within five months. Other studies point out that tungsten can damage the immune system, and attack the body at the level of DNA, and hence belongs in a class called genotoxics. Rory McCarthy, writing in the *Guardian*, in October 2006, interviewed several physicians who said Israel used the DIME weapon in its bombardment of Gaza. (The United States sold those weapons to Israel.) With the Air Force playing a larger role in Afghanistan, we can expect to see America's use of such focused lethality in that country.[147]

What to do? Certainly, citizens cannot require the military to file an Environmental Impact Report whenever it decides to invade a country, or demand it pay for carbon offsets, or enact carbon caps, or plant millions of trees around the world to mitigate its rampant pollution. At the very minimum, however, I would ask that a fair calculation of military greenhouse gases—from land vehicles, planes, helicopters, ships, and munitions factories—be added to the total that this country annually produces, and that that number get factored into the actual and total cost of waging war. As citizens, we have a right to know those figures. We need to be informed. On the model of body counts, why not tabulate daily carbon outputs in Iraq and Afghanistan? Also, people seem to turn against war when it grows too expensive, either in soldiers lost or in dollars spent. If we can turn more Americans against war with transparent accounting disclosures, more power to the truth.

We also need a more honest accounting of all the petroleum products that the military consumes each day, not just a portion of them. Then we might be able to reach a more accurate reckoning of the carbon damage to the globe; we might then see how big a boot the military places on the ground. We need to factor into the war the cost of trying to put the environment back in order after we have contaminated it—indeed, why not include the land and the animals and the lakes in the infrastructure costs when we talk about rebuilding Iraq? Such reimbursements have a limit, of course, for how can we restore the imagination and the innocence of Iraqi boys and girls? How can we bring childhood back? How can we bring back to life any American GI? Obviously, we cannot.

In the end, we can achieve absolutely no meaningful rebuilding of Iraq, for the human infrastructure, along with its land and plants and animals and air, has been thoroughly and perhaps forever compromised. After all, as I have said, the depleted uranium isotope has a half-life of 4.5 billion years; and thus we Americans—all of us—have degraded the Iraqi people for millennia to come. I do not know if they can ever recover, if they can ever again call themselves Iraqis. I cannot imagine what they will wind up calling us Americans.

How can we find a category, or set a dollar amount in determining the cost of malformed fetuses? Those terms we now so easily throw about—"surgical strikes," "precision bombing," and "collateral damage"—need redefining, especially when we consider the new DIME munitions, for we have managed, with our new weapons, to contaminate the entire population of Iraq, no matter age, gender, or tribal affiliation. Under the mechanized hatred and evil that we call war, every single Iraqi constitutes collateral damage—and the children those Iraqis dream of having, well, they too have turned into collateral damage. The most shocking and silent horror here may be that we have laid waste to the people and the land and the animals with the careful deliberation of a highly skilled surgeon. Military leaders are surely aware of not just everything they destroy, but also the cruel and painful and tortuous way they kill things off. Otherwise, they would not ask for more and more lethal weapons. We reserve the word "torture" for Abu Ghraib and Guantanamo, but that's what has been going on for nearly six years throughout the whole of Iraq.

People used to tell a funny story not so long ago: since TV waves take some time to travel through space and not much seems to interrupt them, if there is life on Mars then those creatures are now watching *I Love Lucy*, and not in re-runs. Likewise, since CO_2 takes ninety years or more to dissipate fully from the atmosphere, hovering high above our heads are greenhouse gases from the Vietnam War, Kosovo, various Israeli bombings of Gaza, and, of course, Gulf War I. One can find traces of World War II and, if you look closely enough, even some scant fallout that still persists from World War I. But those earlier layers of pollution are like short stories compared with the monstrously long and dense novels that are Iraq and Afghanistan. Technological improvements in warfare have made contemporary pollution more varied and frightening, and certainly much more lethal. Pollution is an instance of the Hermetic principle of "as above, so below," except reversed: the actions we take down here on the land reverberate up in the skies. We kill down here and simultaneously destroy up there.

Whether you believe strongly in the reality of global warming, or only half-heartedly embrace the idea, the emerging data seem incontrovertible, that the earth simply cannot absorb any more serious CO_2 pollution. It certainly will reach its limit much faster than any scientist has argued given the rate at which the military pollutes in Iraq and Afghanistan. To repeat an earlier point: Even if every person, car, and factory in the world stopped generating greenhouse gases this moment, the military is still propelling us to the very brink of disaster—and indeed over the edge. And yet, in his final months in office, what did the President of the United States, George W. Bush, set his sights on?—The development of a new hydrogen bomb.

Indeed, if scientists are correct in telling us that we must reduce the burning of fossil fuels by seventy percent now just so that the atmosphere can return to normal levels in the next several decades, then surely we must see the obvious: We must put a stop to war. In the twenty-first century, given the precarious state of this planet, we must begin to see war as an outmoded method of solving political problems, real or imagined, actual or trumped-up. As stewards of the earth for these many millennia, who can praise us? Or even give us passing marks? But at least millions of ordinary citizens around the world have now begun to recognize the enormity, not of the problem—that word comes from a simpler time—but of the *crisis*. As responsible citizens, as politicians, as parents, as students and teachers, we must begin to fold into the conversation about our deep-seated fear of "terrorism" the more deep-seated illness of the planet. We have turned the so-called war on terror into a war on *terroir*—a war on the earth.

Perhaps we all accepted war more easily when we viewed the earth as more vigorous, a time long before we began to hear of polar bears drowning, ice caps melting, sea levels rising, bees disappearing, penguins and walruses dying, Iraqis turning radioactive, and on and on. If our politicians cannot find a way to end our long-standing fascination with war—and such a move seems highly unlikely—then the earth is going to do it for us. For all of us. The planet is now speaking the truth to anyone who will listen: settle your problems with diplomacy, or you will have nothing left to negotiate. After centuries of dissipated living, we have left ourselves with no other choice. Global warming trumps all other crises. And, unlike most so-called crises up to this point, we cannot buy our way out of this one. The tactics of capitalism, even the lure of green capitalism, just will not work. In fact, a capital economy exacerbates this particular crisis. Likewise, we cannot engineer our way out this one. Technology will not, as it has so often in the past, come to our rescue. And, besides, technological solutions often behave like medical solutions, creating side-effects that require people to call in ever more technology to fix the newly created problem. And the cycle goes on and on.

Opinion polls indicate that over seventy percent of Americans believe that as a society we should do "whatever it takes" to protect the environment. According to a study undertaken by the Yale Center for Environmental Law and Policy, and made public in March 2007, eighty-three percent of Americans view global warming as a "serious problem—up from seventy percent in 2004." Those numbers cut across political lines. Some right-wing evangelicals, for instance, have joined with liberals and progressives in addressing the crisis of global warming, most prominently the Reverend Richard Cizik, the longtime lobbyist for the National Association of Evangelicals. Risking being reviled by his fellow Christians, especially Jim Dobson of Focus on the Family, Cizik insists that "it's time we return to being people known for our love and care of the earth and our fellow human beings."[148]

It is the one subject, the fate of the earth, that, in this country offers the chance of generating any real communitarian action. The civil-rights movement of the 60s provides an historic example of the way that, in America, disparate people can at times come together to grapple with and solve critical, seemingly insurmountable social problems. And that is the spirit, multiplied 10 thousand-fold, that we will need if we hope to make it out of the polarized world in which we now live. A Coalition of the Willing acts quite differently and thinks quite differently from a Community of the Concerned.

Mark Hertsgaard, an independent journalist and author, who writes about climate change, points out that "environmental justice groups like West Harlem Environmental Action are developing real political clout while proving that affluent white people aren't the only ones who care about clean air and water. And there has been an explosion of student activism, particularly around global warming."[149] For our survival, we will need to see hundreds of thousands of people, perhaps even millions, with their various attitudes and ideas about saving the environment, filling the streets, marching and chanting and demanding an end, not just to the wars in Iraq and Afghanistan, but also to all wars anywhere and everywhere—now and in the future. The anti-war movement must become a No-War movement working alongside those who believe that, if we act now and with determination and without equivocation, it may still be possible to live on this planet decades and even centuries from today.

Citing morgue and hospital statistics across Iraq, the United Nations reported, in January 2007, that an average of ninety-four Iraqi civilians died each day in the war in 2006. The UN says that those numbers were running at double the number for 2005.[150] Roughly every fifteen minutes, another Iraqi human being—a mother or father, a brother or sister, a husband or wife, a son or daughter—died. Roughly every fifteen minutes, another loved one was ripped from a house, or torn from a family. As awful and grim as that sounds, when global warming takes its full effect, we can expect geologic changes of historic proportions, particularly at the equator, especially among poor people, and deaths in numbers we have never before witnessed. As I say, the poorest people, those least able to withstand severe change, will be hardest hit—dry lands most profoundly affected. Remember: two-thirds of the continent of Africa consists of dry land or desert.

Because of changing weather patterns caused by global warming, millions of sub-Saharan Africans may find themselves starving to death. As the rate of desertification accelerates, UNESCO predicts that, from 1997 to 2020, an astonishing 60 million Africans will have migrated to places like North Africa and Europe in search of food and water.[151] Global demand has already depleted many of the rivers in Africa of their fish. The world will divide even more than it does today between the haves and the have-nots. More important, the United States will not give up its top-tier position, and it will need more and more oil to keep this first-world machine grinding away at its maximum capacity. The overwhelming majority of Americans enjoy a comfortable way of life, and they will not easily or willingly give up their luxuries.

The national security think-tank, the CNA Corporation (Center for Naval Analysis), of Virginia, brought together a group of eleven three- and four-star retired admirals and generals, to form a Military Advisory Board, which issued a thirty-five-page report titled "National Security and the Threat of Climate Change." In it, those military professionals describe global warming with a strange sound-ing name, a "threat multiplier," particularly in "already fragile regions." By "threat multiplier," they mean a threat to that comfortable way of American life so many of us know so well. They indicate that the next thirty or forty years will see intense wars over water and food supplies: "Weakened and failing governments, with an already-thin margin for survival, foster the conditions for internal conflicts, extremism and movement toward increased authoritarianism and radical ideologies. The US will be drawn more frequently into these situations."[152] I guess by "drawn more frequently into these situations," military ex-perts mean that we Americans, above all others, will have to defend ourselves, since those experts know only too well that Americans have no desire to see their way of life diminished.

Our occupation of Iraq may thus be a mere dress rehearsal for the really big performance: the safeguarding of America's precious commodities—food and water—of which we have, over the centu-ries, taken our disproportional share. We are now trying to secure that other precious commodity, oil, in the Middle East. When all is done —when we have it all—then perhaps we will all find the safe-ty and security that the US government claims to be so desperately seeking. By then, we will be fairly alone on a fast-dying planet.

A good many Americans believed Bush's argument following 9/11 about the connections between al Qaeda and Iraq. Six years later, polls indicate that the majority of those same people have grown more wary, and more weary—Bush may even be greatly responsible for making them feel that way. We need to start telling a new story, one that describes the overwhelming majority of the earth's popula-tion, not at odds with each other, but moving ever closer and closer together. Climate change is a global issue, and thus only a truly vast communitarian spirit can confront the vastness of its dreaded fallout. What stops some congressional leaders from voting for immediate withdrawal from Iraq is the fear of even greater ensuing chaos. But imagine the chaos in Iraq, facing the most significant global challenge in history, with its infrastructure and fertile land fairly well destroyed.

Much of the world underwent retooling to prepare for the electronic revolution in the 80s and 90s. America led the way. If the world is to survive even the least dire predictions of global warming, people will have to entertain a new kind of retooling. America can assume its position again as world leader by showing a new and more intelligent way to live on the planet.

The neo-cons have had their day; but a question remains about just how much their ideas have permeated the thinking of the general population. They may be gone, I would argue, but they have left behind a precise and dangerous way of looking at global issues. Richard Perle, chairman of the Defense Policy Board, made up of a group of advisers to the Secretary of Defense, and David Frum, former speechwriter for George W. Bush, wrote a book titled *An End To Evil*. In that book, the two authors give us the following astonishing sentence: "There is no middle way for Americans: it is either victory or holocaust." Odd, I think, for two Jews to toss around the word holocaust so freely. But that's exactly what they see: A world peopled with those who think and act and live like us, or absolute extermination of the entire human population.

They never entertain the possibility, which many experts now believe, that too many people in positions of authority greatly exaggerated the importance of al Qaeda. Tariq Ali, for instance, in his new book *The Duel: Pakistan on the Flight Path of American Power*, points out that al Qaeda "unleashes sporadic terror attacks and kills innocents, but it does not pose any serious threat to U.S. power," and then goes on to provide substantial evidence for his position. Likewise, Bruce Riedel, in *The Search for al Qaeda: Its Leadership, Ideology, and Future*, argues that al Qaeda has no real following in the Muslim world and stands no chance of taking over a single Muslim country.

But Perle and Frum persist in seeing the world one way only, arguing that, faced with utter extinction—not from severe changes in climate, but from Muslim extremists—why wouldn't we do anything, follow any policy, no matter how extreme it might appear or how thoroughly it might erase another country or population? We cannot remain strong without a powerful and mighty military. Indeed, we cannot achieve peace without such a military. Should you somehow miss their point, Perle and Frum let you have it right between the eyes: "A world at peace will be brought into being by American armed might and defended by American might, too."[153] Perle and Frum never ask the obvious: What if we pick up arms and there is no one left to shoot?

In a very real sense, our foreign policy under the Bush administration took much that shape: Bring 'em on and on until no one of them is left standing or, in more polite Washington terms, taking the fight against terrorism to the enemy. It is fair to ask just what his policy of pre-emption has accomplished. Our occupation of Iraq has created more and more religious extremists. It has turned a good deal of the Middle East against us. It has destabilized places like Pakistan and Iran and Saudi Arabia. And, in the end, it has turned this nation into a corporation that has entered deeply into Chapter Eleven bankruptcy. We have gone well beyond our budgetary surplus; we are deeply in debt, which we have now, at least tacitly, agreed to pass on to several generations to come. And the greatest surprise of all: we are no safer, no more secure, than we were on September 11, 2001, when all the war-time horror began.

But we should not consider the war in Iraq as an oddity, an aberration in our great history of successful wars. That we found no weapons of mass destruction should surprise no one, for each war has its own crystallizing event—its rationale—that raises ire in Congress and gets sold as fear to the public. Each war has its equivalent of the evanescent but deadly weapons of mass destruction. The war in Iraq simply brought the issues that war always generates into a crisp focus. For one thing, we were enabled to see the stupidity of war up close because so many inept bureaucrats ran that particular administration, and its salesmen and women could not articulate a consistent policy over time. But such unnecessary killing, such duping of the public, has fueled war in this country since its inception. We need only remember the supposed naval crisis in the Gulf of Tonkin, in 1964, that triggered the Vietnam War, a protracted and ugly war that just wore on and on, resulting in the death of 50,000 to 60,000 Americans and as many as 2 million Vietnamese, and finally lost any public backing whatsoever. And recall the trumped up reasons for the invasion of the Bay of Pigs that turned into a political embarrassment for this country.

Let us learn a key lesson from our experience in Iraq and Afghanistan. If we can put an end to war, we can then decide to put an end to an even greater impending round of terrorism—the fight, not over ideology, but over food and water. General Anthony Zinni, Bush's former Middle East envoy and one of the generals who drafted the CNA report on climate change, says it plainly: "It's not hard to make the connection between climate change and instability, or climate change and terrorism." Here's his solution: "The DoD should conduct an assessment of the impact on military installations worldwide of rising sea levels, extreme climate change…"[154] The report remains blind throughout its thirty-five pages to just the opposite problem—the impact of the military on such geologic catastrophes as rising sea levels and extreme climate change.

On March 29, 2007, the non-partisan General Accountability Office (GAO) issued a report that startled many for its frankness. It carried the title: "Crude Oil—Uncertainty About the Future Oil Supply Makes It Impossible to Develop a Strategy for Addressing a Peak and Decline in Oil Production." Just in case the title did not reveal its argument clearly enough, the GAO warned that "worldwide oil production will eventually grind to a halt and the US has no strategy in place to deal with the possible catastrophic results." Matt Simmons, the president of Simmons and Company International, one of the largest investment banks for the oil industry, decries the fact that "the industry has no new technology coming on line." He claims that oil production peaked in 2005; and that we now need "a heroic effort to awaken our country to this threat to the survival of the economy."[155] The GAO and Simmons, once again, miss the most obvious point, one to which thousands of scientists worldwide call our attention: the threat is not to the survival of the economy. It is to the survival of the planet itself. I am reminded here of Pogo's famous line: "We have seen the enemy and he is us."

VIII
AFGHANISTAN

Afghanistan was payback, retaliation. Attacking Afghanistan, our President told us, presented the best chance of getting that mastermind of the attack on the Twin Towers and founder of al Qaeda, Osama Bin Laden. But, alas, he got away. Even with all that high-level intelligence and surveillance, fly-overs with jets and unmanned drones, bombing and cluster bombing and bunker busting, somehow in the ruggedness of the White Mountains in Eastern Afghanistan, Osama Bin Laden gave the Americans the old-fashioned slip.

Everything I have said about military pollution in Iraq can be said about Afghanistan, though the numbers for the latter—the number of sorties, of bombs dropped, of rockets fired, troops employed, and so on—have been, at least up to January 2009, a bit smaller. With hindsight, the invasion of Afghanistan now looks like a mere warm up, a dress rehearsal, so to speak, for that really big one—the invasion of Iraq. Indeed, many of the books about the Bush Administration point out that the planning for the take-down of Saddam Hussein had been talked about by his administration many years before those nineteen hijackers flew their airplanes into the Twin Towers. One could argue just as well that Iraq offered just the right diversion for our failure in Afghanistan.

Almost nine years later, the United States occupation of Afghanistan has come back into the news, but grinds on for the great majority of Americans without commanding very much attention or newsprint, as the on-again, off-again, mostly forgotten war.[156] Americans turned their attention, in those moments when they did turn their attention, to Iraq. But that war has practically vanished from view. Still, after touting a lull in the violence in Iraq, the military resumed its bombing on January 10, 2008. On that morning, two American B-1 bombers and four F-16 fighter jets dropped 40,000 pounds of bombs, ten minutes south of Baghdad. Colonel Terry Ferrell, commander of the Second Brigade, Third Infantry Division, as if describing some stirring musical performance at Carnegie Hall, called the attack "an extraordinary amount of firepower." And yet that "extraordinary" event—40,000 pounds of explosives—appeared only on page eight of the *New York Times*. At one point, not so long ago, twenty tons of molten metal dropped on some village might have made the first or second or third page. Fatigue sets in fast—the economy turns sour, the election looms, the winter or the summer approaches, but more than anything else, the economy heads south. People need to eat. They need to pay bills. They need to find jobs. How can they possibly find Iraq or Afghanistan on a map? And so the world grinds on and on.

News about Afghanistan, on the few occasions when we do read about that remote place in, say, the major newspapers in this country, usually turns on our parallel war in Afghanistan against opium production. But even after seven long years, the poppy wars are not going well for the United States. Not only has the United States military failed to eradicate the Taliban, or smoke Bin laden out of his cave, but, like the Taliban, opium production—revenue from which crop helps to finance the Taliban—in spite of America's spraying and cutting and ploughing of the fields, opium production has managed to remain robust year after year. In 2007, Afghani farmers produced record amounts of the poppy plants. Afghanistan now supplies ninety-three percent of the world's opium, the main ingredient in heroin. Opium farms may represent the one aspect of the country's environment that has not been horribly and irreparably degraded. Indeed, instead of eradicating opium farms, the war has resuscitated opium farming as one of the very few ways the Afghani people can survive economically.

While we think of the war beginning in 2001, we should bear in mind that the Afghani people have been under siege for more than three decades—three invasions from Britain, followed by a ten-year occupation by the Soviet Union, from December 1979 until February 1989. We have had a presence in that country for close to thirty years. When the Soviets finally withdrew, they left behind 1.5 million dead Afghanis, 5 million more disabled, and 5 million more as drifting, bewildered refugees.[157] For the next twenty years, Afghanistan underwent a period of tremendous civil war and unrest. Various factions occupied and then lost control of the capital city, Kabul. The United States supported one of those violent factions, the Mujahideen, with money and rocket launchers and grenades to help oust the Soviets—support that remained covert until the mid-1980s. But that aid accomplished America's goal, at least for a short time: The Mujahideen held a tight grip on Kabul until 1996, at which moment the Taliban took control of the capital city.

One terrible side effect from that protracted civil war is that Afghanistan now holds the distinction as the most heavily landmined country in the world. One estimate, by the United Nations Mine Action Program, places the number of landmines buried by the Soviets throughout the country at 10 million, which each day wound or kill, on average, three people—many of the victims young children, who had the misfortune of playing in the wrong open field. To the number of landmines scattered across the country from previous wars, we must add the unexploded cluster bombs (CBU-87) that the United States has dropped on that country over the last seven and a half years. The United Nations Mine Program places that number at a staggering 25,000.

As we have seen in the section on Iraq, human rights groups have almost universally condemned the use of cluster bombs as inhumane weapons (though I think the distinction between humane and inhumane weapons for killing is a useless and even ludicrous one). On October 25, 2001, Chief of Staff, General Richard Myers announced that "yes, we have used cluster bomb units…There have not been a great deal of them used, but they have been used." If you're a military person instead of a civilian on the ground, "not a great deal" sounds like it might mean only one or two. But that's far from the case. Between October 2001 and March 2002, the United States dropped 1,228 cluster bombs containing 248,056 bomblets over Afghanistan.[158] In Herat, according to Human Rights Watch, between October 2001 and June 2002 latent bomblets killed 44 percent of their victims, while landmines killed 21 percent.[159] (Again, I think comparative numbers on death and dying are degrading, and I offer them only to make a point about lethality. A parent of a dead child does not care about categories.)

Afghanistan is a land-locked, rugged and mountainous country of 25 million, seemingly built for the military's favorite weapon, the Bunker Buster. There are 4 million people living in the capital of Kabul. Almost every person in the country now conducts his or her life without electricity, forced to cook with wood, which they cut from surrounding hillsides and transport into the city. Soot covers the insides of houses. One reporter likened the smoke-filled air to the worst, heavy, barely breathable, smog-filled days in Mexico City.[160] Abdul Wajid Adil, of the Society for Afghanistan's Viable Environment (SAVE), lamented in the spring of 2002, that "losses of natural resources are beyond estimation. Damage to the environment is second only to human loss." He predicted back in 2002 that, if the country sustained many more years of war, the bombing and related fires could wipe out the entirety of the country's forests.

Doctor Joshua Ginsberg, Asia Director of the Wildlife Conservation Society (WCS), stretches a bit to find a bright spot in all those landmines and cluster bombs. He hopes that the booby traps will keep people out of key wilderness areas and so, in a bizarre way, protect some of the country's few remaining endangered species. But he has serious doubts. For instance, he feels quite certain that the Caspian Tigers have totally disappeared, along with the Siberian Crane, but has a hunch that a few bears still survive, along with some Marco Polo Sheep, various rare birds, and endangered Snow Leopards, of which he believes fewer than 100 still prowl the mountains of Afghanistan. The pelts show up for sale periodically at military bases and fetch high prices—up to 1500 dollars.

In the midst of fighting between rival tribes, the United States, on October 7, 2001, started its bombing raids—but we should keep in mind that we began manipulating that country, through supporting the Mujahideen, at the beginning of the 80s. Now, instead of the Soviet Union, it is the United States that has been in Afghanistan for a protracted time—more than twenty years—using surrogates for a time and then our own troops. And whether Afghanistan remains in the news or not, we are, of course, still very much slowly but deliberately dismantling the infrastructure of that country. In fact, we have, over recent years, actually increased our presence, and not merely through the addition of troops, but, as we shall see, more dramatically in greatly stepped-up air attacks.

In July 2004, Lt. General Norton A. Schwartz, the Joint Staff's Director of Operations, testified before the House Armed Services Committee about the number of United States troops in Afghanistan. Several members of the House Committee expressed complete and utter surprise over the General's revelations. If anything, they had assumed a considerably smaller presence. In fact, they had no clue.

The exchange between John Spratt, Democratic Representative from South Carolina, and General Schwartz, points out just how closely the military guards its numbers, and the extent to which some Senators or House members operate in the dark. Remember, these are not ordinary citizens, but members of Congress: they make the laws, they authorize the invasions, and they allocate enormous amounts of money. They are privy to documents about which we have no clue. They send young American men and women off to war, to stand, as politicians like to say "in harm's way." "We have a huge ongoing mission in Afghanistan," Spratt announced with all the confidence of an insider, "yet we've only got 12,000 troops there. Are we slighting and under-sizing, under-resourcing the mission in Afghanistan because of the demands on the mission in Iraq?" Without missing a beat, the General responded: "In point of fact, right at the moment we have about 17,900 US troops in Afghanistan. And that number is adequate to the mission." To believe the General, Spratt missed the mark by 50 percent.

While the major newspapers did not cover the story, the military paper, *Stars and Stripes*, did report on this little interchange. The author of the article, Lisa Burgess, dismissed the congressional surprise over the number of troops by saying that "keeping tabs on the number of US forces deployed overseas—information that military analysts and commanders call the 'order of battle'—is challenging… The Pentagon does not routinely disclose orders of battle, citing 'operational security issues.'"[161] I find her word choice, *challenging*, interesting. To find out the numbers is more than challenging. It is a frustrating, frightening, and near impossible task. Indeed, the usually reliable and accurate website *Global Security*, set the troop level in Afghanistan, in May 2004, at "nearly 10,000 soldiers and roughly 4,200 Marines"—missing the mark by several thousand—or more. For, as we have seen with the troop levels in Iraq, the General has made public the numbers that the military wants us to know. His word choice, "*about* 17,900" interests me, as well. If Iraq is any guide, however, the *actual* rather than the *about* number probably runs higher than General Schwartz admits.

But even the General can be wrong. While he said that he expected the number of troops to remain steady, commanders in the field repeatedly requested an additional 7,500 troops to maintain what is euphemistically called "the mission" in Afghanistan, a number that Secretary of Defense William Gates says the NATO forces seem unable to supply. Gates consistently turned those field commanders down. Then, with no fanfare, on January 14, 2008, the Associated Press reported that Gates had decided to send an additional 3,200 Marines—a ground and air contingent, along with another battalion—to Southern Afghanistan for a one-time deployment of seven months. Gates expected them to counter what the Pentagon predicted would be a ferocious springtime military offensive from the Taliban. The Associated Press indicated that, as of January 2008, the United States had 27,500 US troops in Afghanistan, the highest numbers since the invasion began in 2001. With Gates' additions, the total would reach a little over 30,000. How did we get all the way to 30,000 or even 27,500, when General Schwartz seemed so adamant, so confident, about the lower number of 17,900? And how did the Associated Press conclude that the troop level stands slightly higher than 30,000?[162] It's all a mystery in the hermetically sealed world of the military—all unfathomable.

At any rate, here's where the numbers stand a year later, January 2009: 32,000 US troops, including 14,000 who serve with NATO forces and 18,000 who conduct training and counterinsurgency operations.[163] In addition, troops under the auspices of NATO number a whopping 70,000. Admiral Mike Mullen, Chairman of the Joint Chiefs under Bush, said in December 2008 that American forces could increase by the summer of 2009 to 60,000. He also said that the US currently has 31,000 soldiers in Afghanistan alongside the 60,000 foreign troops, offering yet another set of numbers from which to choose.[164] The truth here is that the US and NATO control an awful lot of troops in country in Afghanistan, as many as 100,000 and soon, perhaps, 130,000.

Ah, those elusive numbers! As a citizen, I expect to be in the dark about the truth on this issue of military numbers, but one can only wonder how members of Congress could be so off the mark about such a basic fact as troop strength. We entrust the safety of our sons and daughters, our wives and husbands, to those Congressmen and Congresswomen. As they argue, discuss, and ultimately vote, they many times decide the fate of this nation, as well as the fate of other nations. We expect them to make reasoned decisions based on accurate data. We assume that they have access to the classified reports and documents that they need to make those reasoned decisions. Maybe that is not always the case—at least when it comes to matters military. Which leads one to wonder what else about the past seven years in Afghanistan do our senators and representatives also know nothing, or very little, about? What do we, as citizens, know nothing about? It must be an enormous amount.

What about a basic question like, how is the war going? Besides record opium production, United States military deaths and suicide bombings also hit record highs in 2007, and grew even higher in 2008. More than 6,500 civilians died during 2007, along with 117 US troops—in both cases, the highest levels ever reached in Afghanistan. Taliban suicide bombers pulled off a record number of attacks in 2007—140 in all, most of them more sophisticated than in the recent past, and more than in the past five years combined. Those bombs killed more than 300 civilians.[165] Almost 4,500 militants also died. Nearly eight years after the invasion, violence dominates much of the southern part of the country, where the government has little presence, and where militant attacks in Pakistan at the end of 2007 underscore a long-term regional battle with al Qaeda and the Taliban.[166] The assassination of Benazir Bhutto at the end of 2007 served to plunge the country deeper into chaos, and to bring al Qaeda back into prominence. The website *Unknown News* reports that 832,962 people have been killed in Afghanistan since we launched our attack, and that 1,590,895 people have been wounded in both Iraq and Afghanistan.

In the past couple of years the war has fallen apart for the United States; Taliban attacks have increased dramatically and US casualties and deaths have also increased. In June 2008, for the first time more soldiers died in Afghanistan—twenty-eight—than in Iraq. For the first two months of 2009, deaths of GIs increased more than three-fold over the same period in 2008 (twenty-nine as opposed to eight). The total number of GIs killed in Afghanistan since the beginning of the invasion totals 630.[167]

The International Council on Security and Development reports that, as of the end of 2008, the Taliban had its men in 72 percent of the territory of Afghanistan, up from 54 percent in 2007, and is expanding its control beyond the rural south. Like the insurgents in Iraq earlier, the Taliban seem undaunted by the combined might of the United States military and NATO forces. Indeed, they seem likely to morph like those insects that came to thrive on DDT in the 50s and grew stronger, absorbing the military's blows and recharging themselves. On December 8, 2008, the Taliban mounted the largest attack yet on NATO supplies going to Afghanistan, destroying ninety-six trucks and seventy Humvees, at a depot in Northwest Pakistan.

We know something about the dead. What about the disappeared? The *New York Times*, for January 7, 2008, carried the following, intriguing headline: "U.S. Prison Grows Beyond Capacity in Afghanistan." The American "detention center," established at the Bagram military base as a temporary holding tank in 2001, according to the *Times*, now "teems with some 630 prisoners—more than twice the 275 held at Guantanamo." The official name for the camp is the Bagram Theater Internment Facility. In 2004, that "facility" held barely 100 prisoners, and in early 2007, only 500. (Notice that only the *New York Times* uses the word "prison"; the military uses "detention center" and "internment facility.") Mistreatment—both physical and emotional—of some of the prisoners, long before we found out about the horrors at Guantanamo—has elicited strong complaints to the Pentagon from the International Committee of the Red Cross. The *Times* goes on to say that "military personnel who know both Bagram and Guantanamo describe the Afghan site...as far more Spartan. Bagram prisoners have fewer privileges, less ability to contest their detention and no access to lawyers. Some detainees have been held without charge for more than five years, officials said."

As the Taliban have stepped up their attacks, so has the United States Air Force stepped up its bombing. CENTAF provides numbers for Close Air Support sorties, for both Iraq and Afghanistan, and counts as a Close Air Support sortie any time a plane takes off loaded with ground attack weapons, either to wait for a target or to deliver munitions against a specific target. In 2004, in Iraq, American and allied forces dropped CAS munitions that totaled 285; in 2005, 404; and in 2006, 229. These figures do not account for helicopter missions—including attack helicopters.[168] (I am aware that drones— unmanned aircraft—may be slowly replacing conventional aircraft, in a movement called Netcentric Warfare Systems—robots, drones, and communication satellites.) In Afghanistan, on the other hand, the numbers move in the opposite direction: in 2004, CAS munitions dropped totaled 86; in 2005, 176; and in 2006, CAS munitions totaled an astonishing 1,770. The Center for Strategic and International Studies found a 65 percent increase in close air support/ precision bombing raids in Afghanistan for 2006 over 2007, from 1,770 to 2,976. In 2008, there was a further increase of another 31 percent. The war grows uglier day by day. More than 6,000 Afghanis were killed in 2007 alone.

In other words, over half of the total munitions dropped by the United States in the last three years fell on the Afghanistan countryside in 2006. The other weapon drops appear to have been limited. All the drops comprised precision weapons, either GPS- or laser-guided, dumped out of a combination of various Air Force and naval-based jets. These munition counts do not include engagements with cannons, or unguided air-to-surface rockets. CENTAF counts here just the bombs and guided missiles dropped or launched from military aircraft.

But we must be careful with the phrase "precision bombing," and here's a horrifying reason why: On election day, 2008, while millions of Americans waited in long lines for the chance to vote George W. Bush out of office and make a fresh start with Barack Obama, the US Air Force killed forty people, and wounded twenty-eight others at a wedding party in the southern province of Kandahar. I mentioned targeted bombing in a previous chapter—fuel depots, nuclear facilities, power plants, and so on—but I did not mention weddings. It seems preposterous to do so, but this was the "6th wedding party eradicated by American air power in Afghanistan and Iraq since December 2001."[169]

Why would the American military wreak such destruction in what goes by the name of precision bombing runs? In just the last six months of 2008 in Afghanistan, American air attacks have been responsible for the deaths of two brides waiting to recite their marriage vows. It seems more than outlandish that the military bombed six weddings. Such a number takes it out of the category of simple error or coincidence. One wonders if it's a possibility of getting local leaders, drunk and with their guards down, all gathered at an event—more death for the dollar. And so what if some innocents get it in the end?

As I end this essay with the earlier war in Afghanistan, I want to end this section by returning to the beginning of the war, to that evening of October 7, 2001, and to an inventory of munitions that the United States military dropped over Afghanistan or fired into various parts of the country. Besides, that invasion began almost eight years ago, and is a dim memory for most of us. We have some reasonably accurate data for a change, since the military's think tank, the Rand Corporation, prepared a report in 2005 that documents the aerial war that first evening.

Forty or more airplanes led the attack, including two Air Force B-2 Stealth Bombers, each carrying sixteen 2000-pound satellite-guided GBU-31 Joint Direct Attack Munitions (JDAMs, an internal guidance system for the GBU series of munitions). Remember, the GBU-31 Bunker Buster contains one and a half metric tons of depleted uranium. According to Marc Herold, Professor of Economics at the University of New Hampshire, from the beginning of the war in Afghanistan to December 2002, the US dropped between 550 and 600 tons of depleted uranium.[170]

The first night's attack, Rand goes on, received additional support from sweeps by more F-14 and F/A-18 fighter jets. Aegis destroyers also fired a total of fifty Tomahawk land-attack missiles against high-priority targets. The Air Force, with its B-52 bombers, however, delivered the heaviest punishment from the sky. The Rand report says the Air Force "rained down both JDAMs and hundreds of 500-pound Mk 82 unguided bombs." Each Mk 82 contains almost 200 pounds of the explosive tritonal. Multiply that 200 pounds of tritonal hundreds of times—and you get perhaps as much as 60,000 pounds of tritonal, some 30 tons of explosive in a single night. That is an extraordinary number. It's difficult to imagine very much living through such an onslaught.

We can only guess at what the phrase "rain down" might mean in terms of numbers. Rest assured, the people and the land shook and trembled through hundreds of ear-piercing explosions, followed by fire, fright, maiming, and of course death. But if the Taliban did not get the message that first night, they soon would, as over the next five days B-52s and B-1B bombers dropped some 500 JDAMs, 1,000 unguided bombs, and 50 cluster bombs. In addition, 15 F-14 and F/A 18 fighter jets dropped 240 JDAMs, 1,000-pound and 2,000-pound Laser Guided Bombs (though the report neglects to say precisely how many), typically using the BLU-109, Hard Target Penetrator warhead. Recall, the BLU-109 warhead weighs 2,000 pounds, 550 pounds of which is explosive, a good portion of which is depleted uranium.[171]

The website *Global Security* points out some interesting details about all those sorties the first days of the war, which compound the problem of pollution for Afghanistan and elsewhere. For instance, Navy jets flew their missions from carriers in the Arabian Sea, some 500 miles from their targets. Air Force bombers flew six hour round-trip missions from Diego Garcia in the Indian Ocean; and fighter-bombers flew from bases in the Persian Gulf, missions that took eight to nine hours to accomplish. Bombers who conducted missions from Diego Garcia in round-trip sorties, mostly over the Indian Ocean, flew anywhere between 12 and 15 hours, and covered roughly 5,500 miles. Remember, the B-52, with 8 jet engines, burns through 3,334 gallons of jet fuel an hour. Those 12 to 15 hours of flying means that each B-52 burned over 50,000 gallons of fuel![172] CO_2 filled the atmosphere.

If the Rand report is correct in stating that ten B-52s flew missions each night, then just the B-52s each evening consumed 500,000 gallons of fuel. Those planes, you will recall, must be refueled in the air, by huge KC-135 Stratotankers, that themselves gobble up enormous amounts of fuel. The Stratotanker, with its boom assembly, can off load fuel at the rate of 6,500 pounds per minute, or 1,000 gallons per minute. That's roughly enough fuel to keep the average car running for two years.[173] The calculus for just that one kind of airplane produces a nightmare of greenhouse gases.

When did the bombing start to taper off? Well, the Rand report states that, as of October 23—sixteen days into the air war—Air Force B-2, B-1, and B-52 bombers, from the 28th Air Expeditionary Wing, Diego Garcia, had expended more than 80 percent of the tonnage dropped on combat missions over Afghanistan during Operation Enduring Freedom. In doing so, the Air Force had flown more than 600 sorties.

The report continues. On November 20, 2001 senior officials announced that more than 10,000 bombs or missiles had been dropped or fired during the course of the war. By the end of the month, the eight B-1s and ten B-52s operating out of Diego Garcia had reportedly dropped most of the 4,700 tons of munitions delivered by the Air Force. That number represented 72 percent of the war's total by that time. To recast the number of munitions, 4,700 tons equals a staggering 9.4 million pounds of explosives. But, as horrible as that number may seem, the devastation only gets worse. By the end of November 2001, Rand tells us that the Air Force had dropped a total of 10,000 tons of munitions, or a staggering, overwhelming 20 million pounds. In addition, the Air Force dropped 600 cluster bombs: 450 BLU-103s and 150 BLU-87s.

Air operations did not begin to slow down until December 23, 2001. By that time, the military had flown 6,500 strike missions over Afghanistan, and had dropped about 17,500 munitions. The B-1 bombers delivered more bombs than any other aircraft. But Rand is quick to point out that, even as the pace slowed, by March 2002 the Americans had dropped another 2,500 or so bombs, making a grand total of around 20,000 bombs. By mid-September, 2002, the pace seems to have definitely slowed, as the number of bombs dropped had risen only slightly, to 24,000.

I say "risen only slightly" rather sarcastically, as if these were nothing but numbers, but of course they are not. These are bombs and they are instruments of death and torture. They pollute everything in their path, including people's nerves and imaginations and perceptions. These 24,000 bombs dropping from the sky over an entire year—2,000 a month, on average, 500 per week, 70 per day, 3 every hour—have the capacity, besides being able to deliver outright death, of driving a person out of his or her mind.

Notice how easily I use the numbers 24,000; 2,000; 500; 70? As if they were somehow unconnected with the worst sort of deaths imaginable. We Americans do not know fear in such proportions. I have only numbers to register, to translate, all that horror. My language—and the vivid adjectives of death and destruction—lose their power when I write about war, from the safety of this country. Our comfortable experience, our lives always on the periphery of war, somehow belittle the fetid facts of war. How can we possibly imagine ourselves as victims of a saturation bombing raid? I am reduced to writing about numbers. I regret this.

To return: terror works through anticipation of knowing something dreadful might happen, but not knowing precisely when it might happen, or of course where it will happen. In what place—what building, what market, what village—will the next bomb land? When will the next landmine go off? Where is it located? Will one of my loved ones get this one? How have I managed to live? Will I get the next one? Imagine Iraqi mothers or fathers fearing that their children might be playing or walking in some forbidden zone, that is, in some potential zone of death.

Depleted uranium acts as such an instrument of terror. People wonder why they are beginning to feel sick. The source is invisible, the rays lethal. The same is true of landmines. Afghanis feel frightened to walk off the beaten path. Tomorrow or the day after tomorrow, for most of us, can hold great excitement. In Afghanistan, the future only raises more questions, shuts off more possibilities, brings more terror. No one makes plans. People just try to survive—this day, the next, the one after that.

Human Rights Watch reports that the United Front (formerly the Northern Alliance), our allies in the Afghan War, continue the Soviet practice of laying landmines inside Afghanistan, while Russian forces lay them along the borders of Uzbekistan and Kyrgyzstan. Human Rights Watch also asserts that the United States supplied landmines to the Mujahideen fighters during the 80s, now known as the Northern Alliance. The report continues by noting that "landmines have been planted indiscriminately over most of the country. Grazing areas, agricultural land, irrigations systems, residential areas, and roads and footpaths, in both urban and rural areas, are contaminated...Landmines and other unexploded ordnance contaminate at least 724 million square meters of land in Afghanistan. Only two of Afghanistan's twenty-nine provinces are believed to be free of landmines."

The United States is not among the 142 countries that have signed, ratified, or acceded to the 1997 Mine Ban Treaty, which prohibits possession or use of antipersonnel mines. According to the *New York Times*, on the third night of the air attack, the United States reportedly dropped a type of weapon known as "area munitions," which I have not yet mentioned in this essay. The military designation for the so-called area weapon is the CBU-89B Gator, a mixed-mine system containing both anti-personnel and anti-vehicle mines. Recall that the CB designation refers to a munition classified as a cluster bomb, which has a reputation as one of the nastiest kinds of bombs that the United States employs, and is universally reviled by human rights groups. The Gator belongs to that category, with the nastiness ramped up beyond all limits.[174]

The CBU-89B is a 1,000-pound cluster munition, which contains a lethal combination of twenty-two antipersonnel mines and seventy-two antitank mines. Dropped from a plane, the mines arm themselves upon impact with the ground. Trip wires activate the antipersonnel mines. The antitank mines have a much more astonishingly complicated mechanism, activated by a magnetic influence sensor, which can detect and distinguish between a vehicle that has armor and one that does not. According to a military fact sheet on this particular weapon, the mine will detonate, even more astonishingly, when the sensor determines the place where the vehicle is most vulnerable. This is truly an example of the advanced technology of death.

While the military has designed the fuses to de-activate after four hours, field commanders report a very high failure rate—coincidentally, just like all the other cluster bombs—making this a munition that keeps on giving. These mines also have the capability of turning even nastier than the conventional cluster bomb, because of something called the variable time feature, which allows the mine—either antiperson or antivehicle—to explode unexpectedly for a period of up to four days. The military calls these moments of deadly surprise, in another of those euphemisms of the powerful, the "harassment feature."[175] Imagine, then, along with the hidden landmines, the unexpected explosions from probably thousands of these Gator bombs. The United States military has approximately 300,000 of them in its inventory. To own them is to have the itch to employ them. We can only guess where next.

The Department of the Army *Field Manual* refers to another variant on the true landmine, allowing the military to further skirt the prohibitions of the international ban on landmines. The Field Manual points to a particularly insidious little bomb known as the M86, Pursuit Deterrent Munition (PDM), and advises its use mainly by specially trained personnel, "as a deterrent by special-operations forces and in operations where units may be pursued by an enemy or an enemy force."[176] Special Operations Forces include specially trained troops from the Army, Navy and Air Force, and includes the Green Berets, Rangers, and SEALs.

The PDM is a hand-placed, wedge-shaped mine which, when armed, deploys tripwires that are six meters in length. When tripped, the mine suddenly bounds up to a height of two to three meters (about six to nine feet)—just about or above the height of a person— hovers for a split second, and then explodes, spraying an area approximately ten meters at high velocity, with 600 1.5 grain fragments. In plain terms, it explodes with a fusillade of shrapnel. The military has designed the PDM to self-destruct four hours after arming, but once again this weapon, like many others, experiences a surprisingly high failure rate. As if this description were not awful enough, and although the *Army Field Manual* omits mention of it, *Global Security* maintains that the munition contains "a small amount of depleted uranium," without suggesting what a small amount might be. The Pentagon has more than 16,000 of those PDMs in its inventory.[177]

Before too long, the war in Afghanistan, in this new phase, will enter its ninth year. And it will have a new and fresh President championing the cause, pushing it toward rhetorical victory. That will, of course, require that Americans become freshly frightened, as well, and pay a renewed and strict attention to the Taliban and al Qaeda. The air war will, at times, make it to the front page, but probably only when a bombing raid goes awry and kills thirty or forty civilians, including a dozen babies and a few scattered children. Some spokesman from the Air Force will promise an inquiry; Obama will grow indignant. Senators will demand action. And then, slowly, the economy will rebound, erasing the war from the newspapers altogether. We can all write the history out of our memories, without having to rely on our imaginations. There will be arguments on the floor of the Senate about funding, some lone voice will advocate shutting the entire enterprise down, but then the chorus will start: You cannot let our boys down. The funding passes. One or two large demonstrations will fill the streets of Washington, DC or Los Angeles, and the President will once again say, "That's democracy in action." The war will creakily roll on. No one will throw a shoe. But worse yet, very few will speak out for the voiceless, defenseless planet.

CONCLUSION

According to the Intergovernmental Panel on Climate Change, which shared the Nobel Peace Prize with Al Gore in 2007, the world faces a minimum of ninety more years of warming no matter what measures we take to stop it at the present moment. The Panel claims that the reasons are not only atmospheric (greenhouse gases, they claim, remain aloft for nearly 100 years), but perhaps more importantly, political. Our leaders cannot seem to understand the crisis we face and so refuse to pass serious legislation. America, the grossest offender in the world, must lead the way. Jay Gulledge of the Pew Center on Global Climate Change says that, at present, the atmosphere contains 385 parts per million of carbon dioxide. By mid-century it will reach 450 parts per million, which will bring us to a crucial point, a tipping point, if you will.

Which is to say that a serious environmental movement needs to begin here, in the United States, not just because we contribute more carbon per capita than any other country—20 tons for every man, woman, and child. Such a statement is, for many people, an abstract notion. To make it more concrete, I recast it this way: We need to lead the environmental movement for radical change because we are responsible, with our way of life and our military, for murdering the planet faster and more effectively than any other country in the world. It turns out that the effects of 385 parts per million are far worse than predicted: Arctic sea ice is melting faster than scientists had predicted, and global sea levels are rising faster than they ever expected. The IPCC predicts that melting glaciers will result in "glacier lake outbursts of floods."[178] Tens of millions of Bangladeshis and other impoverished people living in coastal regions will be under water.

In the end, our efforts must expand exponentially, into a communitarian movement across the globe the likes of which no one has ever witnessed, one that refuses to make compromises about a basic respect for life—human and non-human, rich or poor, white or people of color, upper or working class—especially in the most vulnerable and environmentally fragile parts of the world. Thomas Friedman, writing in the *New York Times Magazine*, hopes that "the next president will rally us with a green patriotism. Hence my motto: 'Green is the new red, white and blue.'"[179] I hope that we can step out of the predictability of patriotism, out of the confines of country and nation, to entertain a much larger and grander vision.

An Inconvenient Truth makes the point that if we hope to have any chance at all in limiting severe climate change, we will all need each other—small countries and large, poor countries and wealthy ones. In the face of this planetary emergency, terms like "First World," "Second World," or "Third World" no longer make sense. Al Gore has inspired an important beginning. His Nobel Peace Prize is a testament to that fact. It is up to the rest of us now to provide that beginning with energy and ideas and to keep it expanding until it turns into a powerful movement. Barack Obama seems to believe in the truth of global warming. As Commander in Chief, he will need to be educated about the mess his military is making of the environment.

We can truly call a coalition of no-war and pro-environmental activists "grass roots," for the name refers both to the actions of the people, and to the earth, each at a very basic level. As Bush said when he announced his Iraqi Surge, we have one more chance to get it right. We may indeed have one more chance, but it's not about success or victory or stability in Iraq, or the eradication of the Taliban or al Qaeda in Afghanistan. It's a chance for all of us to truly live in some kind of reasonable way, but that goal demands something unthinkably difficult—an end to the Earth's most potent nemesis: War. It is we, Americans, who launch the largest and fiercest wars around the world. And so it seems only logical that the citizens of this country do everything possible to help put an end to those wars in Iraq and Afghanistan, and to prevent a possible future one in Iran.

Secretary of Defense Robert Gates asked Congress, in the fall of 2007, for an additional 50 billion dollars for fiscal 2007–2008, to fund the war in Iraq.[180] That's on top of the 23 billion dollars congress had already approved for the war, making a total of close to 173 billion dollars for the year, or roughly 3 billion dollars a week to fund the ongoing devastation. In 2007, Congress funded the war in Iraq at 173 billion dollars; and, in 2008, the most costly year up to that point, at 195 billion dollars. Through 2008, the Iraq war alone had racked up a cumulative cost of over 600 billion dollars—more than the Korean war and nearly as much as the Vietnam war.

The Department of Defense budget request for fiscal 2009, without allocations for the wars in Iraq and Afghanistan totals 515.4 billion dollars. When we factor in monies for emergency discretionary spending and supplemental spending, the total comes to 651.2 billion dollars. At the very same time he requested that money, Gates announced that he was inclined to spend an extra 3 billion dollars to accelerate the expansion of the troops on active duty. We might recall that, in January 2008, when Bush announced his intention to deploy an additional five combat brigades for his so-called surge, he also approved a plan—not very well covered by the press—to increase the size of the active-duty Army by 74,000 soldiers over five years—from 512,000 to 586,000. (That will cost yet another 3 billion dollars.)

Gates also announced plans to expand the Marine Corps by an undisclosed number of recruits. Neither Secretary Gates nor President Bush talked about how much more greenhouse gas such an expansion would add to the atmosphere, an omission that should come as no surprise. Such a question may not cross our minds: We are not accustomed to think about the military and carbon output. But this is the Earth in the twenty-first century, on the brink of catastrophe; and we need to be asking different questions and confronting every department of the government, every corporation and business and institution, and most assuredly, we must be confronting ourselves. We need to think differently about the way we conduct our lives, and the way we impose ourselves on the lives of others—most of whom live half way around the world, in places we cannot locate on a map, or the names of whose countries and leaders we cannot or will not pronounce correctly.

This is not an easy task, for no one seems able to stop this juggernaut known as the military. I mean something beyond just shutting down the wars in Iraq and Afghanistan. I mean trying to erase the way the military has worked its way into the imagination of every American—young and old—over the centuries, so that even most liberals find it very difficult to conceive of solving global problems through anything other than military might. Not education, not the church, not marriage, certainly, only the military in the twenty-first century, has assumed the rank as the most sacrosanct institution in America. From its lofty position, the United States need brook no criticism, answer no objections, and make no real corrections.

The metaphors of combat and war have infiltrated almost every aspect of daily life—sports, religion, business, medicine, music, and even personal relationships. Camouflage clothing, Army boots, military haircuts, and huge Hummer vehicles, now serve as key fashion statements. For centuries, children have been singing joyously about "the rockets' red glare" and "the bombs bursting in air." We "snipe" at each other's statements, "attack" each other's character, "stick to our guns," "blow people out of the water," and declare outright war on drugs, crime, mental illness, and even poverty. What else but the bellicose can we expect from a culture so deeply marked by metaphors of war? Power and the exercise of war drive, not just our foreign and domestic policy, but also direct so much of the way we deal with each other, even those we care deeply about. Bobby Fischer, the chess wizard, while playing in the United States, described his favorite game in the most brutal terms: "Chess is war on a board. The object is to crush the other man's mind."

War did not always occupy the central position that it so much enjoys in the west today. I was prompted to think about this idea because of a poem by Mary Oliver, "The Esquimos Have No Word for 'War.'" I wondered about the English language. The *Oxford English Dictionary* surprised me by introducing the entry for war with a strangely cautionary note. The *OED* is a staid and conservative work; the editors pride themselves in making fine, correct, and incredibly precise linguistic distinctions. In this case, their parsing of the word war should give us all pause about the course of history:

> It is a curious fact that no Germanic nation in early historic times had in living use any word properly meaning "war," though several words with that meaning survived in poetry, in proverbial phrases, and in compound personal names. The Romanic-speaking peoples, who were obliged to avoid the L. bellum on account of its formal coincidence with *bello*- beautiful, found no nearer equivalent in *Teut*, than *werra*.

The word for modern warfare, then, has a history that affords us all a good deal of hope. For the idea of war takes some time to enter the English language: *werra* dates from the middle of the twelfth century. In fact, however, *werra* does not really translate as the modern notion of war. It means something much closer to "confusion," "strife" or "quarrel," or even less than that, plain and simple "worry." What the

OED calls "avowed active hostility"—our notion of warfare—does not appear in English until late in the fourteenth century.

Like Mary Oliver's Esquimo, we were once a people who lived without the concept of war. Unfortunately, the world has perfected that most alien concept over more than 600 years, from the fourteenth century on. The idea has been, for the most part, an absolute failure. Perhaps it might be possible to return to that earlier time.

But if such a change is indeed possible, it will not come from this president or a future president; it will not come in the form of an institutional response. We should not count on any member of Congress to confront the military. A senator or a member of the House might think of it, but would never take action, would never speak out against the solidity of the military at this moment, or the continually expanding military and its needs for more and better equipment, out into the far distant future. The average citizen, also, has a hard time criticizing military strategy. (Who could be opposed to cops walking a beat? Don't you want to feel safe?) Even if no one knows exactly what it means, "Support Our Troops" has assumed the status of a mantra that has a built-in immunity from any questions or criticism. We are expected to accept such slogans without thinking critically about them—a perfect corollary to the way we are expected to accept, without questioning, the wars in Iraq and Afghanistan.

And, always, in hushed tones, one hears that ultimate threat: withholding funds from the military. But, who would ever dare to take such a bold leap? In this country, the military seems to have its way, with very little consequence. Following hours and even days of sometimes heated debate, Congress passes the next and then the next bloated military budget. Children's health care, corporate emission standards, OSHA standards, along with money for education, for the homeless, for the poor, or those wrongly imprisoned—these things all routinely get turned down. But not the Pentagon. No one turns down the Pentagon.

Meanwhile, the worst atrocities committed by United States soldiers against Iraqi civilians—so called "enemy combatants"—such as the horrors that happened at Guantanamo Bay, or the outright murders at Haditha, end with reprimands, or the dismissal of all charges. Or, in the case of the many slaughters of civilians by one private defense contractor or another, very little, if anything, happens at all. On June 27, 2004, L. Paul Bremer, head of the Coalition Provisional Authority, signed Order Number 17, exempting private contractors in Iraq from prosecution, making it certain that Blackwater and other such corporations would answer to no one and to no agency. Private contractors conduct their business in Iraq and Afghanistan outside of any law—domestic or foreign. Part of the recent Status of Forces Agreement between the United States and Iraq—and one of the principle points of contention—was a provision for holding to account American contractors working in Iraq. Maybe that will hold, but most likely not. Meanwhile, the drumbeat goes on and on. And so the military and its intimate associates—dare I say its mercenaries—get a pass, a free ride.

The armed forces grow larger and larger, Pentagon leaders boasting of more equipment and greater technological advances. Like every other aspect of capitalism, each military branch must, of necessity, grow larger and fatter each year; expansion is the lifeblood of imperialism. Each year, the Pentagon builds more and more strategically-placed bases around the world. That's what the strongest nation in the world requires to maintain its position as number one. At least, that's what all the politicians and the leaders—both Republican and Democrat—tell us. Each beribboned general proclaims, to whoever will listen, that this is the best and boldest, most able and powerful military we have ever witnessed in the history of human civilization. Whatever that general says immediately turns into the gospel truth. Very few, if any, senators had the nerve to confront, let alone contradict, General Petraeus as he testified, in the summer of 2007, before congress on the success, against enormous odds and numerous naysayers, of the so-called surge.

The only way to end the war in Iraq, or Afghanistan, we should all now realize, is to cut off all funds. To end all war requires more of the same strategy. The United States Status of Forces Agreement with Iraq establishes that American forces will withdraw from Iraqi cities by June 30, 2009, and that the US will be completely out of Iraq by December 12, 2011. But, if roadside attacks increase, who knows what President Obama will do? In the end, no one can pry this nation from the military's crushing hold, just as no official in the Bush White House was ever able to describe what success might look like. One would be hard-pressed to say that success even exists in war—any war. And, as I have said, no politician will risk his or her career making that foolish move of drawing in the purse strings as tightly as possible, and saying no, you cannot continue your policy of outright aggression in Iraq or Afghanistan or some other country of current interest. No politician—Democrat or Republican—wants to look soft on defense. But, that's the only way to stop the military, the only way even to slow it down—cut off its lifeline of money—and that simply cannot happen. For the military comes first in this country, before everything else—before education, healthcare, and certainly before the needs of the poor and the destitute.

Americans have come to confuse having a large and powerful military with feeling safe and secure. They want to move through their neighborhoods absolutely and totally without fear, and local politicians convince them that the solution is to place more police on the streets—in cars and on foot. Likewise, the government now has us convinced that a huge and mighty military is the only solution to the threat of terrorism: more troops, more firepower, more shock and more awe, more contract workers—it's always more and more. And yet, as we also know, the insurgency in Iraq does more than just go on and on. It has morphed and grown and expanded within the country. The insurgents themselves have changed their tactics, staying one or two steps ahead of the Americans.

Al Qaeda in Iraq has, likewise, splintered into several different groups, grown more clever and, at the same time, more vicious. It has exported its tactics and means and personnel to other countries. Meanwhile, in Afghanistan, the Taliban not only refuses to be bombed into submission but, indeed, according to every news report, has grown stronger and stronger, and more crafty, within the country. According to our own Director of National Intelligence, Michael McConnell, the insurgency has regrouped and reformulated in Pakistan. As I have said, America will soon deploy more troops to confront the Taliban resurgence, as if might could best maneuverability, as if cannons could eliminate cunning.

Four days before he exited the White House, George W. Bush spoke to the nation. One of the things he bragged about was that the United States had not suffered a terrorist attack on its soil since September 11, 2001, which he attributed to his diligent efforts and far-reaching policies. What he didn't say, mainly because he doesn't understand it, I think, is that terrorism works in the same way as partial reinforcement—attack once and then keep your victims guessing. When will the next hit come and where will it come from?

But the tactics of terror are even more sophisticated and elusive than that: the attack of September 11 is still going on. Terrorists have been attacking us for eight long years. America is terrorized, plain and simple. We are practically broke, having spent our monies on military attacks and the creation of new agencies and the protection of airports and sea ports, and on and on. The military is hopelessly short on troops. (A bad economy might fix that, as people search for jobs, any jobs.) We are the victims of the most sophisticated terror attack, and we have been scaring ourselves for so long now we no longer recognize the a normal state of affairs. We have become the terrorists; we have internalized the fear. We spy on each other, turn each other in, distrust the dark-skinned other with the funny-sounding name.

Vietnam provided a potent historical lesson: the largest and mightiest military in the world could not defeat a population who, to use a bit of hyperbole, took on the world's number one superpower with little more than sharpened bamboo sticks, bicycles, and an elaborate system of tunnels. That war gave the world key phrases like "hearts and minds," "domino effect," and "quagmire." We can achieve no victory, military experts repeatedly tell us, without winning the hearts and minds of the people. If that's true—and I am not certain what the phrase actually means—no one can accomplish that goal with tanks and guns. For every war will produce its own gruesome version of the atrocity known in Vietnam as My Lai. We already have witnessed several of them in Iraq. Such atrocities offer guaranteed ways of losing people's hearts and cracking their minds wide open.

The point here is not just the absolute autonomy that the military enjoys in this country, but the way it exploits its position, as well. The military establishment is arrogant. It conducts its affairs facing little criticism and even less restraint. The Pentagon answers solely to itself. It writes its own rules. The price we all pay for that uncontested arrogance and secrecy is now a heavy one: the ultimate destruction of the planet. The subject of the military never comes up in high-level, policy discussions of the environment. And it probably never will. As I have said, it takes more than bravery to confront the military. One risks being a traitor, a turncoat, something other than a pure patriot, when one takes on the military.

To rein in the military will take a wholesale change in thinking in this country. It will require thinking beyond force, beyond might and power. We will need to think not about driving people apart but bringing them together. Only with such a radical shift, however, can we begin to make significant changes toward confronting the crisis of global warming. Perhaps we find ourselves in Iraq for a series of reasons, but Doctor King surely hit on one of strategic importance—oil. We need that precious stuff to keep our habit going, to fuel consumption in this country. It appears that we Americans are willing to go to great lengths to attain the oil we need to maintain the lives we love.

This government places huge corporations in the same exempt category as the military. At a two-day summit on climate change at the White House on September 27th and 28th, 2007, Secretary of State Condoleezza Rice refused to impose goals or set deadlines for cutting greenhouse emissions. She could bring herself to do nothing more than make a plea that all the major polluting nations, including the United States, work toward setting caps on greenhouse emissions.

We simply cannot afford to dampen the economy, she said; setting limits and deadlines will cost too many jobs, cause too much slowdown in production. And then she uttered a feeble statement about solutions, demanding that all developing nations "cut the Gordian knot of fossil fuels, carbon emissions and economic activity. The current system is no longer sustainable, and we must transcend it entirely through a revolution in energy technology."[181]

Those revolutionary new technologies, she predicted, would lift the world out of this looming disaster. That's the promise. Politicians have always held out the promise of change of a better life—success through this technological innovation or that spectacular invention. Maybe that will happen. I doubt it, but maybe buried in her promises and platitudes one might find a glimmer of hope. She also did not mention that the Bush administration tried to censor and intimidate federally funded institutions that work on climate science, like the Environmental Protection Agency (EPA), the National Oceanic and Atmospheric Administration, and NASA. The administration doctored scientific reports and went so far as to try to put the muzzle on arguably the world's best-known and most-respected climate scientist, James Hansen.[182]

This essay offers something concrete, and it starts with the biggest single source of pollution in the country, the military. Of course, our Secretary of State said nothing about the military and pollution. For her, of course, playing the role of advocate for the most bellicose administration in modern times, the military had to remain far off limits. How many times must we hear, "We are at war. We will be at war for a very long time—perhaps for as far as we can see into the future. We will win this war; and we will win it with military might"? GWOT, the Global War on Terrorism, has grabbed hold of our collective imagination and simply will not let go. This vigilance—this way of being in the world, in which we lead with our firepower—will last for the rest of our lifetimes, the Bush administration warned us. Terrorism is with us to stay: it is the New World; the new "clash of civilizations." As Bush put it, our wars constitute the New Crusade.

We must struggle against such a vision, doing everything we can to prevent ourselves from falling into that kind of easy and clichéd way of thinking about the rest of the world—particularly since most of the rest of that world means people of color.

That martial attitude follows closely on the government's second most important objective: the protection of big business. At the White House summit, it was not an environmental advisor but the Secretary of the Treasury, the person responsible for the budget, who came to Bush's defense for refusing to ratify the Kyoto Protocol. The Protocol, an amendment to the United Nations Framework Convention on Climate Change, requires industrialized countries to reduce their greenhouse gas emissions to 5.2 percent below 1990 levels by 2012. One of Bush's first acts as President was to repudiate the Protocol and refuse to bring it to the Senate for ratification. Thus, the Kyoto emission caps, set to expire in 2012, have no binding power in this country.

If the US government makes any move to reduce emissions, it will certainly be tempered by the desire to protect big corporations, most assuredly the oil and the coal industries. As evidence, the Bush Administration, in April 2007, went so far as to argue in the Supreme Court that carbon dioxide did not constitute a pollutant. The Court rejected the Bush contention and "ordered it to review its environmental policies." Dozens of states have made their displeasure with the Bush administration known by passing their own caps on the greenhouse gases.[183]

But, Bush is not the only villain. Opposition to Kyoto crosses party lines. While Bill Clinton professed to agree with the Kyoto Accords, he waited until the very last day of the deadline, in 1998, to sign the treaty, which he did without fanfare, without the usual ceremonial backdrop of the Rose Garden. The President does not, of course, have the power to negotiate treaties alone. He must have the consent of the Senate. And over the course of his next three years in office, Clinton did not take the treaty to the senate for ratification, for it had already expressed its disapproval to any restrictions on economic output.

Something else, something besides concessions to factory output and GDP prevents any administration from signing such accords. And that, of course, is the country's deep and abiding commitment to a powerful and military *free of any restrictions*. If we had an education program in this country that taught about the amount of military pollution and the way its numbers remain off the books, about how the military's principle enemy is the earth, then we might be more easily able to make the radical changes needed to slow down the on-going crisis of global warming. President Obama made greenhouse gases a hallmark of his campaign; he promised reductions without specifying how much or how to do it. We will see just what he will attempt to do, and just what he will manage to accomplish. But, if he is serious about the crisis, he must confront the fact that he is Commander in Chief of an intensely revved up military that is menacing the entire planet. In the end, it seems highly unlikely that the military will not win out over something as abstract as climate, that the heft and muscle of a tank will not trump that invisible stuff called CO_2.

At the meeting of the International Panel on Climate Change, in Bali, in December of 2007, members announced new Kyoto emissions targets. (Its agenda ran to twenty pages and did not include a single mention of the military.) They include the need for the so called rich countries to cut emissions by up to 40 percent below 1990 levels by the year 2020; and the rest of the world to cut emissions by 50 percent by the year 2050. The Panel also pointed out that the United States and Europe are chiefly responsible for raising levels of carbon dioxide, the main greenhouse gas produced by the burning of fossil fuels, from 280 parts per million to 380 parts per million. Carbon dioxide levels had remained steady for some 650,000 years until the Industrial Revolution. They have risen steadily since.[184] A study by economists at the Electric Power Research Institute maintains that unless countries begin to curtail emissions drastically, the concentrations of carbon dioxide by 2040 could exceed 450 parts per million, "a threshold that many scientists say could set in motion harmful changes for centuries to come."[185] I have mentioned these changes earlier in this essay.

In an article in the *Los Angeles Times*, August 5, 2007, titled "Road Kill," the author, Gregg Easterbrook, points out an often neglected fact: traffic deaths are the fastest-rising cause of death in the world. In this country, an astonishing 42,642 people died on the road last year, more than fourteen times the number killed by terrorists in the Twin Towers. The principal cause for the high number of traffic fatalities in this country, Easterbrook argues, is a yearly rise in horsepower in our cars, SUVs, and pickup trucks. For example, 20 years ago, the average new passenger vehicle boasted 119 horsepower and went from 0 to 60 miles per hour in 13 seconds. By 2007, the comparable figures were 220 horsepower and 0 to 60 in 9.5 seconds.

Higher horsepower means not just higher fuel consumption but also greater greenhouse gas emissions. Easterbrook points out that if manufacturers reduced horsepower by one-third, miles-per-gallon efficiency would also rise by one-third. Now here's the kicker. It is such an astonishing fact that I want to quote it directly from Easterbrook himself: "One decade of sales of new vehicles with one-third higher horsepower accounts for the amount of oil the United States imports from the Persian Gulf region. Reduce horsepower by a third and end U.S. Persian Gulf oil dependence."[186] It's that simple, he says. What Easterbrook does not point out is that, even with all that horsepower increase, the average speed on America's highways, because of congestion and speed limits, has not increased. In fact, it has gone down.

But no matter, for Easterbrook offers us more than a solution. He presents us with a strategy, a way of beginning to deal with this impending disaster called global warming. It is one that we do not often hear. In order to move forward, he says very flatly, we will need to take more than a couple of steps to the rear. Indeed, he compares the horsepower race to the arms race: in each case, an end can never be reached. Power and the desire for power will not allow any limits.

In the context of this essay, the military will just keep expanding and expanding, with no end in sight. We must move beyond war.

Why should we entertain the idea of a military with limits? After all, surely we want our military to be as strong as it can possibly be. That means a military that brooks no restrictions on money, on equipment, on man and woman power. But, as I have tried to point out, for America's most sacred institution, the military, that kind of expansive attitude no longer makes much sense. Kennedy, Johnson, Nixon, Clinton, and the two Bushes—all have shown us that war always turns counter-productive and comes back to bite us.

But now we have an additional reason: the Earth, as I say, simply cannot absorb any more abuse. The Science for Peace Institute at the University of Toronto found that an astonishing 10 to 30 percent of all global environmental degradation comes from worldwide military activities. While the Institute does not focus on pollution, it does conclude, however, that the armed forces of the world hold the distinction as the single biggest polluters on the planet.[187] The American military, however, is not the only culprit. Every military unit in every country acts with the same ruthless abandon once the government lets its troops loose on another, foreign and unprepared population.

In fact, if we are serious about saving the planet from total destruction, we must face an essential fact: the largest single source of pollution on the planet, and of the planet, must radically eliminate its damage *to* the planet. If the military were a corporation, and operating with no restraints whatever, we might at least be holding discussions about such arrogance. But the price of imperialism demands an unbridled military, one that we must allow to decimate whatever it wishes on its way to total control, even over the earth itself. We might question that corporation, undertake rational discussions about whether we want some restrictions, some legislation, or even exercise whatever power we have in a capitalist society and withhold our purchases. We might even file an anti-trust against the military. But most of us back off from such actions. We all, quite literally, find ourselves forced into buying into its ethos and philosophy. After all, once we pay our taxes, we act as if we support the government without exception—we quite literally "buy into" the whole system.

For the sake of the planet, the military has to take many steps backwards or, more accurately, someone or some group will have to screw courage to the sticking point and confront the military. That is why I call Easterbrook's conclusion a significant and important strategy, for if we are indeed serious about reversing greenhouse gas emissions, Americans will need to heed that lesson themselves and throttle back their consumption, not just of fossil fuels, but also in all sorts of other areas. But we should agitate to have the military, as the country's single largest abuser of the environment, lead the way. Obviously, military leaders will not change course willingly, will not do it on their own. We, the American people, have to agitate for a reduced military, along with a reduced military presence in the world.

If America consumed oil in line with its percentage of the world's population, then this country would have to cut its daily ration of oil by a whopping 80 percent—from 25 percent down to 5 percent—which would mean reducing its current consumption of 20 million barrels a day to 4 million barrels a day. If the military took that same cut, its current consumption of 1 million barrels a day would turn into a measly 200,000 barrels a day, about the same level as Cuba or the Czech Republic. Such a drawdown would make it difficult indeed to take on many nations. This last figure is skewed, of course, because our active-duty military numbers 1.5 or 2 million—that number, as we know, varies according to source—a scant percentage of the global population of some 6.5 billion people. Nonetheless, the figure gives us a look at a military that would more nearly match our size in the world.

For obese people, some doctors recommend radical surgery, suturing closed part of the stomach, reducing its size drastically. Patients balk; they kick and scream. But if they do not do something like that, they know they will die. In the end, most feel relieved and much healthier. Moreover, most of them survive.

I like that analogy. It is to say that putting limits on our military will not be an easy task. Indeed, it may not even be possible. But, it will be worthwhile to try. The military, as I have said, is probably the last place any patriotic American wants to see cuts of any kind. And a reduced military will radically alter the way America conducts its foreign policy. Backing off from the military will necessitate conducting international politics with fewer bombs dropped and more diplomats shuffled around. People need to recognize that severe and serious reductions must take place in that one sector—the military—that is responsible for bringing the world to the brink of extinction faster than any other.

800 TOMAHAWK CRUISE MISSILES
ONE EVERY FOUR MINUTES DROPPED BY THE
US AIR FORCE INTO THE HEART OF BAGHDAD
MARCH 20-21, 2003

⊢⊢ = 3,000 lbs.
800 lbs depleted uranium

AFTERWORD

On Saturday, January 10, 2009, the forty-first President of the United States, George H.W. Bush—out of office sixteen years—received one of the highest honors this country can bestow on a president. George H. W. Bush had a Nimitz class, nuclear-powered aircraft carrier named after him. The *USS George H.W. Bush*, built at a cost of 6.5 billion dollars, sat in dry dock that Saturday afternoon, awaiting its full compliment of 6,000 sailors and marines. More than three football fields long, the *USS Bush* takes its place alongside a fleet of other presidential carriers—Republicans and Democrats, founding fathers and bright lights, cruising side by side in search of the next country to invade, "save," or "police"—the *USS George Washington*, *Abraham Lincoln*, *Theodore Roosevelt*, *John F. Kennedy*, *Dwight D. Eisenhower*, *Harry S. Truman*, and *Ronald Reagan*. Bush obviously saw the ship as a military extension of the nation, as he told the crowd: "The crew will form an unbroken line of patriots protecting this special piece of American territory"—a maritime version of manifest destiny.

Having one's name written across the side of such a huge vessel is an honor that may indeed rank higher than having a presidential library in one's name. For a library, presidents must raise their own money and then fill the building with their own papers and a few hundred books with respectable and meaningful titles. But an aircraft carrier, well, the Pentagon buys that for you in the name of every democratic ideal that the country holds dear. Bush's sister, Doro Bush Koch, held a bottle of champagne aloft and sent it crashing cross the ship's bow, christening the carrier, as if it were an innocent newborn, in the name of peace and democracy.[188]

Most of the issues that I raise in this essay come together and are made obvious with that January 10 commission: an enormous budget dedicated to furthering all things military; an overweening pride in the country and in the military; a deep connection between technology and killing; an even deeper nexus between political power and war; the easy and false connection between armament and national security; the consecration of war heroes. Finally, and most importantly, the launching of that monstrous vessel makes clear an absolute and utter disregard for the health of the planet. Recall the fuel consumption of the *USS Independence*. And even though the *USS George H.W. Bush* is nuclear powered, as I pointed out earlier, such carriers still heavily pollute the sea, the sky, and eventually all life. A radiation leak of even the smallest proportions would be devastating for the seas and skies.

Imagine, if you will, a room filled with politicians and bureaucrats sitting around tables discussing the wisdom of developing a 6 billion dollar monster of war. Upon hearing of such a project, civilian critics like to raise the issue of tradeoffs: what would that 6 billion dollars buy, in terms of food and shelter and education for the poor in this country? But such discussions are really beside the point, because no one in authority ever entertains such a question, or wonders about such a tradeoff. The choices are made with bureaucrats arguing over the size and scope of the project, and how much money will come back to their home state. In the end, the military trumps every other priority. The bulk of the federal budget always makes its way to the military. Discussions about spending cuts and alternate priorities turn out to be *pro forma* at best.

The Pentagon has always gotten its way, no matter what, while each day we citizens grow more fearful and distrustful of the world around us. More carriers will be commissioned and more troops deployed, and the number of insurgent groups around the world will continue to grow. When Hillary Clinton testified before the Senate, on January 13, 2009, about her confirmation as Secretary of State, she didn't take long to say that this country would resort to war where and when it was necessary. She went on to point out that the new threat, intelligence reveals, will come from terrorists waging a bio-war on our soil. Without actually making anything explicit, Clinton made the case that every citizen should begin feeling even higher and higher levels of fear and panic. Day One of the new confirmation hearings, and the old rhetoric was still on the march. Listen closely to those familiar beats of the drum: they sound out a warning that we can expect even larger military budgets in the coming years.

I have argued in this book that lowering thermostats and changing light bulbs will have little effect in turning aside the enormity of the global warming crisis. Just a few years ago, environmental scientists told us we had about ninety years before climate change reached the point of no return. At that moment, nothing we could do would reverse the course of warming trends. Those same scientists say we have no more than forty, though maybe even fewer years, to take the most decisive action possible. Conditions, they say, have grown seriously worse. In the recent past, climatologists told us we needed to cut greenhouse gases by 70 percent, and then they demanded 80 percent. Now, many argue that greenhouse gases need to be reduced by an astonishing 90 percent. The Greenland icecap has already begun to turn to slush, and because of that melt, climatologists earlier predicted that the oceans would rise by two feet this century. They now expect them to rise much higher. If the icecap completely disappears, and the data suggest that the melt is occurring much more rapidly than any of the models had predicted, scientists expect the oceans, worldwide, to rise some twenty-two feet.

Similarly, cutting the budget for the Department of Defense, decommissioning some ships, or converting from lead bullets to zinc will hardly matter. It also makes little sense to subject the military to oversight restrictions like the Clean Air Act, the Superfund Laws, or the Resource Conservation and Recovery Act. What if the military did in fact agree? Would we then feel that the environment was really being protected? I think not. I have already talked about the absurdity of a green military, of the possibility of some Orwellian concept called pollution-free decimation. So what if the military switched to millions and millions of low-energy light bulbs? The United States military remains in the business of the wholesale destruction of life on this planet. We cannot take incremental steps toward the elimination of war, or hide behind the greening of death. We can settle for no less than the most politically impossible move: the end of war.

One more comment about commissioned ships: Consider the *USS Constitution*. I find in the naming of that carrier an even deeper and more potent connection than one honoring a president. How astounding: a behemoth of war named for what most people in the country view as its most sacred and founding document. At first glance, it seems blasphemous. In a strange way, the naming reveals the truth, of course, that the roots of war grow deeply in the very founding of the republic, and spread out and travel through the entirety of the nation's history. But it seems clear that war has run its course: the roots now threaten to choke us all.

In his magnificent preface to Frantz Fanon's *The Wretched of the Earth*, Jean-Paul Sartre urges his French brothers and sisters to read Fanon, an Algerian stranger, if they wanted to understand the intense pain of colonialism:

> Fanon reveals to his comrades—above all to some of them who are rather too Westernized—the solidarity of the people of the mother country and of their representatives in the colonies. Have the courage

to read this book, for in the first place it will make you ashamed, and shame, as Marx said, is a revolutionary sentiment.[189]

I do not claim for myself the stature of Frantz Fanon, but I do hope that the reader will feel a measure of shame after reading *The Green Zone*. What we Americans have done, not just over the past eight years—for that is obvious—but from the inception of this country by pushing the agenda of war, has been shameful. Damage to the environment, human and non-human, has become more obvious in the recent past because Iraq has for some time been on the front pages, as well as the fact that we have been subject to a most dreadful administration and that the earth now cries out mightily for mercy. And while the new weapons of war—amazingly powerful jet aircraft, horrifically destructive bombs, and depleted uranium—produce staggering amounts of pollution, we must realize that this country has been generating pollution on some level since men with rifles began their confrontation with Native Americans early in our history. We polluted as we expanded west, and then we polluted as we moved off our shores to other countries. We pollute as we purportedly advance democracy using the most powerful machinery of death in the world. We pollute as we consume. We pollute as we colonize. We pollute as we kill.

It doesn't make much difference to shut down the war in Iraq while still pursuing the war in Afghanistan and carrying the threat of war to other countries. We will not survive, plain and simple, without the total and complete elimination of war. The phrase reverberates anew: There is no reason on Earth, anymore, to entertain the possibility of war. Barack Obama cannot shut down all war. No president or politician can do that. Obama may get us out of Iraq—that war has dragged on and on, grown massively expensive, and has had its day. Anyway, he has public opinion behind him. Nonetheless, Obama cannot take a stand against all war. To do that, he would have to break the hold of the biggest corporations in this country. While he pledges to expand the war in Afghanistan, his Secretary of State talks hawk-ish on Iran.

Only we can affect a radical change. But how can that happen? I think there is only one way to stop the machine from grinding on and on. Which takes us to the reality beneath the issue of oil that Doctor King talked about, and that is money. Like all federal agencies, of course, the Pentagon runs not just on money, but on barrels and barrels of money. The defense budget takes up at least 54 percent of the total federal budget—even more if we add in monies for related areas like NASA, Department of Energy nuclear bombs, veterans benefits, and interest on past military debts. Even in the worst of financial times, the Pentagon's budget expands. Even in the worst of financial times, political leaders do not hesitate to double the number of troops in Afghanistan. All this somehow in the name of making us safer.

According to Steve Martinot of San Francisco State College, the military "is now connected and conjoined to 50 percent of all economic activity in the US." He goes on to explain how intertwined the military is in the ordering of the economy: "This doesn't mean that 50 percent of all production is military production; it means that 50 percent of all economic activity is associated with the military, either in the production of military hardware, the running of bases, or in ancillary industries whose major customer is the military, and thus who owe their existence and functioning to that major customer."[190]

Martinot is saying something that, for many of Americans, may sound astonishing: big corporations are the military—simply out of uniform. There is big money to be made in war, we know that, even beyond the obvious examples of Halliburton; Blackwater USA; Parsons Engineering; and Kellogg, Brown & Root. Military might has spread out through the entire system; a huge number of people have a financial stake in its health and strength. The CEO of Raytheon does not salute the military, he bows down in front of every service member in uniform. To cut war out of the economy will be as big a shock to the system as the meltdown of Bear Stearns and Lehman Brothers, as telling as the folding of Bernard Madoff's Ponzi empire. In 1967, in this same speech, "A Time to Break Silence," Dr. King called us "a society gone mad on war." "Somehow," he declared, "this madness must cease. We must stop now."

We can shut the military down one way only and that is by cutting off its funds. Congress has shown no will for such a tactic. Few politicians can risk losing their re-election by taking such a radical position. Only we, as citizens, can call a halt to war. We have a voice when we protest. And we make our loudest protest, in this country, through money, and most significantly through our taxes. In the 60s, to help fund the increasingly unpopular war in Vietnam, the Johnson administration added a surtax to everyone's telephone bill, which many people refused to pay. What change might take place if an overwhelming majority of Americans decide to withhold that amount of their federal taxes that go to pay for the defense budget? Resistance may offer the only course—a resistance to the machine that is killing the environment abroad and in this country, as well. War is so deeply embedded in the democratic system—in fact, in many ways it is the system—that we may need to grab it where it lives, and dies, and that's at the level of money.

So, here's something to at least think about. A colleague tells me that, for 2007, he paid federal income taxes at an effective rate of 17.9 percent. This means that he worked for the government the first nine weeks of the year to help pay for all those goods and services, from education to Social Security, that I am certain he finds necessary and essential. He did not begin pocketing his own wages until roughly the first week of March. But, here's the kicker. If roughly 54 percent of the federal budget goes to the Department of Defense—and that is a conservative figure—then he spent four and a half of those nine weeks helping to pay for the wars in Iraq and Afghanistan and for new weapons of destruction.

His tax bill for 2007 was approximately 25,000 dollars, 54 percent of which—or approximately 13,000 dollars—went to the Department of Defense. To make my example more vivid, I ask you to do the following two things: First, figure out how much you effectively gave to the Pentagon last year. Second, and much harder, imagine yourself writing out a check for that amount, paid to the order of the Pentagon, and signed by you. In the case of my colleague, as I say, that would amount to 13,000 dollars. Now imagine placing that check carefully in an envelope, sealing it, stamping it, and sending it off in the mail. Most of us would hesitate, or even balk, at doing such a thing. And yet, in effect, that's exactly what happens: we send our money to that proxy for Washington DC, the Internal Revenue Service.

The only people who escape this system are those who do not earn enough to pay any taxes, but many of those people pay an even higher price by sending off their sons and daughters to fight—and perhaps even die—in a foreign country. Which might begin to happen with greater frequency as the economy sinks, and more and more young people who cannot find jobs sign up for the military as a last resort.

We must find a way, finally, to lead our collective lives as free people without being enslaved to the military. I am certainly not a commander, and I am definitely not in uniform, but I do reek of that old military/industrial/civilian complex. I cannot exclude myself from it. I am complicit. I am not happy about it; but I am an essential part of the whole plan. I do more than Support Our Troops, I support the military at a most basic level, the level of money.

Refusal to pay taxes will not, of course, appeal to everyone—nor should it. Which means that each person will have to find his or her own way to put a halt to the impending death of the planet at the hands of the United States military. It reveals something about those in high office that now ex-Vice President Dick Cheney, with his intimate and long-standing connections to Halliburton, can so unashamedly find ways of making money from the war. Senator Frank Lautenberg reported that, in one year, alone Cheney's stock options in Halliburton rose 3,281 percent. His 433,333 options increased dramatically from 241,498 dollars in 2004 to 8 million dollars in 2005. We do not need to look very far to discover why his stock shot up so high, since by the end of 2005 Halliburton had amassed a profit from the war in Iraq in excess of 20 billion dollars.

We must discover new and innovative ways of doing much the opposite of what the vice president has so cynically managed to achieve. Cheney's was an easy task, ours will be difficult. His was opaque, ours must be transparent. His was mean-spirited and destructive. Ours will be liberating.[191]

NOTES

1 *Miami Herald*, January 7, 2009.

2 Andrew D. Selsky, "AP Confirms Secret Camp Inside Gitmo," February 6, 2008.

3 Pamela Hess, Associated Press, December 11, 2008.

4 Chalmers Johnson, *Blowback: The Costs and Consequences of American Empire* (Henry Holt and Company, 200), p. xi.

5 The unclassified report, "Operation Iraqi Freedom—By The Numbers," signed by Lt. General Teed Michael Moseley, Commander of CENTAF (Central Command Air Force), I found tremendously useful for statistics on the first months of the war. One can find the report posted on John Pike's rather useful website, http://www.globalsecurity.org. Pike is a well-known writer on military and intelligence policies.

6 The results of this study appeared in the *New England Journal of Medicine*.

7 Martin Luther King, Jr., *I Have A Dream: Writings and Speeches that Changed the World*, ed. James M. Washington (San Francisco, Harper San Francisco, 1992), p. 176.

8 Michael T. Klare, "Garrisoning the Global Gas Station, in *TomDispatch*, http://www.tomdispatch.com, June 13, 2008.

9   "US Troop Totals May Be Higher At End Of Surge," MSNBC, September 14, 2007. See also Stewart M. Powell, "Second Iraq Troop Surge Starts," Hearst Newspapers for May 21, 2007; and see http://www.globalsecurity.org/military/ops/iraq_ofbat.htm.

10   See Stewart Powell, *Seattle Post-Intelligencer*, May 21, 2007.

11   *Washington Post*, May 30, 2008.

12   "Iraq: Summary of US Forces Overview," Congressional Research Service, July 18, 2005.

13   Chalmers Johnson, "America's Empire of Bases," *TomDispatch*, January 15, 2004.

14   Op cit.

15   Johnson, "Empire of Bases."

16   Chalmers Johnson, "737 U.S. Military Bases—Global Empire," Information Clearing House, February 19, 2007.

17   Gar Smith, "How Fuel Efficient Is The Pentagon? The Military's Oil Addiction," Environmentalists Against War, *Earth Island Journal*, Winter 1990–91, accessed from http://www.envirosagainstwar.org/know/read.php?itemid=593, September 10, 2003.

18   "Operation Iraqi Freedom By The Numbers," USCENTAF, April 30, 2003, 15.

19   Tara Copp, "Conflict With Iraq: Ground Forces Get Key Air Support," *Naples Daily News* (Florida), Scripps Howard News Service, March 23, 2003.

20   Nick Turse, "Bombs Over Baghdad: The Pentagon's Secret Air War In Iraq," *TomDispatch*, February 8, 2007.

21   *Air Force Link*, official website of the United States Air Force, April 9, 2003.

22   Harlan Ullman, in interview with David Martin, a CBS reporter, July 30, 2006. See also: http://www.commondreams.org/views03/0127-08.htm: November 2003. Along with James P. Wade, Ullman formulated the concept now known as "shock and awe." Ullman, a senior associate at the Center for Strategic and International Studies, published a book in 1996 titled, *Shock and Awe: Achieving Rapid Dominance*. On CBS, Ullman went on to talk about how the missiles would destroy everything that makes life in Baghdad livable: "You take the city down. You get rid of their power, water. In two, three, four, five days they are physically, emotionally, and psychologically exhausted."

23   Report compiled by the Director of Research, Iraqi Museum, the British Museum, and UNESCO, April 29, 2003.

24   Valentinas Mite, "Iraq: Archives, Libraries Devastated by War, Looting."

25   See http://www.rferl.org/featurearticleprint/2000/07/e5d79a8f-ab28-4ebc.

26   Bob Nichols, "Environmentalists Against War," August 3, 2004. http://www.onlinejournal.com/SpecialReports/071304Nichols/071304nichols.html.

27   Robert Bryce, "Gas Pains," *The Atlantic Monthly*, May 2005, p. 35.

28   Sohbet Karbuz, "US Military Oil Pains," *Energy Bulletin* (on-line), February 21, 2007. Karbuz is the former head of non-OECD energy statistics section of the International Energy Agency. See also *2006 Air Force Almanac*, *2006 Navy Almanac*, and *Congressional Budget Office*, the US Congress, August 2006.

29   Karbuz, "US Military Oil Pains."

30   Ibid. As of September 30, 2005 the Air Force had 5,986 aircraft in service. At the beginning of 2006, the Navy had 285 combat and support ships, and around 4,000 operational planes and helicopters. At the end of 2005, the Army had a combat vehicle fleet of approximately 28,000 armored vehicles.

31   "Guns and Global Warming: War, Peace and the Environment," Scientists for Global Responsibility, http://www.sgr.org.uk/ArmsControl/NFPAGMnotes_feb07.html. And see http://www.organicconsumers.org/perchlorate.com, and see "Guns and Global Warming: War, Peace and the Environment," at http://www.sgr.org.uk/armscontrol/NfPAGnotes_February 2007.html.

32   *CENTAF Fact Sheet* website.

33   Bryce, "Gas Pains," p. 34.

34   See Sohbet Karbuz, "US Military Energy Consumption—Facts and Figures," *Energy Bulletin* (on-line), May 20, 2007, Fact 14, p. 2.

35   Bryce, "Gas Pains," p. 34.

36   Karbuz, "US Military Energy Consumption."

37   Helen C. Caldicott, "Nuclear Power Still A Deadly Proposition," *Nuclear Age Peace Foundation* (on-line), August 17, 2004

38   As with almost everything else with the military, determining their exact oil consumption is puzzling and confusing. The official data comes from the DoD's annual energy management report, Federal Energy Management Program's annual report to congress, EIA/DoE's *Annual Energy Review*, and *DESC Factbook*. (The first three publications do not add fleet vehicle oil and non-fleet vehicle oil.) See also http://www.energyandcapital.com/article/print.php. According to the Defense Logistic Agency's website, as of November 2005, the military had used 2.1 billion gallons of fuel (cited in Karbuz, "US Military Energy Consumption").

39   Karbuz, "Military Energy Consumption."

40   Op cit.

41   Op cit. See also Janet Ginsberg, "The Most Fuel-Efficient That The Military Can Be," *Business Week*, March 28, 2005. What the military spent on fuel, Ginsberg maintains, "was only a tiny portion of the fuel bill. Far more money is spent on delivery."

42   http://www.energyandcapital.com/article/print.php. According to the *CIA World Factbook* (2006), only 35 countries out of 210 consume more oil per day than the Pentagon. See Karbuz, "US Military Oil Pains."

43   *Agence France-Presse* reports that "later, the Kuwaitis sought nominal payment for fuel supplied to US forces remaining in Iraq after Saddam's ouster."

44   See http://www.abovetopsecret.org.

45   See the website, *National Defense*, entry dated November 1, 2005.

46   Karbuz, "Military Energy Consumption."

47   Elizabeth Book, "Pentagon Needs Accurate Accounting of Fuel," *National Defense Magazine*, March 28, 2005.

48   http://www.energyandcapital.com/article/print.php.

49   Richard Lardner, "In Iraq, Private Contractors Outnumber US Troops," Associated Press, September 20, 2007. See also Sarah Meyers, "Iraq Security Companies and Training Camps," *Brussels Tribunal*, May 17, 2006.

50   See Jeremy Scahill, *Blackwater: The Rise of the World's Most Powerful Mercenary Army* (New York: Nation Books, 2007).

51   August Cole and Neil King, Jr., "Blackwater Furor May Alter Way US Contractors in Iraq Do Business," *Wall Street Journal*, October 3, 2007, p. 1. See also Robert Collier, "Global Security Firms Fill In As Private Contractors," *San Francisco Chronicle*, March 28, 2004.

52   Smith, "How Fuel Efficient Is The Pentagon?"

53   Op cit.

54   US Navy Official website, "Status of the Navy," as of November 28, 2007.

55   *TomDispatch*, January 15, 2004.

56   *Wikipedia*—"USS Abraham Lincoln."

57   Karbuz, p.1.

58   Ibid., p.4.

59   Tom Cutler, *The Armed Forces Journal*, July 1989.

60   Smith, "How Fuel Efficient Is The Pentagon? Military's Oil Addiction."

61   Karbuz, "US Military Energy Consumption." See also Tom Cutler on fuel efficiency, in *The Armed Forces Journal*, July 1989.

62   Janet Ginsberg, "The Most Fuel-Efficient The Military Can Be," *Business Week*, March 28, 2005. http://www.businessweek.com/magazine/content/01_36/b3747102.htm.

63   "Energy Statistics oil consumption (most recent by country)," *NationMaster*, http://www.nationmaster.com/red/graph/ene_oil_con-energy-oil-cons.

64   Karbuz, "US Military Energy Consumption—Facts and Figures."

65   Op cit.

66   "America's Secret Air War."

67   Bradley Graham, "Commanders Plan Eventual Consolidation of US Bases in Iraq," *Washington Post*, May 22, 2005.

68   Gar Smith, "How Efficient Is The Pentagon: The Military's Oil Addiction."

69   See Renae Merle, "Running Low on Ammo," *Washington Post*, July 12, 2004.

70   American Forces Press Service, "The M-16 Round's 'Friendly,' But Still Deadly," March 3, 1999.

71   See Friends of the Earth, "Green Group Calls for End to Bunker Fuel Use," November 13, 2007: "A study released last week found that more than 60,000 people died worldwide from shipping emissions in 2002, due in large part to the use of bunker fuel." (See also http://www.foe.org/)

72   George Monbiot, "We Are All Killers," *The Guardian*, February 28, 2006. See also Gregory Lamb, "Flying The Cleanly Skies?," *Christian Science Monitor*, February 12, 2007.

73   Meng-Dawn Cheng, "Research in Military Aircraft Emissions," SERDP (Strategic Environmental Research and Development Program), Oak Ridge National Laboratory.

74   Joachim D. Pleil, Leslie B. Smith, and Sanford D. Zelnick, "Personal Exposure to JP-8 Fuel Vapors and Exhaust at Air Force Bases," *Environmental Health Perspectives*, vol. 108, number 3, March 2000.

75   D.T. Harris, D. Sakiestewa, R.F. Robledo, and M. Witten, "Immunotoxicological Effects Of JP-8 Jet Fuel Exposure," in PubMed: www.pubmed.gov:1997 Jan–Feb, 13:43–55.

76   Jamais Cascio, "Fly Green," March 1, 2006: http://www.worldchanging.com/archives/004.164.html.

77   "U.S. Projects Increase in CO_2 Gases," Associated Press, *MSNBC.com*, March 3, 2007. See, too, Energy Information Administration, "Official Energy Statistics from the US Government"; and "Bush Climate Report Shows U.S. Greenhouse Gases Skyrocketing," *Environmental News Service* (on-line), March 5, 2007.

78   In 1998, the United States Department of Defense spent 2 billion dollars cleaning up installations in the states and its territories, but only a total of 18.6

million dollars cleaning up its bases in Great Britain, Germany, Belgium, Italy, Japan, and South Korea. The DoD allocated no money to the Philippines or Panama. See Michael Satchell, "What the Military Left Behind," *US News and World Report*, 128(3):30, 2000.

79   See Satchell.

80   op cit.

81   See   http://www.globalministries.org/index2.php?option=com_content and table.

82   John Lindsay-Poland and Nick Morgan, *Overseas Military Bases and Environment*, Volume 3, Number 15, June 1998.

83   See http://www.viequesisland.com/navy/georgiau.html. Porter is Associate Dean and Josiah Mcigs Distinguished Professor, University of Georgia, Odum School of Ecology, School of Marine Programs.

84   Katherine T. McCaffrey, *Military Power and Popular Protest: The U.S. Navy in Vieques, Puerto Rico* (Rutgers University Press, 2002).

85   Kimberly Hefling, "Data Sought On Veterans' Suicide," Associated Press, December 12, 2007.

86   "Jobless After War: Veterans Find Tough Going," Associated Press, February 7, 2008.

87   For a discussion of Depleted Uranium, see Mark H. Gaffney's long and detailed essay, "US Use of Radiological Weapons Calls For An International Tribunal," published on-line on a website that has been there from the beginning of the wars: http://www.informationclearinghouse.org, August 23, 2007.

88   Bob Nichols, "Radiation in Iraq Equals 250,000 Nagasaki Bombs," Environmentalists Against War, August 3, 2004. http://www.onlinejournal.com/SpecialReports/071304Nichols/071304nichols.html.

89   See Robert James Parsons, "America's Big Dirty Secret," *Le Monde diplomatique* (March 2002): "The US conducted the first real operational tests against Baghdad in 1991. The war in Kosovo provided further opportunity to test, on impressively hard targets, DU weapon prototypes as well as weapons already in production. Afghanistan has seen an extension and amplification of such tests. But at the Pentagon there is little transparency about this."

90   Op cit. See also Larry Johnson, "Use of Depleted Uranium Weapons Lingers as Health Concern," *Seattle Post Intelligencer*, August 4, 2003.

91   Brita May Rose, "America's Radioactive War," *CounterPunch*, November 11, 2004.

92   op cit.

93   Larry Johnson, "Iraqi Cancers, Birth Defects blamed on U.S. Depleted Uranium," *Seattle Post Intelligencer*, November 12, 2002. See also Mark Gould and Jon Ungoed-Thomas, "UK Radiation Jump Blamed on Iraq Shells," *The Sunday Times* (London), February 19, 2006. And see also Larry Johnson, "Use of Depleted Uranium."

94   See Mark H. Gaffney, "U.S. Use of Radiological Weapons Calls For An International Tribunal," http://www.theinformationclearinghouse.org, August 23, 2007.

95   Robert James Parsons, "America's Big Dirty Secret," *Le Monde diplomatique*, March 2002.

96   Quoted in *Project Censored*, Number 15, 2004.

97   Johnson, "Use of Depleted Uranium."

98   Johnson, "Iraqi Cancers." See also Deborah Hastings, "Sickened Iraq Vets Cite Depleted Uranium," *The Boston Globe*, August 12, 2006.

99   Quoted in James P. Tucker, Jr., "Depleted Uranium Death Toll Among US War Veterans Tops 11,000," *Global Research* website, October 29, 2006." http://www.americanfreepress.net/html/du_death_toll.html.

100   Quoted in Christopher Bollyn, "Depleted uranium Blamed for Cancer Clusters Among Iraq War Vets," Nuclear Age Peace Foundation, August 15, 2004.

101   "Depleted Nuclear Weapons, Genocide and That's Right—The United States," June 27, 2005: http://tabacco.myblogsite.com/.

102   Cited in Johnson, "Iraqi Cancers."

103   "Does Iraq's Depleted Uranium Pose A Health Risk," *The Lancet*, volume 351 (9103), February 28, 1998, p. 657.

104   "War or Not, Iraq's Environment a Casualty," *Environment News*, in http://www.environmentalistsagainstwar.org, March 18, 2003.

105   *The Lancet*, 657.

106   Cited by Johnson, in "Iraqi Cancers."

107   See Christopher Bollyn.

108   op cit.

109   *Life* magazine, May 1995. Riegle was a Democrat from Michigan.

110   See Michael Williams, UN Environmental spokesperson, in "Weapons Dust Worries Iraqis. US Concerned," by Thomas D. Williams, *The Hartford Courant*, November 6, 2004, http://www.environmentalistsagainstwar.org. See also Gaffney.

111   Gaffney.

112   Alexandra C. Miller, et al, "Depleted Uranium-Catalyzed Oxidative DNA Damage: Absence of Significant Alpha Particle Decay," *Journal of Inorganic Biochemistry*, vol. 91(2002), 246–52.

113   Interview with physicist Michio Kaku, in *Poison Dust*, a film by Sara Flanders and Su Harris, 2005.

114   "Depleted Uranium in Iraqi Soil, Air May Cause Health Issues," interview with Diane Henshel and Hina Alam, in *Indiana University Daily Student* (http://www.ids news.com), November 2, 2003.

115   MSNBC News Service, March 1, 2006. Williams, "Weapons Dust": "More than 230,000 of the 697,000 US soldiers who served in that war [Enduring Freedom] have filed disability claims for various maladies, the majority of which fall under the broad category of gulf war syndrome."

116   See Gaffney.

117   See http://www.hrw.org/reports/2003/usa/203/10.htm.

118   Seymour Hersh, "Up In The Air: Where Is the Iraq War Headed Now?" *The New Yorker*, December 5, 2005.

119   USCENTAF Fact Sheet.

120   Nick Turse, "Bombs Over Baghdad: The Pentagon's Secret Air War In Iraq," *TomDispatch*, Februrary 7, 2007.

121   http://www. globalsecurity.org. Guided Bomb Unit 28 (GBU-28). See also the Military Analysis Network, Guided Bomb Unit-28. http://www.globalsecurity.org: "BLU-82 Commando Vault, Daisy Cutter.

122   See the website http://www.ucsusa.org, May 2005.

123   Parsons, *Le Monde diplomatique*, March 2002.

124   See *The London Daily Mail* reporter David Williams on http://www.workingforchange.com, November 8, 2001.

125   Richard Norton-Taylor, "The return of the B-52s," *The Guardian*, November 2, 2001.

126   Paul Walker, "US Bombing: The Myth of Surgical Bombing In The Gulf War," deoxy.org/wc/wc-myth.htm. See also globalsecurity.org: "BLU-82 Commando Vault, Daisy Cutter."

127   See *Human Rights Watch Backgrounder*, http://www.HRW.org, "Cluster Bombs in Afghanistan," October 2001.

128   Nick Turse, "The Air War In Iraq Uncovered," *TomDispatch*, May 25, 2007. http://www.tomdispatch.com/index.mhtml?pid=198624.

129   Op cit. See also Vernon Loeb, "Group Says U.S. Broke Law In Use of Cluster bombs in Afghanistan," *Washington Post*, December 18, 2002.

130   Op cit.

131   Op cit.

132   Marshall Brain, "How Bunker Busters Work," on http://www.howstuff-works.com.

133   http://www.globalsecurity.org GBU-43B, "Mother Of All Bombs" and MOAB-Massive Ordnance Air Blast Bomb.

134   Canadian Centre for Occupational Health and Safety, December 23, 1997. http://www.ccohs.ca/oshanswers/chemicals/chem_profiles/aluminum_powder/health_alu.html.

135   "Pentagon Renews Attack on Public Health and the Environment," March 3, 2005, http://www.commondreams.org.

136   See http://www.organicconsumers.org/perchlorate.com, and see Scientists For Global Responsibility, "Guns and Global Warming; War, Peace and the Environment," at http://www.sgr.org.uk/armscontrol/NfPaGnotes_February 2007.html.

137   "War Or Not, Iraq's Environment A Casualty," *Environment News*, March 18, 2003.

138   See *GlobalSecurity* on the subject of napalm.

139   See Andrew Buncombe, "US Admits It Used Napalm In Iraq," *The Independent*, August 10, 2003; *Daily Kos*: "Fallujah: Napalm By Any Other Name" http://www.dailykos.com/story/2004/11/21/32937/834.; James W. Crawley, "Officials Confirm Dropping Firebombs On Iraqi Troops," *San Diego Union-Tribune*, August 05, 2003; and Lindsay Murdoch, "Dead Bodies Are Everywhere," *Sydney Morning Herald*, March 22, 2003.

140   UK Ministry of Defense letter to Alice Mahon, http//:www.rainews24.rai.it/ran24/inchiesta/foto/documento_ministero.jpg.

141   See Murdoch, "Dead Bodies Are Everywhere."

142   *CBS News*, "Cold War Water Pollution," Los Angeles, January 7, 2003. See also "Guns and Global Warming: War, Peace and the Environment," Scientists for Global Responsibility.

143   Laurie Duncan, "Kuwait Oil Fires, Persian Gulf War," http://www.espionageinfo.com, December 18, 2007.

144   Ben Feller, "War Costs for Iraq and Afghanistan Hit 850 Billion," *Huffington Post*, June 30, 2008.

145   Joseph E. Stiglitz and Linda Bilmes, *The Three Trillion Dollar War: The True Cost of the Iraq Conflict* (New York: W.W. Norton, 2008).

146   Robert Bryce, "As Green As A Neocon: Why Iraq Hawks Are Driving Priuses," http://www.slate.com, January 25, 2005.

147   See the following: Rory McCarthy, "Gaza Doctors Say Patients Suffering Mystery Injuries After Israeli Attacks," *The Guardian*, October 18, 2006; "Embedded Weapons-Grade Tungsten Alloy Shrapnel Rapidly Induces Metastatic High-Grade Rhabdomyosarcomas in F344 Rats," Kalinich et al, *Environmental health Perspectives*, vol. 113, Number 6, June 2005. http://www.eponline.org/members/2005/7791/7791.html; Noah Shachtman, "Cancer Worries For New U.S. Bombs," Noah Shachtman.com, May 2, 2006.

148   Lisa Miller, "Belief Watch: Tree Hugger," *Newsweek*, March 19, 2007.

149   Mark Hertsgaard, "Green Goes Grassroots: The Environmental Movement Today," *The Nation*, July 31/August 7, 2006, p. 11.

150   Sabrina Tavernise, "Iraqi Death Toll Exceeded 34,000 in 2006, UN Says," *New York Times*, January 16, 2007. *The Lancet* created some controversy when it reported, in October 2006, that 650,000 Iraqis had been killed up to that point. The figure represents 2.5 percent of the entire population of the country.

151   United Nations Desertification Conference, Nairobi, 2003. http://www.wateryear.2003.org/en/ev.php CRI.

152   The CNA report is dated April 16, 2007. To illustrate the very tight links between these conservative think tanks: Harlan Ullman, the man who conceived of and promulgated the strategy of "shock and awe," serves as senior vice-president of CNA.

153   Richard Perle and David Frum, *An End To Evil: How To Win The War On Terror* (New York: Random House, 2003).

154   "Global Warming May Be Security Factor," Associated Press, April 16, 2007.

155   Matt Simmons, "Future Energy Challenges: Are We In Denial Or Facing Hard Truths?" Sand Ridge Energy, September 23, 2007.

156   Harris Poll, July 26, 2005, "U.S. Adults Paying Less Attention to the Events in Afghanistan Than Those in Iraq," http://harrisinteractive.com/harris_poll/index.asp?PID=587.

157   See Sonali Kolhatkar and James Ingalls, *Bleeding Afghanistan: Washington, Warlords, and the Propaganda of Silence* (New York and London: Seven Stories Press, 2006), p. 12.

158   See Human Rights Backgrounder, "Cluster Bombs in Afghanistan," and "UN Slams Use of Cluster Bombs as 8 Die," *The News International* (Pakistan), October 26, 2001.

159   See "Afghanistan: UN To Clear Coalition Cluster Bombs," UN Office for the Coordination of Humanitarian Affairs, *IRINnews*, January 2, 2002, http://www.irinnews.org/report.asp?ReportID=18295&SelectRegion=Central_Asia; "Fatally Flawed: Cluster Bombs and Their Use by the United States in

Afghanistan," *Human Rights Watch Report*, Volume 14, no. 7 (G), http://www. HRW.org, December 2002.

160   Michael Kamber, "Afghanistan's Environmental Casualties," *Mother Jones*, March 6, 2002. "Half of the world population and 80 percent of rural households in developing countries cook with solid fuels like wood, coal, crop residues and dung. In many instances, women cook around open fires, typically with a pot atop three large stones and a wood fire in the middle:

> Indoor air pollution, including smoke and other products of incomplete combustion like carbon monoxide, is a major environmental risk factor, usually ranking behind lack of lean water, poor sanitation and malnutrition. The problem does not only afflict the poorest populations. Many affluent households cook on traditional biomass stoves or open fires by choice or because they live in rural areas without electricity or access to modern fuels. "The World Health Organization estimates that 1.6 million people a year die of health effects resulting from toxic indoor air. The problem disproportionately falls on women and children who spend hours each day around the hearth. "Of that 1.6 million, one million children die of pneumonia, and 600,000 women die prematurely of chronic obstructive pulmonary diseases like bronchitis and emphysema. (Amanda Leigh Haag, "Stove For the Developing World's Health," *New York Times*, January 22, 2008.)

161   Lisa Burgess, "U.S. Troop Presence in Afghanistan at 17,900, and Expected To Hold Steady," *Stars and Stripes*, July 9, 2004.

162   Lolita C. Baldor, "Marines Prepare to Send 3,200 Troops to Afghanistan," January 14, 2008.

163   *Army Times*, July 5, 2008.

164   *USA Today*, December 20, 2008.

165   See the conservative Jamestown Foundation for statistics on the number of suicide attacks and the number of civilians killed.

166   On opium production and statistics in general about Afghanistan, see Jason Straziuso, "US Casualties in Afghanistan Hit Record," Associated Press, December 32, 2006.

167   "In 2008, Afghanistan Claims record Number of Soliders Killed," *Agence France-Presse*, January 3, 2009.

168   For data about CAS, besides CENTAF, see http://www.snappingturtle. net/flit/archives/2007_04.html.

169   Tom Englehardt, "Don't Let Obama Break Your Heart," *TomDispatch*, November 11, 2008.

170   See Marc Herold's website, *Archivistan*.

171   Steve Komorow, "Military's Fuel Costs Spur Look At Gas Guzzlers," *USA Today*, March 8, 2006.

172   Benjamin Lambeth, "Air Power Against Terror: America's Conduct of Operation Enduring Freedom," Rand Corporation, 2005.

173   See http://www.globalsecurity.org.

174   Michael R. Gordon and Steven Lee Myers, *New York Times*, "Taliban's Troops Hit As Allies Plan For Commando Raids," October 11, 2001.

175   See http://www.military.com: "National Guard."

176   Department of the *Army Field Manual* (FM 20-32), "Mine/Countermine Operations," May 29, 1998, Chapter Four.

177   See the *Landmine Monitor Report*, 1999, p. 330.

178   See Sharon Begley, "Learning to Love Climate 'Adaptation,'" *Newsweek*, December, 31, 2007.

179   Thomas Friedman, "The Power of Green," *New York Times Magazine*, April 15, 2007.

180   Robert Burns, "Gates Considers Army's Expansion Plan," Associated Press, September 27, 2007.

181   John Heilprin, "Rice Urges Nations To Find Cleaner Fuels," Associated Press, September 27, 2007.

182   New Scientist, "US Agencies Accused of Muzzling Climate Experts," February 25, 2006.

183   *New York Times*, December 15, 2007.

184   Thomas Fuller, "Climate Plan Looks Beyond The End Of Bush's Tenure," *New York Times*, December 16, 2007.

185   "Closing The Fuel Carbon Cycle," *EPRI Journal*, Spring 2007.

186   "Road Kill," August 5, 2007.

187   See Zoltán Grossman, "U.S. Military Consumption," at http://www.scienceforpeace.ca

188   Deb Reichman, "A Presidential Welcome for USS George H. W. Bush," Associated Press, January 10, 2009.

189   Frantz Fanon, *The Wretched of the Earth* (New York: Grove Press, 1963)

190   Steve Martinot, "The Military and Global Warming," *Synthesis/Regeneration* 42 (winter 2007).

191   See "The Raw Story," on-line, October 11, 2005.

SUPPORT AK PRESS!

AK Press is a worker-run collective that publishes and distributes radical books, visual/audio media, and other material. We're small: a dozen people who work long hours for short money, because we believe in what we do. We're anarchists, which is reflected both in the books we publish and the way we organize our business: without bosses.

Currently, we publish about twenty new titles per year. We'd like to publish even more. Whenever our collective meets to discuss future publishing plans, we find ourselves wrestling with a list of hundreds of projects. Unfortunately, money is tight, while the need for our books is greater than ever.

The Friends of AK Press is a direct way you can help. Friends pay a minimum of $25 per month (of course we have no objections to larger sums), for a minimum three month period. The money goes directly into our publishing funds. In return, Friends automatically receive (for the duration of their memberships) one free copy of every new AK Press title as they appear. Friends also get a 20% discount on everything featured in the AK Press Distribution catalog and on our web site—thousands of titles from the hundreds of publishers we work with. We also have a program where groups or individuals can sponsor a whole book. Please contact us for details.

To become a Friend, go to www.akpress.org.